CUISINE DU TERROIR
THE LOST DOMAIN OF FRENCH COOKING

The authors of *Cuisine du Terroir* are the Maîtres
Cuisiniers de France, a distinguished association
of 300 or so chefs who work at some of the
world's best restaurants. The editor is the French
cookery writer Céline Vence, who brought them
together and pooled their knowledge and
research to produce this book.

Cuisine du Terroir
THE LOST DOMAIN OF FRENCH COOKING

———

Original recipes collected by the
Master Chefs of France

AND EDITED BY
CÉLINE VENCE

for the English edition
SUE LERMON AND SIMON MALLET

CORGI BOOKS

CUISINE DU TERROIR
A CORGI BOOK   0 552 13375 2

Originally published in France as *Les Recettes du Terroir des Maîtres Cuisiniers de France*
Published in Great Britain by Blenheim House Publishing

French edition published 1984
Blenheim House edition published 1987
Corgi edition published 1988
Adviser on bread, cakes, and pastries: Jacques Charrette
Translation and adaptation from the French by Sue Lermon
Professional adviser on the English edition: Simon Mallet
Book designed by Kate Simunek
The cover shows a detail from 'The Vegetable Seller' by Joachim
Bueckelaer in the collection of the Louvre, reproduced by courtesy
of Giraudon/Bridgeman Art Library

Corgi Books are published by Transworld Publishers Ltd., 61-63
Uxbridge Road, Ealing, London W5 5SA, in Australia by
Transworld Publishers (Australia) Pty. Ltd., 15-23 Helles Avenue,
Moorebank, NSW 2170, and in New Zealand by Transworld
Publishers (N.Z.) Ltd., Cnr. Moselle and Waipareira Avenues,
Henderson, Auckland.

Printed in Great Britain by
Richard Clay Ltd, Bungay, Suffolk.

CONTENTS

PREFACE TO THE ENGLISH EDITION

It was the French cookery writer, Céline Vence, who had the idea of bringing together the Maîtres Cuisiniers de France and pooling their knowledge of and research into traditional French domestic cookery, in order to record and perpetuate an important but receding part of culinary history.

This distinguished association of chefs (for a complete list, see p.227) sought out the recipes, organising their selection on the basis of the old provinces (e.g. Alsace, Provence) rather than on present-day administrative boundaries, either departmental or regional, and highlighting certain areas (e.g. the Pays Basque) of distinctive character, but without provincial status. These appear in the chapter headings in smaller type, and on the map at each end of the book.

Minor modifications were made to the old recipes to take account of modern tastes and conditions (and in particular the existence of utensils, such as blenders, which eliminate the drudgery), and Madame Vence, who acted as overall editor, wrote an introduction to each chapter. These introductions have been slightly abridged for the present edition, though each still gives, I hope, a clear sketch of the region in question.

The only significant change from the French edition is the omission of thirteen recipes.* Lark and thrush recipes have little relevance in the UK, where the law reflects a profound cultural difference between the two sides of the Channel; similarly, few people will want to bleed a chicken to death to make *poulet en barbouille*. *Tripous* calls for such a variety and quantity of tripe that even in France it is difficult to make on a private scale, while the Basque wedding cake, *gâteau à la broche*, requires a special wooden mould for spit-baking (it is built up in layers as it turns over the fire) and, indeed, a certain dexterity if all is not to be lost in the flames. Otherwise, it has been a lack of proper ingredients or, in one case, the cooler British oven, that has discouraged inclusion.

The question of availability of ingredients is thorny: some, such as *fromage blanc* or *frais*, have become more current since preparation of the translation began. Almost every cheese mentioned can be bought in London as can goose fat and *confit*. On the other hand, people outside the capital may find it easier to get offal, real sausage skins, wild rabbit, or certain kinds of fresh fish; and should be able to roast a goose that will fill several storage jars with fat.

It is worth remembering that the original cooks had to improvise and it is within the spirit of the book to do so, as long as the substitutes are of good quality. Dried herbs, for instance, are not a good alternative to fresh ones; better either to use different herbs or freeze-dried herbs which seem to retain something of their true taste.

Those concerned with precise quantities should, ideally, follow the metric measurements, the imperial ones making slight concessions to convenience and to the fact that these are not traditionally recipes demanding great exactitude. Similarly, oven settings are often not given, such indications as 'moderate', 'hot', or 'low' being felt adequate for the cook who knows his or her oven – again the devisers and users of these recipes could not control temperature as closely as we can.† They did, however, use good thick pots and pans which are much better conductors of heat, allowing very slow simmering or hard, fast cooking.

As to wine, the recommendations given with each recipe are no more than a guide. Usually the wines are modest, befitting the domestic nature of the cookery, and many of them are easily found in the UK.   *Sue Lermon*

---

* *Alose farcie, Tripous, Gâteau à la broche, Poulet en barbouille, Grives en cocotte, Grives à la dauphinoise, Petites galettes de gaudes au maïs, Côte de boeuf villette, Pieds de mouton rouennaise, Cul de bicot à l'ail vert, Lapin en paquets à la brignolaise, Tarte de cardons à la moelle, Pâté d'alouettes de Pithiviers.*

†For comparative oven temperatures, see p. 250.

1
ALSACE

Culinary terms in Alsace can make the cookery sound strange and forbidding; at least the spelling is usually phonetic, with variations reflecting local differences of accent. The cooking itself is rich and regulated by an ancient calendar, each dish having its day, each festivity its speciality, thus, *stollen* cakes for New Year's Day; a joint of lamb and *oeufs à la neige* for Easter; *brioche de foire* for Midsummer's Day; roast goose and a large bretzel with new wine for 11 November, St Martin's Day. There are always filling soups as well, bulked out with homemade pasta (*consommé aux riweles*), hops, or pearl barley, sauerkraut and sausage, or red cabbage and juniper-flavoured sausage.

Of freshwater fish, salmon and char are just a memory. Pike, eel, perch, trout, formerly dried, nowadays smoked, and carp are still available. Since the war sander has made a discreet appearance; it is braised in Riesling and served with fresh pasta. The only sea fish to reach so far inland were herring.

Tarts and pies have always been prominent on the menu: onion tart; *flamme-küeche* or *tarte flambée*, an unmoulded bread dough tart, filled with onions and bacon and thick cream and cooked on a wood fire; or foie gras in brioche. The smoke house, like the salting-tub, is well stocked with bacon, shoulders of pork, pork chops, ox-tongues, and the breasts of fattened geese – these last, when smoked, being a part of the Jewish cookery which has contributed to the region's eating habits. Among the clusters of sausages hanging up to dry, will be *bierwurst*, made from tongue with beer, mustard, mace, cloves, and other spices, *zungenwurst*, another tongue sausage, bright scarlet, this one, and Montbéliard sausages, eaten hot with horseradish sauce. Horseradish, which is also freshly grated into cream or into a béchamel sauce, is a constant accompaniment, particularly to salt pork.

Those geese not fattened for their liver are spit-roasted, stuffed with chestnuts or pears, or casseroled. Pheasant are eaten with sauerkraut, partridge with Chartreuse and white cabbage, but more popular are hare and venison, this last with bilberries or dried pears.

As an alternative to sauerkraut, red cabbage or kohlrabi is cooked in lard or goosefat and served with onions and vinegar, or prepared with bacon, chestnuts, or apples. Turnips, like cabbage, are grated spaghetti-thin, then salted and fermented raw, as *navets salés* (see pp. 7 and 223). Potatoes come in salads with bacon and onions, or are grated, raw or cooked, to make potato cakes fried in goose fat. Asparagus and hop shoots are wrapped in bacon or ham and served with three sauces.

Munster is the most important cheese, made from the milk of cows who have spent the summer on the summits of the Vosges. It may be noted that Munster *au cumin* is not a reflection of ancient connections with North Africa or the Orient: *cumin des prés* are caraway seeds.

Alsace's links were with Austria, and Austrian (and Rhenish) influences are found in such puddings and pastries as *linzertorte*, *strudel*, with its cinnamon flavour, and *kougelhopf* (see p. 8). Tarts are filled with rhubarb, bilberries, plums of all sorts, and apples (*à l'alsacienne*, with a milk, cream, and egg custard). Rolls and buns are made in a welter of shapes and flavours, sweet and savoury. Thick pancakes, *eierkuchas*, are eaten with a salad or sweetened, in summer, with cherries mixed into the batter. Wild roses are used for jam.

Alsace's vineyards benefit from the Vosges, which protect them from the wet Atlantic winds. A distinction of the wine is to be identified by its grape: Sylvaner, Pinot Blanc, Tokay. The region also makes one of the most successful sparkling wines, Crémant d'Alsace. The fruits of the hedgerow (hawthorn, holly, dog-rose, and elderflower) are picked for *eaux-de-vie*. Better known are those made from cherries (Kirsch), raspberries, mirabelles, quetsches, or pears. Locally-brewed beer is consumed in large quantities.

Consommé aux Quenelles à la Moelle
· CONSOMMÉ WITH MARROW DUMPLINGS ·

For the day after a *pot-au-feu*, when there is a good beef stock which has been refrigerated and can be degreased by simply removing the solid layer of fat from the top. Such a soup, with little marrow dumplings, is served with salads: carrots from the *pot-au-feu*, celery, beetroot, or cucumber, potatoes cooked separately in some of the stock, radishes – and horseradish sauce.

———————————— *Ingredients for 4* ————————————

125 g · 4 oz beef marrow
75 g · 2¹/₂ oz breadcrumbs, from
  stale bread
25 g · ³/₄ oz fine semolina
6 egg yolks

2 sprigs of parsley
2–4 sprigs of chervil
salt, pepper
1–1.5 lt · 1³/₄–2¹/₂ pt well-strained
  beef stock

Pound together in a mortar the beef marrow, breadcrumbs, semolina, and egg yolks, with the finely chopped parsley and chervil, till you have a smooth stiff purée, and season with salt and pepper.

Taking a little of the mixture at a time, make it into walnut-sized dumplings.

Heat the beef stock in a wide pan (it makes the poaching easier), add the dumplings, and simmer for 10 minutes, turning them over once or twice.

Serve them in the soup.

Soupe de Grenouilles
· FROG'S LEG SOUP ·

Although frogs, like snails and freshwater crayfish, are dying out almost every-where, they are still common enough in Alsace to make *froscheschenkëlsupp* a part of everyday cooking. The ground rice is often left out.

———————————— *Ingredients for 6* ————————————

12 pairs frogs' legs
125 g · 4 oz butter
1 onion
1 shallot
200 ml · 7 fl oz white wine
1 lt · 1³/₄ pt stock, preferably fish,
  otherwise chicken

salt, pepper, nutmeg
50 g · 1³/₄ oz ground rice
100 ml · 3¹/₂ fl oz milk
100 g · 3¹/₂ oz watercress
2 egg yolks
100 ml · 3¹/₂ fl oz double cream

Soften the peeled and roughly chopped onion and shallot gently in 50 g (1¾ oz) of butter in a saucepan for 10 minutes.

Add the frogs' legs and sauté for 5 minutes until they are evenly browned.

Pour in the wine and the stock, season with salt and pepper, taking account of the strength of the stock, and add a pinch of grated nutmeg. Simmer, covered, for 15 minutes, then strain, and set aside the frogs' legs.

In a bowl, mix the ground rice into the milk and trickle it slowly into the soup, now returned to a low heat, stirring constantly; let the soup thicken for 20 minutes, giving the occasional stir.

Wash and chop the watercress, discarding the stalks and any dead or discoloured leaves. On a low heat, stir it into 20 g (¾ oz) of melted butter, before adding about 200 ml (⅓ pt) of water. Leave to cook slowly while you bone the frogs' legs.

In another small pan, in a barely bubbling bain-marie, work the egg yolks into the cream and beat until the mixture has virtually trebled in volume.

When the soup has thickened incorporate the watercress, cream, remaining butter, and frogs' legs, and taste for seasoning.

Pâté de Foie Gras en Croûte

Also called *pâté de foie gras de Strasbourg*. The earliest known recipe, entitled 'petits pastés de Foyes gras aux truffes', appeared in 1747 in a volume called *Le Cuisinier gascon*, believed to have been written by Louis-Auguste de Bourbon, Prince des Dombes, and cook to Louis XV.

If a truffle is added, it is cut up raw into tiny wedges, and the liver is studded with it before soaking. In Alsace they don't eat the pastry crust.

———————— *Ingredients for 1 foie gras weighing 700–800 g · 1½–1¾ lb* ————————

500 g · 1 lb fine vol-au-vent dough
   (see p. 225)
20 ml · ¾ fl oz Kirsch
salt, pepper
quatre-épices or allspice
150 g · 5 oz shoulder veal

150 g · 5 oz pork loin
300 g · 10 oz lean streaky bacon
2 shallots
2 tbsp goose fat or lard
1 egg
1 sachet aspic powder

Remove all nerves and sinews from the liver (in Alsace they are very meticulous about this) and put it to soak in the Kirsch, seasoned with salt, pepper, and a pinch of *quatre-épices* or, failing that, allspice. Leave for 4 hr, turning the liver over occasionally.

Finely mince together the veal, pork, bacon, and shallots, and brown over a medium heat for 3–4 minutes in half the goose fat or lard. Add salt and pepper, and flavour with a little of the marinade.

Lightly grease a rectangular mould with the rest of the fat and line it with the pastry rolled out to 2 mm (1/10"), leaving a 1 cm (3/8") border all round. With the remaining dough, make a lid the same size as the mould.

Fill it with about three-quarters of the mince. Wipe the foie gras and put it in the middle and surround and cover it with the rest of the mince, pressing it in lightly with your fingers.

Put the pastry lid in place and brush with beaten egg. Fold in the edge of the pastry base over the lid (the egg will make it stick) and brush that with egg too. Use the pastry trimmings, if you like, to make decorations, attaching and brushing them with egg. Make a hole in the centre of the crust and insert a small piece of pastry rolled over your finger to form a funnel (to let out the steam) – or make a little cardboard chimney. Cook in a medium oven for 45 minutes.

Let the pâté cool and poor in a little lukewarm aspic through the funnel.

Recommended wine: an Alsace Tokay.

Matelote de l'Ill
· ALSATIAN FISH STEW ·

Matelote from the river Ill, Alsatian *matelote*, *matelote* from Strasbourg, the name makes little difference, but some say the particular flavour comes from the combination of Riesling and carp; others that pike, tench, eel, and perch, all fish of the Ill, are essential. With such a variety of fish it can hardly be made for less than 6–8 people. Mushrooms may be added, or toast or croûtons served with it.

──────────────── *Ingredients for 6* ────────────────

The following fish, whole or in
  pieces (but keep the heads and
  tails):
  500 g · 1 lb pike
  500 g · 1 lb tench
  500 g · 1 lb carp
  500 g · 1 lb eel
1 onion
1 carrot
1 leek

a bouquet garni: 2 sprigs of parsley,
  1 sprig of thyme, 1/2 bay leaf, 3–4
  tarragon leaves, salt, pepper
130 g · 4 oz butter
50 g · 1 1/2 oz shallots
500 ml · 16 fl oz Riesling
30 g · 1 oz flour
4 egg yolks
250 ml · 8 fl oz double cream
toast or croûtons

Clean and scale the fish, skinning the eel if it is large, wash, and cut into 5–6 cm (2–2 1/2″) pieces, setting aside the heads and tails.

Simmer the heads and tails with the onion, carrot, and leek, all thinly sliced, the bouquet, and salt and pepper, in 2 lt (3 1/2 pt) of water, for 30 minutes, to make a stock. Strain well.

In a large frying pan or sauteuse, brown the chopped shallot and the fish pieces lightly in 50 g (1 1/2 oz) of butter for 2–3 minutes. Pour in the wine and enough stock to cover and simmer for 10 minutes. Take out the fish and keep hot.

Make a roux with 30 g (1 oz) of butter and flour. Beat in 750 ml (1 1/4 pt) of the cooking liquid from the frying pan, and cook for 15 minutes, stirring almost constantly.

In another saucepan, fold the egg yolks into the cream and very gradually add the béchamel. Stir over a low heat till simmering point (whatever you do, don't let it boil) and season if necessary. Away from the heat, beat in the remaining butter a little at a time.

Arrange the pieces of fish on a warm serving dish, coat them with the sauce and garnish with toast or croûtons.

Recommended wine: a Riesling, from a better year perhaps than the one used in the cooking.

Bäckeofe
· PORK, LAMB, AND BEEF CASSEROLE ·

Traditionally, Monday's dish, prepared on Sunday night to cook in the baker's oven while the washing was being done next morning. Its success depends on very slow cooking.

——————————————— *Ingredients for 6* ———————————————

500 g · 1 lb pork spare-rib
500 g · 1 lb shoulder of lamb, boned
500 g · 1 lb beef bladebone, boned
2 leeks, white part only
2 carrots
250 g · 8 oz onions

a bouquet garni: 1 sprig of thyme, 1
  bay leaf, 2 sprigs of parsley, 3
  cloves of garlic
Riesling or a white Pinot
salt, pepper
1–1.2 kg · 2–2½ lb potatoes
50 g · 1½ oz butter or lard

The night before you intend to serve this, cut all the meat into 4 cm (1½") cubes and leave to marinate in a cool place until next day with the cleaned and sliced leeks and carrots, the onions, peeled and cut into rings, the bouquet, and the wine to cover. Season with pepper only, as salt will draw the blood out of the meat.

Next day, peel, wash, and slice the potatoes.

In a casserole, arrange a quarter of the potatoes in a layer, covered with the beef, followed by another layer of potatoes, the pork, a layer of potatoes, the lamb, and lastly the remainder of the potatoes mixed with the onion from the marinade. Salt the marinade and strain it over the meat and potatoes. Dot with the butter or lard.

Seal tightly – if necessary use a strip of dough: flour worked with a little water. Cook slowly for 3 hr and serve straight from the pot.

Recommended wine: a white Pinot.

Choucroute Garnie Alsacienne

The cabbage for *choucroute* (sauerkraut) used to be cut up by a professional *'raboteur'* – and putting the cabbage to soak and ferment was an occasion to celebrate. Garnishes have become less innovative than those of the past which included even snails and herring. Modern *choucroute* is always cooked with an assortment of meat: pork, in all its forms, bacon, green or smoked, smoked or salted hock, salted chops, Strasbourg sausages (like Frankfurters) or *colmarettes* (little sausages from Colmar), liver *quenelles*, sometimes smoked goose breast, or, in Jewish households, smoked rib of beef cooked in goose fat. In Alsace, however, *choucroute* is never eaten with ham, nor with just a single garnish – just bacon, for instance, or just smoked meat. In England, gammon, smoked pork loin (kassler), and salt beef would be worthy accompaniments.

─────────────────── *Ingredients for 4* ───────────────────

2 kg · 4 lb white uncooked *choucroute*
100 g · 3 oz lard or goose fat
2 onions
1 smoked pork blade or bacon hock
1 shin of pork, lightly salted (see
   p. 226)
750 g · 1½ lb pork spare-rib, lightly
   salted
400 g · ¾ lb lean streaky smoked
   bacon

2 cloves of garlic, 2 sprigs of thyme,
   1 bay leaf, 2 cloves, 10 juniper
   berries, 10–12 peppercorns, 5–6
   coriander seeds
500 ml · 16 fl oz Riesling
250 ml · 8 fl oz stock
potatoes – as required
8 Frankfurters (or Strasbourg
   sausages)
400 g · ¾ lb fresh (Toulouse)
   sausages

Wash the *choucroute* thoroughly, separating it, until the rinsing water runs clear. Squeeze it as dry as you can, by hand, then drain in a colander.

Blanch all the meat (see p. 221).

Soften the peeled and finely chopped onions for 7–8 minutes in a third of the fat in a large casserole with a well-fitting lid.

Cover the onion with half the *choucroute* and put the blanched meat on top. Add the garlic tied up in a muslin bag with the other herbs and flavourings, and cover with the rest of the *choucroute*. Pour over the wine and the stock. Dot with the remaining fat. Cover tightly and cook very gently for 2 hr.

Twenty to thirty minutes before the end of the cooking time, prepare the potatoes: either peel and steam them, or boil them in their skins. Ten minutes before the end of the cooking time, poach the Frankfurters slowly in water and grill the sausages.

Take the meat out of the pot and slice it. Put the *choucroute* on a large dish with the meat, the Frankfurters, and the sliced sausages arranged alternately on top, and the potatoes (peeled if they were boiled in their skins) all round the edge.

Recommended drink: an Edelzwicker wine, or beer.

Tourte de la Vallée de Munster
· VEAL AND PORK PIE FROM MUNSTER ·

A traditional wedding dish, cooked in a terracotta pie dish.

─────────────────── *Ingredients for 8* ───────────────────

400 g · 14 oz flaky pastry (see p. 225)
30 g · 1 oz butter
2 white milk rolls
100 ml · 4 fl oz milk
50 g · 2 oz onions
400 g · 14 oz fat pork

400 g · 14 oz shoulder veal or
   chicken
1 clove of garlic
2 eggs
salt, pepper, nutmeg

Roll out two-thirds of the pastry to 3 mm (⅛″), butter a pie dish, and line it, leaving a 1 cm (⅜″) border all round. Roll out the other third to 2 mm (¹⁄₁₀″) and make a lid the exact size of the dish. Leave in a cool place.

Warm the milk and crumble the bread into it to soak.

Peel and slice the onions, and soften them for 7–8 minutes in the butter remaining after greasing the pie dish.

Mince together coarsely all the meat, the onion, the peeled garlic, and the bread, squeezed as dry as possible. Stir in an egg, salt, pepper, and a pinch of grated nutmeg, and mix well.

Fill the pie dish with the mince, and if you have a pie funnel place it in the centre. Fold the border in over the filling and brush the upper surface with beaten egg. Put the pie lid in position and press it down all round to seal it. Make a pattern on the crust with a knife or fork or use the pastry trimmings to make decorations – stick these on and brush the whole pie top with the egg. If you do not have a pie funnel, make a small hole in the centre of the crust, and insert a pastry (or cardboard) chimney.

Place in a hot oven, and after 15 minutes, lower the temperature to medium and continue cooking for 30 minutes. Serve hot.

Recommended wine: Sylvaner or Riesling.

Navets Salés

· PICKLED TURNIPS ·

In Alsace, these much loved turnips, shredded, salted, and fermented like *choucroute*, are usually served as here. Potatoes boiled in their skins are an obligatory accompaniment, bacon an optional one. To prepare salted turnips, see p. 223.

———————————— *Ingredients for 4* ————————————

1.5 kg · 3 lb salted turnips
1 kg · 2 lb smoked pork bladebone
    or bacon hock
150 g · 5 oz onions
100 g · 3 oz lard

2 cloves of garlic
2 cloves
10 peppercorns
350 ml · 12 fl oz white wine
potatoes

Leave the pork or bacon under running water for 3–4 hr to remove the salt and then blanch (see p. 221).

Wash the turnip until the water runs clear. Drain.

Soften the finely sliced onions in a third of the lard in a large saucepan or casserole for 7 or 8 minutes. Put half the turnip on top, having pressed it lightly between your hands to dry it a little. Add the pork, and the garlic, cloves, and peppercorns tied in a muslin bag, and the rest of the turnip. Pour over the wine and an equal quantity of water. Dot with remaining lard. Seal the pot well and leave on a low heat for 1½ hr.

Thirty minutes before the end, boil the potatoes in their skins.

Serve the turnip very hot, piled high in a dish, surrounded by the peeled potatoes, with the meat sliced on top.

Recommended drink: Edelzwicker or Sylvaner wine, or beer.

Tarte au Fromage Blanc

This is known as *käsküeche* locally. It should be made with well-drained *fromage blanc* – called *bibbelkäs* or *bibeleskäs* in Alsace. Flavourings vary: vanilla, grated lemon peel, raisins soaked in rum. The tart is turned upside down after cooking, and that is the key to its impressive appearance.

─────────────────── Ingredients for 6 ───────────────────

20 g · ³/₄ oz butter
400 g · 14 oz shortcrust pastry (see
  p. 224)
5 eggs
500 ml · 17 fl oz milk
1 vanilla pod

100 g · 3¹/₂ oz castor sugar
80 g · 2¹/₂ oz ground rice
500 g · 17 oz well-drained *fromage
  blanc*
icing sugar

Butter a 25–30 cm (10–12″) tart tin. Roll out the pastry to 3 mm (¹/₈″), prick it, turn it over, and line the tin with it. Brush the border with a beaten egg and bake blind (i.e. covered with greaseproof paper and weighted down, e.g. with dried beans) for 10 minutes in a medium oven.

Bring the milk to the boil with the vanilla pod and let it cool.

Cream the remaining egg yolks with the sugar until the mixture is smooth and pale, with all the sugar dissolved. Fold in the ground rice and the milk, vanilla pod removed. Thicken over a low heat – it must not boil – stirring constantly.

Fold in the *fromage blanc*, then the stiffly beaten egg whites.

Pour the mixture into the tart shell immediately, and brush with the rest of the beaten egg. Bake in a medium oven for 20 minutes.

Remove the tart from the oven; as soon as it is cool enough to handle turn it out on to a cake rack and leave it upside down until it is cold, to stop it sinking. Turn carefully the right way up and dust with icing sugar.

Recommended wine: a Muscat d'Alsace.

Kougelhopf

Kügel was supposedly a cake-maker from Ribeauvillé, who gave hospitality to the Three Kings on their way back from Bethlehem and in return they made him a cake in a special mould. Either that, or the *kougelhopf* is a legacy of Alsace's spell under Austrian rule. The traditional glazed clay mould does, incidentally, make the best cake.

─────────────────── Ingredients for 6–8 ───────────────────

100 g · 4 oz (Muscat) raisins
200 ml · 7 fl oz milk
20 g · ³/₄ oz baker's yeast (very fresh)
75 g · 2¹/₂ oz castor sugar
5 g · ¹/₆ oz salt

500 g · 17 oz flour
2 eggs
220 g · 7¹/₂ oz butter
100 g · 4 oz peeled almonds
icing sugar

Soak the raisins in warm water.

Warm half the milk (but not hot enough to 'kill' the yeast), dissolve the yeast and a teaspoon (5 g) each of sugar and salt in it, and stir in 50 g (1¾ oz) of the flour, to make a soft mixture. Cover with a damp cloth and leave in a warm place for 20–30 minutes to double in volume.

When the yeast has proved, mix together the rest of the flour and sugar in a bowl, make a well in the centre, and gradually fold in the eggs and the remaining milk, also warmed. Knead hard to make a smooth dough.

Work in 200 g (7 oz) of butter, softened but not melted, and when it has been absorbed, add the yeast mixture and knead until you have a smooth dough. Cover with a damp cloth, and leave to rise for 2 hr.

Butter a fluted mould carefully to ensure it is evenly greased everywhere, and place a whole almond at the point of each flute. Knead the dough again, incorporating the drained raisins, and fill the mould. Leave in a warm place, without covering, until the dough reaches the brim.

Cook in a medium oven for 45 minutes, keeping an eye on it and, if the top browns too quickly, protecting it with buttered greaseproof paper.

Turn out on to a cake rack, sprinkle generously with icing sugar and leave to cool.

Recommended drink: white coffee, Gewürztraminer, or Muscat d'Alsace.

Bretzels

Introduced by the Protestants who settled in Alsace after the revocation of the Edict of Nantes in 1685. Nowadays bretzels are eaten with cheese and beer, or served with goose on festive occasions. Large bretzels with egg (*brioche*) are made for breakfast and children's parties.

———————————— *Ingredients for 300 g · 10 oz flour* ————————————

100 ml · 3½ fl oz milk, full-cream or
    curdled
5 g · ⅙ oz salt
15 g · ½ oz very fresh baker's yeast

50 g · 1¾ oz butter
bicarbonate of soda
1 tbsp caraway seeds
1 tbsp coarse salt

If you use full-cream milk, heat it gently (hand-hot) and, away from the heat, add a teaspoon (5 g) of salt and the yeast. If you use curdled milk (which gives a better flavour), mix the salt and the yeast into 2 tablespoons of either whey or water and then add the curds. Stir 50 g (1¾ oz) of flour into the yeast mixture and cover with a damp cloth. Leave in a warm place until it has doubled in volume, about 30 minutes.

Work the rest of the flour with 25 g (¾ oz) of softened butter and enough water to make a smooth dough. Knead well. Incorporate the yeast and leave for 2 hr covered with a damp cloth (which stops the dough forming a hard crust).

Divide the dough into small portions, and on a lightly floured board roll them into sausages 7–10 cm (3–4″) long and the thickness of your little finger. Make these into rings, tying the ends once, and arrange them on a dish between floured cloths. Leave for 45 minutes, then refrigerate for a further hour to make them firm.

Boil a large pan of water. Leave to cool, before dissolving 25 g (¾ oz) of bicarbonate of soda per litre (1¾ pt) of water. Return the pan to a medium heat and drop the bretzels in, transferring each one as it surfaces to a baking sheet covered with well-buttered greaseproof paper. Sprinkle them with caraway seeds and coarse salt before baking in a very hot oven for 5 minutes. Detach them from the paper while they are still warm and leave to cool.

Recommended drink: vin nouveau *or beer.*

2
ANGOUMOIS · AUNIS SAINTONGE

More readily recognised as the Charentes, the area takes in Charente, Charente-Maritime, and the islands of Ré and Oleron. Angoulême, La Rochelle, and Saintes were the old provincial capitals. Whether or not the inhabitants resemble the snails (*cagouilles*) of which they are so fond as to have acquired the nickname Cagouillards, the cooking, long and slow, with wine and cognac, matches the gastropod's pace.

The presence of the rich Atlantic seaboard is reflected in a preference for fish as an hors d'oeuvre rather than soup or *charcuterie*. The extensive mussel beds are said to have originated with an Irishman, shipwrecked in the bay of Aiguillon in the thirteenth century: trying to survive by trapping low-flying birds, he noticed that the long poles he had stuck in the sea to hold his nets were coated in mussels – the first *moules de bouchot*, prized not only for their flavour, but also because suspended on their stakes they escape the little parasitical crabs that normally harbour in the shells.

Oyster culture has suffered repeated setbacks. Thus, even the Portuguese oysters, which were established by chance after a contaminated cargo was thrown overboard in 1868, and which flourished in the wake of the declining Marennes Plates and Claires, have in turn become scarce, giving way to the giant Pacific oysters.

On the other hand, the clams that were accidentally introduced in the 1900s by the discharge of an American cargo into the Seudre estuary have thrived. Langoustine are another successful twentieth-century addition to the repertoire. But there were already countless shellfish and molluscs along this marshy coast, many of them eaten simply with a vinaigrette well-seasoned with shallots: crabs, razor-shells, carpet-shells, cockles, winkles, limpets, murex, scallops, shrimps; while, on the Ile de Ré, squid were dried in the sun.

The predominant fish are sole, of all sizes, particularly the *solette* and the *céteau* (the latter distinguished by a 'z' mark under the gills), sardines, eaten fresh and raw with sea salt and bread and butter, grey mullet, skate, ray, sea-bream, whiting, sea-bass, monkfish, and eels. At night, in the early part of the year, you can see the strange will o'the wisp dance of lanterns as the fishermen go out to catch the eels newly arrived from the Sargasso Sea. These might be fried, poached, or cooked in omelettes.

And on terra firma? There are pigs with Yorkshire blood, cattle which were introduced after the phylloxera epidemic of the 1870s destroyed the vineyards, and sheep which enjoy the alluvial pastures – *les misottes* – between sea and dykes. A leg of lamb must always be well-studded with garlic to be worthy of the table or of a Vieux Pineau wine; and it is served with flat beans (see p. 16).

Around the town of Confolens, at the moment of a woman's confinement, a chicken broth used to be prepared, the soup for her, the bird for her husband. Wild rabbit and young hare were 'washed' in cognac, coated in sea salt, and stuffed with rosemary for roasting. Game pâtés continue to be made at Confolens, partridge pâtés at Ruffec, lark at Excideuil; and the poor woodcock, who kill themselves flying into the Chassiron lighthouse on Oleron, are still eaten although now protected from hunting.

The climate is good for spring vegetables and fruit, particularly Charentais melons, and wild mushrooms. Samphire (*perce-pierre*) is collected before it flowers in mid-June and pickled in vinegar. Mustard seed from the marshes is served with oysters.

Of cheese there is little other than fresh curd cheese, such as Caillebote, which is flavoured with *chardonnette* (a wild artichoke, whose blue flowers are dried in the dark), and Jonchée which is cow's milk in Saintonge and sheep's milk on Oleron – and goat's milk in neighbouring Poitou. It is drained on reeds and often sweetened. Ruffec is a goat's cheese. As for wine, it is the province of cognac. There is an angelica liqueur, too, but Fenouillette de Ré, another liqueur, very popular in the eighteenth century, has disappeared.

Mouclade
· MUSSELS WITH CREAM ·

Moucles is the local word for *moules* – those from the nearby Charron beds are regarded as the best. The curry powder is a reminder that the Dutch spice traders' route to the Indies was via La Rochelle.

—————————— Ingredients for 8 ——————————

300 ml · ½ pt white wine   2 sml tsp curry powder
80 g · 3 oz shallots   2 eggs
80 g · 3 oz butter   300 ml · ½ pt double cream
3–4 kg · 6–8 lb mussels   salt, pepper

Let the wine, the peeled and chopped shallots, and the butter bubble gently in a large pan for 10 minutes.

Meanwhile, scrape and clean the mussels, which should have been covered with cold water and salt, or a wet cloth, or soaked in milk and oatmeal, beforehand. Reject any that are broken, already open, or whose half-shells slide against each other. Add the mussels to the wine, cover, and turn the heat right up; when steam starts escaping, remove the lid and turn the mussels over. Take them out individually as they begin to open.

Strain the cooking liquid through a cheesecloth or muslin and reduce by a third. Meanwhile, throw away the empty halves of the mussel shells and arrange the full ones in an oven-proof dish.

Mix the curry powder, egg yolks, and cream together, and trickle very slowly into the reduced liquid, stirring constantly; bring to simmering point, not hotter, and pour over the mussels. Put under the grill for 1 minute.

Recommended wine: a white Haut-Poitou (Sauvignon).

Éclade
· MUSSELS COOKED IN PINE NEEDLES ·

For an *éclade*, which is quite easy for anyone conversant with barbecues, in the quantities given below, you will need up to a metre square of pine, at least 1 cm thick, and plenty of very dry pine needles (or straw, in the tradition of the Ile de Ré). The mussels must be hinge-end uppermost and tightly packed together so they can't open and lose their liquid; the other way up, they will do so and will let in the ash. Remember to check which way the wind is blowing before lighting. Eat the shellfish in your fingers with bread and butter. (The same dish is known as an *églade* when the mussels are wedged together with clay.)

———————————— *Ingredients for 4* ————————————

2–3 kg · 4–6 lb mussels

Scrape and wash the mussels. Dampen the wood.

In the middle, place the 4 largest mussels together. Pack the rest of the mussels tightly round them, hinge-side up, in an ever-expanding circle, so that they can't move or open too much.

Cover with a thick layer (3 cm) of pine needles and set them alight.

When the fire goes out, fan it to disperse the ashes.

Recommended wine: a white Ile de Ré or Gros-Plant.

Sauce de Lavignons
· TELLINS IN WHITE WINE ·

The *lavignon* (tellin) or *lavagnon* as it is incorrectly known in the Charentes, is nowadays found only on this coast. So this is a true *terroir* recipe. The tellin resembles a small clam, which can be used instead, but it hasn't the same peppery taste.

———————————— *Ingredients for 4* ————————————

2 kg · 4 lb tellins
coarse salt
80 g · 2 oz butter
100 g · 3 oz shallots
250 ml · 8 fl oz white wine (Ré or
   Oleron or Gros-Plant)

fine salt, pepper
8 sprigs of parsley
1 lge clove of garlic
100 g · 3 oz homemade breadcrumbs
2 egg yolks
250 ml · 8 fl oz thick cream

Leave the shellfish for an hour or so in a basin of salted water – 35 g (1¼ oz) of coarse salt to 1 lt (1¾ pt) of water.

Soften the chopped shallots slowly for 7 or 8 minutes in 20 g (¾ oz) of butter in a sauteuse or frying pan, turning them over now and then and not letting them brown. Pour in the wine, cover, and simmer for 10 minutes.

Rinse the shellfish in plenty of water and put them on their own in a covered pan over a high flame. When they start to steam, remove the lid, stir them round, and take them out as they open.

Strain the water given off by the tellins, and pour it into the shallots. Season with salt and pepper as necessary.

Chop up the parsley and garlic and mix into the breadcrumbs and sauté in the remaining butter for 2 or 3 minutes.

Discard the empty shells, remove the shallots from the heat, and arrange the full shells on top of them. Cover with the breadcrumbs and the egg yolks mixed into the cream, and return to a medium heat.

Serve hot, at the first bubble.

Recommended wine: Muscadet-sur-Lie.

Chaudrée
· FISH CHOWDER ·

There are endless variations of this fishermen's soup whose common theme is to use the unsaleable fish. It might include grey mullet, sole, plaice, eels, or tiny sole (3–4" long); the combination of flat fish, small skate, and cuttlefish or squid is however essential. Some old recipes include potatoes.

————————————— *Ingredients for 4* —————————————

300 g · 10 oz of each of the following:
    cuttlefish or squid, mantles only
    sole, plaice, or *céteaux* fillets
    small skate, filleted
    small eels, preferably from the sea
    grey mullet
100 g · 4 oz butter

500 ml · 17½ fl oz white wine
    (ideally a Ré or a Chassiron)
a bouquet garni: 1 sprig of thyme,
    ½ bay leaf, 2 sprigs of parsley
2 onions
2 cloves of garlic
salt, pepper
croûtons, fried in butter (optional)

Cut the cleaned cuttlefish or squid (see p. 37) mantles into rings and put with half the butter, the thinly sliced onions, and the whole peeled garlic cloves in a cooking pot that you can bring to the table. Stew gently, covered, for 15 minutes, shaking frequently.

Add the wine, 1 lt (1¾ pt) of water, and the bouquet; simmer for 30 minutes.

Clean, scale, and slice the other fish. Put the thickest, firmest pieces on top of the cuttlefish, season with salt and pepper, and cook for 5 minutes.

Add the rest of the fish and butter. Take the pot off the heat when the butter has melted and mixed with the cooking liquid.

Remove the bouquet and the garlic; serve with croûtons if you like.

Meuilles d'Arvent
· GREY MULLET FROM ARVENT ·

Meuilles is the local word for grey mullet, abundant on this coast. The best are said to be those with yellow marks (*oreilles jaunes*) on the gill-covers. If you can't get grey mullet, try sea-bass or John Dory, or even codling.

————————————— *Ingredients for 4* —————————————

4 grey mullet, c. 200 g · ½ lb each
600 ml · 1 pt dry white wine
100 g · 4 oz onions
1 clove
a bouquet garni: 2 sprigs of thyme,
    ½ bay leaf, 2 sprigs of parsley

salt, pepper
170 g · 6 oz butter
6 cloves of garlic
8 more sprigs of parsley
400 g · 14 oz tomatoes

Make a *court-bouillon* with 2–3 lt (4–5 pt) of water, 500 ml (¾ pt) of wine, an onion, peeled, quartered, and stuck with a clove, the bouquet, and salt and pepper. Let it bubble gently for 20 minutes.

Add the scaled, gutted, and cleaned fish to the *court-bouillon* and simmer another 6 minutes. Drain.

Peel and chop the garlic finely, and stew gently with 150 g (5 oz) of butter, until it just melts. Away from the heat add the finely chopped parsley.

Butter an oval oven-proof dish, arrange the fish in it head-to-tail, and pour over the remaining wine. Cover with the rest of the onions, thinly sliced, the tomatoes, peeled, seeded if you like, and sliced, and the garlic, parsley, and butter mixture. Season lightly.

Cook in a medium oven for 10 minutes, and serve straight from the dish.

Recommended wine: a white Haut-Poitou or a Bourgueil.

Daube Saintongeaise

A clear *daube*, bound only with a calf's foot. Not worth making in small quantities, but it improves with reheating, and can be eaten cold when it will form a light jelly. You can use a pig's trotter, easily available from butchers.

--------------------------------- *Ingredients for 8* ---------------------------------

2–2.5 kg · 4–5 lb stewing beef
  (shoulder or chuck)
3 tbsp oil
200 g · 7 oz onions
a bouquet garni: 2 sprigs of thyme,
  1 bay leaf, 3 sprigs of parsley
1 tbsp coarsely ground pepper
1 bottle robust red wine
50 g · 1½ oz butter

250 g · 8 oz lean green streaky bacon
1.5 kg · 3 lb carrots
2 doz shallots
50 ml · 1¾ fl oz cognac
1 calf's foot or pig's trotter,
  blanched (see p. 221) and boned,
  + bones
3 cloves of garlic
salt, pepper

Cut the meat into 4 cm (1½″) cubes and marinate for 12–24 hr in a cool place with 2 tablespoons of oil, half the onions, peeled and chopped, the bouquet, the coarsely ground pepper (best done with a pestle and mortar), and the wine.

Take the meat out with a draining spoon, wipe it, and brown in a casserole, over a medium flame, using the last spoonful of oil and half the butter. Remove from the casserole.

Blanch the bacon (see p. 221) and cut into small lardons. Brown gently in the casserole in the rest of the butter, along with the scraped, washed, and sliced carrots, the remaining onions, peeled and quartered, and the shallots, peeled.

Meanwhile, strain the marinade into a saucepan, setting aside the bouquet. Pour in the cognac and boil for 3–4 minutes.

Return the meat to the casserole, with the calf's foot and bones, the bouquet from the marinade, the garlic, peeled, but left whole, and the boiled marinade; add salt, and pepper if necessary. Cover tightly and cook slowly for 4 hr.

Recommended wine: a red Haut-Poitou (a Gamay).

Mojhettes Piates ou Haricots Plats au Jus

· FLAT HARICOT BEANS WITH CARROTS AND ONIONS ·

These flat beans are a local speciality, grown only in the Charentes and the Marais Poitevin, but other beans can be used for this dish. They need slow cooking without too much water to begin with, boiling water being added as the cooking liquid evaporates. Remember to change the water if you soak the beans for more than twelve hours, to prevent fermentation. Should you be using unshelled fresh beans (such as you can buy in France in late summer), there is no need to soak them.

─────────── Ingredients for 8 ───────────

1–1.2 kg · 2–2¹/₂ lb dried beans
200 g · 7 oz onions
200 g · 7 oz carrots
50 g · 2 oz butter
3 cloves of garlic

a bouquet garni: 2 sprigs of thyme,
2 sprigs of parsley, ¹/₂ bay leaf, 1
clove
salt, pepper

Soak the beans for about 12 hr in plenty of cold water.

Soften the sliced onions and the scraped, washed, and roughly diced carrots slowly in 20 g (³/₄ oz) of butter in a thick pan, stirring frequently, for 10–15 minutes.

Mix in the drained beans. Turn them over for 2 or 3 minutes before adding the peeled and crushed garlic, the bouquet, and just enough water to cover. Simmer gently for 1¹/₄–1¹/₂ hr, with the lid on, continually checking that everything is immersed in the liquid and replenishing with hot water if necessary. Season with salt and pepper after about 45 minutes.

Remove the bouquet and stir in the remaining butter.

Galette Charentaise

A crumbly cake, eaten as a pudding, or as an apéritif with a Pineau de Charentes, or as afternoon refreshment with a cup of coffee. The Charentaises make it after their guests arrive so it can be eaten warm. You need a large baking tin because the *galette* must be very flat. Sometimes a little chopped-up angelica is added.

─────────── Ingredients for 8 (2 galettes) ───────────

4 eggs
250 g · 8 oz castor sugar
¹/₂ sml tsp salt
500 g · 16 oz flour

¹/₂ sachet dried yeast
195 g · 6 oz butter
2 tbsp granulated sugar

Cream the eggs and the castor sugar until the mixture forms the ribbon, i.e. is smooth, pale, and creamy, with no grains of sugar visible.

Fold in very gradually the salt, flour, yeast, and 125 g (4 oz) of softened butter.

Butter 2 baking tins and spread half the mixture evenly over each. Sprinkle with the granulated sugar and bake in a hot oven for 15 minutes (if your oven won't hold both *galettes* together, don't sprinkle the second one until it goes in, as the sugar's function is to melt during the cooking, thereby browning the top).

Merveilles
· FRITTERS ·

Traditional fare for Lenten festivities. They will keep several days in an airtight container but nothing quite matches a hot, crisp, freshly cooked *merveille*.

——————————— *Ingredients for 4* ———————————

10 g · ¹/₃ oz fresh baker's yeast
100 ml · 3¹/₂ fl oz milk
500 g · 17 oz flour
¹/₂ sml tsp salt
200 g · 7 oz castor sugar + sugar to
   sprinkle over after cooking

4 eggs
150 g · 5 oz butter
1 sml tsp orange flower water
1 tbsp cognac
oil for frying

Dissolve the yeast in the warmed milk.

Mix the flour, salt, and sugar together; make a well and gradually stir in the eggs, one at a time, the softened butter, the orange flower water, the cognac, and the yeast. Make into a ball and leave for at least 2 hr in a warm place, covered with a damp cloth.

Roll out the dough to about 2 mm (¹/₁₀″) and cut it into strips of 2 × 10 cm (³/₄ × 4″). Make a knot in each one.

Plunge into very hot oil, a few at a time so that the oil doesn't cool (and make the fritters greasy). Turn them over with a draining spoon as they surface. When they are golden brown, drain them and sprinkle with sugar before serving.

Recommended wine: a sparkling white Seudre or Monbazillac.

3
ANJOU · MAINE
Perche

Anjou, along with its neighbour Touraine, lays claim to being the garden, or at least the northern garden, of France. Maine and Perche, in complementary fashion, breed cattle, pigs, and poultry – chickens, capons, guinea-fowl, turkeys, geese – these last all reared with a healthy suspicion of battery methods.

Soups were lush and various: cultivated mushroom, *soupe de piochons* (cabbage heart soup), peapod, turnip, lettuce. Pork had its place in the soup-pot, and in the Sarthe, after the ritual spring killing, the head would be served in a soup; in Maine, pig's ear soup is a speciality. Nearer Brittany, the soups were made clear for bread to be added, recalling that *soupe* originally meant the slice of bread that was put into the *potage* – contents of the pot – and served for a modest evening meal, *le souper*. Incidentally, in this part of France, when a little wine is poured into the dregs of the soup, it is not a *chabrot* or *chabrol* but a *soupe au perroquet*.

For this landlocked area, the Loire was the chief source of fish. There may be no more sailing barges or boatmen to enliven the river at water level, but life goes on below, if in diminished quantities, in the form of shad (which is stuffed with sorrel), perch, bream (which is stuffed with garlic-and-herb-flavoured bread and cooked with constant bastings of white wine), a few salmon, and pike. For the amateur fisherman's line and frying pan, there are gudgeon, small perch, and bleak.

In the Maine, around Craon, the hams, especially the smoked ones, have a distinctive flavour, the result of the pigs' diet of flour and potatoes. As in all pork-producing regions, there are *andouilles* and black puddings, but the Anjou also makes a giant blood sausage, *la gogue angevine* (see p. 21). Modern farming methods have unfortunately made some dishes, like *foie de veau à la bourgeoise*, virtually impossible to prepare as they require meat from a calf that has been exclusively milk-fed.

In the past, the evening meal might have consisted of potatoes cooked in their skins (*trompe-bonhomme*), then peeled on the plate and eaten with cream, a sprinkling of chopped onion, parsley, and shallot, each element separately served. Nowadays, artichokes stuffed with chopped mushrooms, breadcrumbs, parsley, garlic, and butter are preferred. Cabbage is eaten simply boiled with plenty of butter (butter is always on the table). Fairy-ring mushrooms (*mousserons*) from Anjou's sandy slopes go into omelettes, fricassées, and stews; when they are out of season, cultivated mushrooms, which are produced in large quantities hereabouts, replace them.

The province's sole claim to a place on the cheese map is that Port Salut originated in a Cistercian monastery near Laval, before it was taken over for industrial production and given its name. The monks' cheese can apparently still be bought from them. Otherwise, there is a goat's cheese from Montreuil-Bellay, and Chouze which is a *fromage blanc* drained and mixed with whipped cream and drained again through muslin.

Fruit from the Anjou includes the famous pears, as well as cherries, strawberries, plums, hazelnuts, chestnuts. Apples are plentiful in the Maine – Reinettes, Reine des Reinettes, Reinettes Clochard.

The region's wine list is impressive: Anjou, Saumur, including the red Saumur-Champigny, Coteaux du Loir, particularly the white Jasnières, and the Coteaux de la Loire, under the *appellation* Savenniers and counting two Crus:

Coulée de Serrant and Roche-aux-Moines. The white Coteaux du Layon are comparable to the great Bordeaux whites. And, as well as Calvados and cider, *marc* and pear *eau-de-vie*, there is Cointreau, made at Angers.

Rillettes

From the old French *rille*, a little piece of pork. Rillettes vary with the regions: pure pork, pork and rabbit, pork and goose; textures differ too.

─────────────── *Ingredients for about 1 kg · 2 lb* ───────────────

250 g · 8 oz fat from around the pig's
   kidney (*panne de porc*) – can be
   obtained from butchers
1 kg · 2 lb meat to include:
   700 g · 1½ lb pork bladebone or
   spare-rib

300 g · 8 oz goose – these
   proportions may be varied
a bouquet garni: 2 sprigs of thyme,
   1 bay leaf, 2 cloves
salt, pepper

Break the pork fat up into small pieces, and remove any skin (best done by hand). Melt it very slowly in a thick-bottomed pan with 2 cm (¾″) of water.
   Following the grain, cut the pork and goose into 2 cm (¾″) wide strips.
   When the fat has melted, add the meat and the bouquet and leave to cook, to pale gradually – without the fat ever bubbling – for 3–4 hr, very low, stirring occasionally. If you have a solid-fuel stove, the slow oven is ideal.
   Take out the bouquet and leave to cool.
   With a small ladle, remove and set aside a little of the surface fat. Season the meat with salt and pepper, mixing well.
   Pack the rillettes into small jars, leaving half an inch free at the top. Pour a little reserved fat into each. When the rillettes are cold, cover and store in a cool place.

Recommended drink: for rillettes as a snack: a white, red, or rosé Anjou, a Cabernet d'Anjou or de Saumur, a red or white Coteaux du Loir, or cider; for rillettes as an hors d'oeuvre: a white from the region or whatever red is to follow on the menu.

Rillauds, Rillots, Rillons

Can be eaten hot or cold, as a snack, or as a main course with a green salad. The lard left over from the final cooking can be used for sautéing vegetables.

─────────────── *Ingredients for about 1 kg · 2 lb* ───────────────

1 kg · 2 lb lean belly pork
25 g · ¾ oz coarse salt

300 g · 10 oz lard
2 tbsp castor sugar

Cut the belly pork, including the rind, into 30–40 g (1–1½ oz) cubes. Leave in a bowl with the salt for 24 hr, turning the meat over several times.
   Drain and wipe the pork and put it in a thick pan with the lard. Simmer gently – the fat must not bubble – for 3 hr, stirring occasionally. The slow oven of a solid-fuel cooker is excellent for this purpose.

Drain off and save as much fat as possible.

Return the meat to the pan, sprinkle with sugar, and brown slowly stirring constantly until it has taken colour all over.

Recommended wine: as for rillettes above.

Saumon, Beurre Blanc

There is a traditional dispute as to whether *beurre blanc* is from Nantes or Anjou. While the Nantais claim that it originated with a failed *béarnaise* made by la Mère Clémence, cook to the Marquis de Goulaine at the turn of the century, the Angevins regard *beurre blanc* as the apogée of their cooking, only conceivable with the local shallots which give it its subtlety. Cream should never be added to stop the *beurre* separating: the art of *beurre blanc* is, say the locals, to start with a little of the residue from clarifying butter (whey casein) in a bain-marie and to work a tablespoon of boiling water into this before beating in the butter and the reduced shallot.

The classic recipe, from the banks of the Loire, was for pike, but fashions have changed and pike is now considered too bony, while salmon, once so common that household cooks' contracts stipulated that it should not be served more than once or twice a week, has become a rarity, and consequently sought after. Salmon have returned to the Loire, thanks to local efforts.

—————————————— *Ingredients for 8* ——————————————

2 carrots
2 onions
a bouquet garni: 1 sprig of thyme,
  ¹/₂ bay leaf, 2 sprigs of parsley
1 bottle white wine
25 g · ³/₄ oz coarse salt
1 sml tsp roughly crushed
  peppercorns

a salmon 1.7–2 kg · 4–4¹/₂ lb

FOR THE BEURRE BLANC
100 g · 3¹/₂ oz shallots
100 ml · 3¹/₂ fl oz dry white wine
200 ml · 7 fl oz white wine vinegar
250 g · 8³/₄ oz butter
salt, freshly milled white pepper

Make a *court-bouillon*, in a fish kettle, with 3 lt (5 pt) of water, the carrots and onions, peeled and sliced, the bouquet, the wine, coarse salt, and crushed peppercorns. Boil for 20 minutes, then allow to cool.

Leave the salmon unscaled, but gut and clean it. Immerse it in the cooled stock, bring it back to the boil, and simmer gently for 25–30 minutes.

The *beurre blanc* needs preparing so that it is ready at the same time as the fish. Peel the shallots, discarding the hard layers under the skin and any sprouts, and chop them very finely, as there should be no more than a hint of their presence. Cook them very slowly with the wine and the vinegar until the liquid has evaporated and the shallots are reduced to a pale purée. Heat a large saucepan in a bain-marie, pour a tablespoon of boiling water into it and, beating constantly, incorporate very gradually a third of the butter divided into nut-sized pieces, the shallot purée, and the remaining butter also in small pieces. (The temperature of the water in the bain-marie is all important: too cold and the liaison won't take place, too hot and the butter will turn – if that happens, take another suacepan, pour a tablespoon of boiling water into it and gradually beat in the contents of the first saucepan.) Season with salt and pepper.

Drain the fish, skin it, and arrange it in fillets on a hot dish. Serve the *beurre blanc* separately in a sauce-boat.

Recommended wine: Coteaux de Saumur or a Jasnières.

Gogue Angevine
· ANJOU BLOOD SAUSAGES ·

A sort of stocky *boudin*, made in the large intestine of a pig or cow. It is sliced and eaten either cold or lightly fried.

———————————— *Ingredients for c. 2 kg · 4 lb* ————————————

500 g · 1 lb Swiss chard leaf (i.e.
  from a 2 kg · 4 lb bunch)
  or half chard, half lettuce
200 g · 7 oz onions
spices to taste
a few thyme leaves
10 g · ¹/₃ oz coarse salt

pepper
100 g · 3¹/₂ oz pork flair fat
400 g · 14 oz cold bacon fat
1 lt · 1³/₄ pt pig's blood
cleaned sausage skin, from large
  intestine, if possible

Wash the chard leaf well and the lettuce if you are including it. Spin it in a salad-dryer and snip it into a bowl. Chop the onions finely and add them to the green stuff, along with the spices and thyme, and sprinkle with coarse salt and pepper. Leave for 12 hr.

Drain with great care and lightly fry in half the pork flair, having broken it all up into small pieces by hand. Return to the cleaned out bowl.

Dice the bacon fat and sauté fairly hard so that it is crispy rather than melted, in the rest of the flair fat. Add to the bowl.

Beat the contents of the bowl, incorporating the blood; adjust the seasoning.

Knot one end of the skin and fill it, using a special short, wide, round-ended funnel which won't pierce the skin. Tie it roughly every 20 cm (8″), ensuring it is not overful and liable to burst during cooking.

Simmer in water for about 1 hr, without letting it boil, and turning the sausages over occasionally. Leave to cool in the liquid. (This last can be used for soup, particularly if the *boudin* has split open.)

Once cold, drain off the liquid, and hang the sausages for 48 hr in a dry and airy place before cutting them.

Recommended wine: Cabernet de Saumur, Cabernet d'Anjou rosé, Gamay d'Anjou.

Cul de Veau à l'Angevine
· LOIN OF VEAL FROM ANJOU ·

In Anjou, the *cul de veau* is the *quasi-entier*, i.e. the whole hind loin plus the rump. The meat should be well browned before the liquid is added. Braised celery hearts or, in season, morel mushrooms *à la creme* go well.

--- *Ingredients for 8* ---

a hind loin of veal, including rump
250 g · 9 oz fresh pork rinds
200 g · 7 oz onions
800 g · 1¾ lb carrots
½ bottle dry white Anjou
2 tbsp cognac or *marc*

a bouquet: 2 sprigs of thyme, ½ bay
  leaf
stock, preferably beef
salt, pepper
200 ml · 7 fl oz thick cream

Line the bottom of a casserole with the pork rinds, fat side down. Peel the onions, wash and scrape the carrots, slice them all finely, and arrange them in layers on top of the rinds. Put the joint on top and roast uncovered in a medium oven for 20 minutes, turning the meat over after 10 minutes.

Add the wine, the cognac, the bouquet, and stock to cover. Season with salt and pepper, taking account of the strength of the stock. Cover, return to the oven, and cook slowly for 2 hr.

Remove the veal and the pork rinds and, away from the heat, stir the cream into the cooking juices. Keep this sauce warm while you carve the joint (with a well-sharpened knife) then pour it over the meat.

Recommended wine: Coteaux de Saumur or Saumur-Champigny.

Oie Farcie de Segré
· STUFFED GOOSE FROM SEGRÉ ·

Segré holds a goose fair at the beginning of December and this is the time for the young geese which are suitable for stuffing. Locally, they would be accompanied by an assortment of vegetables – quartered artichoke hearts, salsifis (first cooked in water), mushrooms, little onions – all sautéed in butter.

--- *Ingredients for 8* ---

500 g · 1 lb chestnuts
100 g · 3 oz shallots
100 g · 3 oz butter
200 ml · 7 fl oz Madeira
250 g · 8 oz pork bladebone or spare-
  rib
1 young goose + giblets
4 sprigs of parsley

4 sage leaves
salt, pepper
1 bottle white wine
200 ml · 7 fl oz double cream
1 lemon
optional: 2 tbsp homemade tomato
  sauce

Peel the chestnuts: heat them gently in cold water, and take them out as they split. Otherwise, use whole tinned chestnuts.

Sauté lightly a third of the shallots, chopped, in a thick casserole, with a third of the butter and the chestnuts, for 5–6 minutes. Add the Madeira, cover, and cook, shaking the pan occasionally, for 20 minutes (the chestnuts should not be completely cooked). Do not drain.

Mince the pork with the goose heart, liver, and gizzard, and the parsley and sage and stir in the chestnut mixture. Season with salt and pepper. Stuff the bird with this and truss it.

Brown the goose lightly all over, in the casserole, using another third of the butter. Remove the bird and drain off the fat from the pan.

In the same casserole, gently soften the remaining shallots, finely sliced, in the last third of butter, for 5–6 minutes, stirring frequently.

Return the goose to the casserole, pour over the wine, and season with salt and pepper, taking account of the strength of the stuffing. Cover and cook for 40 minutes, turning the bird over at halftime.

Take out the goose. Pressing lightly, strain the cooking liquid into a saucepan and add the cream (and the tomato sauce); leave to reduce slowly while you carve.

Serve everything separately: the goose, the stuffing, the sauce, and the vegetables.

Recommended wine: red: Anjou, Coteaux du Loir, Coteaux de l'Aubance, or Saumur-Champigny.

Pâté de Prunes
· GREENGAGE PIE ·

Pâté means a preparation encased in pastry like *pâté en croûte*, or a pie. This is sometimes made *en pâté pantin*, i.e. without a mould, the pastry being shaped by hand on the baking tray.

——————————— Ingredients for 8 ———————————

400 g · 14 oz shortcrust pastry (see
  p. 224)
1 kg · 2 lb greengages

20 g · ¾ oz butter
100 g · 3 oz castor sugar
1 egg

Wash, dry, and stone the greengages.

Divide the dough into two: two-thirds, one third. Roll out the larger piece to about 3 mm (⅛″) and the smaller one a little thinner. Cut the latter the same size as the pie dish.

Prick the larger piece with a fork and, turning it over, line the buttered dish; cut off the excess dough, leaving a 3 cm (1″) border all round.

Fill the pie with the fruit and sprinkle with the sugar; if you like, insert a pie funnel. Cover with the pastry lid, brush it with beaten egg, fold over the edge of the pastry base, and brush that with egg. Make a hole for the pie funnel – if you are not using one, insert a small pastry or cardboard chimney in the hole.

Put straight into a medium oven (before the fruit soaks into the dough) for 25 minutes.

Recommended wine: Coteaux de Saumur or Saumur-Champigny.

4
THE AUVERGNE
Gévaudan · Velay · Vivarais

The Auvergnats have always retained their identity. Even after years away it clings to them like the mud of their harsh and inaccessible region deep in the Massif Central, where their artistic and cultural autonomy has managed to survive fairly intact.

The Auvergne's reputation is perhaps too strongly founded on pork and cabbage, *potées* and *soupes* which simmer all day. Although soup was often the only course – bacon, chestnut (*la bajane*), and cold milk (*le brézou livradois*) soups enlivened the repertoire. And in the long spells of isolation brought by winter, potatoes, milk, flour, and eggs would be the basic ingredients, to be eked out as inventively as possible in omelettes, pâtés, gratins, and *galettes*.

Far from the coast, their only traditional sea fish was stock fish (i.e. dried but unsalted cod), but the many rivers and lakes provided trout, shad, eels, salmon, and crayfish. Frogs remain plentiful, with a market at Aurillac, and snails, which are eaten with sorrel, are still found in the Clermont region and in the Vivarais.

Hams hang in proliferation from the joists, enjoying the lofty, clean air so propitious to the drying process. Delicious raw, they are also marinated whole, roast, and served with chestnuts *à la clermontoise*, or cooked in bread dough, as at Lezoux. The rest of the pig is not neglected: *saucissons*, *saucisses sèches* (in a U-form, now found all over France), trotters with dried beans, ears – with cheese in the Cantal or with almonds in Bourg-Saint-Andéol – and *boudins*, filled with chestnuts in the Ardèche, further enrich the Auvergnat's diet.

From the cattle which climb high and can be seen silhouetted on the top of distant escarpments where the gentians grow, comes an array of cheeses which were already popular in Paris in the Middle Ages: Tome, Cantal, Bleu d'Auvergne, Fourme d'Ambert, Bleu du Velay, St-Nectaire, which should be matured on a bed of rye straw, and Murol, a round cheese with a hole in the centre, the part that has been removed being sold separately as Trou de Murol. Gaperon or Gapron is made from buttermilk curds, flavoured with herbs or pepper; Tome de Vivarais is cow's milk in winter and goat's milk in summer.

A rugged region with special blessings, rocks that secrete precious stones and the purest of water, it has wine, too, made here since Roman times: Côtes d'Auvergne, mainly red, Corent rosé, often called Corent Gris or Oeil-de-Perdrix, and, on the right bank of the Rhône, the northern Côtes du Rhône, particularly the fruity St-Joseph, the Cornas, and the white St-Péray, a sparkling champagne wine. From Aubrac comes a gentian liqueur and there is yellow and green Verveine from the Velay.

∾

Petites Tourtes de Brioude
· SALMON PIES FROM BRIOUDE ·

A traditional New Year dish for the salmon that once came up the river Allier as far as Brioude. Usually served as one large pie, this is a slightly more festive recipe for individual pies.

──────────────── *Ingredients for 8* ────────────────

750 g · 1¹/₂ lb shortcrust or puff
  pastry (see p. 224)
1.5 kg · 3 lb fresh salmon fillets
200 g · 7 oz fresh mushrooms (fairy-
  ring mushrooms, ideally)
350 g · 12 oz butter

150 ml · ¹/₄ pt fresh cream
salt, pepper, nutmeg
2 lemons
1 egg
6 sprigs of chervil
6 tarragon leaves

Have the salmon cut thinly and set aside the eight best slices. Chop up the rest of the fish with the cleaned mushrooms and pound the mixture in a mortar with 150 g (5 oz) of butter and the cream. Season with salt, pepper, a pinch of grated nutmeg, and the juice of half a lemon.

Divide the pastry dough into three or four portions. Roll each one out to a thickness of 3 mm (¹/₈″), and cut out eight pastry bases, each 3–4 cm (1¹/₂″) larger in diameter than the tart tins (which should be about 12 cm / 5″), and eight pastry pie lids the exact size of the moulds.

Butter the moulds and line them with the pastry bases, leaving a 1.5–2 cm (¹/₂–³/₄″) border all round. Fill the shells with half the salmon mixture, place a slice of salmon in each, and cover with the rest of the mixture.

Put the pie lids in place and brush with beaten egg. Fold the borders of the pastry shells over the lids and brush these with egg. Then make a hole in the centre of each pie top and insert a small piece of pastry rolled round your finger as a funnel to let the steam escape. Cut out pie decorations from the pastry trimmings if you like, sticking them on and brushing them with egg too. Bake in a medium oven for shortcrust pastry and in a hot oven for puff pastry, turning the heat down to medium after 10 minutes, for the latter. In both cases, cook for 20 minutes altogether.

Melt the remaining butter in a saucepan over a hot flame with the rest of the lemon juice (i.e. from 1¹/₂ lemons). When the boiling butter forms an emulsion season with salt and pepper and remove from the heat. Snip the herbs finely on to the butter and serve separately.

Recommended wine: St-Péray or Corent rosé.

Pounti
· SWISS CHARD WITH HAM AND BACON ·

Also called *pountari*. Prunes or raisins are sometimes added.

──────────────── *Ingredients for 4* ────────────────

150 g · 5 oz lean green streaky bacon
1 bunch of leafy Swiss chard
150 g · 5 oz uncooked ham
4 sprigs of parsley
250 g · 8 oz flour

4 eggs
milk
salt, pepper
thinly cut bacon rashers

Blanch the green streaky bacon (see p. 221) and drain.

Wash the chard leaf, and chop it up with the blanched bacon, ham, and parsley. Add the flour gradually, then the eggs, one at a time, and lastly a little milk to soften the mixture. Season with salt and pepper.

Line a terrine with the bacon rashers, and fill it with the mixture, smoothing over the top. Cook for 1 hr uncovered in a medium oven. The top should be well browned and a skewer or knife blade should come out clean. If not, continue cooking, covered with buttered greaseproof paper, if necessary, to stop the crust burning.

Unmould and serve hot as a first course.

Recommended wine: Côtes d'Auvergne rosé or St-Péray.

Potée Auvergnate

Pork and cabbage dishes (*potées*) are found in most regions. Nowadays, the pig's head is not always included. Try to use salted meat which will still be a nice pink, rather than grey, after cooking. You can add dried haricot beans, previously soaked, or a few handfuls of lentils.

―――――――――――――――― *Ingredients for 8–10* ――――――――――――――――

½ a pig's head (can be ordered from a butcher)
500 g · 1 lb lean green streaky bacon
1 pork bladebone, lightly salted (see p. 226)
500 g · 1 lb pork spare-ribs, lightly salted
1 boiling sausage
1 dried sausage (*saucisse sèche*)
1 lge onion
2 cloves

1 bouquet garni: 1 sprig of thyme, 1 bay leaf, 2 sprigs of parsley, 1 celery stalk
50 g · ½ oz lard
1 firm green cabbage
vinegar
400 g · 14 oz carrots
400 g · 14 oz small turnips
salt, pepper
800 g · 1¾ lb potatoes
rye bread

Put the pig's head, bacon, bladebone, and spare-ribs in a large round casserole, covered with plenty of cold water, and bring slowly to simmering point. Cook without boiling for 15 minutes and drain.

Rinse out the pot. Return the meat to it with 4 lt (7 pt) of hot water, the onion, peeled, quartered, and studded with the cloves, the bouquet, and the lard. Let bubble very gently for 2 hr, having skimmed it.

Discard the outer leaves and main stalk of the cabbage, and cut into eight sections. Wash in water to which a drop of vinegar has been added. Blanch by bringing slowly to the boil, covered in fresh cold water, and drain.

At the end of the 2 hr, draw off and set aside enough stock from the *potée* to cook the potatoes, and add to it, the sausage, the carrots, cut into 2 or 4 lengthways, and the whole turnips. Cook for a further 30 minutes. Adjust the seasoning, add the cabbage, and simmer another 20 minutes.

Meanwhile, cook the peeled potatoes in the reserved stock, for 20–30 minutes, according to size.

Extract all the meat from the pot, slice it, and arrange it on a dish; take out the vegetables with a slotted spoon and arrange them with the potatoes round the meat. Eat with slices of rye bread.

For the next meal, reheat the stock, letting it simmer for 7–8 minutes, and pour over slices of rye bread in a soup bowl.

Recommended wine: a red Côtes d'Auvergne or a neighbouring red, like a St-Pourçain.

Boeuf aux Herbes de Massiac
· BEEF WITH SPRING VEGETABLES ·

At Massiac, a cow was killed to celebrate Midsummer's Day. Spring vegetables (*les herbes*) being at their very best just then, they were added in generous proportions.

Ingredients for 8

400 g · 14 oz lean green streaky bacon
3–4 kg · 6–8 lb beef brisket
100 g · 4 oz fat: lard or butter
1 bottle white wine
a bouquet garni: 2 sprigs of thyme, 1 bay leaf, 4 sprigs of parsley, 2 celery stalks
4 young lettuces
1 kg · 2 lb new carrots

500 g · 1 lb new turnips
800 g · 1¾ lb Toulouse sausage
200 g · 7 oz white or spring onions
2 kg · 4 lb peas, unshelled weight
10 basil leaves
salt, pepper
1 dozen sml gherkins in vinegar
2 tbsp capers
2 tbsp strong Dijon mustard
200 g · 7 oz homemade breadcrumbs

Blanch the bacon (see p. 221), drain, and cut into thin slices.

Cut the beef into 4 cm (1½") cubes and sauté in a casserole, over a medium heat, in a third of the fat, until a good colour all over.

Add the bacon, the wine, brought to the boil in another pan, the bouquet, and water to cover. Seal with a close-fitting lid and cook slowly for 2 hr.

Scrape the carrots, peel the turnips, and plunge these, along with the lettuce, into boiling water for 5 minutes. Prick the sausages and blanch separately, for 3 minutes.

At the end of the cooking time, turn the beef over and add the blanched vegetables and sausages, the onions, and, if the liquid has reduced too much, boiling water to cover. Replace the lid and cook for a further 20 minutes.

Shell the peas and at the end of the 20 minutes stir them in together with the basil leaves, salt, and pepper. Cook, still covered, for another 10 minutes.

Grease a large oven-proof dish, strew the bottom with the bacon, and place the thickly sliced sausages in the centre, and the beef and vegetables round the edge, alternating. Scatter the sliced gherkins and capers on top. Mix the mustard with enough of the strained cooking liquid to come about halfway up the dish. Sprinkle with breadcrumbs and dot with the remaining fat.

Put in a medium oven for 20–25 minutes. Serve very hot.

Recommended wine: St-Joseph or a red Boudes.

Montayrol
· HAM, BEEF, AND CHICKEN WITH SAFFRON ·

Still a dish for festive occasions although saffron is no longer cultivated locally. The stock is eaten as soup and it is one of numerous country broths to which, when you have only a little left, you add some wine, and abandoning your spoon, drink directly from the bowl. A comforting habit in cold weather.

----------------------------- *Ingredients for 8–10* -----------------------------

500 g · 1 lb uncooked ham on the
   bone – very dry
1.5 kg · 3 lb beef – brisket, chump,
   or silverside
1 chicken, drawn and trussed
a bouquet garni: 1 sprig of thyme, 1
   bay leaf, 2 sprigs of parsley
1 firm green cabbage
vinegar

1 turnip
1 kohlrabi
1 celeriac
600 g · 1¼ lb good white leeks
400 g · 14 oz carrots
salt, pepper
rye bread – slightly stale
1 pinch of saffron

Cover the ham with cold water and cook gently for about 15 minutes after the water has reached simmering point. Drain.

Rinse out the pan, return the ham to it with 4 lt (7 pt) of water and the bouquet, and bring to the boil. Add the beef, and let it cook, covered, for 1½ hr, skimming at the outset.

Meanwhile, remove the outer leaves and main stalk from the cabbage, and cut it into 8. Wash, adding a little vinegar to the water. Bring slowly to the boil, covered with cold water, and drain. Prepare and wash the turnip, kohlrabi, celeriac, leeks, and carrots.

When the ham and beef have cooked for 1½ hr, add the chicken, all the vegetables, and salt and pepper, and continue cooking, covered and scarcely bubbling so that none of the flavour is lost, for 1–1½ hr or until the chicken is ready. Add hot water if necessary.

Cut the bread into fingers and put them in an oven-proof pot with the saffron and enough of the cooking liquid to give everyone some soup. Leave in a moderate oven for 30 minutes.

Serve the soup first, followed by the meat, sliced and surrounded by the vegetables. There should be gherkins, mustard, coarse salt, and mayonnaise on the table.

Recommended wine: red, e.g. a Chanturgue.

Fetchoulette
· KID WITH SORREL ·

The sorrel gives flavour to what is fairly bland meat (which can be obtained from Halal butchers). This is not however a recipe for the squeamish cook.

----------------------------- *Ingredients for 4* -----------------------------

1 forequarter of kid + heart and liver
250 g · 9 oz lean green streaky bacon
50 g · 1½ oz butter
1 tbsp flour
200 ml · 7 fl oz white wine

1 bouquet garni: 2 sprigs of thyme,
   a bay leaf, 2 sprigs of parsley
4 cloves of garlic
1 kg · 2 lb sorrel
salt, pepper

Blanch the bacon (see p. 221), drain, and cut into small lardons.

Detach the legs from the joint, cut the breast into pieces along the ribs. Peel off the fine skin that covers the heart and cut it into approximately 3 cm (1″) cubes, removing the blood vessels and clots.

Brown the lardons and the pieces of kid, including the heart, all over, in half the butter, on a medium heat.

Lower the heat, sprinkle the meat with the flour, and cook a further 2 or 3 minutes. Add water just to cover, the wine, the bouquet, and the garlic, peeled but whole. Cook, covered, for 30 minutes.

Trim off all but 2 cm (³/₄") of the sorrel stalks, wash well, snip, and cook briefly, 2 or 3 minutes, in the other half of the butter.

Turn the meat over at the end of the 30 minutes, season with salt and pepper, add the sorrel, cover and cook a further 10 minutes.

Meanwhile, remove and discard the fine skin encasing the liver, cut it into cubes and mix well into the other ingredients. Leave on the heat for 5 minutes, and serve.

Recommended wine: white Côtes du Vivarais, a still St-Péray, or Chateaugay for those who insist on red.

Coq au Vin

This should not be made with chicken, which is no substitute for a mature cockerel. Whether or not it is first marinated in wine is a matter of taste – and of the bird's quality. Those who prefer to let the cockerel's flavour predominate dispense with the marinade and choose a light red wine for the cooking. If you do have the blood, it will improve the sauce.

———————————— *Ingredients for 8* ————————————

1 lge cockerel, cut into pieces, and, if possible, its blood
1 bottle Côtes d'Auvergne or other red wine
2 tbsp oil
2 sprigs of thyme
1 bay leaf
3 sprigs of parsley
1 sml tsp coarsely ground pepper
200 g · 7 oz lean green streaky bacon
70 g · 2¹/₂ oz butter

60 ml · 2 fl oz cognac
20 g · ³/₄ oz flour
2 cloves of garlic
salt
2–3 doz sml onions
1 sml tsp castor sugar
freshly milled pepper
150 g · 5 oz small field or cultivated mushrooms
1 lemon

Beat the blood with 2 tablespoons of the wine and refrigerate until needed.

Marinate the cockerel, covered, for 12–15 hr in a cool place, with the oil, wine, thyme leaves, crumbled bay leaf, chopped parsley, and the coarsely ground pepper.

When the cockerel is ready to be taken out, blanch and drain the bacon (see p. 221) and cut into lardons.

Remove the cockerel from the marinade, strain the liquid and bring it to the boil, then leave to simmer.

Wipe the pieces of meat and sauté lightly all over in a casserole with a third of the butter and the lardons. Pour in the cognac and set light to it. When the flames die down, sprinkle in the flour, and turn the meat over two or three times to give it more colour but without letting it burn. Add the hot marinade and the crushed garlic; season with salt. Cover and cook gently for 1 hr.

Meanwhile, soften the whole onions in another third of the butter for 10 minutes, shaking them frequently, and sprinkling sugar over them at the last minute to brown them. Add them to the casserole at the end of the cooking time, turning the cockerel pieces over, and tasting the sauce for seasoning. Cook another 15 minutes.

Clean the mushrooms and stew slowly, covered, with the rest of the butter and the juice of the lemon, for 5–6 minutes, shaking occasionally. Add to the pot and simmer a further 15 minutes.

To serve, transfer the cockerel and its accompaniments to a hot platter with a draining spoon. Away from the heat, beat some of the blood gradually into the sauce, and pour over the meat.

Recommended wine: what was used for the sauce or a Quercy or Cahors.

Chou Farci
· STUFFED CABBAGE ·

Don't be put off by the quantities, it will all get eaten, and it goes well with meat left over from a joint, either cold or sliced and lightly fried in butter.

————————————— *Ingredients for 4* —————————————

1 very large Savoy cabbage (or 2 medium ones)	12 sprigs of parsley
1 bunch Swiss chard or celery	12 sprigs of chervil
500 g · 1 lb lean green streaky bacon	1 doz chives
fat streaky rashers	salt, pepper, nutmeg
500 g · 1 lb carrots	4 tbsp buckwheat flour
1 clove of garlic	250 ml · 8 fl oz double cream
3 shallots	10 eggs

Discard the main stalk and the outer leaves of the cabbage. Separate out the other leaves, cutting away any thick stalks, and wash them. Bring them slowly to the boil in cold water. Drain.

Wash and set aside the green part of the chard. Prepare the stalks, peeling off the film-like skin, cutting them into lengths, and plunging into boiling water. Add the chard leaves after 5 minutes and blanch a further 2 minutes. Drain. If using celery, blanch it a minute or two longer.

Blanch the bacon (see p. 221) and drain. Thinly slice the cleaned carrots.

Cover the base of a terrine with a layer of fat streaky bacon and half the carrots. Then line the terrine completely with the largest cabbage leaves, ensuring some overhang all round the rim; spread a few additional small leaves in the bottom.

Chop up together fairly finely, the lean streaky bacon, the chard (leaves and stalks) or celery, the garlic and shallots, and the parsley, chervil, and chives. Season with salt, pepper, and a little grated nutmeg. Mix in the flour and cream, then the eggs, one by one.

Spread a 1 cm (½") layer of this stuffing in the bottom of the terrine, then alternate layers of cabbage leaves and stuffing, so that the second layer of cabbage reaches just halfway up the terrine and the third layer two-thirds of the way up; the following layers of cabbage should be only one leaf thick, and the final layer should be cabbage.

Fold the overhanging leaves in over the top, cover with fat streaky rashers and the rest of the carrots. Seal tightly with greaseproof paper and string and cook for 2 hr in a medium oven.

Remove the paper, drain the juice off, and unmould.

Recommended wine: if served as a starter or cold, a Corent rosé; otherwise a red Côtes d'Auvergne, Côtes du Vivarais, or St-Joseph.

Aligot
· POTATOES WITH CHEESE AND CREAM ·

Some people prefer to rub the cooking pot with garlic, others to chop a little into the mixture. It is important not to overbeat or overheat the cheese, as it will ruin the texture.

———————————— *Ingredients for 4* ————————————

600 g · 1½ lb potatoes
300 g · ¾ lb cheese – in France, full-
  fat Tomme; in England,
  Camembert will do

150 g · 6 oz butter
140 ml · ¼ pt double cream
1 sml clove of garlic
salt

Boil the potatoes in their skins for 20–30 minutes according to size.

Cut the cheese into thin slivers.

On a low heat, mix the butter, cream, and a pinch of crushed garlic together in a thick pan; season with salt according to the saltiness of the cheese. Beat in the potatoes, peeled and mashed, and very hot.

Add the cheese all at once and beat vigorously bringing the spatula higher and higher.

Serve the moment the purée has risen and is smooth, or it will lose its texture.

Recommended wine: wine is an indigestible accompaniment and not therefore advisable.

Milliard aux Cerises
· CHERRY FLAN ·

For a true *milliard*, you need black cherries – unstoned, as the stones provide the flavour even if they are a slight inconvenience. When cherries are unavailable, apples will do.

———————————— *Ingredients for 8* ————————————

200 g · 7 oz flour
200 g · 7 oz castor sugar
a pinch of salt
6 eggs

400 ml · 14 fl oz milk
1 kg · 2¼ lb black cherries
25 g · ¾ oz butter
a little flour for the tin

Mix the flour, sugar, and salt together in a bowl; make a well in the centre and work in the eggs, one at a time, very gradually, or the mixture will be lumpy, and the milk.

Wash and tail the cherries; let them dry so they do not make the dough soggy.

Butter a mould or tart tin and dust it with flour, shaking off the excess.

Mix the cherries into the dough, pour it all into the tin, and bake immediately at mark 6 / 200°C for 45 minutes.

Serve warm or cold.

Recommended wine: a sparkling St-Péray.

5
BÉARN
The Pays Basque

Although Béarn and the Pays Basque were made into a single department in 1790 (the Basses-Pyrénées, renamed the Pyrénées-Atlantiques later, when any suggestion of inferiority was removed from departmental names) and no one argues any more about the superiority of his beret (Béarnais = black, Basque = red) over the other, the two cookery traditions remain distinct. Béarnais cooking has much in common with neighbouring Bigorre (see map), which, like Béarn, was part of Navarre. Basque cooking is essentially coastal.

Tuna, cod, sardines, anchovies, hake, sea-bream, sea-bass, squid, langoustine, prawns, and crabs are the seafood of the Pays Basque. Olive oil, onions, tomatoes, sweet peppers, ham, salted and dried (from Bayonne, and right up the Adour valley), and, most important of all, *le piment d'Espelette* – chilli peppers which are tied in bunches on balconies to dry – are the flavourings. Next to the peppers, hang the heads of sweetcorn which will fatten the poultry and game and go into savoury *galettes*, *broye* (maize porridge), and different sorts of dumplings (*bourrétade* or *miques* – see p. 114).

Chicken and lamb compete for a place on the Basque table. Mutton is made into *boudins* (*tripotcha*), the stock being used for a *potée au mouton*. In a region of few cows, ewe's cheeses predominate, Arneguy, Ardigasna, and Esbareich, which is soft when young but which matures into a strong hard grating cheese. L'Abbaye de Belloc is a monastery cheese produced semi-industrially near Urt. The only wine to suit the hot, spicy diet is the local Irouléguy, but there is a local cider and a liqueur, Izarra.

The Béarnais, on the other hand, live off the fat of their green land and the fish of the cold mountain streams (*gaves*), firm-fleshed fish like trout and gudgeon, though minnows are not disdained for omelettes. But the typical dishes are soups, filled with vegetables, sorrel, spinach, leeks, wild endive, mallow (*la cousine* while the soup is *cousinète*), and cabbage, which could be called the 'national' vegetable. Chestnuts, less important than they used to be, are grilled with cider. For festive occasions it is the *poule-au-pot* that rules (not the *sauce béarnaise*, created far away in a Paris suburb). The stuffed bird is poached in a beef stock prepared the day before, the stock is then served with vermicelli as a soup, followed by the chicken and stuffing with vegetables.

As in Gascony, the preserving of goose, duck, and pork is a cornerstone of the cookery, providing not only a well-stocked store cupboard, but a valuable cooking fat, all the better for being flavoured with garlic, thyme, and parsley. The Béarnais also enjoy milk-fed lamb (sautéed with peppers), beef, pigeon, woodcock, quail, larks, hare, and wild boar, roast when young, casseroled later.

Again the cheeses are ewe's milk, Oloron or Tardets, and Laruns or Fromage d'Ossau, matured at Gabas. The best-known wines are Madiran, a keeping wine, which goes well with garlic, its white brother, Pacherenc du Vic-Bilh, especially good around Portal, and Jurançon, which comes in dry and mellow versions.

Ttoro de Saint-Jean-de-Luz
· FISH SOUP ·

Pronounced 'tioro', and enjoying numerous spellings. At one time, this Basque soup was made with the water from cooking a salt cod, vegetables and herbs being added, plus grated potato to thicken it. Habits changed, and fish heads, commonly hake, were used to make the stock. But the present-day *ttoro*, a soup enriched with shellfish, is acquiring the reputation of bouillabaisse.

The recipe given includes Dublin Bay prawns (*langoustines*), but along the Basque coast where crawfish (*langoustes*) are common, they are often used instead.

——————————————— Ingredients for 8 ———————————————

2 fish heads (hake or conger eel)
1 carrot
1 leek
2 medium onions
100 ml · 3 fl oz olive oil
2 cloves of garlic
1 sml stalk of celery
6 lge firm tomatoes
1 pinch of saffron
1 small green pepper

1 dried red chilli
2 kg · 4 lb assorted fish in slices or
    steaks: e.g. hake, monkfish,
    gurnard
salt, pepper
8 Dublin Bay prawns
1 kg · 2 lb mussels
flour
small slices of bread
parsley

Clean the fish heads and split in two; wash and slice the peeled carrot and the white part of the leek; slice the onions thinly. Sauté heads and vegetables together gently in a large saucepan with 1 tablespoon of olive oil for 7–8 minutes, stirring frequently.

Add the crushed garlic, celery, tomatoes, skinned, seeded (if you like), and roughly chopped, the saffron, and the pepper and chilli, both tailed, seeded, and cut in rings. When this has reduced by half, add 2.5 lt (4 pt) of water and cook gently for 1 hr.

Meanwhile, ensure all the fish is well scaled, wipe it, and rub each side with salt, pepper, and flour; rinse the prawns, clean the mussels, and fry the bread in a little oil.

When the stock is ready, brown the fish in the rest of the oil, two minutes per side, and arrange in a pot that you can heat and bring to the table. Add the prawns and, having removed the celery stalk, strain in the stock, pressing it through the sieve. Check the seasoning, simmer for 5 minutes, add the mussels, and let the soup bubble until they open.

Serve garnished with the fried bread and sprinkled with chopped parsley.

Recommended wine: a dry Jurançon.

Ouillat
· GARLIC SOUP ·

Tourri, tourin blanchi, tourin à l'ail, all mean garlic soup. The *ouille* is the glazed clay pot in which it is made. You can also use beef stock, or green bean, pea, or broad bean water.

―――――――――――――― *Ingredients for 4* ――――――――――――――

150 g · 5 oz onions
1 head of garlic
1 tbsp goose fat or olive oil
20 g · ³/₄ oz flour

1.5 lt · 2¹/₂ pt chicken stock,
  preferably skimmed
salt, pepper
2 eggs
a trickle of vinegar

Slice the onions and garlic finely and stew very gently (they must not brown) in the fat or oil, covered, in a thick pan, for 10 minutes, shaking them occasionally.

Mix in the flour and stir for a minute or two before adding the stock. Bring to the boil and simmer for 30 minutes. Towards the end of the cooking time, adjust the seasoning. Put through a food mill.

Separate the eggs, whip the whites lightly, and beat the yolks with the vinegar.

When the soup is about to be served, remove from the heat and very gradually beat in first the whites, then the yolks. Do not reheat, as the egg will cook and make the soup granular.

Recommended wine: an Irouléguy, red or rosé.

Garbure Béarnaise
· BEARNAIS VEGETABLE SOUP ·

Speculation has ranged widely on the origins of the word *garbure*, meaning a collection of fresh green vegetables, the most convincing suggestion being that it comes from the Béarnais word *garbe* meaning a sheaf, and, by extension, a bunch.

The soup varies with the seasons: the one given here is autumnal in flavour. In winter you might add turnips or chestnuts, previously grilled; in spring, cabbage is replaced by spring greens or turnip tops, and by broad beans, peas, green beans, even, and new potatoes. Whatever the season, the ham bone (*le trébuc*), or a piece of ham or salt pork, and the *confit*, be it preserved goose, duck, or pork, plus its fat, are essential, but tinned *confit* will do.

In the days of open fire cookery, the Béarnais would spread the *confit* fat on the surface of the soup and set light to it. They would then put hot embers on the lid while the soup cooked and this would give it a crust. And the *garbure* has worked if the ladle stands up in it, like a skittle.

―――――――――――――― *Ingredients for 8* ――――――――――――――

500 g · 1¹/₄ lb fresh white beans,
  shelled weight, or dried and
  soaked haricots
1 ham bone with a little meat
  attached *or* 200 g · 7 oz good ham
  in the piece
800 g · 1³/₄ lb potatoes
200 g · 7 oz carrots
200 g · 7 oz leeks
100 g · 3 oz turnips

1 lge onion
a bouquet garni: 1 sml piece of
  celery, a little parsley
1 red chilli
1 cabbage, white or green
salt, pepper
c. 500 g · 1 lb *confit* of goose, duck,
  or pork + surrounding fat
2 cloves of garlic
a little stale bread

Put 4 lt (7 pt) of water in a thick pan with the beans, the ham, the potatoes, carrots, leeks, turnips, and onion, all peeled or scraped, cleaned, and diced, the bouquet, and the chilli, tailed and seeded; cover and cook on a medium heat for 1 hr. The soup must constantly bubble gently, so have some boiling water to hand in case of evaporation.

Cut out the stalky parts of the cabbage, wash and shred the rest, add to the pan, and continue cooking another 30 minutes.

Add the *confit* and all but a tablespoon of its fat, along with the chopped garlic, salt, depending on the saltiness of the meat, and pepper. Cook a further 30 minutes.

Put some thinly sliced bread into a heatproof serving-bowl (a clay *pignate* in Béarn), transfer to it from the pan enough broth for everyone, cover, and leave to simmer. Set aside the meat, discard the bouquet and the chilli, and pour the vegetables and remaining liquid into an oven pot (a glazed clay one, ideally). Pour the reserved spoonful of *confit* fat on the surface and leave in a low oven until ready to serve. Slice the meat and keep hot to eat with the vegetables, following the soup.

Recommended wine: Madiran.

Piperade

A piperade, whatever may be argued elsewhere, always includes eggs. That said, there are various ways of adding them: stirring beaten eggs into the cooked vegetables; breaking eggs individually into little hollows in the bed of vegetables; mixing breadcrumbs, previously soaked in water and squeezed out, into the eggs and vegetables. If a slice of ham is served, it is fried separately and placed on top, the dish becoming 'piperade with ham'. The true recipe is for the small green peppers (*piments doux*) only grown in south-west France, but it is made with large ones when these are unavailable. If there is no ham fat, olive oil is used. Piperade can be refrigerated for several days, if the eggs have not been added.

———————————— *Ingredients for 8* ————————————

100 g · 4 oz uncooked ham or thin
  gammon rashers, fat and lean
3 tbsp olive oil, more if the ham is
  very lean
200 g · 7 oz onions

400 g · 14 oz sml green peppers
1 kg · 2¼ lb tomatoes
3–4 cloves of garlic
salt, pepper
8 eggs

Dice the ham and brown it lightly in a tablespoon of oil in a thick-bottomed pan. Add the onions, sliced thinly, cover, and stew gently for 20 minutes, shaking the pan from time to time.

Tail the peppers, split them in two to seed them, and cut into thin strips. Cook these gently in a frying pan in the rest of the oil, turning them over occasionally.

When the onions are ready, add the peppers, together with the tomatoes, peeled, seeded, and quartered, the crushed garlic, and salt and pepper. Cook gently for 15 minutes.

Beat the eggs and mix them into the vegetables. Remove from the heat the moment they set.

Recommended wine: Irouléguy rosé.

Chipirons à la Guipuzcoane
· SMALL SQUID STEWED WITH ONIONS ·

Chipirons are tiny squid, not more than 4–5″ long, caught on the Biscay coast in high summer. They are usually stuffed, the stuffing being held in place with cocktail sticks, or served as here.

———————————————— *Ingredients for 4* ————————————————

250 g · 8 oz onions
3 tbsp olive oil
1.5 kg · 3 lb small squid
6 cloves of garlic

salt, pepper
a pinch of cayenne
150 ml · ¼ pt very dry white wine

Peel and chop the onions and soften them slowly in the oil, without letting them brown, for 10–12 minutes, turning them over frequently.

Meanwhile, remove any inkbags by gently detaching the squids' heads, working over a bowl into which you drop each bag, to save as much 'ink' as possible.

To prepare the squid: clean out the mantles (the body part) with a finger or a spoon handle, throw away the entrails and the pen (the transparent backbone). Save the white gelatinous part if it is formed. Remove the film-like outer skin of the mantle, detach the fins, if they've not come off with the skin, and, if you wish, skin the tentacles (done most easily by rubbing with a rough cloth); cut the head to remove the hard piece of beak. Wash the mantles, fins, tentacles, and the white part in plenty of water and cut up. This procedure is much easier and less disagreeable than it sounds.

When the onions are soft, add the squid, chopped garlic, salt, pepper, cayenne, wine, and the inkbags and any ink, rinsed out of the bowl with a little water. Cover and cook for 2 hr or longer if necessary, shaking occasionally.

Recommended wine: dry Jurançon or Txaccoli, a very dry white, hard to come by, from Zarauz, near Saint-Sébastien.

Crabe Farci à la Labourdine
· STUFFED CRAB FROM THE LABOURD ·

———————————————— *Ingredients for 4* ————————————————

4 crabs of about 500 g · 1 lb each
1 lge crab weighing 1 kg · 2 lb
a *court-bouillon* (see p. 222),
    seasoned with a pinch of cayenne
1 carrot
1 onion
5 shallots
3 cloves of garlic
3 tbsp olive oil
250 ml · 8 fl oz white wine

a bouquet garni: thyme, bay leaf,
    parsley
4 tomatoes
salt, pepper
2 sprigs of parsley ⎤ or a little fresh
6 chives   ⎦ mint
6 tarragon leaves
50 g · 1¾ oz homemade
    breadcrumbs

Cook the crabs in the *court-bouillon*, 10 minutes for the small ones, 18 for the large one. Leave to cool.

Scrape and wash the carrot. Soften the thinly sliced carrot and onion, together with the finely sliced shallots and the chopped garlic, in 2 tablespoonfuls of oil. Pour over the wine and the *court-bouillon* and add the bouquet. Reduce by half before putting in the tomatoes, peeled, seeded, and roughly chopped. Cook down gently to a light purée. Remove the bouquet.

Scoop the crab meat out very carefully, saving the creamy tomalley, the coral, and any roe as well. Reserve the 4 small shells.

Strain the sauce and mix in all the crab meat and the herbs, very finely chopped or snipped. Taste for seasoning which should be strong.

Fill the 4 shells with the stuffing, sprinkle with the breadcrumbs, and moisten with the last spoonful of oil. Cook at mark 6 / 200°C for 10 minutes.

Recommended wine: dry Jurançon or Txaccoli (see previous recipe).

Thon aux Oignons
· TUNA WITH ONIONS ·

This can only be made with fresh white tuna, red is not suitable.

──────────────────────── Ingredients for 8 ────────────────────────

1.5 kg · 3 lb onions   ½ sml tsp castor sugar
2 tbsp olive oil   salt, pepper
1.5 kg · 3 lb white tuna in the piece   vinegar
3 cloves of garlic

Stew the finely sliced onions in the oil in a thick-bottomed pan over a low heat, covered, for 30 minutes, shaking the pan regularly but not opening it, so that the onions are reduced virtually to a compote and are hardly coloured at all.

Rub the tuna skin with a rough cloth to ensure it is well scaled.

When the onions are ready, add the crushed garlic, the sugar, salt and pepper, and a couple of drops of vinegar. Bury the tuna in the onion, and cook for 15 minutes, with a lid on, turning the fish over at halftime if the onion does not completely cover it.

Skin the tuna before serving.

Recommended wine: an Irouléguy rosé.

Estouffat Béarnais

Like all *daubes*, this improves with reheating and the 4–5 hour cooking can be done in two stages. It is best cooked in a cast-iron casserole (ideally with a concave lid which can be filled with water) and in the oven where the heat is more evenly distributed.

─────────────── *Ingredients for 8* ───────────────

100 g · 3 oz uncooked ham or
  gammon fat (or lard)
100 g · 3 oz uncooked ham or
  gammon lean
500 g · 1 lb onions
4 cloves of garlic
2 good carrots
bacon rashers or a fresh pork rind

2–2.5 kg · 4–5 lb braising steak, in
  1 large piece if possible
1 bottle of Madiran or other heavy
  red wine, e.g. a Cabernet
2 sprigs of thyme
1 bay leaf
2 cloves
salt, pepper

Dice the ham fat, let it melt slowly in a cast-iron casserole.

Chop the lean ham, onions, garlic, and scraped and washed carrots very finely and stir into the ham fat. Cover, and stew for 15 minutes, shaking occasionally. Remove from the casserole with a slotted spoon.

Line the bottom of the casserole with the bacon or the pork rind, fat side down; fill it with half the ham and vegetables, and lay the beef on top, pour the wine over, add the thyme, bay leaf, cloves, and salt and pepper, and cover with the remaining ham and vegetables.

Seal tightly, fill the lid with water, and leave in a low oven for 4–5 hr, adding water to the lid when necessary. Serve from the pot.

Recommended wine: a Béarn rosé or Madiran.

Lotte à la Basquaise
· MONKFISH WITH PEPPERS, ONIONS, AND TOMATOES ·

Lotte is the name for *baudroie* (monkfish or angler fish), once it has arrived, headless, on the fishmonger's slab.

─────────────── *Ingredients for 4* ───────────────

200 g · 7 oz onions
100 ml · 3 fl oz olive oil
1 kg · 2 lb tomatoes
salt, pepper

a pinch of castor sugar
250 g · ½ lb sml green peppers
half a head of garlic
1 kg · 2 lb monkfish, in 8 slices

Stew the thinly sliced onions gently in a thick frying pan with half the oil, covered, for 30 minutes. Shake the pan frequently but do not take off the lid.

Peel, seed, and quarter the tomatoes; add them to the onions at the end of 30 minutes, and season with salt, pepper, and a pinch of sugar. Continue cooking for 15 minutes.

Meanwhile, tail the peppers, cut them in half to seed them, and slice in julienne strips. Sauté them quickly in 2 tablespoons of oil, with 1 clove of finely chopped garlic. Avoid overcooking as they'll lose their colour. Drain.

In the same pan, over a medium flame, brown the fish, 4 minutes a side, in the remaining oil, which should be nice and hot. Add salt, pepper, and the rest of the garlic, cut into thin strips, when you turn the fish over.

To serve: arrange the hot tomatoes and onions on the bottom of a warmed dish and put the fish, covered with the garlic and the peppers, on top.

Recommended wine: Irouléguy rosé.

Riz à la Gachucha

· A BASQUE PILAFF ·

Gachucha means 'gracious' in Basque. Short-grained rice is used for this recipe because it is easier to mould.

———————————— *Ingredients for 4* ————————————

150 g · 5 oz green olives, stoned
150 g · 5 oz lean green streaky bacon
100 ml · 3 fl oz olive oil
100 g · 3 oz onions
250 g · 8 oz short-grained rice
100 g · 3 oz homemade tomato purée

1 chorizo sausage
salt
a lge pinch of cayenne
500 g · 14 oz sml peppers
20 g · ³/₄ oz butter

Drop the olives into boiling water; drain as soon as the water comes back to the boil. Blanch the bacon (see p. 221). Drain and dice.

Pour all but a spoonful of the oil into a thick-bottomed pan or casserole over a low heat and soften the finely sliced onions for 7–8 minutes. Add the rice, having shaken it in a cloth (there is no need to wash it), and stir until it has absorbed the oil and become translucent.

Mix in the tomato purée and pour over enough boiling water to come about 2 cm (³/₄″) above the rice. Then, without stirring, add two-thirds of the olives, roughly chopped, two-thirds of the chorizo, skinned and sliced, salt, and the cayenne.

Cover, and leave to cook very slowly for about 25 minutes or until all the water is absorbed. Do not be tempted to stir.

Meanwhile, tail and seed the peppers, and cut them into thin strips, and sauté the bacon in the last spoonful of oil. When it begins to brown, take it out with a draining spoon and soften the peppers in the rendered fat.

Butter a savarin mould and, using the butter to stick the garnish to the sides of the mould, arrange the rest of the chorizo, skinned and finely sliced, the bacon, and the remaining olives, also roughly chopped, around the interior. Fill with the rice when it is cooked.

Unmould and put the peppers in the centre.

Recommended wine: Irouléguy – red or rosé.

Gâteau Basque

Made in the past with black cherry jam, but nowadays usually with rum-flavoured *crème pâtissière*. If you prefer jam, you will need 300 g (10 oz) for the proportions given.

———————————— *Ingredients for 8* ————————————

250 ml · 9 fl oz milk
1 vanilla pod
200 g · 7 oz castor sugar
5 eggs
300 g · 10 oz flour

180 g · 6 oz butter
¹/₂ sachet dried yeast
1 sml tsp orange flower water
optional: 2 tbsp dark rum

Start with the *crème pâtissière* so it has time to cool: bring the milk to the boil with the vanilla pod, and set it aside. Beat together 50 g (1¾ oz) of sugar and two eggs until they are creamy and smooth; beating constantly, sift in 30 g (1 oz) of flour and fold in the warm milk (having removed the vanilla pod) very gradually. Pour the mixture into a saucepan, and, over a gentle heat, stir it constantly until it comes to the boil; remove from the heat immediately and dot with 10 g (⅓ oz) of butter in tiny pieces to stop a skin forming.

To prepare the sponge, cream 150 g (5 oz) of butter and continue beating, having added the rest of the sugar, until pale and smooth. Gradually fold in 2 eggs, all but a tablespoon of the flour, the yeast, and the orange flower water.

Butter a sandwich tin and dust with the last of the flour, shaking off the excess. Cover the bottom of the tin with two-thirds of the sponge mixture, using either a spatula or a forcing bag and working from the outside in with a circular movement.

Beat the *crème pâtissière* (adding the rum at this point), and spread it over the sponge, leaving a border all round the edge (the width of a coil) as the cake will not rise properly if the filling touches the tin.

Cover with the rest of the sponge mixture, working in from the edge again with the same spiral movement. Beat the last egg and brush the surface with it. Bake for 40 minutes at mark 6 / 200°C.

Let it cool completely before turning it out on a rack.

Recommended wine: a mellow Jurançon.

6
BERRY

In France, this central province, whose boundaries are not perhaps very well-known to the outsider, is famous for its lamb, which goes so far as to figure in the coat of arms, and its turkeys, the first *poule d'Inde* having been brought back from the East and presented to Charles VII at his residence in Bourges, the capital of Berry, in the fifteenth century.

The cooking of the Berrichons (or Berriois, or indeed, Berriauds) is robust, with lots of traditional soups. If *la fromentée*, a soup where the wheat is cracked in water then cooked in milk, has disappeared, many others, cabbage, pumpkin, turnip and cream, *velouté berrichon* (potato, bean, onion, and parsley) still form part of the daily menu. And for newly weds, to follow an invigorating *routie* (Reuilly wine and chocolate boudoir biscuits, presented to the happy couple in a chamber pot), there is, should they need it, a special wine and onion soup.

Another landlocked region, once dependent on freshwater fish, the Berry too has seen a decline in supply and variety, though crayfish can be caught, by stirring up the river mud, and eels and trout are there; but the gudgeon of the Cher and the lamprey at Vierzon are virtually gone. Carp survive in the ponds of the dank La Brenne region.

A Berrichon is reputedly a loud-mouth – *ferlaud* in local dialect – and the substantial pancakes (*fonds de culotte*), *galettes*, and tarts and pies that he enjoys are known collectively as *ferlauderie*. The pastry, as is often the case here, even with sweet pastry, is made with the goat's cheese (see *pâté de Paques*, below) that comes in all shapes and sizes: flattened pyramids (Valençay, Levroux), tall pyramids (Pouligny, St-Pierre) and *crottins*, such as Chavignol, Sancerre, Crezanay, and Santranges.

As well as lamb, there is veal, stewed in red wine, or with cream; calf's head comes *aux appétits*, an old term once used all over France to designate salad vegetables. Ox-tongue is cooked with gherkins, chicken is stuffed with chestnuts and casseroled. Rabbit goes into sausages and partridge into a salad strongly seasoned with shallots. Morels, chanterelles, ceps, parasol mushrooms are all gathered for the cooking pot. Chestnuts edge into the Berry from neighbouring Limousin.

The Romans discovered the local inhabitants of the Cher making wine, and Pliny sung its praises. He probably still would, if he could taste a Sancerre, a Quincy, a Reuilly, or a Gris de Châteaumeillant, or even one of the lesser known Gris from the Coteaux du Cher or de l'Arnon.

Pâté de Pâques au Biquion, en Chaussons
· EASTER PASTIES ·

An imposing pie for Easter, it can also be made, as here, in the form of lighter individual pasties.

─────────────────── *Ingredients for 4* ───────────────────

FOR THE PASTRY
250 g · 9 oz flour
110 g · 4 oz butter
70 g · 2½ oz fresh Valençay or other
  goat's cheese, salted and drained
  for 4 days

FOR THE FILLING
75 g · 3 oz hand or neck of pork
75 g · 3 oz shoulder veal
75 g · 3 oz shoulder or leg of kid
1 sml onion
3 sprigs of parsley
6 eggs
salt, pepper, nutmeg
oil

Make a puff pastry dough (see p. 224), folding and turning it six times, having first worked the crumbled cheese well into the butter.

For the filling, chop up the pork, veal, kid, onion, and parsley; mix in an egg yolk, salt, pepper, and a pinch of grated nutmeg.

Hardboil 4 eggs.

Roll out the pastry to 2.5 mm (¹/₁₀″) and with a pastry-cutter, cut out four ovals about 16 cm (6″) long and fairly wide, and put a quarter of the filling on half of each one with a hardboiled egg on top. Fold the other half of the pastry over the filling and seal it like a pasty, pinching it together with your fingers.

Paint the surface with beaten egg and cook on a lightly oiled baking sheet for 20 minutes in a medium oven.

Recommended wine: Pinot Noir de Reuilly.

Soupe à l'Ortruge (Ortie)
· NETTLE SOUP ·

Best made in spring before the nettles become bitter. Garlic is sometimes added.

─────────────────── *Ingredients for 4* ───────────────────

500 g · 1 lb young nettle shoots
4 shallots
100 g · 3 oz butter
2 lge potatoes

slightly stale bread, for croûtons
salt, pepper
250 ml · 8 fl oz thick cream

Wash the nettles, and snip a third of them very finely.

Chop up the shallots equally finely, and soften them in 20 g (¾ oz) butter, stirring occasionally. Peel, wash, and dice the potatoes.

When the shallots are soft, add the uncut nettles, and stir for a minute before adding the potato and 1 lt (1¾ pt) of water. Simmer for 20 minutes.

Dice the bread and fry it in the remaining butter.

When the soup is cooked, put it through a food-mill. Season with salt and pepper and return to the heat with the chopped nettles. Simmer briefly (it must be served hot) and turn out into a soup tureen.

Spoon a quarter of the cream into each soup bowl and pour the soup on to it. Serve the croûtons separately.

Recommended wine: either no wine, or, possibly a white that will also go with the next course.

Galettes de Pommes de Terre
· CHEESE AND POTATO CAKES ·

To be eaten on their own or to accompany a main dish.

———————————— Ingredients for 4 ————————————

200 g · 7 oz potatoes
75 g · 2½ oz Valençay or other goat's
   cheese – fresh, salted, and drained
   for 4 days
50 g · 1¾ oz unsalted butter

2 eggs
200–250 g · 7–8 oz flour – the
   quantity depending on the
   quality of the potatoes
oil

Bake the potatoes.
  Skin them and work into them, by hand, the crumbled cheese, the butter, which should have been softened and creamed till quite white, an egg yolk, and enough flour to give the mixture the consistency of a softish shortcrust pastry dough. Set aside for at least an hour.
  Roll out to 1 cm (⅓″) thick and cut out four 10 cm (4″) or eight 5 cm (2″) circular pieces, according to how many *galettes* you want. Brush with beaten egg and arrange on a lightly oiled baking tray.
  Cook for 20 minutes in a medium oven.

Carpe Farcie au Pinot Noir de Reuilly
· STUFFED CARP ·

All the old recipes call for a potato purée stuffing; done in the oven, the potato holds together better and has more flavour.

———————————— Ingredients for 4 ————————————

500 g · 1 lb potatoes
a carp weighing c. 1 kg · 2 lb
100 g · 3 oz mushrooms
120 g · 4 oz butter
1 lemon
100 g · 3 oz finely minced pork (or
   French sausagemeat)
2 shallots
3 sprigs of parsley

6 chives
1 egg
salt, pepper
50 g · 1½ oz carrots
50 g · 1½ oz onions
1 sprig of thyme, ½ bay leaf
1 bottle Pinot Noir de Reuilly (or a
   red Burgundy)

Bake the potatoes and in the meantime prepare the carp: scale it; expose the backbone by making an incision along it, and cut through it just behind the head and before the tail, and pull it out, disturbing as little flesh as possible; gut the fish, saving any roe; wash and wipe it inside and out.
  Clean and chop the mushrooms and sweat them in an open saucepan with 20 g (¾ oz) of butter and the juice of half a lemon, turning them over now and then until all the liquid has evaporated.
  Skin the potatoes and mash them with a fork, mixing in the mushrooms, the roe (if any), the pork, the shallots and parsley, finely chopped, the snipped

chives, the egg, and salt and pepper. Stuff the carp and sew up the opening with tough thread.

Make a bed of finely sliced carrot and onion in an oval oven dish; on it, place the thyme, bay leaf, and carp. Pour over the wine and season, taking account of the strength of the stuffing. Bake in a medium oven for 50 minutes.

Transfer the fish to a hot serving dish, strain the carrot and onion mixture, pushing it lightly through the sieve, and beat in the remaining butter; pour over the carp having removed the stitching. Serve the fish in slices.

Recommended wine: a Pinot Noir de Reuilly.

Foie de Veau Farci
· STUFFED CALF'S LIVER ·

A whole calf's liver once would have been used, but as that is now too expensive, this otherwise traditional recipe has been modified, the liver being made into *paupiettes*.

──────────── Ingredients for 4 ────────────

80 g · 3 oz stale bread, without crust
100 ml · 3½ fl oz beef stock, well
   skimmed
50 g · 1¾ oz shallots
150 g · 5 oz butter
150 g · 5 oz sorrel
3 eggs
½ clove of garlic
8 chives
8 tarragon leaves
salt, pepper

100 g · 3½ oz onions
100 g · 3½ oz carrots
1 tbsp oil
a bouquet garni: 1 sprig of thyme,
   ½ bay leaf, 2 sprigs of parsley
300 ml · 10 fl oz Gris de
   Châteaumeillant (or a rosé)
8 finely cut slices of calf's liver,
   about 80 g · 3 oz each
piece of caul fat

Crumble the bread and soak it in the beef stock. Gently soften the chopped shallots in 20 g (¾ oz) of butter in a thick-bottomed pan, for 5–6 minutes, stirring frequently. Remove the stalks and any dead or discoloured leaves from the sorrel; wash well and snip into the shallots. Cover and stew for 5 minutes. Hardboil 2 eggs.

Away from the heat, stir the crushed garlic into the shallots and sorrel, along with the mashed hard-boiled eggs, the remaining raw egg, the chives and tarragon, finely snipped, and the bread, squeezed as dry as possible. Season with salt and pepper before removing the mixture from the pan.

Sauté the roughly chopped onions in the pan together with the carrots, scraped, washed, and grated, in 20 g (¾ oz) of butter and the oil, for 7–8 minutes, stirring frequently. Add the bouquet and the wine and cook hard still stirring for 5 minutes; transfer to a buttered oven dish.

Divide the stuffing into 8 portions and place one on each slice of liver; roll the liver round loosely. Soak the caul fat in warm water to make it more supple, stretch it, and cut into 8. Wrap each roll of stuffed liver in a piece of it and trim off the excess.

Arrange side by side in the oven dish, cover with foil, and cook in a moderate oven for 20 minutes; remove the foil and turn the rolls over at halftime.

Take out the *paupiettes*, discard the bouquet, very gradually incorporate the butter into the onion, carrot, and wine mixture, pour over the *paupiettes*, and serve hot.

Recommended wine: Gris de Châteaumeillant, Pinot Noir de Reuilly, or a red Sancerre (or the rosé used in the cooking).

Poirat
· PEAR PIE ·

Use whatever pears are in season. Tinned pears are not suitable.

———————————— *Ingredients for 4* ————————————

500 g · 1 lb fresh pears
4 tbsp brandy
50 g · 1¾ oz castor sugar
freshly milled pepper

400 g · 14 oz shortcrust pastry
oil
1 egg

Wash, peel, core and dice the pears. Pour over the brandy and sugar, and season with pepper (some ten turns of the mill – the pepper brings out the flavour). Leave to soak.

Divide the pastry in two and roll out to make two circular pieces about 3 cm (1¼″) thick.

Prick one of the pieces with a fork and turn it over on to an oiled baking sheet; arrange the diced pear on it and cover with the other piece of pastry, pressing top and bottom firmly together with your fingers all round the edge.

Brush the surface with beaten egg; make a small hole in the centre and insert a pastry or cardboard chimney to allow the steam to escape.

Bake for 45 minutes in a medium oven.

Recommended wine: a Vouvray, demi-sec, if eaten as a pudding, otherwise a Sauvignon de Reuilly or a Quincy.

Gâteau Raferdi de Tante Renée
· AUNT RENÉE'S PUDDING ·

Raferdi means cold in Berry dialect; so this is a pudding to be made the day before.

———————————— *Ingredients for 4* ————————————

100 g · 3½ oz mixed crystallised
   fruit, diced
100 ml · 3½ fl oz Kirsch
8 eggs

150 g · 5 oz butter
8 tbsp castor sugar
125 g · 4 oz sponge fingers
optional: *crème anglaise* (see p. 221)

Leave the diced fruit to soak in half the Kirsch.

Hardboil 4 eggs.

Work the hardboiled yolks, while they are still warm, with the softened butter, and add the sugar, the 4 raw egg yolks, and the fruit. Then fold in the raw whites stiffly beaten.

Pour 150 ml ($^1/_4$ pt) of water into a bowl with the remaining Kirsch and dunk the unsugared side of the sponge fingers, briefly, one by one, so that they don't absorb too much liquid; line a charlotte mould, ensuring the fingers are tightly pressed together. Fill with the fruit mixture and cover with the remaining fingers, also dunked and packed together well.

Cut out a piece of cardboard to fit the circumference of the mould neatly; insert it under the rim, and refrigerate, with a weight on top, for 24 hr.

Unmould and serve chilled – hand round the *crème anglaise* separately.

Recommended wine: Vouvray, demi-sec, or Gris de Châteaumeillant.

7
BRITTANY
The Pays Nantais

Much of Brittany's cookery serves as a reminder that it was once an impoverished region making the best of resources. Yet, it enjoys the benign influence of the Gulf Stream, of which it has taken advantage in modern times to provide early vegetables to less privileged parts of Europe, and it has a long intricate coastline which shelters a huge stock of fish and shellfish.

The shellfish, eaten raw, stuffed, sautéed, or stewed, include oysters, from some of France's best beds, mussels, scallops, carpet-shells, cockles, winkles, whelks, and clams. There are also squid, lobster, sea-urchins, ormers (made into a pâté), crawfish, and langoustine, and all sorts of crabs. On the islands, goose-necked barnacles are found and eaten with a vinaigrette or bread and butter.

The staple diet of salt cod no longer comes from Newfoundland, caught by the 'Terre-Neuvas', as the Breton fishermen were known, nor is it simply desalinated and hung in the fireplace for each person to cut himself a slice, grill it on the embers, and wash it down with a bowl of cider. But it is still eaten with potatoes and cream, or butter and herbs or in croquettes or fritters. Nearer to home the catch includes sardines, mackerel (from St George's Channel), tuna, monkfish, and turbot. Brill is cooked with oysters and prawns, sole with Muscadet, mussels, prawns, and a tomato sauce, conger eel with cider. A sweet cake is made out of seaweed, and samphire is collected from the rocks. As for freshwater fish, the Loire offers young eels, in the estuary, and upstream, shad, lamprey, salmon, and pike (on whether the Nantais invented *beurre blanc* to go with the latter, see p. 20).

The land sustains the *pré-salé* lamb of the Mont St. Michel salt-marshes, and cattle. Young veal was so respected in the Ille-et-Vilaine in the nineteenth century that when a girl got engaged, her father had to kill a calf and prepare twenty-five dishes from it for the customary meal. Pigs, as elsewhere in France, are turned into black puddings, brawn, and chitterling sausages. *Andouille de Guémené* is salted and smoked, then desalinated and washed and lengthily poached, either on a bed of hay or with potatoes. *Casse rennaise* is a typical ragout of pig's head, mesentery, calf heel, bacon, pork rinds, and herbs (a *casse* was the pot in which it cooked over the fire). Teal and cormorant are hunted along with partridge, woodcock, deer, and wild duck.

Little of Brittany's milk goes into cheese, though curd cheeses are made at home, and Mingaux is made at Rennes from a blend of fresh and day-old milk, the formula a closely guarded secret. Most milk becomes buttermilk or butter, the latter, given abundant salt-pans, usually being salted.

A modest but robust part of the Breton diet is made up of *farz*, which come in numerous forms, resembling dumplings, puddings, and porridge. *Far pod* is tied in a bag to poach in stock; after cooking it is removed from the bag and beaten till it crumbles, and then eaten with plenty of salted butter. There are also sweet *farz*, known as *farz lichouserich*, a dialect word blending French and Cornish. One *far* still current is *far fourn*, which contains prunes and grapes, and is baked like a flan.

In the seventeenth century, Brittany brought in vines from Burgundy and these provide three *appellation* Muscadets. There is also cider and an *eau-de-vie* (*lambig*) made from it: add some to a cup of coffee and you have a *mic*. And at Rosporden, in south-west Brittany, *chouchen*, a strong fermented honey drink, is produced.

Galette de Sarrasin
· BUCKWHEAT CAKES ·

From the Rennes area where they constituted the main meal on Fridays, usually filled with fried eggs (broken directly on to the hot *galetière* in the hearth). A huge batch would be made to be eaten subsequently instead of bread, or stuffed, often with grilled sausages (known as *galettes robiquettes* after Robiquet, a suburb of Rennes).

————————— *Ingredients for 500 g · 1 lb of buckwheat flour* —————————

2 eggs
20 g · ¾ oz salt
a lump of green fat bacon

Make a well in the flour.

Incorporate the eggs and very gradually enough water (in which the salt has been dissolved) to give the dough the consistency of a pancake batter, beating hard to make it light.

Cook like pancakes, using, if possible, a large, low-rimmed frying pan; grease it with the bacon after each *galette*.

Recommended drink: dry cider is best – otherwise Gros-Plant or Groslot de Retz, depending on the accompanying dish.

Soupe d'Étrilles
· FIDDLER CRAB SOUP ·

The rice is sometimes replaced by tapioca. Fiddler crabs can be found on the southern and western coasts of England.

————————————— *Ingredients for 4* —————————————

1 carrot
2 medium onions
250 ml · 8 fl oz Muscadet
a bouquet garni: 1 sprig of thyme,
  ¼ bay leaf, 2–3 sprigs of chervil
80 g · 3 oz rice (preferably short-
  grain, it binds better)

salt
1 kg · 2 lb fiddler (or other small)
  crabs
pepper
a pinch of cayenne
sml slices of slightly stale, good
  bread

Slice the carrot thinly and chop the onions roughly. Put to boil with the wine and bouquet in 2 lt (3½ pt) of water for 20 minutes.

Cook the rice for 17 minutes in boiling salted water.

Scrub the crabs in plenty of water and drop them into the boiling stock. Cook for 5 minutes after they come back to the boil.

Remove the bouquet and extract the crabs, carrot, and onion with a draining spoon. Mix these with the drained rice, and put through a blender (in several batches).

Press the resulting mixture gently through a sieve into a clean saucepan, and pour in the stock. Season with salt if necessary, pepper, and cayenne. Simmer for 5 minutes.

Pour into a tureen on to the bread, lightly toasted.

Recommended wine: depends on the rest of the menu, otherwise, possibly, a well-chilled Gros-Plant.

Cotriade
· BRETON FISHERMEN'S SOUP ·

This was prepared on board ship with whatever was to hand, the constant ingredients being mackerel and plenty of herbs. The word *cotriade* is thought to come from *cotret*, the support for the cauldron. The fish is eaten first, with a couple of spoonfuls of soup and vinegar or pickles, followed by the soup, served with potatoes.

──────── *Ingredients for 4* ────────

a lge handful of sorrel
2 onions
50 g · 1³/₄ oz salted butter
1 kg · 2 lb potatoes
a bouquet garni: parsley, chervil,
    tarragon, marjoram, etc. + a little
    thyme

salt, pepper
1 kg · 2 lb assorted fish, e.g.
    mackerel, horse mackerel,
    sections of conger eel (head or
    tail), whiting, gurnard
vinegar
a little stale bread

Discard the sorrel stalks and snip the leaves, and stew these with the chopped onions in a large, covered, frying pan, in 20 g (³/₄ oz) of butter, for 10 minutes, shaking frequently.

Add the potatoes, peeled, washed, and sliced, the bouquet, 2–3 lt (3–5 pt) of water (the fishermen would use sea water), and salt and pepper. Simmer hard for 10 minutes.

Scale, gut, and clean the fish, cut up the biggest, and add to the semi-cooked potato, the firmest pieces first, then the rest, making sure everything is covered with water. Simmer until ready (10 minutes or so depending on the size of the pieces).

Transfer the fish to a hot dish and pour a little soup over it, flavoured with vinegar.

To serve the soup, cut the bread in thin strips into the soup tureen, dot with the remaining butter, put in the potatoes, and strain in the soup.

Recommended drink: the strong presence of vinegar limits the choice. Try a dry cider.

Gros Pâté Breton

A coarse pâté from the Rennes region. It is unusual for being cooked uncovered. It must be strongly seasoned: after you have minced all the meat, weigh it, and calculate 20 g (³/₄ oz) salt, and 5 g (¹/₅ oz) of freshly milled pepper per 1 kg (2¹/₄ lb) of meat.

──────────────── *Ingredients for c. 2.5 kg · 5 lb of pâté* ────────────────

750 g · 1½ lb fresh pork rinds
500 g · 1 lb hand of pork
1 kg · 2 lb cold fat bacon
500 g · 1 lb pork liver
1 pig's heart
a pig's melts

200 g · 7 oz onions
12 sprigs of parsley
salt, pepper
2 sprigs of thyme
1 bay leaf
a lge piece of caul fat

Line the bottom of a terrine dish with a third of the pork rinds, fat side down. Put the other rinds in a pan, covered with cold water, and boil for 10 minutes. Drain and chop fairly finely.

Grind all the meat, onions, and parsley, medium fine; mix in the chopped rinds, and season with salt and pepper (see above).

Put the thyme and bay leaf in the bottom of the terrine with the mince on top, and cover with the caul fat.

Cook for 1 hr 40 minutes in a pre-heated oven, first at mark 10 / 250°C, turned down to mark ¼ / 100°C after 10 minutes. Leave to cool and keep in a cool place for a further 24 hr before eating. Serve without unmoulding.

Recommended drink: good cider is if the pâté is eaten as a snack, the first wine on the menu if it is an hors d'oeuvre.

Coquilles Saint-Jacques à la Bretonne

The scallop is a hermaphrodite: the grey coral is the male part, the orange the female, the latter becoming more prominent as laying-time approaches; since at such times, a creature may not be at its best, a pronounced orange coral is sometimes thought to indicate poor flavour, but others take it as the sign of a good scallop. In the past, the beards or mantles were used to improve the stock, but this is rarely done now as they require long cooking.

──────────────── *Ingredients for 4* ────────────────

8 good scallops
100 g · 3½ oz onions
75 g · 2½ oz butter
200 ml · 7 fl oz white wine

a handful of homemade
  breadcrumbs
1 doz sprigs of parsley, chopped
salt, pepper

Wash carefully the white part of the scallops (having removed the membrane) and the corals if you are using them; scrub the deep half of the shells.

Soften the finely chopped onions gently in a saucepan in 25 g (¾ oz) of butter without letting them brown; pour in the wine, cover with a close-fitting lid, and cook slowly for 15 minutes. If you want to include the beards with the wine, leave to simmer very slowly for 2–3 hr.

Slice the washed scallops thinly and add to the pan; season with salt and pepper. Bring to the boil and remove from the heat. Sprinkle with two-thirds of the breadcrumbs and all the parsley.

Divide the scallops up between the cleaned shells. Sprinkle with the rest of the breadcrumbs, dot with the last of the butter and toast lightly under a hot grill.

Recommended wine: Muscadet-sur-Lie or Muscadet.

Homard à la Morbihannaise

Leaving aside the discussion of lobster *à l'américaine* and *à l'armoricaine*, it may be noted that Brittany has always had a *sauce armoricaine*, originally made with crabs flambéed in cider *eau-de-vie* and eaten with cuttlefish. This related recipe, for the small lobster of which the Bretons are particularly fond and which they also roast, grill, or braise in cider, was very popular all along the Lorient coast at the end of the last century, to the extent that Édouard Nignon, the nineteenth-century chef, set it down (as here). To conform with modern tastes, the flour can be omitted and the liaison made simply with the butter.

——————————————— *Ingredients for 4* ———————————————

4 small live lobster, c. 500 g · 1 lb
  each
250 g · 8 oz butter
1 tabsp oil
2 tabsp of cider *eau-de-vie* (Calvados)
3 onions
3 cloves of garlic

400 g · 14 oz firm tomatoes
1 sml tsp of curry powder
salt, pepper
200 ml · 7 fl oz white wine
20 g · ¾ oz flour (optional: see
  above)

Cut the lobster in two lengthways, on a board with a channel to catch the lymph, and remove the grit pouches and the black gut running through the tail meat. Save the creamy parts and the coral, and any eggs, setting these to one side with the lymph. Detach and crack the claws.

On a hot flame, sauté the half-lobsters and claws in 50 g (1¾ oz) of butter and the oil till the shell goes pink; pour over the *eau-de-vie* and set light to it.

When the flames die down, reduce the heat, add the chopped onions, cover, and stew for 4–5 minutes, without letting the onions brown; add the crushed garlic, the tomatoes, peeled, seeded, and chopped, the curry powder, and salt and pepper. Stir well before pouring in the wine. Cover and simmer for 15 minutes.

Work the rest of the butter with the flour, if using it, and the rest of the lobster (lymph, etc.).

Transfer the half-lobsters and claws to a hot dish with a draining spoon. Beat the worked butter hard into the onion and tomato, and pour over the lobster to serve.

Recommended wine: Muscadet-sur-Lie.

Thon aux Légumes de Concarneau
· TUNA WITH VEGETABLES AND MUSCADET ·

As with all such classic recipes, there are numerous variations, for example, braising the tuna on its own with the shallots, the vegetables being cooked separately, with or without tomatoes. But the tender early summer vegetables provide the best flavour. A dish worth preparing in quantity as it is delicious cold.

―――――――――――― *Ingredients for 8* ――――――――――――

a thick fresh tuna steak,
   1.2–1.5 kg · 1³/₄–3 lb
1 tbsp oil
25 g · ³/₄ oz butter
100 g · 4 oz shallots
600 g · 1¹/₄ lb carrots
2 lettuces

salt, pepper
6 sprigs of parsley
250 ml · 9 fl oz Muscadet
250 ml · 9 fl oz stock
1 sprig of thyme
1 kg · 2 lb peas, unshelled weight
250 g · 9 oz long-grain rice

In a casserole, cook the tuna gently in the oil, 5 minutes a side. Remove and clean out the pot.

Return it to a low heat and sauté the chopped shallots and the finely sliced carrots in the butter for 8–10 minutes, stirring frequently.

Wash the lettuces whole, quarter them, and plunge into boiling salted water. Drain carefully as soon as the water comes back to the boil.

Skin the tuna, and add it to the shallots along with the chopped parsley, the wine, and the stock. Season with salt and pepper according to the strength of this last. Put in the thyme and cover the fish with the lettuce leaves. Cook in a closed pot for 30 minutes.

Shell the peas and mix them in; cook another 15 minutes.

Meanwhile, boil the washed rice in plenty of salted water and drain.

Serve the tuna on a bed of rice, covered with the vegetables and juices.

Recommended wine: Groslot de Retz or a red Coteaux d'Ancenis.

Morue à la Brestoise
· SALT COD WITH LEEKS ·

The combination of salt cod and leeks is unexpectedly good.

―――――――――――― *Ingredients for 4* ――――――――――――

800 g–1 kg · 1³/₄–2 lb potatoes
600–800 g · 1¹/₂–1³/₄ lb salt cod,
   soaked under running water for
   at least 12 hr (see p. 222)
4 lge white leeks

1 onion
50 g · 1³/₄ oz butter
1 tbsp flour
salt, pepper
4 sprigs of chervil

Boil the potatoes in their skins for 20–30 minutes, according to size. Peel and slice thinly.

Bring the salt cod, covered with cold water, very slowly to simmering point, remove from the heat, and leave to stand.

Wash and slice the white part of the leeks, and chop the onion. Toss them together in 25 g (³/₄ oz) of butter for 7–8 minutes on a low heat, then sprinkle in the flour, stir for 2 minutes, pour in 250 ml (9 fl oz) of the salt cod's cooking liquid, and let bubble for 5 minutes, stirring constantly. Taste for salt, and add pepper and the chervil leaves.

Butter an oven-proof dish, arrange the drained, skinned, and boned salt cod on a bed of potatoes, and pour over the leeks and onions.

Bake for 10 minutes in a medium oven.

Recommended wine: Musadet or Groslot de Retz.

Rognon de Veau de Haute-Bretagne
· CALF'S KIDNEYS WITH CIDER ·

Buy the kidneys still in the fat if you can. In Haute-Bretagne, this dish is cooked with cider, elsewhere with Muscadet. It is worth doing with lamb's kidneys if calf's are unavailable.

──────────────── *Ingredients for 4* ────────────────

3 calf's kidneys (or lamb's – 3 per
　person)
250 g · 9 oz lean green streaky bacon
200 g · 7 oz small onions
4 cloves of garlic
200 ml · 7 fl oz cider

1 tbsp Calvados
salt, pepper
100 g · 3½ oz butter, for the sauce
　(+ additional butter if there is no
　kidney fat)

Reserve the kidney fat. Remove the thin membrane covering the kidneys, cut them in half, and having carefully cut out and discarded all the white sinewy bits inside, chop them roughly.

Blanch the bacon (see p. 221) and dice.

Break up a little kidney fat and melt it (if you don't have any, use butter) in a large thick frying pan; turn up the heat and brown the kidneys quickly all over. Reduce the heat and continue cooking a further 6–8 minutes – the kidneys should be pink. Drain and keep hot.

Return the frying pan to a low heat, put in a little more kidney fat (or butter) with the bacon, the peeled onions, and the unpeeled garlic, and cook for 5–6 minutes, shaking occasionally. Pour in the cider and the Calvados and cook, still shaking from time to time, until the sauce is reduced to a syrupy consistency; season with salt and pepper.

Away from the heat, incorporate 100 g (3½ oz) of butter into the sauce, check the seasoning, and pour over the kidneys (leaving the garlic in).

Recommended wine: Groslot de Retz.

Gigot à la Bretonne

A la bretonne refers not to the cooking of the lamb, but to the bean and tomato accompaniment. In Brittany, the lamb would always be *pré-salé* – reared on the salt-marshes.

──────────────── *Ingredients for 8* ────────────────

1 kg · 2 lb white haricot beans
2 or 3 onions
2 big tomatoes
a bouquet garni: 2 sprigs of savory
　or thyme, 1 bay leaf, 2 sprigs of
　parsley

salt
2 cloves of garlic
2 kg · 4½ lb leg of lamb
100 g · 3½ oz butter
pepper
2 shallots

Soak the beans in plenty of cold water for at least 12 hr, but changing the water if you leave them longer, to prevent fermentation.

Drain the beans and cook them in fresh unsalted water – salt hardens the skins – with the peeled onions, the tomatoes, and the bouquet, for ³/₄–1¹/₄ hr, or until the beans are ready, adding salt approximately two-thirds of the way through the cooking.

Peel the garlic and insert it along the bone of the meat. Remove the hard outer skin and place the joint in a buttered dish or roasting tin. Dot it with butter, season with salt and pepper and, roast in a hot oven to taste (10–12 minutes per 500 g (1 lb) is very rare).

Towards the end of the beans' cooking time, sauté the shallots, together with the onions and tomatoes extracted from the cooking pot, all chopped, in 50 g (1³/₄ oz) of butter, for 7 minutes, in a pan large enough to take the beans. Using a slotted spoon, add the beans to the sautéed vegetables along with a couple of spoonfuls of the cooking liquid. Season with pepper and keep hot.

Serve the lamb sliced, on top of the beans and coated with its own cooking juices, deglazed and diluted with 1–2 tablespoons of bean liquid.

Recommended wine: a red: Coteaux d'Ancenis, Saumur-Champigny, Bordeaux Cru, Burgundy, Madiran, or Cahors.

Bardatte à la Nantaise
· CABBAGE STUFFED WITH HARE ·

A traditional harvest-supper dish. The Bretons would have stuffed a whole cabbage (rather than making small packets as in this recipe) and served it surrounded by roast quail. The hare would have been caught during harvesting.

───────────────── *Ingredients for 4* ─────────────────

2 leverets or 1 hare, completely
   boned, + offal and blood
a little vinegar
2 tbsp Calvados or brandy
¹/₂ bottle of Muscadet
300 g · 10 oz fat green bacon
100 ml · 3 fl oz thick cream
2 eggs

salt, pepper
plenty of fresh herbs (parsley,
   chervil, tarragon, chives)
1 good, firm cabbage
very thin bacon rashers
50 g · 1¹/₂ oz butter
250 ml · 9 fl oz stock

Beat the blood with the vinegar to stop coagulation and set aside. Bone the hare completely. Cut the leg meat and saddle into fine escalopes and marinate in the Calvados or brandy and an equal quantity of Muscadet for 6 hr.

Mince medium fine the rest of the hare meat along with the hearts, livers, and lungs and the fat bacon. Take the hare out of the marinade; work gradually into the mince, the marinade, the cream, eggs, salt and pepper, and herbs, all finely chopped or snipped, and the blood.

Discard the outside cabbage leaves; wash the inner ones, having removed the thick stalks, and plunge them into boiling salted water and drain the moment it comes back to the boil. This will make the leaves supple. Rinse under cold water to stop further cooking, and dry carefully.

Spread the leaves out, arranging the small ones in pairs, head to tail;

apportion some stuffing to each leaf, or pair of leaves, and a slice or so of hare meat, fold the leaves round the filling and wrap a thin rasher of bacon or two round each parcel.

Put these in a well-buttered heat-proof dish; place on a low flame until the butter starts to colour (but not brown), then pour in the remaining wine. Leave to reduce for 10 minutes.

Turn the packets over, add the stock, cover and cook in a medium oven for 1 hr or until the cabbage is quite soft.

Recommended wine: Groslot de Retz.

Artichauts Rennaise
· GLOBE ARTICHOKES WITH BACON ·

———————————— *Ingredients for 4* ————————————

6 lge artichokes
1 lemon
400 g · 14 oz lean green streaky
  bacon in very thin rashers
100 g · 4 oz butter
200 g · 8 oz onions
200 g · 8 oz carrots

a bouquet garni: 2 sprigs of thyme,
  ¼ bay leaf, 1 sprig of parsley, 2
  cloves
250 ml · 9 fl oz Muscadet
800 ml · ½ pt stock
salt, pepper
3–4 sprigs of parsley

Break off the artichoke stalks and take off the two outer layers of leaves. Cut the tops off the artichokes so that you are left with just the bulbous part; quarter these and, having removed the choke, put into water with the lemon juice.

Blanch the bacon (see p. 221) and drain.

On a low heat, toss the sliced carrots and onions in a heavy pan, with the butter, for 10 minutes. Remove with a draining spoon.

Line the bottom of the pan with the bacon and fill with the carrots and onions, the drained artichoke quarters, the bouquet, the wine, and the stock. Season with salt and pepper, taking into account both the strength of the stock and the saltiness of the bacon. Cover and cook slowly for 1 hr.

Remove the bouquet, transfer to a serving dish, and sprinkle with parsley.

Recommended wine: the wine used in the cooking, unless an accompanying dish calls for something different.

Pommes de Terre de Trébeurden
· POTATOES WITH ONIONS, BACON, AND GARLIC ·

———————————— *Ingredients for 4* ————————————

200 g · 7 oz lean green streaky bacon
200 g · 7 oz onions
150–200 g · 5–7 oz butter – the
  quantity depending on how
  much the potatoes absorb

2 cloves of garlic
1 kg · 2 lb potatoes
salt, pepper
buttermilk

Blanch the bacon (see p. 221) and cut into 2 cm (³/₄″) pieces.

Sauté with the chopped onions in a thick saucepan for 7–8 minutes in 25 g (³/₄ oz) of butter.

Add the crushed garlic, the potatoes, peeled, washed, and quartered, and enough water just to cover, and season with salt and pepper. Simmer until all the water has been absorbed and the potatoes begin to stick but not burn.

Melt the remaining butter in a separate pan. Mash the potatoes with a fork, working in the melted butter; check the seasoning.

Serve with a bowl of buttermilk in which everyone can dip their potato.

Recommended drink: the buttermilk is enough.

Kouigh-Amman
· BRETON BUTTER CAKE ·

Kouigh means cake, and *amman*, butter, in Breton. It keeps for a day or two.

──────── *Ingredients for 4* ────────

500 g · 17 oz flour
20 g · ³/₄ oz salt, or less if you use
   salted butter

20 g · ³/₄ oz fresh yeast
420 g · 14³/₄ oz butter
350 g · 12 oz castor sugar

Pour the flour into a bowl and make a well in the centre. Dissolve the salt and the yeast in 100 ml (3¹/₂ fl oz) of warm water, and mix into the flour. Make the dough into a ball and leave for 20 minutes in a warm place.

Flatten out the dough with your hands to about 1 cm (¹/₃″) thick, spread 400 g (14 oz) of softened butter evenly over it, and cover with 200 g (7 oz) of sugar; turn up the edges of the dough, to hold the butter and sugar in place, and flatten out the dough into a rectangle, using the tips of your fingers. Fold in three as for puff pastry (see p. 224) and leave for 20 minutes.

Move the dough round once so a narrow side is facing you and flatten the dough out again, still with your fingers; fold and leave another 20 minutes. Repeat, moving the dough round in the same direction as previously. Leave it a last 20 minutes.

Butter a round cake tin, dust it with flour, shaking off the excess. Turn the dough upside down into the tin, and press it into shape with your fingers, rinse the cake very quickly under cold water, drain it, and sprinkle with the rest of the sugar.

Bake in a pre-heated oven (mark 6 / 200°C) for 30 minutes.

Recommended drink: ideally, chouchen (see p. 48).

Craquelins

A survival of Medieval cookery, when the dough was poached before being toasted on the fire. *Craquelins* are eaten for breakfast or at any time, either with milk, or buttered with bacon or ham; otherwise they are served with soup instead of bread. Larger ones, *cimeraux*, are made in some parts of the Côtes-du-Nord. *Craquelins* keep for several days in an air-tight container.

—————————————————— *Ingredients for 1 kg · 2 lb of flour* ——————————————————

40 g · 1¼ oz fresh baker's yeast   6 eggs
20 g · ¾ oz salt   flour for working the dough
50 g · 1¾ oz castor sugar

Pour 250 g (½ lb) flour into a bowl and work in the yeast dissolved with the salt and sugar in 200 ml (7 fl oz) of warm water. Cover the bowl with a damp cloth and leave to rise for an hour in a warm place.

Make a well in the remaining flour in another bowl, and mix in the eggs, one by one, then the yeast – you may need to add more warm water if the dough is not malleable enough (but it should be firm). Cover with a damp cloth and leave in a warm place to double in volume (about 30 minutes).

Transfer the dough with floured hands to a well-floured board and roll it out with a rolling-pin; the dough should absorb all this flour and become stiffer.

Cut it into 10 cm (4″) squares. Fold each square's corners in, kneading gently, and flatten and smooth the surface lightly with your fingers. Prick the squares here and there.

In a wide pan, bring the poaching water to simmering point (if the water boils the *craquelins* will not puff out) and drop the *craquelins* in, a few at a time, removing them with a draining-spoon as they surface. Leave to cool.

Immerse the cooled *craquelins* in cold water for 30 minutes. Drain, hollow-side down, for about 1 hr.

Bake them in a medium oven and take them out one by one as they brown.

Recommended drink: a Breton would drink a good glass of cider.

8
BURGUNDY

In the fourth century, the inhabitants of Dijon were already enjoying rabbit with a mustard seed, honey, oil, and vinegar condiment. By the thirteenth century, mustard had achieved not only proverbial status but also economic and political significance when Louis IX's Provost of Paris withdrew Dijon's right to make it and conferred it on the vinegar makers.

Wine may be regarded as the leitmotiv of Burgundian cookery, which may explain a modest selection of soups, though there is a special *potée*, a rich concoction of beef, salt pork, boiling sausage, and cervelat, plus vegetables and potatoes, for feast days.

Freshwater fish, on the other hand, were there for the taking and could only benefit from the wine. Nowadays the fragile balance between supply and demand maintained by the fishing societies, is reinforced by a law prohibiting the sale of river trout to the restaurant trade. The trout is thus the province of the amateur fisherman. The once-abundant burdot (*lote* or *lotte de rivière*, not to be confused with monkfish, *lotte de mer*) was prized for its liver. Burdot was a key ingredient of *la pochouse* (from *la poche*, the fisherman's bag), a dish of many variations, with a history going back to at least the sixteenth century, according to the archives of the Hôpital St-Louis at Chalon-sur-Saône, and calling for at least four kinds of fish to stew in white wine.

The neighbouring Lyonnais may have been more committed to charcuterie and *triperie*, but the Burgundians have nonetheless been inventive in the preparation of the poorer parts of the pig and cow, wine assisting. *Ferchuse* (a name which varies from place to place), was a ragoût made the day the pig was killed and it took care of the liver, heart, melts, and lungs which were cooked with onions and potatoes. Otherwise, the liver might be marinated whole in white wine, wrapped in bacon, and poached in the marinade, to eat cold. Ox-heart would be sliced, larded, marinated, and browned in butter before going to the baker's oven for a long braising with onions and the marinade; while the ox-tongue would be put in coarse salt with two heads of garlic for six days, before being poached in a white wine bouillon. The *andouillettes* were made with Chablis and eaten in a mustard sauce; ham was braised in Chablis.

Almost all the meat dishes depend on wine. The difference between *boeuf à la bourguignonne* and *boeuf bourguignon* is that the former is made with a whole piece of meat larded and marinated in red wine and *marc* before cooking, while the latter is made with cubes of meat which are browned before simmering in red wine. Veal tendrons and rabbit are cooked *en meurette* (i.e. in a red wine sauce); hare with grapes and white wine. *Poulet au verjus* (verjuice) was a dish for an occasion.

The cheese selection is wide, the names evocative: Abbaye de Cîteaux (a Trappist cheese), Époisses, Aisy Cendré, Pierre-qui-vire, Soumaintrain – all cow's cheeses; Bouton de culotte, Charolles, Bessay-en-Chaume, Claquebitou (a little fresh cheese with herbs from Beaune) – all goat's. The Burgundians also have a choux pastry and Gruyère cheese speciality, *la gougère*, said to have originated in the late nineteenth century when a Parisian pastrycook, Léonard, moved to Flogny in the Yonne and started selling *le ramequin*, a cheese confection prepared in the eponymous pots. The locals liked it well enough but complained it was too small, so Léonard dispensed with the ramekins and made it in large rings.

One pudding of note is *la résinaille* or *raisiné*, another wine harvest treat, for which a mass of autumn fruit was cooked in the must while the young danced and the old played cards.

Escargots Beaunoise

―――――――――― *Ingredients for 6* ――――――――――

6 dozen cleaned snails (see p. 134)
2 bouquet garnis: a sprig of thyme,
  1/2 bay leaf, 2 sprigs of parsley, in
  each
2 sml shallots
1 celery stalk

250 g · 8 1/2 oz butter
1 bottle white Burgundy
1 clove of garlic
200 ml · 7 fl oz stock, veal best,
  otherwise chicken
salt, pepper

Wash the snails in plenty of water while bringing a pan of salted water to the
boil with one of the bouquets. Drop the snails into the boiling water and simmer
very gently for 3 1/2 hr. Leave to cool.

Toss the finely sliced shallots, together with the celery, cleaned and sliced
thinly, in 50 g (1 3/4 oz) of butter, in a saucepan, for about 5–6 minutes, on a
low heat. Add the wine, the crushed garlic, and the second bouquet. Reduce
by half.

Once reduced, pour in the veal or chicken stock, and simmer for 30 minutes.
Strain into another pan, check the seasoning, and reheat gently.

Meanwhile, shell the snails and remove the little black bits (their digestive
organs).

Warm up the snails in the sauce and incorporate the remaining butter
gradually.

Recommended wine: the same wine as used in the cooking or a white Côtes de Beaune.

Jambon Persillé
· HAM OR GAMMON IN ASPIC ·

Traditionally made before Easter and served for Easter Sunday lunch. If you
use a calf's foot or two (or pig's trotters, easily obtainable from a butcher), you
shouldn't need gelatine – an ingredient foreign to rural cookery – furthermore
the jelly will be lighter and better-tasting. It will keep several days in the fridge.

―――――――――― *Ingredients for 12–20* ――――――――――

4–5 kg · 8–10 lb uncooked, salted
  ham, or smoked or unsmoked
  gammon joint + the bone
2 calf's feet or pig's trotters
1 kg · 2 lb veal knuckle
100 g · 4 oz carrots
50 g · 2 oz onions
2 cloves

1 bouquet garni: 3 sprigs of thyme,
  1 bay leaf, 4 sprigs of parsley, 4
  sprigs of chervil, 1 sml piece of
  tarragon
1 tbsp peppercorns
1 bottle white Aligoté or Chablis
20 g · 3/4 oz garlic
100 g · 4 oz shallots
1 doz sprigs of parsley

Desalinate the ham under running water for at least 12 hr (not always necessary
for gammon). Bring it very slowly to boiling point in a large pan, immersed in
cold water, and simmer for 30 minutes.

Remove the rind from the ham or gammon and bone it (if necessary). Rinse out the cooking pan, return the ham to it, together with the rind and bone; cover with boiling water. Add the calf's feet or pig's trotters, the veal knuckle, the carrots, the onions stuck with the cloves, the bouquet, peppercorns, and wine. Simmer until the ham feels completely tender when pressed with a spatula, checking about halfway through the cooking to see if salt is required.

Take out the ham, cut it up into large cubes, or mash it with a fork. Dice the meat on the calf's feet and veal knuckle.

Chop up the garlic, shallots, and parsley finely.

Strain the cooking liquid, check the seasoning, let it cool, and skim.

Pour a ladleful of the cooking liquid into a terrine, and tilt the terrine to coat it all over. Leave to set. Cover the bottom with half the diced meat from the knuckle and the calf's feet, using a little additional cooking liquid (if this has set, reheat it gently), to ensure the meat adheres to the sides. Arrange the ham and the garlic, shallot, and parsley mixture in alternating layers, with a final layer of the remaining diced meat on top. Pour in enough of the warmed cooking liquid to cover, making sure it penetrates between the pieces of ham.

Seal and refrigerate. To serve, unmould, by dipping in hot water, and slice. The left-over aspic can be chopped up as a garnish.

Recommended wine: for a snack: a Bourgogne Aligoté – or any good white Burgundy; for a starter: the wine that is to follow on the menu.

Oeufs Pochés Meurette
· EGGS POACHED IN RED WINE ·

A typical Burgundian combination of red wine, bacon, and onions. The lengthy reduction of the sauce thickens it without the addition of flour. The eggs should be very fresh to ensure that the whites hold together; for the sake of the sauce, it is best to poach them separately, as described here.

———————————— *Ingredients for 4* ————————————

100 g · 3½ oz lean green streaky bacon
100 g · 3½ oz onions (or shallots, for a subtler flavour)
120 g · 4 oz butter
1 bottle red Burgundy

250 ml · 8½ fl oz very concentrated stock
8 thin slices of good bread
2 cloves of garlic
50 ml · 1¾ oz wine vinegar
8 eggs
salt, pepper

Blanch the bacon (see p. 221) and cut into small lardons. Sauté gently in 20 g (¾ oz) of butter with the onions or shallots, finely chopped, for 7–8 minutes. Pour in ½ lt (17 fl oz) of wine and the stock, and reduce by two-thirds.

Lightly toast the bread and rub with garlic. Put 2 slices on each plate.

At the same time, bring the remaining wine, with an equal quantity of water, and the vinegar, to the boil, in a deep narrow saucepan; do not add salt as this will stop the whites coagulating.

Reduce the heat to simmering point and break each egg separately into a cup or ladle, bring it as near as possible to the cooking liquid, and drop it in quickly; poach for 3 minutes, remove with a slotted spoon, and place on a slice of bread. If you poach several eggs simultaneously, you need to note the order in which you put them in so that you can fish them out in the same order. Cut off any threads of egg white.

When the sauce has reduced to the required consistency, add salt and pepper, and, away from the heat, gradually beat in the remaining butter. Pour over the eggs.

Recommended wine: the wine used for the sauce, possibly from a better year – or a Volnay.

Andouille aux Haricots

Generally, this dish would be served as here, with the meat and beans separate, but it is also presented as a single dish, the beans and meat arranged in alternating layers, with breadcrumbs sprinkled on top and lightly gratineed.

—————————— Ingredients for 8 ——————————

1.5 kg · 3 lb red kidney or white haricot beans
1 kg · 2 lb chitterling sausages – *andouille de campagne au vin*
1 salted knuckle of pork (see p. 226)
800 g–1 kg · 1¾ lb salted pork spare-ribs
2 snouts and 2 tails, salted
200 g · 7 oz fresh pork rind
3 onions
3 carrots

a bouquet garni: 2 sprigs of thyme, 1 bay leaf, 2 sprigs of parsley, 1 celery stalk
2 cloves of garlic
2 cloves
12–15 peppercorns
1 bottle robust red Burgundy
salt
50 g · 1¾ oz butter
3 more sprigs of parsley

The day before, put the beans to soak and cover the *andouille* with cold water and simmer gently for 2 hr; leave to stand in the cooking liquid.

Drain the beans the next day and put them in a large casserole, over a low heat, just covered with cold water, and bring to the boil.

Put all the salt pork and the pork rind in a panful of cold water and simmer for about 30 minutes.

When the bean water boils, add the onions, peeled and quartered, the scraped, washed, and sliced carrots, and, tied in some muslin, the bouquet garni, the peeled garlic, the cloves, and the peppercorns. Pour over the wine and bring back to the boil.

Drain the salt pork and cut it up or slice it, cube the pork rinds, and add it all to the beans; simmer very slowly for 30 minutes.

Drain the *andouille* and add it to the beans; season with salt if necessary; continue cooking until the beans are soft.

Slice the *andouille* and arrange it in the middle of a dish surrounded by the pork. Serve the beans mixed with the pork rinds and the onion, dotted with butter and sprinkled with parsley.

Recommended wine: the same as for the cooking, but of a better year, or a Hautes Côtes de Nuits.

Queue de Boeuf Vigneronne
· OXTAIL IN RED WINE ·

——————————— *Ingredients for 4* ———————————

100 g · 3½ oz fresh pork rind
1 bottle red Burgundy
½ lump of sugar
c. 1.5 kg · 3 lb oxtail cut into sections
20 g · ¾ oz lard
250 g · 9 oz carrots

3 shallots
1 sml onion
a bouquet garni: 2 sprigs of thyme,
   1 bay leaf, 2 sprigs of parsley
salt, pepper

Blanch the rind (see p. 221); drain. Bring the wine and sugar to the boil.
   In a cocotte or casserole, lightly fry the oxtail in the lard. When it is browned all over, remove it and line the casserole with the blanched rind, fat side down.
   Return the oxtail to it and cover with the carrots, sliced thinly, the whole, peeled shallots, the sliced onions, and the bouquet. Pour in the wine. Season.
   Seal tightly and cook in a slow oven for 4 hr.
   Leave for a few minutes, and skim before serving. Potato or celery purée goes well with this, and is good for mopping up the sauce.

Recommended wine: Côtes de Beaune, or the cooking wine from a better year.

Jambonneau au Mâcon
· PORK KNUCKLE WITH WHITE MÂCON ·

——————————— *Ingredients for 4* ———————————

1 salted knuckle of pork (see p. 226)
1 kg · 2 lb leeks
1 celary stalk
1 carrot
1 clove of garlic
5 shallots

a bouquet garni: 2 sprigs of thyme,
   1 bay leaf, 2 sprigs of parsley
2 bottles white Mâcon
salt, pepper
120 g · 4 oz butter
200 ml · 7 fl oz thick cream
1 tbsp mustard

Blanch the pork knuckle (see p. 221) if it is heavily salted.
   Trim and clean the white part of the leeks and the celery, scrape and wash the carrot, and slice these finely, along with the garlic and 2 shallots. Put into a large casserole with the bouquet, the wine, and an equal amount of water, and bring to the boil. Add the knuckle, cover, and cook very slowly for 1 hr.
   Turn the knuckle over, add salt, if necessary, and pepper; leave to cook a further 40–60 minutes, depending on the size of the knuckle.
   Towards the end of the cooking time, gently soften the other 3 shallots, chopped, in 20 g (¾ oz) of butter, for 5–6 minutes, without letting them take colour. Pour in 2 ladlesful of cooking liquid and the cream, and reduce by a third. Taste for seasoning. Away from the heat beat in the mustard and, gradually, the remaining butter. Slice the knuckle and coat it with some of the sauce; serve the rest of the sauce separately.

Recommended wine: white Mâcon, St-Véran, Pouilly-Fuissé, or Meursault.

Rigodon
· FRUIT AND NUT BRIOCHE ·

This distant cousin of bread and butter pudding would have been put in the
oven when the bread was taken out – the gentle cooking keeps it moist.

──────────────── *Ingredients for 4* ────────────────

750 ml · 1¼ pt milk
1 vanilla pod
150 g · 5 oz castor sugar
a pinch of salt
a pinch of cinnamon
125 g · 4 oz cooked brioche (see
   p. 223)

10 walnuts
5 hazelnuts
7 eggs
2 tbsp rice flour
50 g · 1¾ oz butter
stewed fresh fruit (pears, peaches,
   strawberries, etc.)

Bring the milk and vanilla pod to the boil. Away from the heat, mix in the
sugar, salt, and cinnamon, cover and leave to cool and infuse, stirring once or
twice.

Break the brioche up into small pieces, and soak in 2 or 3 spoonfuls of the
milk. Crush all the nuts roughly, removing any skins.

Beat the eggs, sift and fold in the rice flour, then whip in the milk very
gradually, followed by the brioche and the nuts.

Pour into a deep, well-buttered cake mould. Dot the surface with the
remaining butter. Bake immediately in a pre-heated oven, set low, for 45
minutes.

Cool, unmould, and cover with a layer of stewed fruit. Leave until completely
cold.

Recommended wine: traditionally, Puligny-Montrachet or Meursault.

Flamous
· PUMPKIN FLAN ·

The pumpkin appears in Burgundian cookery as both vegetable – in, for
instance, the now-neglected recipe for *chorlatte* (a dough made with flour, eggs,
cream, salt, pepper, and pumpkin, and baked in cabbage leaves) – and pudding,
as here.

──────────────── *Ingredients for 4* ────────────────

500 g · 1 lb pumpkin
4 eggs
100 g · 3½ oz castor sugar
a pinch of salt

75 g · 2½ oz flour
500 ml · 17 fl oz thick cream
70 g · 2⅓ oz butter

Remove the flesh of the pumpkin, cut it up, and cook in a little water for 15
minutes; drain and mash.

Cream the eggs, sugar, and salt until pale and smooth. Sift and fold in the
flour, then add the cream, pumpkin, and 50 g (1¾ oz) of melted butter.

Pour into a well-buttered sandwich tin. Bake in a moderate oven for 30 minutes. Serve warm.

Recommended wine: a rounded white, like a Meursault.

Pain d'Épices de Ménage
· ANISEED CAKE ·

Dijon, Reims, Orléans, all claimed to produce the best *pain d'épices*. This one keeps very well if wrapped in foil and stored in a cool place.

―――――― *Ingredients for 12* ――――――

FOR THE ANISEED SYRUP
10 green aniseeds
1 cm · 1/2" cinnamon
1 clove

FOR THE CAKE
250 g · 8 1/2 oz honey
30 g · 1 oz candied orange peel

30 g · 1 oz almonds, shelled and
  blanched
a pinch of baking powder
1 sml tsp bicarbonate of soda
2 tbsp of aniseed syrup
150 g · 5 oz rye flour
150 g · 5 oz wheat flour
25 g · 3/4 oz butter

To make the syrup, grind up the aniseeds, cinnamon, and clove, and bring to the boil in 100 ml (3 1/2 fl oz) of water. Leave to cool, and strain carefully.

Heat the honey, without letting it boil, and skim.

Put the orange peel and the almonds through a food mill or blender. Dissolve the raising agents in 2 tablespoons of the cooled syrup – never use a hot liquid as this will destroy their raising power.

Mix together all the flour and the orange peel and almonds. Make a well and work in the honey and the syrup.

Turn into a well-buttered rectangular cake tin, which should be not more than three-quarters full. Bake in a pre-heated slow oven for 1 1/2 hr or until a skewer or knife comes out clean.

Cool slightly before unmoulding.

Recommended wine: a Crémant de Bourgogne.

Tartouillat, Tourtouillat
· CHERRY FLAN ·

In the Charolais, this was cooked on a cabbage leaf in a bread oven.

―――――― *Ingredients for 4* ――――――

250 g · 8 oz flour
250 g · 8 oz castor sugar
1 tbsp vanilla sugar
10 g · 1/3 oz table salt
4 eggs

50 ml · 1 1/2 fl oz dark rum
100 ml · 3 fl oz milk
50 g · 2 oz butter
500 g · 1 lb very ripe black cherries
icing sugar

Work the sugar, vanilla sugar, salt, eggs, and rum into the flour, and add the milk slowly.

Grease a deep round tart tin thickly with butter; fill it with the cherries, washed, tailed, and dried well, but not stoned. Cover with the flan mixture.

Bake for 25 minutes in a medium oven.

Unmould while still hot, sprinkle with icing sugar; cool before eating.

Recommended wine: a white Montagny.

9
CHAMPAGNE

Champagne includes the plateaux and valleys of the French Ardennes. The cooking, not surprisingly, is enlivened by the wine.

Like other northern areas, it has hearty soups, *la soupe au boeuf des Ardennes*, for instance, which despite its name contains a quantity of vegetables, cabbage, swede, leeks, carrots, potatoes, and purslane (a fleshy-leaved herb favoured in sixteenth-century English cooking), and *la potée champenoise* or *des vendanges*, traditional round Reims and Épernay at wine-harvest time, and requiring five kinds of meat and five vegetables including the purply leaves of a *chou d'Écury*.

The plentiful fish in the rivers took well to poaching in white wine or champagne, but two pike specialities from Reims, a Lenten fish cervelat of pike, potatoes, eggs, and butter, and *le pain à la reine*, a sort of fish mousse, eaten with a crayfish coulis, are now almost forgotten, and frogs are no longer eaten since they are a protected species in the region.

Among scores of savoury tarts and pastries were: *ouyettes*, little goose pies, made in quantity for St. Martin's Day (11 November); *la palette à la viande*, a sort of flat pork, veal, and bacon pie, from the Ardennes; *le frotté de l'Argonne*, a kind of quiche; and the pasties filled with veal which were sold on the streets of Reims on New Year's Eve.

With little beef or lamb, pork was a staple. The pork butchers were resourceful, and *andouillettes de Troyes* and *pieds Sainte-Menehould* (pronounced *menou*), pig's trotters, tightly wrapped in linen and cooked in stock till the bones crack, helped carry their reputation beyond provincial boundaries. Bacon is prominent here, especially in salads, which have a local flavour of endive, cos lettuce, or dandelion. Bacon would also be cooked with ham on a fork on an open fire, while lard was eaten on toast, sprinkled with salt.

Meanwhile, the family pig would have been consigned to a swineherd who would take it along with the other families' pigs to fatten up on acorns in the woods. Pork is still cooked a good deal at home, quite simply, pork chops with sage, for example, or pot-roasts. Hams were smoked over broom or cooked whole, closely sealed, in a little water, for twenty-four hours. Sliced ham was cooked in wine or breaded after cooking with herbs and seasonings. There were poultry and game to help ring the changes: *le coq au Bouzy*, or *la poularde au champagne*, or *le civet de lièvre au Bouzy*.

Bread was as important a part of the meal as vegetables and it was sold in 6–12 lb loaves (*miches*). Slices were cut out of smaller loaves (*michettes*) to serve as plates for the meat. Loaves under 2 lb (*le souvendier* or *le pain commun*) were sold for making *casse-croûte* to eat at work, with bacon, or studded with cloves of garlic. There were several excellent cow's cheeses to go with the bread, quite apart from Brie de Meaux: Chaource, Langres, Rocroi, and Carré de l'Est, among others.

Too solid for modern tastes, many puddings and cakes are no longer made, but there are still aniseed cakes, spice cakes, meringues with almonds (*caisses de Wassy* or *de Joinville*), pink biscuits to eat with champagne, myrtle or quetsch tarts from the Ardennes, and sugared almonds from Châlons. They reflect the varied supply of fruit and nuts, but some, like the Saint-Gilles walnuts, noted for their green kernels, the little Rousselet pears which were dried, and the wild plums, Noberte or Balosse, from which jellies were made, have disappeared, and so too has wild asparagus.

As well as champagne, there are red and white Coteaux Champenois or Bouzy, and a rosé from the Riceys. '*Vin de cochon*', a concoction put together with the residue of grapes after fermentation, sugar, water, and sometimes raisins, is just a memory; as is the homemade beer that was drunk with crumbled bread and sugar. But there is *marc de champagne* and cider, and Kirsch from Tourteron.

Soupe au Lait
· MILK SOUP ·

The fresher the milk the better; ideally, it should be unpasteurised.

———————————— *Ingredients for 4* ————————————

750 ml · 1¹/₄ pt milk   salt, pepper
20 g · ³/₄ oz castor sugar   4 level tbsp fine vermicelli

Bring the milk to the boil with 150–200 ml (5–7 fl oz) of water, the sugar, and salt and pepper.
   Add the vermicelli, making sure it separates properly, and cook gently for 10 minutes.
   Serve very hot.

Pissenlits au Lard
· DANDELION AND BACON SALAD ·

Although found in other regions, this dish is paid particular attention here, the lardons being honoured with numerous names – *cretons*, *curtons*, or *quertons* in the Ardenness; *chaïons*, *choïons*, or *chons* around Châlons and in the Argonne. Although potatoes and garden herbs are sometimes added, none of the other additions, such as croûtons or eggs, are part of local tradition. It is a spring salad, to be made before the end of May while the dandelions are small and very green and bitter.

———————————— *Ingredients for 4* ————————————

250–300 g · 9–10 oz small wild   1 shallot
   dandelion leaves   1 onion
150 g · 5 oz potatoes   2 tbsp wine vinegar
150 g · 5 oz lean green streaky bacon   salt, pepper

Wash the dandelion, discarding any dead or discoloured leaves, dry in a salad-spinner, and split each plant in half or quarters, according to size.
   Boil the potatoes in their skins for 20–30 minutes, peel, and mash.
   Cut the bacon into 1 cm (¹/₂″) pieces and sauté gently in their own fat until crisp.
   Put the dandelion in a thick pan, adding the shallot and onion, both finely chopped, and the mashed potato. Heat very gently (the dandelion should soften without actually cooking). Meanwhile, pour the vinegar over the bacon and let it just boil – two or three bubbles – before adding to the dandelion. Mix well, and add salt, unless the bacon is very salty, and pepper.
   Serve at once.

Brochet Braisé au Champagne
· BAKED PIKE OR SALMON WITH CHAMPAGNE ·

The once-abundant pike is nowadays often replaced by salmon or sander.

─────────────── *Ingredients for 6* ───────────────

a pike, salmon, or sander,
  1.5 kg · 3 lb, scaled and gutted
300 g · 9 oz butter
2 medium shallots
1 sprig of thyme
1 bay leaf

salt, white pepper
1 bottle dry white wine
300 ml · 9 fl oz single cream
250 g · 8 oz small button mushrooms
1 lemon
100 ml · 3 fl oz dry champagne

Wash and wipe the fish. Grease generously (using about 100 g / 3 oz of butter) an oval baking dish (or a fish kettle), large enough to hold the fish, and a sheet of greaseproof paper.

Strew the finely chopped shallots, the thyme leaves, and the crumbled bay leaf in the bottom of the dish.

Season inside the fish with salt and pepper, put it in the baking dish, and pour in the wine and cream. Cover with the greaseproof paper, butter-side down. Bake in a medium oven for 30–40 minutes according to the size of the fish, basting from time to time with the cooking juices to keep the fish moist.

Clean the mushrooms meanwhile, cut off the stalks, and sprinkle with lemon juice to stop them discolouring.

Transfer the fish very carefully to a warm dish, cover with greaseproof paper, and keep hot. Pour 100 ml (3 fl oz) of the strained cooking juices into a saucepan with the mushrooms and stew slowly, covered, for 8–10 minutes.

At the same time, reduce the rest of the strained cooking juices to a coating consistency.

Skin the fish, arrange it on a serving dish, and continue to keep hot, still under greaseproof paper.

Pour the reduced sauce into a deep bowl and gradually beat in the rest of the butter, softened, until the sauce is creamy, then add the cooking liquid from the mushrooms, and the champagne. Taste for seasoning.

Surround the fish with the mushrooms and coat with a little sauce, the rest being served separately.

Recommended wine: a dry champagne, or a Blanc de Blancs or Coteaux Champenois.

Rôti de Sanglier en Cocotte
· POT-ROAST WILD BOAR ·

The wild boar is the emblem of the Ardennes. It may be casseroled or roasted depending on the cut, or – as here – pot-roasted. This is also a good way of cooking pork.

———————————————————————— *Ingredients for 8* ————————————————————————

2 shallots
2 cloves of garlic
4 sprigs of parsley including stalks
1 sprig of thyme
1 bay leaf
pepper

a joint of wild boar, 1.5–2 kg · 3–4
  lb, on the bone (shoulder or loin)
75 g · 2½ oz lard
salt
200 ml · 7 fl oz white wine

Chop up the shallots and garlic and parsley, including the stalks; mix in the thyme leaves and the crumbled bay leaf, and season with pepper.

Rub this mixture well into the meat and leave, covered, in a cool place for 24 hr.

In a casserole, brown the joint all over in the lard, over a medium heat. Season with salt, cover, and cook slowly for 30 minutes.

Turn the meat over, pour in the wine, and continue cooking very gently for 1 hr, turning the meat over again once; if at this point the sauce seems to have reduced too much, add a little boiling water, but without pouring it directly on to the meat.

Carve in slices and serve the sauce separately.

Recommended wine: Bouzy, Beaune Cru, St-Émilion, or Pomerol.

Épaule d'Agneau à la Farce Champenoise
· STUFFED SHOULDER OF LAMB ·

The stuffing in this recipe can be used for any meat or game, and even for vegetables. Ask your butcher to remove the bladebone from the shoulder, but to leave in the knucklebone.

———————————————————————— *Ingredients for 6* ————————————————————————

1 boned shoulder of lamb (see
  above)
3 carrots
4 onions
a bouquet garni: 1 sprig of thyme,
  1 bay leaf, 2 sprigs of parsley,
  1 clove of garlic
1 bottle dry white wine
2 tbsp white wine vinegar
3–4 juniper berries
pepper

1 shallot
1 other clove of garlic
3 more sprigs of parsley
1 chicken liver
450 g · 1 lb finely chopped pork
salt
75 g · 2½ oz lard
4 very firm large tomatoes
200 ml · 7 fl oz dry champagne
50 g · 1¾ oz butter

Put the lamb in the piece, together with the carrots and 3 onions, all thinly sliced, the bouquet, all but 100 ml (3½ fl oz) of the still wine, the vinegar, juniper berries, and pepper, in a bowl just large enough to hold everything. Leave to marinate for 24 hr in a cool place, turning the meat over once or twice.

To prepare the stuffing, chop up the remaining onion, the shallot, and the second clove of garlic, together with the parsley and the chicken liver. Mix with the pork and the reserved still wine and season with salt and pepper.

Take the meat out of the marinade and wipe it. Put the stuffing in place of the bladebone, roll the joint up tightly round it, and tie it. Brown all over in a casserole in the lard, on a medium heat.

With a slotted spoon, transfer the seasonings from the marinade to the meat, cover the casserole, and cook slowly for 10 minutes.

Now pour in the marinade liquid, and season with salt, taking account of the strength of the stuffing. Seal and cook for 2–2½ hr according to the size of the shoulder. Turn the joint over halfway through and, 20 minutes before the end, add the peeled, seeded, and chopped tomatoes.

When the joint is ready, take it out. Strain the cooking juices, pressing the vegetables through the sieve, and leave to stand for a few minutes to let the fat rise to the surface before skimming. Return to a low heat, add the champagne and let it reduce to a coating consistency, check the seasoning, and away from the heat, beat in the butter.

Pour a little of the sauce into a serving dish and arrange the lamb, sliced, in it. Serve the rest of the sauce separately.

Recommended wine: Bouzy Rouge or a Mercurey.

Bayenne
· POTATOES WITH ONION AND GARLIC ·

There is neither fat nor liquid in this recipe despite the meaning of its Old French name: 'split in boiling water'.

―――――――――――――― *Ingredients for 4* ――――――――――――――

1.2 kg · 2½ lb medium-sized
  potatoes
500 g · 1¼ lb onions

1 clove of garlic
salt, pepper

Wash but don't peel the potatoes; cut them in half. Slice the onions and garlic thinly.

In a cast-iron casserole, arrange a layer of potatoes, skin side up, then a layer of onions, garlic, salt, and pepper, another layer of potatoes, and so on, until all the the ingredients are used up.

Seal with a close-fitting lid. Bake for 1 hr, turning the heat from medium to low after a few minutes.

Gâteau Mollet

A *gâteau mollet* is eaten warm, with mousses, creams, fruit desserts, or just with a hot drink. In the past, it would have been cooked in a cocotte; nowadays, a ridged mould, with a central funnel, like a *kougelhopf* mould, is used.

―――――――――――――― *Ingredients for 4* ――――――――――――――

5 g · ⅙ oz salt
10 g · ⅓ oz castor sugar
20 g · ¾ oz fresh baker's yeast

250 g · 9 oz flour
3 eggs
200 g · 7 oz butter

Dissolve the salt, sugar, and yeast in 3 tablespoons of warm water. Stir in 50 g (1³/₄ oz) of flour and leave in a warm place until it has doubled in volume (about 20 minutes).

Pour the remaining flour into a bowl and make a well in the centre, fold in the eggs, one by one, then the yeast. Work it hard to make a smooth firm dough.

Mix in gradually 175 g (6 oz) of butter, softened but not melted. Make into a ball. Cover the bowl with a damp cloth and leave to rise in a warm place for 2 hr.

With lightly floured hands, flatten the dough and shape it to fit into a large buttered mould which should not be more than half full. Cover with a damp cloth again and leave in a warm place until it is 2 cm (³/₄″) from the top of the tin.

Cook in a pre-heated oven, mark 7–8 / 225°C, for 25 minutes. Test with a skewer or a knife which should come out clean.

Recommended wine: champagne, demi-sec.

Galette au Sucre

Ingredients for 6
---

500 g · 17 oz brioche dough (see
  p. 223)
80–100 ml · 3–3¹/₂ fl oz thick cream

150 g · 5 oz castor sugar
75 g · 2¹/₂ oz butter

When the dough has risen well (see pp. 223–4), flatten it out and shape it with your fingers to fit a wide, shallow tart tin. Cover with a damp cloth and leave to rise another 30 minutes.

Spread the cream over the dough with a spatula, sprinkle with the sugar and dot with the butter.

Bake for 15 minutes in an oven pre-heated to mark 10 / 250°C.

Unmould on to a rack. Serve hot – with coffee.

10
DAUPHINY

Dauphiny, which became the departments of the Isère, the Hautes-Alpes, and the Drôme, forms a watershed between Alpine Savoy and Mediterranean Provence, and although popular myth has it that the Dauphinois live on four dishes, all gratins: millet, pumpkin, crayfish (see over), and potato (see p. 77), in fact the province's dual nature is echoed in a diet as rich in olive oil (from the famous olives of Nyons) and anchovies, as in butter, cream, and milk. A typical dish is a *bouillée*, a sort of fish stew with trout, pike, eel, and crayfish, made in the Rhône area, and served with croûtons spread with anchovy butter.

As in other mountainous regions, the air is conducive to fine-tasting hams and these used to put under the ashes of the fire to cook. The various sausages and *saucissons* also benefit from the altitude, two notable ones being the fennel-flavoured *murçon de la Mure*, which is served hot with boiled or steamed potatoes, and a winter *saucisson de chou*, made near Briançon.

Cattle and sheep are nourished on gentians and other aromatic mountain plants. For Easter, half a side of beef would be marinated with twenty or so chickens in a highly spiced, highly alcoholic marinade, in preparation for a *daube viennoise*. Both beef and veal are cooked with anchovies: in a *grillade marinière*, slices of beef are layered with onion, and seasoned halfway through the cooking with crushed anchovies, chopped parsley and garlic, vinegar, and olive oil; veal chops are studded with bacon and anchovies and stewed with onions, spices, and *eau-de-vie*. Milk-fed lamb goes into a *blanquette*.

There are plenty of chickens as the Easter *daube* suggests. They are also cooked with crayfish or spit-roasted over a wood fire, and both chickens and eggs are eaten with the numerous wild mushrooms that grow here, morels, chanterelles, and ceps, as well as black Périgord truffles (the name indicates the variety, not the source). Although many birds are now protected, quail, partridge, and pheasant still appear on the table, the latter cooked in Chartreuse. It is an area where unusual game was prized, including squirrel, which was eaten in a white wine fricassée.

The Dauphinois cook has been ingenious with potatoes, not stopping at the invention of *gratin dauphinois*, but sautéing them *à la dauphinoise* (i.e. with garlic and vinegar), filling tarts with them, stuffing them with eggs, *fines herbes*, or whatever was to hand, or mashing them with an equal quantity of chestnuts for a *pounti*, a staple winter dish, saved from dryness by the addition of milk or wine. The other vegetables eaten here are rather foreign to modern British taste: cardoons, picked before Christmas and stored in the dark to whiten, pumpkins and marrows, and Swiss chard.

The excellence of Dauphinois dairy products gives the cookery its finesse, and, in the past, a suitor could assess his chances of success with the lady of his choice by the amount of grated cheese she put on his soup. The range of cheese is broad: Tomes (or Tommes as they are called commercially) from cow's or goat's milk; Bleu de Lavaldens and de Sassenage, both cow's cheeses; and Saint-Marcellin, once a goat's cheese from the left bank of the Isère, now a cow's cheese from the right bank. Fresh goat's cheese is the basis of *pétafine*, a mixture of cheese, cream, and *eau-de-vie*, left to mature, and eaten with bread.

Dauphiny is walnut country, the walnuts from Grenoble being regarded as some of the best in France. They find their way into cakes, sweets and pastries. Further south there is nougat – from Montélimar.

Besides Côtes du Rhône, there is Hermitage and Crozes-Hermitage, Coteaux du Tricastin, and the sparkling Clairette de Die, which must not be left more than two years or it will be flat. Chartreuse originated here, the first, the green, at the hand of Père Maubec in 1737; the second, the yellow, the work of Frère Bruno Jacquet a hundred years later.

Soupe de l'Ubac
· POTATO AND MILK SOUP ·

L'ubac is the side of the mountain in shadow. The milk is good in these high pastures and such a soup would have constituted a whole meal.

―――――――――――――― *Ingredients for 4* ――――――――――――――

1 kg · 2 lb potatoes
500 ml · ³/₃ pt milk
salt, pepper
a veal bone, preferably a knuckle

bread
100 g · 3 oz grated Gruyère
50 g · 1½ oz butter

Peel and wash the potatoes, cut them up roughly.

Boil the milk with 2 lt (3 pt) of water, in a casserole. When it boils, add salt and pepper, the potatoes, and the knuckle, and simmer for 1 hr.

Slice the bread into thin strips and arrange them in layers, alternating with the grated cheese, in the bottom of a soup tureen. Dot the top with butter. When the soup is ready, remove the bone and pour into the tureen.

Gratin de Queues d'Écrevisses
· FRESHWATER CRAYFISH GRATIN ·

Surprisingly, although crayfish are *the* shellfish of Dauphiny, there is no trace of a recipe for this most typical of local dishes before 1850, perhaps because any Dauphinoise cook worth her salt would have known how to make it. As for the crayfish, they only had to be caught . . .

―――――――――――――― *Ingredients for 4* ――――――――――――――

500 ml · ³/₄ pt white wine
1 onion
1 carrot
a bouquet garni: 1 bay leaf, 2 sprigs
   of parsley
salt, pepper
2 dozen freshwater crayfish

175 g · 6 oz butter
50 g · 1³/₄ oz flour
250 ml · 8 fl oz milk
250 ml · 8 fl oz thick cream
4 eggs
100 g · 3½ oz grated Gruyère

Make a *court-bouillon* in advance, with 2 lt (3 pt) of water, the wine, onion, peeled and quartered, carrot, and bouquet. Leave to bubble gently, uncovered, until reduced by half. Season with salt and pepper.

Add the crayfish and cook gently for 6 minutes. Drain, keeping about 100 ml (4 fl oz) of the stock.

Detach the crayfish heads and pick out any flesh inside. Shell the tails carefully so as not to damage them. Crush the head and tail shells in a mortar or blender and melt them gently in 100 g (3½ oz) of the butter. Press lightly through a sieve into a bowl of iced water, and extract the hardened butter.

Butter a gratin dish. In a thick pan, mix the remaining butter with the flour to make a roux, and whisk in the milk, warmed. Let it bubble for 5 minutes, stirring constantly. Add the cream and the reserved stock and reduce by a third, still stirring frequently.

Away from the heat, beat in the separated egg yolks, and the crayfish butter. Add the shelled crayfish. Taste for seasoning.

Pour into the gratin dish, sprinkle with the Gruyère, and put under the grill for a few minutes until the cheese has risen slightly and is golden brown on top.

Recommended wine: a white Hermitage.

Omelette au Fromage

The village of Les Andrieux, high in the Alps, spends a hundred days a year in shadow, so deep is it set in its valley. To celebrate the sun's annual reappearance on 10 February, all the villagers used to gather on the main bridge to offer omelettes to the celestial light before dancing and making merry.

––––––––––––––––––––– *Ingredients for 4* –––––––––––––––––––––

8 eggs
2 tbsp thick cream
100 g · 3½ oz coarsely grated
  Gruyère

salt, pepper
50 g · 1¾ oz butter

Beat the eggs together and continue beating, adding the cream.

Mix in the cheese, and season with salt according to the strength of the cheese, and pepper.

Heat two-thirds of the butter in a frying pan on a medium heat, and just before it starts to smoke, pour the eggs in quickly. Using a spatula, stir the eggs, working inwards from the edge in a spiral. As soon as the omelette sets, fold it, and slide it out on to a buttered oven-proof dish.

Brown under the grill, ensuring that the inside remains slightly runny.

Recommended wine: a white: Châtillon-en-Diois or Coteaux du Tricastin.

Rioles de Corps
· POTATO QUENELLES ·

Similar to Italian *gnocchi*. Here the potato is mixed with cheese, cream, and eggs, a trio dear to Dauphiny.

––––––––––––––––––––– *Ingredients for 4* –––––––––––––––––––––

600 g · 1¼ lb large potatoes
1 fresh goat's cheese
200 ml · 7 fl oz thick cream
50 g · 1¾ oz butter

1 egg
salt, pepper
100 g · 3½ oz grated Gruyère

Wash the potatoes and boil them in their skins for 20–30 minutes.

Peel and mash them while they are still hot, adding the goat's cheese, half the cream, half the butter, and the egg, beaten; season with salt and pepper. Taking small portions of the mixture, roll them one at a time between your fingers to make tiny sausages (*rioles*), the size of corks.

Bring a large pan of salted water to the boil and drop in the *rioles* in batches, turning them over with a draining spoon and fishing them out as they rise to the surface. Drain well.

Place them in a buttered oven dish, pour over the remaining cream, and sprinkle with the Gruyère. Brown in a medium oven for 8–10 minutes.

Recommended wine: if they are being eaten on their own, white Crozes-Hermitage, or Coteaux du Tricastin or Châtillon-en-Diois rosé; otherwise, depending on what they are accompanying.

Ravioles
· DAUPHINOIS RAVIOLI ·

Nowadays, ravioli is associated with Italy, but *ravioles* have always been enjoyed in Dauphiny, and are still made in France, with numerous different fillings, an enrichment of the past when goat's cheese was the principal stuffing. Serve them plain with a bowl of grated Gruyère or Beaufort cheese.

—————————————— *Ingredients for 8* ——————————————

FOR THE PASTA
500 g · 17 oz flour
4 eggs
100 ml · 3½ fl oz oil
10 g · ⅓ oz salt

FOR THE FILLING
50 g · 2 oz parsley (chopped weight)
25 g · ¾ oz butter

60 g · 2 oz grated Gruyère
350 g · 12 oz fresh Saint-Marcellin
cheese (or other soft French
cow's cheese, with 50% fat
content)

FOR COOKING THE PASTA
3 lt · 5 pt well-skimmed chicken
stock

To prepare the pasta: pour the flour into a bowl and make a well in the centre. Work in, very gradually, 2 whole eggs, plus 2 whites, the oil, and the salt dissolved in a tablespoon of hot water. Knead well, adding a little water if the dough is not elastic enough – in theory this should not be necessary, but in practice it depends on the quality of the flour. Make into a ball and leave for at least 2 hr covered with a damp cloth.

For the filling: chop the parsley finely and stew it, slowly, uncovered, in the butter until it has just softened – it should not take colour. Mix in the Gruyère, the Saint-Marcellin, and the two remaining egg yolks, with a spatula. Remove from the heat.

Divide the dough into two equal parts and roll out very thinly, with one piece thinner (and thus larger) than the other.

On the smaller sheet, arrange little mounds of filling, the size of a hazelnut, in rows, just over 3 cm (1″) apart. Cover with the second sheet of pasta. Press the two together around the mounds of filling with your fingers, and cut each *raviole* out, with either a pastry wheel, which helps seal the pasta together as well as giving a crenellated edge or, failing that, a knife.

Bring the stock to the boil in a wide pan, and drop in a few *ravioles* at a time so that they don't stick together; when the stock comes back to the boil, lower the heat and let the *ravioles* simmer for 5 minutes. Remove them with a slotted spoon and proceed with the next batch.

Recommended wine: as for rioles *above.*

Bettes à la Voironaise
· SWISS CHARD WITH EGGS AND GRUYERE ·

Chard leaves are often incorporated in fillings and stuffings. This is a recipe for the stalks. To stop them losing their colour, they are sometimes cooked in a flour and lemon *blanc* (see p. 220). More simply, lemon juice may be added to the cooking water.

─────────────────── *Ingredients for 4* ───────────────────

the stalks from a 1 kg · 2 lb bunch
  of chard
salt
optional: 1 lemon
80 g · 2¹/₂ oz butter

80 g · 2¹/₂ oz grated Gruyère
pepper
2 eggs
optional: 2 tbsp well-skimmed stock

Trim and wash the root end of the chard and remove the film-like skin which covers the stalks, with a small knife. Slice into 4–5 cm (1¹/₂″) sections, boil in salted water – with lemon juice if you like – for 30 minutes, and drain.

In a big frying pan, sauté the chard in the butter for 7–8 minutes. Sprinkle on the Gruyère, turning the chard over to coat it in the cheese; season with salt, if necessary, and pepper.

Beat the eggs (adding the stock, if you are including it), pour into the frying pan, and stir with a spatula until they set.

Serve at once, very hot.

Recommended wine: if served on its own, a local white.

Gratin Dauphinois

A dish that has done the *tour de France* if not of Europe, not always to advantage. Its success, however, depends less on faithfulness to a recipe than on the quality of the potatoes and the cream – it should be single cream, not milk. To the south-west of Grenoble, in the Pays des Quatres-Montagnes, they will tell you that you need waxy yellow potatoes, that cheese is out of order, that the potatoes should only just show through the cream, that the surface should be dotted with butter, and that, above all, the gratin dish needs special attention, as explained here.

─────────────── Ingredients for 4 ───────────────

1 kg · 2 lb waxy potatoes
1 clove of garlic
1 sml turnip
50 g · 1¾ oz butter

salt, pepper, nutmeg
single cream, the quantity
depending on the size of the gratin
dish

Peel the potatoes, and cut them into thick (2 cm / ¾″) slices, wash and wipe carefully.

Rub the inside of a gratin dish big enough to hold the potatoes in not more than 3 or 4 layers, with a peeled clove of garlic and the turnip, peeled and cut in two; butter the dish with half the butter.

Arrange the potatoes in the dish in layers, adding salt, pepper, and a pinch of nutmeg to each layer. Pour over the cream, just to cover, no more; dot with the remaining butter.

Bake in a low oven for 1–1½ hr, increasing the heat 15 minutes before the end to brown the top slightly.

Pogne, Pougna, Pugna
· EASTER CAKE ·

Would be made from a portion (*une poignée* – a handful) of dough set aside during the bread-making, worked together with butter, eggs, and a flavouring, to make an Easter cake. Sometimes a little pumpkin was added to give colour. Made into figures of soldiers, they became known as *suisses*, after Napoleon's army.

─────────────── Ingredients for 4 ───────────────

20 g · ¾ oz fresh baker's yeast
10 g · ⅓ oz salt
100 g · 3½ oz castor sugar
500 g · 17 oz flour + a little for
  working the dough

1–2 tbsp orange flower water
6 eggs
300 g · 10 oz butter
a little oil

Dissolve the salt and 20 g (¾ oz) of sugar in 70–80 ml (2–3 fl oz) of warm water, and add the yeast. Stir in 100 g (3½ oz) of flour to make a soft mixture. Cover the bowl with a damp cloth and leave in a warm place to double in volume (about 20 minutes).

Mix the remaining flour and sugar together. Make a well in the centre and gradually work in the orange flower water, the eggs, one by one, and the yeast mixture, beating well to give the mixture body. Lastly, incorporate the softened butter.

Make into a ball, cover the bowl with a damp cloth and leave for 2 hr. Deflate the dough with floured hands, reshape into a ball, and leave, covered, for a further 4–5 hr.

Flour your hands, and form the dough into 2 large rings on a lightly oiled baking tray. Leave another 20–30 minutes before baking.

Wet a knife in cold water and make a few incisions in the rings. Bake in a medium oven for 30 minutes, testing with a skewer or knife which must come out clean.

Unmould on to a rack straightaway.

Recommended drink: a Muscat from the nearby Vaucluse – Beaumes-de-Venise or Rasteau; or a sparkling St-Péray or a young Clairette de Die.

Gâteau aux Noix
· WALNUT CAKE ·

A light homemade cake that brings out the flavour of the local walnuts. It can be decorated with whole nuts or iced with pale caramel.

———————————— *Ingredients for 4* ————————————

200 g · 7 oz castor sugar
6 eggs
2 tbsp dark rum
1 sml tsp coffee

6 *biscottes* / French toasts (or crisp homemade breadcrumbs)
250 g · 8–9 oz shelled walnuts
20 g · ³/₄ oz butter

Cream the sugar and egg yolks until the mixture is smooth and pale, and all the sugar dissolved. Add the rum and coffee and mix well.

Crumble the *biscottes* finely, crush the walnuts, and add to the cake mixture. Beat the egg whites till they peak and fold them in carefully.

Pour the mixture into a buttered sponge-cake tin which should not be more than three-quarters full as the cake will rise. Bake for 45 minutes in a slow oven, until a skewer or knife comes out clean.

Reverse the tin on to a rack, but wait a few minutes before unmoulding. Let the cake cool.

11
FLANDERS · HAINAUT
Avenois

A province which does not respect modern political boundaries and which makes up for a bleak landscape and an uncertain climate with a continuing tradition of warm hospitality (coffee – with chicory – is always on the hob), a full calendar of *fêtes*, fairs, and festivals, and a passion for clubs and societies (archery, *boules*, pigeon-fancying).

The cooking is long and slow, a subtle blend of sweet and sour. A beer-drinking region, the beer often finds its way into the cooking pot. And there are plenty of soups to keep out the chill, including cherry and red wine, beer (flavoured with cinnamon, a touch of sugar, and cream), onion, beetroot, pumpkin and leek, and *soupe flamande* (potato, leek, celeriac, tomato, tapioca, and chervil).

Beef, poultry, and game are all submitted to a lengthy simmering process – *carbonade de boeuf* (see p. 84), duck with raisins, turkey or duck stuffed with bacon, chestnuts, and apple, sweet and sour *civet de lièvre*, boar with hop shoots, for example. It is notable that there are no pigeon recipes here, perhaps because every town has its homing pigeons and its *rue des coulons* in their honour. Pork also has its sweet accompaniments, for instance, *boudin noir* which may itself contain raisins, is eaten with cinnamon-flavoured apples, and pig's liver is cooked with plums.

However there is a salty, smoked side to the diet. The fish are familiar to us on the English side of the sea, and certain tastes and even names are shared (kippers, haddock – only for the fish once smoked), though the Flamands prefer their herrings lightly salted and smoked like bloaters; these are known as *craquelots* or *bouffi* and are eaten with potatoes which have either been baked or cooked with garlic and very little water (in an enamelled pan called an *étouffoir*). Smoked haddock is the basis of a *carbonade de poissons*. Ox-tongue also goes into the smoke-house before being filled with layers of foie gras to make a luxurious dish called *langue de boeuf de Valenciennes* or *Lucullus*.

It is also the land of *steack-frites* – the bulls, it is said, come up to Lille, because their meat is more appreciated there. But the *gens du Nord* enjoy potatoes cooked in other ways – and vegetables in general. Asparagus, hop shoots, leeks, chicory, are all eaten hot with melted butter and egg yolk, one yolk on each plate to be mixed with the butter. Carrots are served with bacon (in this part of France, it is not Father Christmas who comes, but St Nicholas, on 6 December, and carrots are left out for his donkey), and garlic from the peatbogs of Arleux contributes its smoky tang to the cooking.

The cheeses are strong, with Maroilles topping the list. Boulette d'Avesnes is a whey cheese kneaded with *fines herbes* and mixed with beer before being left to dry, nailed, in the past, to planks of wood hung on the window frame. Gris de Lille is also called le Puant Macéré, a vivid enough name. Mont-des-Chats was a Trappist cheese now become the ubiquitous and indifferent Saint-Paulin.

It is impossible in a short space to mention all the puddings, cakes, pastries, and sweets. As well as tarts, pies, waffles, pancakes, and brioche, there are *clouches*, little balls of pasta which are poached in milk or water, sautéed in butter, and served with sugar and the milk if that was used. *Croquandouilles* are made in the shape of St Martin on his donkey (on which he apparently disappeared in the dunes of Dunkerque). *Couques* are light raisin cakes, while *couquebaques* are buckwheat pancakes, and *couquebootram flamand* is a large brioche.

Péninque or *péningue* (sugar and wheat glucose), also known as *la bêtise de Cambrai*, merits its own festival.

Cider is made here, and Dutch gin (*genièvre*), a drop or two of which in a cup of coffee makes *l'bistouille*, but it is beer that is consumed by the *pot*, *pinte*, or *canette*.

Potjevleisch en Terrine
· CHICKEN, RABBIT, AND VEAL TERRINE ·

A dish from the Dunkerque area, blessed with numerous names, *pot de viande*, *terrine flamande*, *pâté flamand*. It cannot be made in small quantities but keeps well in the fridge.

———————————— *Ingredients for 8–10* ————————————

legs and wings from a good boiling fowl
back and front legs of a large rabbit – the saddle is too dry
300 g · 10 oz shoulder veal
200 g · 7 oz shallots
10 sprigs of parsley
200 g · 7 oz cold lean streaky bacon
salt, pepper
optional: 1 lemon
dry white wine
2 sprigs of thyme
1 bay leaf
1 fresh pork rind, to cover the terrine dish

Cut the chicken, rabbit, and veal into large pieces, without boning. Chop up the shallots and parsley. Dice the bacon.

Fill a terrine dish with the meat, alternating the different kinds, and packing it well down. Insert a little of the shallot mixture, salt and pepper, and lemon slices (if you like), between layers, and slip the bacon in the holes between the meat.

Pour in enough wine just to cover, arrange the sprigs of thyme and the bay leaf on top, and spread the pork rind over, fat side down. Seal the terrine tightly with foil.

Stand the terrine in a container of water in a slow oven for 3 hr, during which time you should continually be able to hear it bubbling gently.

Remove from the oven, leave to cool, set aside the pork rind, and take out the herbs, and the bones if you wish. Put the pork rind back, press the pâté down and, when it is quite cold, refrigerate.

Unmould to serve.

Recommended wine: Mâcon-Viré, St-Véran, Chablis, or even Beaujolais-Villages, chilled.

Goyère de Valenciennes
· MAROILLES CHEESE TART ·

Possibly the invention of a certain Gohier in the early sixteenth century, it appears on the menu of a wedding feast in Lille, dated 17 June 1587, as *gohière*. For *aficionados*, it must puff up like a soufflé.

——————————————————————— *Ingredients for 12* ———————————————————————

half a soft Maroilles or Munster   100 g · 3¹/₂ oz grated Gruyère
180 g · 6 oz flour   salt, pepper
1 kg · 2 lb *fromage blanc*, well drained   400 g · 14 oz enriched shortcrust
5 eggs   pastry dough (see p. 224)
                                        20 g · ³/₄ oz butter

Work the Maroilles or Munster well into the flour. Stir in the *fromage blanc*, 4 eggs, one by one, and Gruyère; add salt, if necessary, and pepper.

Roll out the pastry to 2 mm (¹/₁₀″), prick it with a fork, and line a deep, buttered tart tin; build up a thick border and brush with beaten egg.

Fill with the cheese mixture and cook for 25 minutes in a medium oven. Serve hot.

Recommended drink: a good blond French or Belgian beer.

Anguilles au Vert
· EELS WITH HERBS ·

Eels are caught in the canals of Flanders and cooked with fresh herbs and vegetables – some fourteen in all, if possible, plus, sometimes, a little aniseed.

——————————————————————— *Ingredients for 4* ———————————————————————

1.5 kg · 3 lb small skinned eels   2 garlic stems ⎤ or spring onion
flour   2–4 shallot stalks ⎦ tops
150 g · 5 oz sorrel   80 g · 2¹/₂ oz butter
100 g · 3 oz spinach   500 ml · 17 fl oz white wine
150 g · 5 oz watercress   salt, pepper
50 g · 1¹/₂ oz young white nettle   1 sml sprig of green winter savory
  shoots   1 sml sprig of green thyme
20 g · ³/₄ oz parsley   ¹/₂ fresh bay leaf
20 g · ³/₄ oz chervil   4 eggs
12 tarragon leaves   200 ml · 7 fl oz thick cream
10 g · ¹/₃ oz young salad burnet   1 lemon
4–5 sage leaves

Slice the eels into 5 cm (2″) sections and rub with flour. Stalk the sorrel, spinach, watercress, nettles, parsley, chervil, tarragon, and salad burnet; wash all these together with the sage and garlic and shallot stems and snip finely.

On a moderate heat, sauté the eel in half the butter. Pour in the wine, season with salt and pepper, reduce the heat, and simmer for 10 minutes until the flesh comes away from the backbone easily. Take the eel out of the liquid.

Soften the chopped herbs and vegetables separately in the remaining butter, adding savory and thyme leaves to taste, and the half bay leaf, broken up small.

Beat the eggs, cream, and a trickle of lemon juice together, over a bain-marie. Continue beating while adding the wine in which the eel cooked and all the greenery. Check the seasoning.

Coat the pieces of eel in the sauce and serve either at once or cold.

Recommended drink: if hot: Chablis or St-Véran; if cold: continental lager or light beer.

Lapin aux Pruneaux
· RABBIT WITH PRUNES ·

─────────────── *Ingredients for 8* ───────────────

1 large rabbit, cut up, with its liver
1 bottle of red wine
3 tbsp of oil
100 ml · 3½ fl oz red wine vinegar
a bouquet garni: 2 sprigs of thyme,
   1 bay leaf, 4 juniper berries, 2
   sprigs of parsley
1 sml tsp coarsely crushed
   peppercorns

2 dozen prunes
50 g · 1¾ oz raisins (optional)
250 g · 9 oz lean green streaky bacon
flour
50 g · 1¾ oz butter
200 g · 7 oz shallots or onions
salt
1 tbsp of redcurrant jelly

The day before you intend to eat this, cover the liver with some of the wine and leave in a cool place, and put the rabbit pieces to marinate in 1 tablespoon of oil, all but 100 ml (3½ fl oz) of the remaining wine, and the vinegar, plus the bouquet, and pepper, for 18 hr, turning the meat over a couple of times.

The following day, soak the prunes (and raisins) in the reserved wine.

Blanch the bacon (see p. 221). Cut into lardons.

Take the meat out of the marinade, wipe well and rub with flour to dry it; brown in a thick pan or casserole, over a medium heat, with 20 g (¾ oz) of butter and 1 tablespoon of oil, and remove from the pan.

Reduce the heat, add the rest of the butter and oil, and soften the finely sliced shallots or onions.

Strain the marinade into a saucepan and boil for 10 minutes.

When the shallots or onions are ready, return the rabbit to the pan, with the marinade, and salt; cover and cook for 40–60 minutes, depending on the age of the rabbit.

Ten minutes before the end of the cooking time, add pepper, if necessary, and the whole liver, plus its marinade.

When cooked, arrange the rabbit in a deep dish with the liver sliced in escalopes on top. Stir the redcurrant jelly into the cooking juices and pour over the meat.

Recommended wine: Givry, Morey-St-Denis, Corton, red Bandol, Cahors, or Madiran.

Hochepot de Queue de Boeuf
· OXTAIL STEW ·

There are endless interpretations of the word *hochepot*, familiar, of course, to English ears as hotchpotch and, perhaps, hot pot. Not surprisingly for a recipe current by 1392, there are many variations, but the oxtail is always present. A Flemish *hochepot*, for example, also includes top rib of beef, shoulder of lamb, pig's head and ears, pork belly, all sweated or blanched before the liquid is added, and a selection of vegetables (leeks, carrots, turnips, celeriac, celery, parsnips, cabbage, potatoes) and herbs, including juniper, and the broth is served first with toast and grated cheese.

---------------------------------- *Ingredients for 4* ----------------------------------

1 fresh pork rind, the size of the
  cooking pot
100 g · 3½ oz onions
2 cloves
a bouquet garni: 2 sprigs of thyme,
  1 bay leaf, 2 sprigs of parsley
600 g · 1¼ lb carrots
1.5 kg · 3 lb oxtail, cut up

2 pig's ears (can be obtained from
  butchers)
1 sml firm Savoy cabbage
vinegar
200 g · 7 oz turnips
400 g · 14 oz Toulouse sausage
50 g · 1¾ oz butter
50 g · 1¾ oz flour
10 sprigs of parsley

Line the bottom of a casserole with the pork rind, fat side down. On top, spread the onions, cut into eighths, and stuck with the cloves, the bouquet, and the sliced carrots. Put in the oxtail and the whole pig's ears. Seal tightly, and cook in a medium oven for 30 minutes.

Meanwhile, remove the outside leaves and cut the cabbage into eight; cut away the thick stalks, and wash in acidulated water. Bring slowly to the boil, covered with cold water, and drain.

Put the quartered turnips and the cabbage into the casserole, along with hot water just to cover, and salt and pepper. Seal and cook in a low oven for 2 hr.

Add the sausage and leave to cook, still covered, another 5 minutes.

Melt the butter slowly in a saucepan, and make a roux with the flour. Pour in 600–700 ml (1–1¼ pt) of the cooking liquid and let bubble for 10 minutes, stirring constantly. Away from the heat, check the seasoning and add the parsley, finely chopped.

Serve the vegetables and sauce separately. Cut the pig's ears up small and slice the sausage.

Recommended drink: red Mâcon, Beaujolais Cru (Chiroubles, Fleurie, Juliénas), Pauillac, St-Julien, or beer – preferably a bière de garde.

Carbonades Flamandes

The secret of this well-known dish lies in the combination of braising or stewing steak (rather than a roasting joint), lard, brown sugar, vinegar, light beer, and mustard, with bread to bind the sauce.

---------------------------------- *Ingredients for 4* ----------------------------------

800 g · 2 lb lean braising or stewing
  steak, sliced thinly, on the bias, if
  possible
50 g · 2 oz lard
250 g · 9 oz onions
1 tbsp soft brown sugar
1 tbsp wine vinegar

a bouquet garni: 2 sprigs of thyme,
  1 bay leaf
salt, pepper
500 ml · 17 fl oz light beer or lager
1 slightly stale slice of good bread
1 tbsp strong smooth Dijon mustard

In a thick-bottomed casserole, brown the meat on both sides, over a medium heat, using half the lard, and remove from the pot.

Reduce the heat, add the rest of the lard, and toss the sliced onions in it for 10 minutes. Stir in the brown sugar and the vinegar and cook 2–3 minutes.

Return the meat to the pot, layering it alternately with the onions, and placing the bouquet in the middle. Season with salt and pepper. Pour in the beer. Crumble the bread and sprinkle it in. Cover and cook in a slow oven for 3 hr.

Transfer the meat to a hot serving dish and mix the mustard into the sauce. Check the seasoning and pour over the meat.

Recommended drink: as for previous recipe.

Coq à la Bière

Cock-fighting is a traditional pastime around Tourcoing and Roubaix. It is, however, the farmyard cockerel that goes into the cooking pot.

──────────────── *Ingredients for 8* ────────────────

125 g · 4 oz lean green streaky bacon
20 g · ³/₄ oz lard
1 young cockerel, 2.5 kg · 5 lb
  (available from game suppliers),
  cut into pieces
2 tbsp Dutch or juniper gin
1 tbsp flour
500 ml · 17 fl oz light beer or lager
50 g · 1³/₄ oz shallots

1 clove of garlic
1 bouquet garni: 1 sprig of thyme, 1
  bay leaf, 2 sprigs of parsley
salt, pepper
2 dozen sml onions
50 g · 1³/₄ oz butter
250 g · 8 oz button mushrooms
100 ml · 3¹/₂ fl oz thick cream
  (optional)

Blanch the bacon (see p.221). Dice and brown two-thirds of it gently in a casserole, in half the lard. Remove with a draining spoon.

Raise the heat, and sauté the cockerel legs in the remaining lard, adding the rest of the bird after five minutes. Put in the browned bacon. Pour in the gin and set light to it; when the flames die down, sprinkle in the flour, and stir for 2–3 minutes. Add the beer, the finely chopped shallots and garlic, the bouquet, and salt and pepper. Cover and cook in a moderate oven for 1¹/₂ hr.

Half an hour before the end of the cooking time, peel the small onions, and, leaving them whole, sauté gently with the remaining bacon, in half the butter, shaking the pan occasionally.

Clean and tail the mushrooms and mix into the browned onions with the rest of the butter. Cover and stew for 15 minutes, shaking the pan at intervals.

When the bird is cooked, transfer the pot to a low flame. Extract the cockerel pieces, arrange them in a pre-heated dish, and keep hot. Discard the bouquet. Pour the mushrooms, onions, and bacon into the meat juices and add the bird's liver, chopped (and green gall removed). Check the seasoning, and simmer 2–3 minutes (with the cream if you are using it).

Pour over the meat and serve.

Recommended drink: red Sancerre or Moulis – or a strong lager.

Salade de Chicots
· CHICORY SALAD ·

Made with the white chicory that the French call *endive* or, in this region, a major producer, *chicots* or *chicons*.

──────────────── *Ingredients for 8* ────────────────

500 g · 1 lb potatoes
salt
500 g · 1 lb sml firm heads of chicory
4 tbsp oil
2 tbsp wine vinegar
pepper

1 lge onion
4 sprigs of parsley
5–6 chives
100 g · 3 oz smoked lean streaky
    bacon

Boil the peeled and washed potatoes in salted water for 20–30 minutes according to size.

Meanwhile, if the chicory is clean, simply wipe the outside, and cut a cone shape out of the base and rinse it out; otherwise, wash it, but do not leave it to soak as that brings out the bitterness. Slice and set aside.

Mix a vinaigrette of oil, vinegar, salt, and plenty of pepper in a salad bowl. Add the finely chopped onion.

Purée the potatoes in a food mill and mix into the vinaigrette. Stir in the chicory and the herbs, chopped or snipped finely.

Cut the bacon into thin lardons, and fry until just crisp.

Pour the bacon with its hot fat over the potato salad and serve.

Chou Rouge à la Flamande
· RED CABBAGE WITH ONION AND APPLE ·

Goes well with goose, turkey, or venison, as well as pork and sausages.

──────────────── *Ingredients for 4* ────────────────

c. 1 kg · 2 lb red cabbage
1 lge onion
50 g · 1³/₄ oz lard
1 tbsp soft brown sugar

salt, pepper
red wine
250 g · ¹/₂ lb apples

Remove the outer leaves of the cabbage and cut off the end of the main stalk. Wash, quarter, and shred the rest.

In a large thick pan or casserole, soften the chopped onion gently in the lard.

Mix in the cabbage, brown sugar, salt and pepper, and pour in enough wine to come halfway up the cabbage. Cover and cook for 30 minutes.

Meanwhile, peel, core, and dice the apple. Stir it into the cabbage and continue cooking another 30 minutes.

Recommended drink: depending on what the cabbage is to accompany, otherwise the wine used in the cooking, from a better year, or a chilled Beaujolais-Villages – or beer (Newcastle Brown or stout).

Gaufres à l'Chitrouille
· PUMPKIN WAFFLES ·

Waffles are eaten at any time of day with a cup of the coffee that endlessly simmers here.

———————————————— *Ingredients for 8–10* ————————————————

1 kg · 2 lb pumpkin, peeled and
  seeded
salt
200 g · 7 oz flour
5 eggs
10 g · ⅓ oz fresh baker's yeast
200 ml · 7 fl oz milk

75 g · 2½ oz butter
30 g · 1 oz castor sugar
1 sml tsp dark rum
a piece of fat bacon for greasing the
  waffle-iron
icing, castor, or soft brown sugar

Cut the pumpkin into cubes and cook in salted water until tender but not collapsed; drain and squeeze as dry as possible in a cloth.

Put the flour in a bowl, make a well, and mix in the separated egg yolks, one at a time, the yeast dissolved in half the milk, slightly warmed, the butter, melted, a little salt, 30 g (1 oz) of castor sugar, and the rum.

Mash the pumpkin with the remaining milk. Beat it into the flour and fold in the stiffly beaten egg whites – the batter should coat the spoon but still be runny.

Heat a large honeycombed waffle-iron, spear the piece of bacon with a fork, and grease the inside of the iron carefully. Use the first waffle to 'prove' it.

With a small ladle, take a little batter and pour it on to the waffle-iron, tilting the iron this way and that to spread the batter evenly; close and set on the heat, batter-side down, turning it over to brown the top. Grease the waffle-iron between waffles.

To serve, sprinkle with sugar.

Recommended drink: depending on when you are eating them: a Tokay, or beer, or cider.

Tarte à l'coloche
· APPLE TART ·

Despite the pepper, a sweet tart and a feast for the eyes: *coloche* refers to the appearance of the cooked sugar which should puff up in a bell-shape – like a *cloche*.

———————————————— *Ingredients for 8* ————————————————

400 g · 14 oz enriched shortcrust
  pastry (see p.224)
2 kg · 4 lb eating apples, such as
  Coxes
5 eggs
200 g · 7 oz castor sugar

150 g · 5 oz sugar lumps
2 drops of vinegar
500 ml · 17 fl oz thick cream
5 g · ⅙ oz milled white pepper
70 g · 2½ oz butter
a little flour

Make the pastry dough a good 2 hours before you need it.

Peel, core, and cut up roughly half the apples. Reduce these slowly to a purée in 1 cm (⅜") of water. Leave to cool.

Cream 4 eggs with 100 g (3½ oz) of castor sugar until the mixture is pale and smooth and all the sugar dissolved.

Heat the sugar lumps slowly, with a little water, until they turn to caramel, and add the vinegar.

Beat the cream into the egg and sugar mixture and stir, with the pepper and caramel, into the apple purée.

Roll out the pastry to 3 mm (¹/₈″) and prick it with a fork. Turning it upside down, line a deep tart tin, buttered and floured in preparation. Make a decorative border and brush with beaten egg.

Peel and core the other apples, slice them into eighths, and sauté them in the butter left over after greasing the mould for 1–2 minutes; mix in the rest of the castor sugar and toss the apple until the sugar just begins to brown – not too much as the apple will be further cooked in the oven.

Fill the tart tin with the puréed apple mixture and arrange the sliced apple on top. Bake for 15 minutes in a moderate oven, Then increase the heat slightly and cook another 10 minutes.

Recommended drink: Sauternes or, if eaten between meals, cider.

Pain Perdu

Known as *pain crotté* in Belgium and around Douai and Valenciennes.

―――――――――――――――――― *Ingredients for 4* ――――――――――――――――――

4–8 slices of slightly stale bread
   (depending on size)
milk

50 g · 1³/₄ oz butter
2–3 eggs
castor or soft brown sugar

Arrange the bread in one layer in a shallow dish, and pour over enough milk to moisten but not soak it.

Heat a little butter in a large frying pan (or cook the bread in two batches).

Beat the eggs, coat the bread in it, slice by slice, and transfer quickly to the sizzling butter. When they begin to brown underneath, turn them over and add more butter.

As soon as both sides are golden-brown, sprinkle with sugar and serve.

Recommended drink: as for previous recipe.

12
FRANCHE-COMTÉ
Bresse · Bugey · Dombes · Pays de Gex

It was in the Franche-Comté, where an aroma of rich cooking prevails, that Brillat-Savarin was born. A mountainous area shading into Savoy and Switzerland (the Pays de Gex enjoys duty-free status between the latter and France), its cookery draws its distinctive flavour from the cheese, notably Comté, which is a Gruyère, wild mushrooms, and the late-flowering wines, *vins de paille* and *vins jaunes*.

As elsewhere, the freshwater delicacies (trout, crayfish, frogs) have become scarce, but there are still pike (*à la crème*, and in *quenelles*, made as part of the filling for *timbales vésuliennes*, sort of vol-au-vents in choux pastry), carp, tench, barbel, and char, this last the basis for several sumptuous modern dishes.

Another high airy region, it has good hams and sausages, smoked sausages from Montbéliard, sausages seasoned with caraway from Montbozon, boiling sausages from Morteau, and *saucisson de Belley*, which is a distant cousin of mortadella. Beef is also salted, smoked, and dried to become *le brézi*.

If the beef recipes are otherwise unexceptional, those for poultry (with the much-prized *poulet de Bresse* on the doorstep) and game are alluring: *mousse de foie de volailles bressanes, rissoles du Bugey* – made with turkey, tripe, and raisins for Christmas – spring chickens fed on *broin* (a cornflour, bran, and whey cake), *pigeon en croûte*. Protection of rare species has meant the disappearance of grouse and hazelhen from the menu, but partridge and thrushes still appear, the latter seared in *marc* from Arbois and then cooked with grapeseeds.

Potatoes are a staple, served as a gratin with milk and Comté; or stuffed with sausagemeat; or cooked with onions, a little water and vinegar, and a bouquet garni, when they become *fierrottes*; or baked in their skins, the insides then mashed up with butter, cream, Comté, egg, chives, and sliced *jésus* sausage, and returned to their skins for a final browning. They are mashed with flour, milk, and yeast and baked as a flat cake, or sautéed with onions *à la casse* (a long-handled black frying pan used in Bugey). Other filling country dishes which were made as hors d'oeuvres or supper dishes were *croûtes* (morel mushrooms or Comté cheese on toast covered with a cream béchamel sauce), croquettes with Comté, and heavy pancakes, now forgotten, known as *matafans*, *matefaims* ('kill-hunger'), or, more familiarly, *tape-culs*. Ears of corn, hardly ripe, were eaten toasted, while leeks, turnips, cabbage, spinach, cardoons, kidney beans, lentils, and sweet corn added a further vegetable element to the diet.

If Comté is one of their best cheeses, Morbier, from the village of the same name in the Jura, is one of the oldest. It was made by spreading a layer of soot, taken from the underside of a copper pan, between two layers of curds, before pressing. Vacherin Mont d'Or (also made in Switzerland) gets its bitterness from the corset of spruce bark in which it matures.

The residue from clarifying butter (*la craîche*) and the skin from boiled milk are used for cake-making in an area very partial to galettes, waffles, cracknels, fritters (flavoured in spring with the accacia flowers from the trees which support the vines), charlottes, *pâtes de fruits* (quince and apple), jams (notably bilberry and watermelon), and other sweet dishes.

Both *vins de paille* and *vins jaunes* are made from late-harvested grapes, the former dried out on beds of straw, the latter matured in oak for six years without any replenishment of what evaporates. As a physical reminder of the process, the 63 cl left from every original litre of grape juice, are bottled in a special bottle (*le clavelin trappu*) of that capacity. The result is a wine that will keep a minimum of twenty and a maximum of a hundred years. Not for people in a hurry, but the Comtois have a reputation for being as lively as a dish of *gaudes*, a kind of maize porridge of which they are supposedly inordinately fond. They also enjoy a good egg flip (*le lait de poule*) not to mention a wide selection of *marcs* and *eaux-de-vie*.

Cassolettes d'Écrevisses aux Morilles et au Vin Jaune
· CRAYFISH AND MOREL CASSOLETTES ·

In the days when freshwater crayfish were everyday food, they would be cooked, not in a *court-bouillon*, but dry with salt, just 10 minutes on a medium heat. In the Jura, they would sauté them with shallots, finely chopped and softened in seasoned butter, would add equal amounts of *vin jaune* and water, and cook for 10 minutes, the crayfish then being taken out, and a bowl of cream mixed into the cooking juices. A *cassolette* is a type of ramekin.

———————————————— *Ingredients for 4* ————————————————

40 freshwater crayfish
1 tbsp oil
100 g · 3½ oz butter
50 g · 1¾ oz carrots
20 g · ¾ oz shallots
salt, pepper
1 lge firm tomato

100 ml · 3½ fl oz *vin jaune*
250 ml · 9 fl oz thick cream
200 g · 7 oz fresh morels
50 g · 1¾ oz crayfish butter (see
    p.220)
chives

Sauté the crayfish in the oil and half the butter until their shells begin to redden.

Reduce the heat, add the finely diced carrot and shallot, salt and pepper, and the tomato, peeled, seeded, and roughly chopped. Let the moisture from the vegetables evaporate for a few seconds before pouring in the wine and cream. Bring to the boil and cook hard for 5 minutes. Take out the crayfish so as not to overcook them.

Shell them, remove the black intestines, and set aside the best shells. Break up and add the remaining shells to the sauce.

Stew the cleaned morels slowly for 10–12 minutes, covered, in the last of the butter.

Pour the liquid given off by the mushrooms into the sauce and reduce to a syrupy consistency. Strain as much as possible through a sieve, beat in the crayfish butter, and check the seasoning.

Mix in the morels, crayfish, and the good shells, and reheat gently to blend the flavours together.

Share out between the warmed *cassolettes* or ramekins. Serve at once.

Recommended wine: vin jaune.

Jésus de Morteau Vigneronne
· BOILING SAUSAGE WITH VINE SHOOTS ·

A big boiling sausage, made from the large intestine (some 10 cm in diameter), and eaten for Christmas lunch – hence, undoubtedly, the name, which makes the current fashion for writing *jésu* incorrect.

————————————— *Ingredients for 4* —————————————

vine cuttings
2 onions
3 cloves
a bouquet garni: 1 sprig of thyme, 1
  bay leaf, 2 sprigs of parsley
white wine
salt, pepper

2 *Jésus de Morteau*, or other boiling
  sausage, 400–450 g · 14–16 oz
  each
1 kg · 2 lb firm potatoes
150 g · 5 oz thin rashers of smoked
  streaky bacon
more parsley
butter on the table

Arrange a deep bed of broken vine cuttings (20–25 cm / 8–10″ long), in the bottom of a deep stew-pot, inserting the whole onions, stuck with the cloves, and the bouquet. Season with salt and pepper, and pour in enough wine and water to leave about 2 cm (³/₄″) of the vine shoots uncovered, the proportion of wine to water being 250 ml of wine to 2 lt (½ pt to 4 pts) of water. Cover and simmer for 1 hr.

Meanwhile, prick the boiling sausage three or four times, peel and wash the potatoes, and cut the bacon into lardons. Add the sausage to the vine shoots, which should by now come about 3–4 cm (1–1½″) above the liquid, and put the potato and bacon on top. Cover and stew for 35–40 minutes.

Arrange the vine shoots on a serving dish, with the sausage, in thick slices, bacon and potato on top. Garnish with parsley and serve butter separately.

Recommended wine: an Arbois or a Pupillin rosé.

Veau Farci de Bugey
· VEAL STUFFED WITH FAIRY-RING MUSHROOMS ·

In the Valromey region, this is often served with black morels.

————————————— *Ingredients for 4* —————————————

500 g · 1 lb fairy-ring or field
  mushrooms, if possible
100 g · 3½ oz butter
1 kg · 2 lb thick joint of shoulder
  veal
100 g · 3½ oz pork loin
75 g · 2½ oz fat green bacon
50 g · 1¾ oz chicken livers
50 g · 1¾ oz shallots
2 sprigs of parsley

2 sprigs of chervil
salt, pepper
thin streaky bacon rashers
250 ml · 8 fl oz white wine
100 ml · 3½ oz chicken stock
1 sml onion
1 clove
1 sml celery stalk
250 ml · 8 fl oz thick cream

Clean the mushrooms, dice a quarter of them and put to stew gently for 5 minutes, covered, in a saucepan, with 20 g (³/₄ oz) of butter, shaking the pan occasionally.

If you haven't got the butcher to do so, cut out a circular piece of about 200 g (8 oz) from the centre of the veal joint.

Mince half this piece of veal, together with the pork loin, fat bacon, chicken livers, shallots, and herbs. Mix in the stewed mushrooms, and the remaining veal, diced, and salt and pepper. Fill the cavity in the veal with this forcemeat, and tie two or three rashers of streaky bacon round the joint.

Brown it all over in a casserole, on a medium heat, in 20 g (³/₄ oz) of butter. Reduce the heat, pour in the wine and stock, and add the onion, peeled and stuck with the clove, and celery. Adjust the seasoning, taking account of the strength of the stuffing. Cover and simmer for 2 hr, turning the meat over halfway through.

Towards the end of the cooking time, stew the remaining mushrooms in the butter, covered, for 10 minutes (less if using cultivated mushrooms).

When the meat is ready, take it out, and stir in the mushrooms and the cream; reduce until the sauce coats a spoon and the mushrooms are cooked.

Slice the veal and pour the sauce over it.

Recommended wine: a Bugey (Mondeuse).

Poulet Vésulienne

------------------------------ *Ingredients for 4* ------------------------------

50 g · 1³/₄ oz onions
145 g · 5 oz butter
200 g · 7 oz stale bread, crusts
  removed
milk
200 g · 7 oz smoked streaky bacon
1 young chicken c. 1.2 kg · 2¹/₂ lb +
  giblets

10 sprigs of parsley
2 eggs
salt, pepper
400 g · 14 oz fine vol-au-vent dough
  (see p.225)
1 sml tsp oil
1 lemon

Chop the onion and soften in 20 g (³/₄ oz) of butter until it starts to colour. Crumble up the bread and soak it in milk.

Chop up the bacon, giblets, and 3–4 sprigs of parsley. Stir in the onion, along with the bread, well squeezed out, 1 egg, and salt and pepper.

Stuff the bird with this mixture and truss it.

Roll out the pastry to 3 mm (¹/₈″) and wrap the chicken in it. Brush with beaten egg. Decorate it, if you wish, using the pastry trimmings, and attach and brush them with egg.

Place on a lightly oiled baking tray. Roast in a medium oven for 50 minutes.

If the pastry browns too quickly, cover it in buttered greaseproof paper.

When the chicken is ready, heat the remaining butter with the lemon juice, salt and pepper, and the rest of the parsley, chopped.

To serve, break up the crust, carve the chicken and extract the stuffing; pour the sauce over the chicken and arrange the stuffing, sliced, and the bits of pastry, on top.

Recommended wine: a Pupillin.

Coq au Vin Jaune

A Bresse cockerel would be used in the Franche-Comté. Cockerels in England may be bought from game-dealers.

——————————— *Ingredients for 8* ———————————

1 cockerel, 1.5–2 kg · 3–4 lb, cut into
  pieces
salt, pepper
50 g · 1³/₄ oz flour
150 g · 5 oz butter

300 ml · ¹/₂ pt *vin jaune* from Arbois
  or Château-Chalon
300 g · 10 oz fresh morels
750 ml · 1¹/₄ pt thick cream

Rub the cockerel pieces with salt, pepper, and flour, sauté gently in the butter but without letting them brown, cover and cook in a moderate oven for 20 minutes.

Take out of the oven, pour off the fat, and deglaze with the wine. Turn the cockerel pieces over, add the cleaned morels and the cream, adjust the seasoning, and leave on a low heat, without a lid, until the reduced sauce gleams.

Recommended wine: what was used in the cooking.

Gaufres Comtoises
· THE CANONESSES OF BAUME-LES-DAMES' WAFFLES ·

In Franche-Comté, the moulds of the old waffle-irons were a work of art.

——————————— *Ingredients for 4* ———————————

180 g · 6 oz flour
3 eggs
100 ml · 3¹/₂ fl oz milk – or water
30 g · 1 oz castor sugar
30 g · 1 oz icing sugar + a little to
  sprinkle

5 g · ¹/₆ oz salt
1 lemon or orange
50 ml · 1³/₄ fl oz thick cream
a piece of fat bacon or a little oil

Sift the flour into a bowl and make a well in the centre. Work in the eggs, milk or water, all the sugar, and the salt.

Pare the fruit, drop the peel into boiling water, and let bubble for 3 minutes.

Drain and grate finely into the batter. Mix in the cream.

Beat the batter hard and strain through a fine sieve.

Heat a honeycomb-pattern waffle-iron; rub it with the bacon, stuck on a fork, or brush it with oil. Pour in a little batter, and tilt the waffle-iron to spread it evenly. Cook three minutes on each side.

Dust with icing sugar while the waffles are still hot.

Recommended wine: a white Côtes du Jura, Étoile, or Arbois – or a vin de paille *or Château-Chalon.*

Pain aux Oeufs
· CARAMEL CUSTARD ·

--------------------------- *Ingredients for 4* ---------------------------

500 ml · 17 fl oz milk
1 vanilla pod

4 whole eggs
230 g · 8 oz castor sugar

Bring the milk to the boil with the split vanilla pod. Cool.

Cream the eggs with 150 g (5 oz) of sugar. When the mixture is pale and smooth and all the sugar dissolved, add the warm milk gradually.

Heat the remaining sugar slowly with 2 tablespoons of water until it turns a pale caramel; pour into individual moulds or ramekins, ensuring the bottom and the sides are well coated.

Strain the custard into the moulds to within $1/2$ cm ($1/4$'') of the rim and stand the moulds on a folded cloth in a roasting tin. Fill the tin with water to the level of the custard and bake in a medium oven for 25 minutes.

Cool and unmould to serve.

Recommended wine: a vin de paille *from the Jura or a sparkling Arbois.*

Charlotte aux Pommes à l'Ancienne

It was Carême's idea to make apple charlotte with biscuits rather than bread, but bread continued to be used in the domestic kitchen.

--------------------------- *Ingredients for 4* ---------------------------

enough slices of bread, 7 mm · $1/4$''
    thick, to line a pan or cocotte the
    size of a charlotte mould
200 g · 7 oz butter

1.5 kg · 3 lb firm eating apples, such
    as Coxes
125 g · 4 oz castor sugar
5 g · $1/6$ oz cinnamon powder

Brown the bread on both sides, in batches, in about 120 g (4 oz) of butter. Line the bottom and sides of the pan without leaving any gaps.

Peel, core, and cut the apples into eighths. Toss with the sugar and cinnamon in the remaining butter for 5 minutes. Turn into the bread-lined pan, pressing well down.

Stand the pan in a tray of water in the oven, pre-heated to mark $1/4$ / 100°C, for 30–40 minutes.

Unmould while still hot, inserting a knife all round to ensure that the bread doesn't stick.

Serve warm or cold.

Recommended wine: a vin de paille *or a sparkling Jura.*

Sèche
· GALETTES FROM BESANÇON ·

——————————————————— *Ingredients for 4* ———————————————————

300 g · 10 oz flour
5 g · 1/6 oz salt
60 g · 2 oz castor sugar
4 eggs

50 ml · 1³/4 fl oz thick cream
50 ml · 1³/4 fl oz oil
80 g · 2¹/2 oz butter
60 g · 2 oz granulated sugar

Make a well in the flour and pour in the salt, castor sugar, eggs, and cream, and half the oil. Work quickly with your hands to make a stiffish dough.

Oil a sheet of greaseproof paper, itself on an oiled baking sheet. Roll out the dough as thinly as possible and place it on the paper.

Dot with butter and sprinkle with granulated sugar. Bake in a slow oven for 15 minutes. The result will be very crumbly.

Recommended wine: a dry sparkling Arbois.

13
GASCONY
Armagnac · Bigorre · Chalosse

Gascony separates Languedoc from the Atlantic, and Guyenne from the Pays Basque and Béarn; it includes the sandy Landes. From 1152 until the mid-fifteenth century, it was under English rule, yet its cookery is perhaps more foreign to British taste than that of any other area of France. It is a traditionally hospitable region, and if a Gascon is slow to raise his beret, it is owing not to impoliteness but to a sixteenth-century dispensation by Henri IV's mother, Jeanne d'Albret, from so doing.

Soups have a prominent place, with plenty of *pots-au-feu* and *garbures*, as in Béarn, though the ham bone is here replaced by a piece of preserved duck. The daily soup often comes *au farci* – a mixture of bacon (*ventrèche*), bread-crumbs, garlic and beaten egg, cooked in duck or other *confit* fat (i.e. fat rendered during the preparation of preserved duck, goose, or pork, see p. 109) until it sets, and then puffed up by simmering for twenty minutes in the soup.

The Atlantic brings in sea-bass (*loubine* or *louvine*), grey mullet, somewhat disdained here, and sardines, which are very popular. There is salmon, from the Adour river, and shad, which is grilled on bay leaves or baked with sorrel, butter, and a Tursan wine. Lamprey is prepared with red wine, raisins, prunes, and pine kernels, and eels, from the Étang de Léon and Vieux Boucau (= old mouth, once the estuary of the Adour), are cooked with prunes.

Although always an area of cattle- and sheep-farming, where the older inhabitants still tuck into a plate of tripe and onions on Sunday morning, it is poultry that reigns supreme: turkeys (bred for July roasting), maize-fed chickens, geese, and, above all, the *canard gras* from Chalosse. Here, at Dax (the capital of Chalosse), at Montfort, Mugron, Pomarez, and Saint-Séver, the markets over-flow with hot fresh foie gras, *confits* (duck and geese), stuffed necks (without the Guyennais embellishments of truffles and brandy), and all the other parts prepared by the *traiteurs*, restaurateurs, and *conserveurs* – parson's noses, gizzards, tongues, hearts *en brochettes*, the skin, well-crisped, for adding to salads and omelettes – nothing is wasted since even the feathers are sold. Only the beaks and the claws are useless.

This rich diet is little modified by vegetables, which have no place in the great repasts, being reserved for family meals. Ceps, particularly the *cèpe de pin* or '*bleu*' head the menu, every household maintaining a supply conserved, for consumption out of season. Otherwise, there are other mushrooms, asparagus a-plenty on the dunes, tomatoes, and small peppers (*piments doux*) which as in Béarn (see p. 36) are distinguished from sweet peppers (*poivrons*), and which give a special tang to Gascon dishes.

Local cheese is confined to a *fromage blanc* from the Landes, Poustagnacq, made with cow's, goat's, or ewe's milk, and eaten fresh or slightly fermented and seasoned with cayenne and Armagnac; and Amou, a ewe's cheese, named after its village of origin, the place itself said to owe its name to one of Caesar's men who, on seeing it for the first time, let out a cry of admiration, 'Amou'.

On the sweet side, there are *tortillons*, sort of aniseed fritters, for Maundy Thursday and fair days, *la coque de Nadao*, a large aniseed galette for Christmas, madeleines from Dax, barley sugar from Cauterets, and a grated carrot jam, known, charmingly, as *confiture de cheveux d'ange*. The spit-baked cake of Béarn and the Pays Basque was also a part of festivities in Gascony and Guyenne.

The high-tannin Chalosse wines or Vins de Piquepoult earned letters patent from Henri IV in 1600. This permitted their sale abroad and they became particularly popular with the English and Dutch, the latter exchanging their Delft china which led to the establishment of potteries at Samadet. The *vins de sable* which came from the dunes of the Côte d'Argent and went especially well with fish are now rare. Today the chief wines are Madiran, an excellent keeping wine, and its white brother, Pacherenc de Vic-Bilh. But the real drink of Gascony is Armagnac. The region has also produced some of the world's best cork.

Consommé au Confit

This soup would be drunk from a cup.

————————————————— *Ingredients for 8* —————————————————

1 chicken carcass, neck, and pair of
   plump wings
1 onion
2 cloves
2 sprigs of thyme
2 sprigs of parsley

400 g · 14 oz leeks
200 g · 7 oz carrots
100 g · 3½ oz turnips
1 sml celery stalk
500–600 g · 1–1¼ lb duck *confit*
salt, pepper

The day before, put the carcass, neck, and wings to simmer gently for 4 hr, with the onion, peeled and stuck with the cloves, the thyme and parsley, all the vegetables, scraped or peeled, cleaned, and cut up, and covered with plenty of water. Ten minutes before the end of the cooking time, add the *confit* to melt its coating of fat.

Remove the *confit* with a slotted spoon. Strain the stock, let it cool, and refrigerate.

Next day, skim the solid layer of fat off the surface of the stock, and return the latter to the heat, seasoned with salt and pepper. Dice the *confit* very finely, share it out between the cups, and pour in the boiling broth. The giblets and vegetables can be eaten on another occasion, the giblets grilled and the vegetables sautéed.

Recommended wine: a dry Pacherenc or Jurançon or white Graves.

Gratin d'Asperges Landaises
au Jambon du Pays

The asparagus would come from the Marensin sands, the ham from La Gosse (*jambon de Bayonne*), and the wine would be a Tursan.

————————————————— *Ingredients for 4* —————————————————

24 large white tinned or bottled
   asparagus (the locals would
   preserve their own) or fresh if
   available
a little ham fat or lard
24 small thin slices of uncooked
   ham, about 20 g · ¾ oz each

80 ml · 3 fl oz dry white wine
4 eggs
2 tbsp thick cream
40 g · 1½ oz butter
salt, pepper, nutmeg

Drain the asparagus, keeping the water, if preserved; if fresh, prepare and boil in the usual way, setting aside the cooking liquid afterwards. Trim down to 10 cm (4″) spears and put these in a saucepan covered with all but 150 ml (¼ pt) of their liquid.

Using a food-mill (or blender), reduce the trimmings to pulp.

Melt a tiny quantity of the ham fat or lard in a frying pan, non-stick if possible, and brown the slices of ham very lightly on both sides. Keep hot.

In a small pan, reduce the wine and an equal quantity of the asparagus water by two-thirds, over a medium heat.

Pour the remaining asparagus water into the reduced wine, and, on a low heat, beat in the egg yolks and cream until the mixture foams and thickens. Continue beating, adding the butter, and salt and pepper, and a pinch of grated nutmeg.

Spread the asparagus pulp in the bottom of an oven dish, arrange the drained and carefully wiped asparagus spears on top, and wedge the pieces of ham between the spears. Cover with the sauce and brown briefly under the grill.

Recommended wine: a white Tursan or Graves.

Massacanat de Bigorre
· EASTER OMELETTE ·

A thick well-set omelette for Easter morning. In the Landes it is eaten with sausage or *boudin*.

──────────────── *Ingredients for 4* ────────────────

400 g · 14 oz shoulder veal	2 cloves of garlic
150 g · 5 oz onions	3–4 sprigs of parsley
1 good tbsp *confit* fat or lard	8–10 eggs
salt, pepper	

Dice the veal into 1.5–2 cm (½–¾″) cubes. Slice the onions thinly and toss in the fat, in a frying pan, for 7–8 minutes over a low heat.

Add the veal, season with salt and pepper, cover, and stew for 15 minutes, shaking the pan occasionally.

Chop the garlic and parsley finely. Beat the eggs with salt and pepper.

When the veal is cooked, stir in the garlic and parsley, and pour in the beaten egg, spreading it evenly over the pan with a spatula. Leave to set.

Slide onto a serving dish without folding.

Recommended wine: Pacherenc de Vic-Bilh or Tursan rosé.

Escalopes de Foie Gras au Raisin

La Chalosse or Calossia is the area caught between Béarn and the river Adour, a smiling fertile countryside which provides both the duck foie gras and the grapes. Restaurants have enriched this dish by using Muscat grapes or replacing the local wine with a Jurançon or even port, as here. You could try this with chicken livers, though it would obviously be a different dish.

─────────────── *Ingredients for 8* ───────────────

1.2 kg · 2½ lb mature white grapes
200 ml · 7 fl oz white wine
100 ml · 3½ fl oz tawny port
2 duck's foies gras, c. 500 g · 1 lb
   each, a rich light tan colour,
   softish when pressed

salt, pepper
a pinch of castor sugar
3 carrots
2 onions
20 g · ¾ oz goose fat or butter
200 ml · 7 fl oz chicken stock

The day before, wash and peel the grapes and remove the pips (done, in the past, with a sharpened quill). Soak them for 24 hr in the wine and port in a cool place.

Trim the livers, removing any bits that may have been in contact with the gall. Rub all over with salt, pepper, and sugar. Leave in a cool place for 12 hr.

Slice the carrots and onions thinly and spread them in the bottom of a thick casserole. They will both flavour the cooking and stop the livers sticking.

Arrange the whole livers on top and line the lid with greaseproof paper rubbed with the fat. Cook for 25–30 minutes in a moderate oven.

Set aside the livers and keep hot, drain off the fat in the pot, and stir in the stock together with the wine and port in which the grapes have marinated; reduce by half on a medium heat. Strain, pressing the vegetables lightly through the sieve to bind the sauce. Return to the casserole, add the grapes, and reheat for 3–4 minutes; check the seasoning.

Slice each liver into 4 escalopes and coat with the sauce and the grapes.

Recommended wine: Madiran, dry Jurançon, or white Graves.

'Sale' de Porc
· CASSEROLE OF PORK WITH RYE BREAD AND ·
ARMAGNAC

Dishes such as this, where the meat is cooked in a sauce, are still called '*sauce de . . .*'. This one was made the day the pig was killed. It would have been eaten with *escautons* or *cruchades*, cornflour dumplings first poached in the pot in which the *confit* had cooked, with the tiny bits of *confit*, the *frittons*, left in the bottom, then sliced and grilled or fried.

─────────────── *Ingredients for 8* ───────────────

800 g · 1¾ lb neck of pork
800 g · 1¾ lb lean pork loin
2 tbsp goose fat, lard, or olive oil
salt, pepper
1 pinch of *quatre-épices*, otherwise,
   allspice
1 pinch of grated nutmeg
slightly stale (rye) bread, without
   crust

2 shallots
4 cloves of garlic
200 ml · 7 fl oz dry white wine
   (ideally, Chalosse)
200 ml · 7 fl oz stock
1 pig's brain (to thicken sauce; or
   use *beurre manié*)
1 sml tsp Armagnac

Dice all the pork into 1.5 cm (2″) pieces. Brown gently in the fat in a thick pan.

Add salt, pepper, the *quatre-épices*, and nutmeg, and cook slowly, shaking the pan frequently, for 10–15 minutes, so that the meat remains slightly tough.

Meanwhile, crumble the bread and mix in the finely chopped shallots and garlic. Bring the wine to the boil in a saucepan and set light to it.

Drain the excess fat off the meat, return to the pan with the breadcrumb mixture, and sauté another 4 minutes, without browning too much.

Pour in the wine and stock, cover and simmer for 50–60 minutes.

Transfer the meat to a serving dish with a slotted spoon and keep hot. Mix the pig's brain, which should previously have been very carefully soaked, trimmed, and mashed with a fork, into the sauce (or work in the *beurre manié*, see next recipe); stir for 2–3 minutes, checking the seasoning and adding the Armagnac at the last minute.

Pour over the pork and serve very hot.

Recommended wine: Madiran, red Graves, or Saint-Émilion.

Poule Farcie Landaise et sa Sauce

Part of the meal traditionally given to the grape-pickers at the end of the wine-harvest. The immutable menu dictates chicken broth with vermicelli (see below), an entrée, the chicken itself with the stuffing and a bowl of sweet tomato sauce, a roast and a salad, and finally a *tourtière* (see p. 103) or pastis and *eau-de-vie*; the beef or veal joint which cooks with the chicken is served with a white sauce for the following meal. Occasionally, an uncooked ham bone is also put to cook with the bird.

———————————— *Ingredients for 8* ————————————

1 good boiling fowl with its giblets, neck, and feet
800 g · 1¾ lb carrots
2 onions
3 cloves
2 sprigs of thyme
2 sprigs of parsley
1 bay leaf
1 knuckle of veal or a joint of boiling beef, 2 kg · 4 lb
salt, pepper
60 g · 2 oz bread, without crust
2 tbsp milk
3 cloves of garlic
250 g · 8 oz ham, including fat
1 sml tsp *confit* fat or lard

100 g · 3½ oz finely chopped pork
2 eggs
800 g · 1¾ lb leeks
50 g · 1¾ oz turnips

FOR THE SAUCE
2 onions
25 g · ¾ oz ham fat or lard
1 clove of garlic
1 kg · 2 lb tomatoes or 2 14 oz tins of Italian chopped tomatoes
1–2 sml tsp castor sugar
salt, pepper
20 g · ⅔ oz butter
10 g · ⅓ oz flour
½ tbsp vermicelli per person

Set aside the chicken liver and heart. Cut off the wings and trim away any fatty bits (and from the neck and feet).

Put feet, neck, wings, and gizzard in a pot with 4 lt (7 pt) of water, 400 g (14 oz) of carrots, scraped and washed, a peeled onion, stuck with the cloves, the thyme, parsley, and bay leaf, tied in a bouquet, and the veal or beef joint. Simmer for 2 hr. Season with salt and pepper.

Meanwhile, prepare the stuffing: crumble the bread and soak it briefly in the milk; chop up the second onion with the garlic and ham and soften gently in the *confit* fat or lard for 3–4 minutes and leave to cool. Stir in the bread, squeezed dry, the chopped liver and heart, the chopped pork, the eggs, and salt and pepper. Stuff the bird and truss it.

When the stock has cooked for 2 hr, add the chicken, and skim carefully before putting in the leeks, cleaned and loosely tied together, and the rest of the carrots and the turnips, peeled and washed. Cook 1¼–1¾ hr or until the bird is tender.

To make the sauce, soften the finely chopped onion and ham fat gently, stirring frequently, for 3–4 minutes. Chop the garlic, wash and cut up the tomatoes, and mix into the onion, with the sugar. Cook for 30 minutes, stirring occasionally. Put through a sieve or food-mill. Return to a low heat, season with salt, pepper, and more sugar if the tomatoes need it – the final sauce should be sweetish. If the sauce seems too thin, it can be thickened by working the butter with the flour (*beurre manié*), mixing it into the sauce, and stirring over the heat for 10 minutes.

To serve, bring the required amount of chicken broth to the boil, add the vermicelli, and cook for 8–10 minutes. Carve the chicken and take out the stuffing. Arrange the chicken and stuffing, sliced, on a dish and serve the sauce separately. If it were a family occasion, the vegetables would be eaten with salt after the soup, otherwise, the leeks and carrots would be kept back for another meal.

Recommended wine: red Tursan, Madiran, or red Chalosse.

Salmis de Palombes
· ROAST WOOD-PIGEON IN ARMAGNAC AND RED · WINE

The secret of a good *salmis* is to have an extra pigeon (the oldest) for the sauce.

─────────────────── *Ingredients for 4* ───────────────────

4 young wood-pigeons + another
   for the sauce, and their hearts
   and livers
1 onion
30 g · 1 oz shallots
2 carrots
70 g · 2½ oz butter
1 clove of garlic
2 tbsp flour

2 tbsp Armagnac (or cognac)
500 ml · 17 fl oz chicken stock
1 tbsp homemade tomato sauce
500 ml · 17 fl oz robust red wine
1 sprig of thyme, ½ bay leaf, 2
   sprigs of parsley
salt, pepper
optional: croûtons fried in butter

Toss the extra pigeon, cut into small pieces, and the diced onion, shallots, and carrots, in 20 g (¾ oz) of butter, in a large frying pan or sauteuse, for 7–8 minutes. Add the finely chopped garlic and the flour, and stir for 3–4 minutes. Pour over and set light to 1 tablespoon of Armagnac. When the flames die down, add the stock, tomato sauce, all but 2 tablespoons of wine, and the thyme, bay leaf, and parsley tied in a bunch. Simmer for 1 hr, season with salt and pepper.

Towards the end of the cooking time, start roasting the 4 other pigeons (without the giblets) either on a spit with a tray to catch the juice or in a buttered tin. They should be cooked quickly at a high temperature so they are browned but rare.

Strain the sauce, pressing it through the sieve to get all the juices. Return to the frying pan on a moderate heat.

Drain the excess fat from the drip tray or roasting tin, and stir in the finely chopped hearts and livers over a low heat. Add the second tablespoon of Armagnac, set light to it, and when the flames die down, pour in the reserved wine. Let it bubble briefly, and keep hot.

Cut the pigeons in two, saving the juices that escape; immerse them in the sauce in the frying pan and simmer 4–5 minutes. Transfer them to a hot serving dish.

Whip the sauce, incorporating the juice rendered by the birds, the chopped hearts and livers and their sauce, and the remaining butter. Pour it over the pigeons and if you like serve with croûtons.

Recommended wine: a Madiran, St-Émilion, Médoc Cru, or Côtes de Beaune Cru.

Estouffade de Cèpes au Confit

Ceps take the place of vegetables on important occasions and every household conserves its own. Fresh ceps are often prepared *à la viande*, that is, studded with garlic and little bits of ham, stewed and finished with chopped garlic, parsley, and breadcrumbs; or in a *daube* or *estouffade*.

––––––––––––––––––––––––––––– Ingredients for 4 –––––––––––––––––––––––––––––

1 kg · 2 lb very firm ceps	500 ml · 17 fl oz chicken stock
150 g · 5 oz uncooked ham or gammon	salt
100 g · 3½ oz onions	1 sprig of thyme, 1 sprig of parsley, ¼ bay leaf
1 tbsp *confit* fat	5 cloves of garlic
500 ml · 17 fl oz dry white wine	500 g · 17 oz *confit de canard*

Wipe the ceps with a fine cloth, and tail them. Chop the stalks roughly with the ham and onions, and toss them in the fat, in a casserole, for 7–8 minutes, on a low flame.

Bring the wine to the boil in a separate pan, to eliminate its acidity, and pour into the casserole, together with the stock. Season with salt if necessary, but not pepper – ceps do not take to pepper – and add the thyme, parsley, and bay leaf, tied in a bouquet.

Check the tops of the ceps and remove any green spores, before putting them in the casserole along with the chopped garlic. Cover and cook very gently for 3 hr, shaking occasionally.

Toward the end of the cooking time, heat the *confit* slowly in a thick pan, covered, in order to melt its coat of fat. Drain.

Pour the ceps into a dish and arrange the sliced *confit* on top.

Recommended wine: a red Tursan, Madiran, or red Graves.

Tourtière Landaise
· AN APPLE AND PRUNE TART ·

A covered tart, made with puff pastry, in which *confit* fat rather than butter was often used. It can be eaten plain. Try to have someone on hand to help stretch out the pastry.

──────────────── Ingredients for 4 ────────────────

350 g · 12 oz flour
1 sml tsp salt
2 eggs
2 tbsp sunflower oil
50 ml · 1³/₄ fl oz milk
10 prunes

3 tbsp Armagnac (or cognac)
2 apples
80 g · 2¹/₂ oz butter
175 g · 6 oz castor sugar
1 tbsp orange flower water

In a bowl, make a well in 250 g (9 oz) of flour, and put in the salt, eggs, half the oil, the milk, and 50 ml (1³/₄ fl oz) of water. Knead or use an electric beater until the dough is evenly blended and malleable. Cover with a damp cloth and leave for 30 minutes.

Spread a piece of felt or a blanket under a cloth you can wipe (oilcloth or plastic) on a good-sized table (2.5 × 1 m). Sprinkle with flour and, having floured your hands, place the dough in the centre; hit it with a rolling pin, hard, folding the dough inwards between each blow, until it holds together and can be stretched without going into holes or crumbling. Make into a ball, oil all over, and leave in a bowl, covered with a damp cloth, a further 4–5 hr.

Meanwhile:

★ stone the prunes and soak in two-thirds of the Armagnac;
★ peel, core, and shred the apples; soften gently for 4–5 minutes in 20 g (³/₄ oz) of butter and 50 g (1³/₄ oz) of sugar; add the rest of the Armagnac away from the heat;
★ weigh out the remaining sugar required;
★ measure out 150 ml (¹/₄ pt) of water and add the orange flower water;
★ melt the last of the butter.

Flour the tablecloth again, and start pulling the dough outwards from the centre, by hand, working evenly all round, very slowly, until you have a rectangular sheet, approximately 2 m × 75 cm (6′ × 2′¹/₂″). It is for this exercise that it is best to work with someone else, to help ensure there are no folds and no holes. The ragged edges should be trimmed.

Brush the pastry with the melted butter, sprinkle on a little sugar, and damp it down (as you would the ironing) with the water and orange flower water. Fold into three longways, interleaving butter, sugar, and water, still making sure there are no crinkles or pleats; brush the surface with butter, and sprinkle on sugar and water.

At this point, you could simply fold it in two the other way and bake it, but for a filled *tourtière*, spread the apple and the prunes across the middle of the pastry and fold in the two ends over the fruit.

Bake in a shallow buttered rectangular tin for 15 minutes at mark 10 / 250°C.

Chaudeau de Mimizan
· A HOT PUNCH ·

A spicy drink, somewhere between hot wine and egg-flip, it reputedly ensures a good party.

──────────────── *Ingredients for 8* ────────────────

2 lt · 3½ pt veal or chicken stock,   3 cloves
   well clarified and skimmed   6 peppercorns
500 ml · 17 fl oz dry white wine   8 eggs
1 stick of cinnamon   16 tbsp castor sugar

Put the stock, wine, cinnamon, cloves and peppercorns in a saucepan on a medium flame and boil for 20 minutes.

Meanwhile, either take eight large mugs and in each one beat together an egg yolk and 2 spoonfuls of sugar, or beat altogether in a punch bowl.

Continue beating as you gradually pour in the strained liquid. Serve burning hot.

14
GUYENNE
Agenais · Bordelais · Périgord · Quercy Rouergue

There is no formal boundary between Gascony and Guyenne, the latter including several ancient and topographically distinct provinces: the Bordelais, flat coastal country; the Rouergue, hilly pastureland; Quercy, with its limestone plateaux, only suitable for goats, but interspersed with fertile wine-growing valleys; the Agenais, home of the prune in Armagnac; and the three parts of Périgord, Périgord blanc, the chalky district round Périgueux, Périgord noir, truffle country (around Sarlat), and Périgord vert, the undulating green country-side of the Dordogne.

The cooking is similarly varied, ranging from the rustic slow-cooked, spar-ingly spiced dishes of the Rouergue to the foie gras and truffles of the Périgord. Walnut oil, goose fat, and lard are the main cooking mediums; butter was seldom used outside the Rouergue where it was provided by the ewes whose milk makes France's greatest sheep's cheese, Roquefort. Matured in the damp limestone caves, Roquefort almost literally conveys the flavour of the Causses.

There is a large range of soups, notably vegetable *tourains* (*tourins*, or even *tourils*), based on goose or pork fat, garlic or, occasionally, sorrel, and sometimes tomatoes. It is made with vinegar in Périgord, and with turnips or a piece of *confit* in Quercy, when it becomes *tourain à l'archevêque*. A *poule au pot* appears frequently on the table, *à la farce noire*, when bread soaked in the chicken's blood is added, *à la sauce de Sorges* with a vinaigrette of oil, vinegar, egg yolks, shallots, and chopped hardboiled egg. The coastal soups include *soupe arcachonnaise* (leeks, potatoes, and garfish) and *soupe d'Andernos* (made exclu-sively with fish from the Bassin d'Arcachon). Arcachon has little oysters, Gravettes, which are eaten with grilled sausages or cooked with entrecôte steak.

Guyenne is *the* province of *confits*: fattened goose, pork (including the rinds, which are heavily peppered, rolled up, and sealed with lard, for eating later with lentils or beans or a pork stew), chicken (for *galantines* and *ballottines*). Even potatoes are preserved in goose fat. Goose foie gras is sliced and cooked with apples, grapes, chives, vinegar, or capers and served hot. Truffles, supreme luxury, are eaten whole, each one wrapped separately in bacon, and placed in the cinders. And thanks to the truffles, the lamb of the Bordelais salt-marshes become lamb cutlet pie with truffles, while Quercinois *boudin blanc* is pig's cheek and breadcrumbs, plus truffles. Turkeys are filled with truffles, thrushes with foie gras and truffles (and baked *en croûte*).

Red-legged partridge (which went into the Périgueux *terrine de Nérac*), along with woodcock, lark, and snipe, once added to the repertoire. Hare was spit-roasted, basted with bacon fat dripped through a special iron cone with holes in it – *un capucin* – while rabbit was casseroled with prunes, *à l'agenaise*, or stuffed with bacon or ham, bread, garlic, parsley, and shallot.

There was still room for vegetables: globe artichokes cooked in walnut oil; chestnuts steamed in a pot lined with fig leaves; asparagus; ceps; tomatoes (from Marmande, which has given its name to an excellent variety); scorzonera; purslane for salads; pumpkins and marrows.

Besides Roquefort, there is a rich cow's cheese from Rouergue called Laguiole or Laguiole-Aubrac (not to be confused with Cantal). The Périgord has numerous goat's cheeses, some with cow's milk added out of season. Bleu de Causses is a cow's cheese but close to Roquefort.

Puddings and desserts are reserved for special occasions: at Easter, a huge brioche is made, *la coque de Cahors* or *de Gramat*, flavoured with orange flower water and eaten with an orange salad and white wine. For St Bartholemew's Day, a fifty kilo *fouace* (unleavened bread, cooked in the cinders) is carried through the streets of Najac. *Châtaignes truffées* or *rufadou* (from the instrument used to peel them) are prepared with sweetened milk or sweet wine by *énoiseuses* (the women who wield the *rufadou*). Walnuts are stuffed or made into jam. There are macaroons, aniseed cakes, chocolate-coated toffees, and sweet potato fritters, plus melons, plums, grapes, strawberries, and peaches, to sweeten existence between *fêtes*.

The wines include all the Bordeaux, to which the more easterly wines such as Bergerac, Cahors, and Monbazillac are related. In Rouergue, there is Entraygues & Fel, Marcillac, and Estaing. At home, people make a walnut or quince liqueur or Mesclou, a mélange of prune and walnut *eau-de-vie*.

Cou Farci de Quercy et sa Garniture
· STUFFED GOOSE NECK ·

Cou farci is made when the goose is killed for the foie gras and *confit*. This is the classic Quercy stuffing, the sausagemeat sometimes being partially, though never more than half, replaced with goose or with the giblets. Initial preparation of a *cou farci* must be begun three days before it is needed. It will keep for several months, coated in fat.

———————————— *Ingredients for 8* ————————————

2 goose necks, skin intact, + if possible, a piece of skin from the breast
coarse salt
400 g · 17 oz lean coarsely minced pork (reduce the quantity proportionately if adding goose meat)
400 g · 14 oz fresh foie gras

80 g · 2 oz truffles (can be tinned peelings or pieces)
2 eggs
50 ml · 1¾ fl oz *marc*, Armagnac, or cognac
salt, pepper
1 kg · 2 lb goose fat or fat from cooking the *confit*

Three days in advance, take the necks and peel back the skin, like a glove, without splitting it; scrape off and set aside the fat from it, still being careful not to pierce it. Weigh the skin and sprinkle with coarse salt in the proportion 22 g (¾ oz) to 500 g (17½ oz) of skin; leave in a cool place for 48 hr.

The day before the necks are to be cooked, make the stuffing: chop the goose meat if you are including it (you can use the neck meat); dice the foie gras into 2 cm (¾″) pieces; chop up the truffles roughly. Mix these together with the minced pork, eggs, *marc*, and salt and pepper; cover and refrigerate.

Break the goose fat into small pieces, removing the covering skin; put it with 2 cm (¾″) of water in a thick pan and melt slowly.

Carefully wipe any undissolved salt off the neck skins and dry them. Turn the right way in and tie up the larger end with string. Fill with the stuffing without packing it too tightly or the skin may burst during cooking. Tie up the other end.

Place the stuffed necks in the pan of melted fat, in which they should swim, leave to simmer, without allowing to boil, for 1–1¼ hr, turning them over without puncturing at halftime.

They can be served immediately, drained and cut into four, and accompanied by peas, or ceps cooked with parsley and garlic, or with a sorrel purée. Alternatively, they can be reheated in their own fat or in a soup, or they can be drained and eaten a day or so later, cold, in slices, with a dandelion or wild chicory (*barbe de capucin*) salad, dressed with walnut oil.

To conserve, put into storage jars and coat each neck separately in fat; cover and keep in a cool place.

Recommended wine: a young red Graves.

Pibales Sautées
· SAUTÉED ELVERS ·

The initial part of this recipe is included more for interest than for practical guidance, though the following tip could be applied to other recipes: to avoid burnt garlic (essential in this recipe), heat several whole unpeeled cloves in oil and then discard them; they will have given off their flavour, without any attendant bitterness. *Pibales* is a local word for elvers, tobacco a local crop.

———————————— *Ingredients for 4* ————————————

1 kg · 2 lb live elvers
1 tobacco leaf
100 ml · 3½ fl oz olive oil

½ a dried red chilli
5 cloves of garlic
salt, freshly milled white pepper

Leave the tobacco leaf to infuse for 10 minutes, covered, in a saucepan of hot water. Put the elvers in a basin of cold water and add the infusion which will kill and purge them instantaneously. Drain and wash them in plenty of water, transfer to a colander, plunge into boiling water for 5 seconds, and wash under running water until they are no longer sticky. Drain well.

Heat the oil in a large frying pan, add the chilli, seeded and cut finely, the peeled garlic, sliced thinly (or heat it whole, as described above), the elvers, and salt and pepper. Stir-fry for one minute.

Turn them out immediately on to a terracotta dish (pre-heated with boiling water).

Recommended wine: Entre-Deux-Mers or other dry white.

Lamproie à la Bordelaise

Lamprey, like salmon, go up river to spawn, and must be caught before this since they generally die from the wounds they receive during mating. They are now a protected species in France, but they were never easy to sell commercially as they have to be prepared live: once dead for more than two or three hours, they can no longer be divested of their vertebral column which gives them an unpleasant taste. If the wine they are cooked in lacks body, counteract it by adding a few drops, not more, of a good mature Bordeaux – or possibly Armagnac – at the end, without letting it cook.

─────────────────── *Ingredients for 12* ───────────────────

500 g · 1 lb onions
4 tbsp groundnut oil
2½ bottles red wine, strong in
    tannin
6–7 lge white leeks
2 tbsp flour
1 lt · 1¾ pt stock
1 sml head + 2–3 cloves of garlic

2–3 additional cloves of garlic
a bouquet garni: 2 sprigs of thyme,
    1 bay leaf, 4 sprigs of parsley, 1
    sml celery stalk
3 live lamprey of 1–1.2 kg · 2–2½ lb
    each
salt, pepper
small slices of bread

Start with the sauce as it needs lengthy cooking: toss the finely sliced onions for 4–5 minutes in half the oil, in a saucepan or casserole. Meanwhile, put all but a pint or so of the wine to boil. Clean the leeks, discard the dark green part, chop up the pale green part, and add to the softened onions. Turn them over for 2–3 minutes, stir in the flour, and pour in the boiled wine. Beat hard for several seconds, then add the stock, the small head of garlic, peeled and chopped, and the bouquet, tied up. Leave to simmer for 2 hr.

To prepare the lamprey: put some water to boil in a large pan, and when it reaches boiling point, add a little cold water to bring the temperature down to about 85°C. Holding the lamprey with an S-hook, plunge them in, one by one, for 10 seconds. Put them on a table and scrape the blanched skin with the back of a knife to remove the silt. Wash them in cold water, and hang over the sink with a bowl underneath containing the mug of reserved wine. Cut off the tails at the anus, and add these to the simmering sauce. Leave the rest of the fish to bleed into the bowl for 30 minutes.

Unhook them, cut off their heads and add likewise to the sauce. Now cut the fish across the middle to expose the spinal cord without slicing right through, and holding the lamprey at each end, pull it to release and detach the cord. Slice into 4 cm (1½″) sections, pressing out the intestines with your thumbs and discarding them. Wash.

When the sauce has cooked, pour in the mixture of blood and wine and strain the sauce into a deep frying pan or sauteuse; season with salt and pepper. At the same time, blanch the white part of the leeks, in 5 cm (2″) pieces, by dropping into boiling salted water and draining as soon as it comes back to the boil.

Bake the lamprey sections, rubbed all over with salt, in a drip tray in a pre-heated oven, mark 7 / 220°C, for 5 minutes, and drain. Add the blanched leek and the drained lamprey to the sauce and leave to simmer for 15 minutes.

Toast the bread and rub with the remaining garlic. Serve very hot, garnished with the bread.

Recommended wine: a more mature version of what was used in the cooking, or St-Émilion.

Estofinado Rouergat
· STOCKFISH FROM ROUERGUE ·

Stockfish is cod, or occasionally, nowadays, other fish, wind-dried until stiff; it is not salted. Scandinavian sailors used to come and exchange stockfish for salt, hence its presence in the traditional diet of people far from its home. It

needs 3–5 days' soaking, with fresh water every day, and may require beating
as well to soften it up.

———————————— *Ingredients for 8* ————————————

1 kg · 2 lb soaked stockfish
a bouquet garni: 1 sprig of thyme,
  1 sprig of parsley, ¹/₂ bay leaf
1 kg · 2 lb potatoes
5 eggs
4–8 sprigs of parsley

6 cloves of garlic
salt, pepper
100 ml · 3¹/₂ fl oz walnut oil
200 ml · 7 fl oz cream (or half cream,
  half milk)

Bring the stockfish and bouquet slowly to simmering point in cold water.
Remove from the heat, cover, and leave for 20 minutes.
  Boil the potatoes in their skin for 20–30 minutes. Hardboil 3 eggs. Chop up
the parsley and garlic finely.
  Peel the cooked potatoes and mash them into small pieces, with a fork, into
a bowl over a bain-marie. Mix in the drained stockfish, skinned, filleted, and
flaked.
  Heat the walnut oil in one small saucepan, the cream or cream and milk in
another.
  Add the garlic and parsley to the stockfish, along with salt and pepper, and
the last two eggs, beaten; working the spatula constantly, stir in the very hot
oil, drop by drop, and the cream. Mix in the hardboiled eggs, cut into eighths.
  Serve very hot on pre-heated plates.

Recommended wine: Cahors, Estaing, or Marcillac.

Confit d'Oie à la Purée d'Oseille
· PRESERVED GOOSE WITH SORREL PURÉE ·

Confits are made with a boned bird: flattened out, it is cut into four (two wings
and two legs) and the skin left on but excess fat trimmed off. The pieces are
put into coarse salt, using the same proportions as for *cous farcis* (see p. 106),
and left for 48 hr. Thyme leaves may be mixed into the salt. The joints are then
cooked in melted goose fat (see *cous farcis*), 2 hr for the legs, 2¹/₄–2¹/₂ hr for the
fleshier wings. They are cooked when a skewer goes into the meat easily and
the juices run clear – if the juice is pink, continue cooking.
  Confit is eaten cold, the fat previously removed, with a dandelion salad or
an endive and *chapon* (fried garlic bread) salad. Hot, it is served in cabbage
soup with *miques* (see p. 114), or lightly fried in its fat, which must not burn,
and eaten with *pommes sarladaises* (see p. 113), ceps, peas, broad beans, or
asparagus – or with sorrel.

———————————— *Ingredients for 4* ————————————

2 preserved leg joints (making 3
  portions each) or 1 wing (4–5
  portions)
500 g · 1¹/₄ lb sorrel
100 ml · 3¹/₂ fl oz chicken stock

table salt
pepper
4 sprigs of parsley, 6 sprigs of
  chervil

Put the *confit* in a thick pan, covered, and let the fat melt gently and the meat heat through without browning.

Stalk the sorrel and discard the dead or discoloured leaves, wash thoroughly, and immerse in boiling water; drain as soon as it comes back to the boil. Run the leaves under cold water, squeeze as dry as possible by hand, and shred coarsely.

Remove the *confit* from the pan, keep it hot, and drain off all but a tablespoon of fat. Return the pan to a low heat with the sorrel and the stock; add salt, if necessary, and pepper, the finely chopped parsley, and the chervil leaves. Cover and simmer about 20 minutes.

Slice the meat, being careful to divide up the skin fairly, and arrange it on the sorrel.

Recommended wine: Côtes de Bergerac or Haut-Médoc.

Gigot Périgourdine à la Couronne d'Ail
· LEG OF LAMB WITH A CROWN OF GARLIC ·

The garlic, which must be plentiful, is sweetened by the long slow cooking with the meat, in a tightly sealed casserole. In the past, it would all have been simmered in a *tourtière*, a cast-iron pot with feet, that stood astride the fire, and with a hollowed-out lid which could be filled with embers to provide heat above as well as below. The lamb is accompanied by a salad or purée of broad or green beans.

––––––––––––––––– *Ingredients for 8–12* –––––––––––––––––

1 large onion	2 tbsp of *confit* fat or lard
2 cloves	2 tbsp of old *marc* or cognac
3 sprigs of thyme	60 cloves of garlic
1 bay leaf	1 bottle Monbazillac
3 sprigs of parsley	salt, pepper
a leg of lamb, 2.5–3 kg · 5–6 lb	

Boil the onion, peeled, quartered, and stuck with the cloves, along with the thyme, bay leaf, and parsley, in 4 lt (7 pt) of water, for 20 minutes.

Lower the leg of lamb into the bubbling water and boil for 15 minutes. Take it out (this is easiest with a string tied to the knuckle end), and keep the stock for a soup.

Wipe the joint carefully and brown it all over in the fat or lard, in a cast-iron casserole, on a medium heat; pour over and set light to the *marc* or cognac.

When the flames die down, remove the pot from the heat, arrange the whole peeled cloves of garlic round the meat, pour in the wine, and add salt and pepper.

Seal the casserole and cook, undisturbed, in a very slow oven for 5 hr.

Transfer the lamb, with great care as the joint will be very fragile, to a meat dish; encircle it with the garlic, and pour over the cooking juices.

Recommended wine: Cahors, Pécharmant, St-Émilion or Pomerol.

Tourtière de Poulet aux Salsifis
· CHICKEN AND SALSIFY PIE ·

The cast-iron *tourtière* (see above) would have stood in one of the great open fireplaces of the Guyenne, with their built-in benches, one for salt, on either side. Only the name is left, applied nowadays to pies and other pastries (see p. 103), and to yeast cakes. This chicken pie was a carnival dish. It works quite well in modern conditions with a thick pie dish or mould.

—————————————— *Ingredients for 8* ——————————————

1 large chicken (c. 1.8 kg · 4 lb) or 2
    spring chickens, in pieces, +
    giblets and, if possible, wing tips,
    feet, and neck
2 carrots
1 leek
1 onion
2 cloves
a bouquet garni: 1 sprig of thyme, 2
    sprigs of parsley, a sml celery
    stalk, ½ bay leaf
salt, pepper
1.5 kg · 3 lb black salsify

vinegar
a *blanc* (see p. 220)
50 g · 1¾ oz shallots
2 tbsp goose fat or lard
2 tbsp cognac
1 tbsp flour
1 clove of garlic
200 ml · 7 fl oz dry white wine
500 g · 1 lb enriched vol-au-vent
    dough (see p.225)
1 sml tsp oil
1 egg
optional: 2 egg yolks or butter

Bone the chicken pieces.

Simmer the carcass, giblets, bones, wing tips, neck, and feet in a covered saucepan with 2 lt (3½ pt) of water, the carrots and leek, cleaned and sliced, the onion, peeled and stuck with the cloves, the bouquet, and a very little salt and pepper (because the stock will reduce), on a medium heat, for a good hour. Strain the stock and reduce slowly.

Meanwhile, peel the salsify, immersing them in cold acidulated water immediately to stop them going black. Wash and slice into 4 cm (1½") pieces. Drop them into the boiling *blanc* and cook for 1 hr.

Brown the chicken pieces and the chopped shallots in the fat, for about 10 minutes; pour in the cognac and set light to it. When it goes out, sprinkle in the flour and stir for 2–3 minutes. Add the crushed garlic, the wine, and enough stock just to cover; cook gently for 10 minutes.

Drain the salsify, put them in with the chicken, check the seasoning, and simmer another 10 minutes.

Roll out two-thirds of the dough to 3 mm (⅛") and line the oiled mould or pie dish, leaving a 3 cm (1") border all round. Fill with alternating layers of chicken and salsify well coated in the sauce, but without spooning in any more as it will make the pastry soggy. Place a pie funnel, if you have one, in the centre. Cover with the rest of the pastry, rolled out to the diameter of the mould, brush with beaten egg, fold the border of the pie base over the top, and brush that with egg. Make a hole in the centre for the pie funnel or for a small pastry chimney. The pastry trimmings can be used to make decorations, attached and brushed with egg. Bake for 30 minutes in a medium oven.

If you wish to serve the rest of the sauce as an accompaniment, add 200 ml (7 fl oz) of stock to it and leave to simmer while the pie is baking. Thicken by either mixing in 2 egg yolks, stirring constantly and not letting the sauce boil, or beating in some cold butter very gradually. Locally, a little chopped truffle might be dropped in at the end.

Recommended wine: Cahors or Médoc.

Falette
· VEAL BRISKET STUFFED WITH SWISS CHARD ·

Once boned, a brisket of veal conveniently provides a kind of pocket ready for stuffing (the French cut is *poitrine préparée en poche*). Belly pork can be used instead of veal in the stuffing; and the joint can be poached, in which case the lid should be left partially off or the *falette* may burst.

———————————————————— *Ingredients for 8* ————————————————————

1 bunch of leafy Swiss chard or
    spinach (you need approximately
    250 g · 9 oz of leaf)
salt
200 g · 7 oz onions
70 g · 2½ oz fat – lard or butter
50 g · 1¾ oz parsley – flat-leaved, if
    possible, it's more aromatic
400 g · 14 oz shoulder veal
2 eggs

pepper
a brisket of veal, boned, in the
    French way, if possible
a large piece of fresh pork rind
600 g · 1¼ lb carrots
a bouquet: 2 sprigs of thyme, 1 bay
    leaf
250 ml · 9 fl oz concentrated veal
    stock, well-skimmed

Wash the leafy part of the chard (or the spinach) and plunge into boiling salted water. Drain immediately and run under cold water to revive its colour; squeeze it as dry as possible. Gently soften 50 g (1¾ oz) of chopped onions, in 20 g (¾ oz) of fat. Mince together the chard, parsley, and shoulder veal and mix in the softened onion and the eggs. Season with salt and pepper.

Fill the 'pocket' of the joint with this stuffing, sew up the end with a trussing needle, and brown the joint all over in a casserole in the rest of the fat, on a medium heat. Take it out.

Away from the heat, line the bottom of the casserole with the pork rind, fat side down. On it, strew the remaining onions and the carrots, sliced thin, and the bouquet. Return the joint to the pot, pour over the stock, and season with salt and pepper, taking into account the strength of both the stock and the stuffing. Cover tightly and braise in a medium oven for 2 hr.

Slice the veal on to a serving dish and pour over the cooking juices lightly skimmed.

Recommended wine: an Entraygues & Fel, an Estaing, a Marcillac, or a Médoc.

Ragoût de Truffes au Vieux Cahors

This old recipe from Souillac is recorded that it may not be forgotten now that truffles have earned their French nickname, 'diamant'; but should you happen to have some fresh, well-matured truffles between December and February, this is a worthy way of treating them.

—————————————— *Ingredients for 2* ——————————————

2 good truffles, 30–40 g · 1–1¹/₂ oz
  each
3–4 little truffles
1 carrot
1 celery stalk
1 white leek
1 sml onion
1 shallot
70 g · 2¹/₂ oz butter
20 g · ³/₄ oz uncooked ham or
  gammon, lean only

1 clove of garlic
²/₃ bottle mature Cahors or other
  robust red
a bouquet garni: 1 thyme stalk,
  ¹/₄ bay leaf, 1 sprig of parsley
salt, pepper
200 ml · 7 fl oz strained veal or
  chicken stock
1 sml tsp flour

Brush the truffles carefully, and peel them evenly, keeping the skin.

Scrape and wash the carrot, trim and clean the celery and leek, discarding the green, and finely dice them, together with the onion and shallot, before softening them gently in a saucepan with 20 g (³/₄ oz) of butter, the chopped ham, and the crushed garlic, for 7–8 minutes, without letting them brown.

Add the wine and bouquet, and simmer for 20 minutes. Strain and return the liquid to the saucepan with salt and pepper, the truffle skins, the small truffles, sliced, and the veal stock. Simmer and thicken with the remaining butter worked with the flour (*beurre manié*), then dotted on the surface of the sauce and mixed in by shaking the pan. Do not let the sauce boil.

Place the two large truffles in individual oven-proof bowls and share the contents of the saucepan between them. Cover and cook in a low oven for 7–8 minutes to heat the truffles through.

Recommended wine: a mature Cahors or a Pomerol.

Pommes Sarladaises
· POTATOES WITH GARLIC AND PARSLEY ·

These have travelled a bit – losing something on the journey. True *pommes sarladaises* are not sliced but are broken up during cooking, and the inclusion of truffles is a restaurant embellishment. Successfully done, these potatoes are crisp and brown on the outside and soft in the middle.

—————————————— *Ingredients for 8* ——————————————

1.5 kg · 3 lb firm potatoes
3 tbsp goose fat, lard, or olive oil
  (more may be necessary,
  depending on the potatoes)

salt, pepper
4 cloves of garlic
6 sprigs of parsley

Peel, wash, and cut up the potatoes into chunks, quarters or eighths, according to size. Toss them for 15 minutes or until they are brown all over, in 2 table-spoons of the fat or oil, on a medium heat.

Now, using a fork or small knife, break up each piece of potato without mashing it.

Add salt and pepper and the garlic and parsley chopped together finely, and the last of the fat. Continue cooking until the potatoes are soft, turning them over occasionally.

Miques

In the Sarladais, these dumplings took the place of bread with soups, casseroles, *confits*, and salads. They were eaten either cold or sliced and browned in goose fat. Sometimes they would be fried with sugar as a snack. There were *miques* made with maize or bread, wrapped in cabbage leaves, and cooked in stock or in soup; and a yeast *mique*, a bit like brioche, also cooked in stock but without the cabbage. The first two would sometimes contain a bit of chard.

Mique de Pain

──────────────── Ingredients for 8 ────────────────

300 g · 10 oz stale bread with plenty
   of crust – in France, it would be a
   wedge of *pain de campagne*
80 g · 2½ oz blanched streaky bacon
   or salted belly pork
80 g · 2½ oz cold bacon fat
100 g · 3½ oz chicken livers (or the
   bits in the bottom of the *confit* pot
   – the *frittons*, see p. 99)

100 ml · 7 fl oz stock
50 g · 1¾ oz goose fat or lard
2 eggs
flour
blanched cabbage leaves
stock or broth for cooking the *mique*

Dice the bread, bacon, and bacon fat finely, and mix in the chicken livers, previously stiffened in water and mashed, or the *frittons*.

Add the stock, fat, and eggs, and work the mixture with a spatula. Bind it together with a little flour and roll into a ball.

Divide up into small dumplings and wrap in cabbage leaves.

Plunge into the hot broth and boil for 30 minutes, turning them over very carefully.

Mique Levée

──────────────── Ingredients for 8 ────────────────

500 g · 17 oz wheat flour
15 g · ½ oz fresh baker's yeast
2 tbsp milk or stock
10 g · ⅓ oz salt

5 eggs
100 g · 3 oz goose fat or lard
broth or stock for cooking the *mique*

Make a well in the flour and pour in the yeast dissolved in the warmed milk or stock, and the salt; work in the eggs, one by one, and the fat to make a well-blended dough. Make into a ball and leave in a bowl covered with a damp cloth for at least 2 hr.

Knead the risen dough with floured hands and make it back into a ball. Plunge it into the simmering broth.

Turn it over after 30 minutes and leave to cook until it floats to the surface (20–30 minutes).

Massepain et sa Crème Caramélisée
· PÉRIGORD MARZIPAN WITH CREAM CARAMEL ·

This has nothing in common with what is usually called marzipan/*massepain*. It is a very light biscuit, without almonds, intended to accompany a cream caramel, which, in the past, was made by dotting the surface of the custard with lumps of sugar and browning with a hot poker.

————————————— *Ingredients for 8* —————————————

FOR THE MASSEPAIN
6 eggs
200 g · 7 oz castor sugar
1 sml tsp orange flower water
200 g · 7 oz flour
20 g · ¾ oz butter

FOR THE CARAMEL
120–170 g · 4–6 oz sugar lumps

FOR THE CREAM
1 lt · 1¾ pt milk
10 eggs
250 g · 9 oz castor sugar
7–8 g · ⅓ oz vanilla sugar

To prepare the *massepain*: cream the egg yolks and castor sugar until the mixture is pale, smooth, and creamy. Add the orange flower water, sift and fold in the flour, followed by the stiffly beaten egg whites.

Butter a sandwich tin and pour in the mixture which should not more than three-quarters fill it. Bake for 25–30 minutes in a low oven without opening the door. Test with a skewer which should come out clean. Unmould on to a rack.

While the *massepain* is cooking, prepare the caramel: melt the sugar lumps very gradually, stirring constantly, pour in a small cup of boiling water, and let bubble for a few minutes.

To make the cream: boil the milk, let it cool, and cream the egg yolks and the castor and vanilla sugar until all the sugar is dissolved and the mixture is pale and smooth. Add the milk very slowly. Turn into a saucepan and stir constantly over a low heat, without letting it boil, until the custard thickens. Away from the heat, pour in caramel to taste, leave to cool, pour into a serving dish, cover, and refrigerate.

Serve the cream caramel with the *massepain*, sliced, on the side.

Recommended wine: champagne.

15

ILE-DE-FRANCE

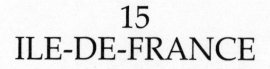

It is difficult to imagine that the Ile-de-France, an area nowadays synonymous with Paris and its extensive suburbs, ever had a tradition of country cooking lurking behind the great creations of the restaurant trade of the nineteenth and twentieth centuries. The Ile-de-France was, however, once a world of small vilages and market gardens, whose names are attached not only to such dishes as *potage Argenteuil, potage Crécy, garniture Clamart, garniture Viroflay*, but to the produce itself, asparagus *d'Argenteuil*, carrots *de Crécy, champignons de Paris, cèpes de Senlis*, peas *de Clamart* or *de Vaugirard*, cauliflowers *d'Arpajon*, cherries from Montmorency, strawberries from the Bièvre and from Vaugirard, milk-fed veal from Pontoise, lamb from Nanterre, game from Marly, wine from Argenteuil and Suresnes, butter from Vanves, bread from Gonesse, as well as Brie de Coulommiers, de Meaux, and de Provins, and Crémet de Fontainebleau, all recalling the rural charm that was once the Pourtour de Paris.

Potage Saint-Germain
· PEA SOUP ·

Not to be confused, as it often is in France, with the Picardian split-pea soup. *Petits pois*, incidentally, means no more than 'shelled peas'.

––––––––––––––– *Ingredients for 4* –––––––––––––––

1 kg · 2 lb peas, unshelled weight
50 g · 1¾ oz lean green streaky
  bacon
70 g · 2½ oz butter

a bouquet garni: 1 sprig of thyme,
  ½ a bay leaf, 2 sprigs of parsley
salt, pepper
3–4 sprigs of chervil

Shell the peas. Chop the bacon and cook gently in 20 g (¾ oz) of butter in a large pan for 5–6 minutes without letting it go crisp.

Stir the peas into the bacon and cook slowly for another 2–3 minutes. Add 1 lt (1¾ pt) of water and the bouquet and simmer for 15 minutes. Season with salt and pepper.

Take a few peas out with a draining spoon and put them in a tureen with the rest of the butter and the chervil leaves. Put the soup through a food-mill or blender, having first removed the bouquet, and pour into the tureen.

Soupe Cressonnière
· WATERCRESS SOUP ·

Part of Paris folklore, along with the watercress sellers. Someone had the good idea of substituting sorrel for the watercress and binding it with egg yolks – *potage santé*.

───────────────── *Ingredients for 8* ─────────────────

1 onion	500 g · 1¼ lb potatoes
2 celery stalks	2 lt · 3½ pt chicken stock
150 g · 5 oz butter	salt, pepper
2 bunches of watercress	500 ml · 17 fl oz thick cream

Slice the onion and the cleaned celery finely, and sweat in a covered saucepan with 20 g (¾ oz) of butter, for 7–8 minutes, giving the pan the odd shake.

Cut off all but 2 cm (¾″) of the watercress stalks, wash the rest, discarding the dead or discoloured bits. Set aside a dozen or so leaves and add the others to the saucepan.

Peel, wash, and dice the potatoes and mix into the pan. Pour over the stock, season with salt and pepper according to the strength of the stock, and cook gently for 20 minutes.

Put through a food-mill (or blender), return to the pan, add the cream, and heat slowly till it starts to thicken. Check the seasoning.

Away from the heat, beat in the remaining butter and pour into a tureen over the leaves set aside earlier. Serve very hot.

Friture de Goujons de Seine
· FRIED GUDGEON ·

The staple dish, and a very popular one, of the *guinguettes*, the little dancing cafés on the banks of the Seine where Parisians would go to escape the city. Gudgeon were a family treat too. If the fish are large, it is best to cook them twice (see below), if small, once should be enough.

───────────────── *Ingredients for 4* ─────────────────

1 kg · 2 lb very fresh gudgeon	oil for deep frying
500 ml · 17 fl oz milk	1 lge bunch of parsley
salt, pepper	lemons
300 g · 10 oz flour	

To gut the fish, press the stomach wall hard with your thumbs; and then scale by rubbing all over with a rough cloth.

Soak them in milk, seasoned with salt and pepper.

Drain and sponge dry and roll in the flour (if the fish are small, you can simply put the flour and the fish together in a plastic bag and shake them).

Dust off the excess flour and deep fry the fish in several batches, ensuring the oil does not cool. Remove as soon as they stiffen.

Return the gudgeon to the oil, which must be very hot, to brown. Drain on absorbent paper.

Dry and fry the parsley, and garnish the fish. Serve with wedges of lemon.

Recommended wine: Sauvignon de Loire or Muscadet or, if you can find it, Suresnes.

Poularde à la Briarde
· CHICKEN WITH CIDER AND MEAUX MUSTARD ·

———————————— *Ingredients for 4* ————————————

a chicken, 1.8–2 kg · 3½–4 lb +
  giblets, and, if possible, the neck,
  feet, and wing tips
3 onions
2 cloves
bouquet garni: 1 sprig of thyme, ½
  bay leaf, 1 celery stalk, 1 leek, 2
  sprigs of parsley

500 g · 17 oz carrots
200 g · 7 oz butter
1 tbsp oil
1 bottle dry cider
salt, pepper
500 ml · 17 fl oz thick cream
4 tbsp Meaux mustard
4 sprigs of parsley

Spear the feet, neck, and wing tips with a fork and singe before putting to cook on a moderate heat with the giblets, 1 lt (1¾ pt) of water, a peeled and quartered onion studded with the cloves, and the bouquet, until needed.

Scrape and wash the carrots and sculpt them into large olives, reserving the peelings. Stew the 'olives' in a covered saucepan, with 50 g (1¾ oz) of butter for 45 minutes, shaking the pan several times (if they seem to be sticking, add 3–4 spoonfuls of boiling water).

Cut the chicken into eight, removing any prominent bones and breaking them up into the stock pot. Soften the carrot peelings and the two remaining onions, chopped, in 20 g (¾ oz) of butter and the oil, in a large frying pan, without letting them take colour. Add the chicken pieces and seal, without browning. Pour in the cider and simmer for 10 minutes. Strain in the stock, season with salt and pepper, and cook gently for 40 minutes, turning the chicken over after 20 minutes.

Take out the chicken, pour the cream into the sauce, and reduce by half. Away from the heat, mix in the mustard and the last of the butter, and taste for seasoning. Return the chicken and the carrot 'olives' to the sauce and simmer until everything is well heated through.

Serve very hot, sprinkled with chopped parsley.

Recommended wine: Coteaux Champenois, Bouzy, Monthélie, Auxey-Duresses, or a red Bellet.

Tête de Veau à la Parisienne
· CALF'S HEAD WITH A MUSTARD SAUCE ·

If the Ile-de-France cannot entirely claim this as a local dish, it has nonetheless long been part of Parisian tradition. It is eaten with a *sauce gaillarde*, also known as *sauce gribiche*, which is excellent with cold meat or brawn.

--- Ingredients for 4 ---

½ a calf's head, cleaned, the brains
  and tongue set aside
2 lemons
3 lt · 5 pt *blanc* (see p. 220)
salt, pepper

FOR THE SAUCE
3 eggs

2 tbsp strong French mustard (some
  think Meaux best)
salt, pepper
40 ml · 1½ fl oz wine vinegar
120 ml · 4 fl oz oil
80 g · 3 oz small gherkins
3 tbsp capers
1 doz sprigs of parsley

Rub the head with a lemon, cut into quarters, before putting into the boiling *blanc* and simmering fairly hard for 30 minutes. These procedures help keep the meat a good clear colour.

Under running water, brush the tongue and rub the brains with a smooth cloth to remove the skin and coagulated blood vessels.

Add the tongue to the *blanc*. Simmer another hour.

Ten minutes before the end, bring a pan of salted water with a squeeze of lemon juice to the boil and simmer the brains for 10 minutes. Pre-heat a serving dish and plates.

To make the sauce: hardboil the eggs, mix the yolks with the mustard and oil in a salad bowl; dissolve a little salt (having checked the strength of the mustard) and pepper into the vinegar and beat it into the oil; add the sliced gherkins, the capers, well-drained, the finely chopped parsley, and the mashed egg white.

Drain the head and cut it up, removing the bones. Bone the tongue, cut away any fat, and slice. Divide the brains into 4 portions. Arrange on the hot dish.

Recommended wine: white Mâcon or red Sancerre.

Blanquette de Lapin à l'Ancienne
· RABBIT BLANQUETTE WITH CIDER ·

--- Ingredients for 8 ---

1 lge rabbit, cut into pieces, + the
  kidneys, well covered in white
  fat, and liver
1 bottle dry cider
150 g · 5 oz carrots
1 lge onion
2 cloves
bouquet garni: 1 lge leek, 2 sprigs of
  thyme, 1 bay leaf, 2 sprigs of
  parsley, 1 celery stalk

salt, pepper
200 g · 7 oz little onions
60 g · 2 oz butter
250 g · 9 oz mushrooms
60 g · 2 oz flour
4 eggs yolks
100 ml · 4 fl oz thick cream
1 lemon

Put all the rabbit pieces except the liver in a shallow pan, covered with cold water, over a low heat. Drain when the water boils. Check all the meat for splinters of bone.

Return the rabbit to the pan with the cider and enough water just to cover. Add the carrots, sliced, the large onion, peeled and stuck with cloves, the bouquet, and salt and pepper. Put it on a strong flame, skim, reduce the heat, and simmer for 50 minutes.

Twenty minutes before the end, cook the little onions in the butter in a large saucepan, to colour lightly. Add the cleaned mushrooms, halved or quartered according to size; cover and stew 7–8 minutes. Remove the lid and let the juices evaporate before mixing in the flour. Pour in 600 ml (1 pt) of liquid from the rabbit pan. Let it bubble gently, giving a frequent stir, for 10 minutes. At the same time, immerse the liver, whole, into the liquid in which the rabbit is cooking.

Transfer the rabbit pieces to a serving dish with the liver, sliced into 8. Incorporate the cream and lemon juice into the egg yolks and trickle this mixture very slowly into the mushroom sauce, on a low heat as it must not boil, stirring constantly. Taste for seasoning and pour over the rabbit.

Recommended wine: a Rully or Coteaux Champenois.

Brioche de Coulommiers
· CHEESE BRIOCHE ·

Difficult to make properly even in France, requiring, as it does, *blanc de brie*, i.e. fresh Brie; well-drained *fromage blanc* can be used instead.

———————————— *Ingredients for 4* ————————————

1 sml tsp salt unless using salted
  Brie, in which case, a pinch
10 g · ¹/₃ oz castor sugar
20 g · ³/₄ oz fresh baker's yeast
2 tbsp milk

500 g · 1 lb flour
250 g · 9 oz *blanc de brie* or drained
  fromage blanc
4 eggs
20 g · ³/₄ oz butter

Dissolve the salt, sugar, and yeast in the warmed milk. Stir in 100 g (3¹/₂ oz) of flour. Leave to double in volume.

Mix together the rest of the flour and the cheese and work in the eggs and the yeast. Roll into a ball, cover with a damp cloth. Leave to rise for 2 hr.

Deflate the dough with floured hands, and put it into a buttered ribbed mould. It should not be more than three-quarters full. Let the dough rise to fill the mould.

Bake in a medium oven for 25 minutes. Cool before unmoulding.

Recommended wine: Coteaux Champenois, Bouzy, Monthélie, Auxey-Duresses, or a red Bellet.

16
LANGUEDOC: *The Mediterranean*
ROUSSILLON · *Catalogne*

Languedoc has a different meaning for the historian from that of the geographer, or the administrator. For the culinary writer, it is an area of great diversity, hence the division here into Mediterranean or lower Languedoc and Toulousain or upper Languedoc.

Olive oil, garlic, chilli, sweet onions, tomatoes, bitter oranges (a variety called Punset), and green rather than black olives, all contribute their distinctive notes to the cookery of the Mediterranean region. *All y oli* (like Provençal *aïoli*, see p. 190, but never made with egg yolks); croûtons, rubbed alternately with garlic, salt, and olive oil (*al pa y all*) and eaten with grape seeds; *l'all crémat*, a sort of bacon or lard, red chilli, olive oil, and garlic sauce, browned and then diluted in soup: these are the flavours of the Bas-Languedoc.

The Mediterranean makes its contribution too: oysters, nowadays Portuguese, from the Étang de Thau, and mussels, bred on ropes (see p. 11), at Bouzigues, where they are eaten raw or grilled and stuffed with spinach or finely chopped pork, and accompanied, in the latter case, by a tomato and chilli sauce. Octopus, crabs, *cigales* or flat lobsters, and rockfish go into *pinyata roussillonnaise*, the Languedoc version of bouillabaisse (see p. 191). Anchovies are cooked fresh as soon as the boats come in, while sardines are grilled on Sundays in a *grangette biterroise* (i.e. from Béziers), *baraquette sétoise*, or a *mazet montpelliérain* or *nîmois*. Monkfish is roasted in the piece, studded with garlic, on a bed of aubergines, tomatoes, and onions. Sea-bass (*loup de mer*) and tuna are caught all along the coast.

Fishermen also pick up forkbeard, grouper, and scorpion-fish or rascasse, and these are poached in water and sea-salt, before being cooked in a purée of garlic, chilli, vinegar, and olive oil. When shad was common in the estuaries of the Hérault and the Aude, it was braised with calf's foot, ham, and white wine, in the baker's oven. Salt cod, if not made into *brandade nîmoise*, (see p. 128) is cooked with spinach, pine kernels, and prunes or is sautéed in olive oil with onion, tomato, chilli, and garlic, *à la catalane*.

Turning away from the sea, it is the snail (known here as the *cagaraoule*) that rules the table. For a *cargolade*, friends are invited to eat snails, barbecued with a seasoning of salt, bacon, and garlic, and served with an *all y oli*, and hunks of bread to soak it up. Excess consumption may be countered by an *ascaldada*, an infusion of garlic, thyme, olive oil, and boiling water.

All the meat dishes are eclipsed by *le cassoulet de Castelnaudary* (see p. 128), at least in terms of reputation. But the people of Pézenas are partial to tiny pastries filled with mutton, kidney fat, bone marrow, soft brown sugar, and citron, little delicacies apparently devised by an Oriental cook to satisfy an English lord and master who required to nibble constantly. Similar pastries are made at Béziers and Nîmes. Pork and partridge are prepared with bitter oranges. Liver was cooked with bacon, tomatoes, and raisins, but the dish is now forgotten. Chicken is often accompanied by aubergines, courgettes, and green peppers, a favoured mixture, sometimes with onion as well, and also served with fish.

There is not much cheese, though there are goat's cheeses, from the Cévennes and the Haut Gard, Pélardons, which are preserved in olive oil with thyme and bay leaf, or in *marc*; and tiny ewe's cheeses, Pérails. On the other hand, there is so much fruit, cherries, melons, apricots, peaches, pears, figs, medlars, jujubes (of Syrian origin), it may have stifled the cake-maker's initiative. But there is the nut and honey *touron*, liquorice from Uzès, and various biscuits and aniseed cakes.

The Aude and Hérault departments produce enormous quantities of wine, the *appellations* including Corbières (Fitou), St-Chinian, Picpoul de Pinet, Côtes du Roussillon and Côtes du Roussillon-Villages, Minervois, Costières du Gard, Lirac, and Tavel, and, of course, Côtes du Rhône. Bas-Languedoc has numerous Muscats as well as the *vins des sables*: Clairette du Languedoc and de Bellegarde and Blanquette de Limoux. And there is vermouth (Noilly-Prat).

Gâteaux au Poivre de Limoux
· PEPPER BISCUITS ·

To accompany Blanquette de Limoux as an apéritif. The biscuits can be made lighter and more crumbly by mixing in a little dried yeast at the kneading stage. Traditionally rather large, they can equally be turned into small squares, sticks, or rings, like modern cocktail biscuits. They keep well in a tin.

———————— *Ingredients for c. 500 g · 1 lb of biscuits* ————————

400 g · 14 oz flour	1 sml tsp salt
150 ml · ¼ pt olive oil	2 eggs
5 g · ⅙ oz freshly milled white pepper	1 sml tsp groundnut oil

Blend together the flour, olive oil, and pepper and salt, to a powdery dough, in a mixer (you can knead it by hand but it's hard work).

Add a whole egg and about 150 ml (¼ pt) of water, to make it smooth and malleable. Ensure the pepper is evenly distributed and shape into a ball. Wrap and leave in the salad box in the fridge for 4–5 hr.

Divide the dough into small pieces and roll it out, a piece at a time, to the thickness of a pencil and cut into equal lengths, of about 3 cm (1¼"). Arrange in pairs and twist each pair together. Form into rings, sticking the ends together with a little beaten egg. Place on a lightly oiled baking tray and brush with the rest of the egg.

Bake in a medium oven for 20 minutes.

Recommended wine: Blanquette de Limoux or Clairette Rancio.

Soupe de Fèves
· BROAD BEAN SOUP ·

Almost everywhere in France, broad beans are eaten raw, sometimes with cream cheese with herbs, often with pork, butter, and salt. In Languedoc, you find them stewed with salt pork or with spring onions, or in a light soup like this colourful and aromatic one.

--------------------------- *Ingredients for 8* ---------------------------

3 kg · 6 lb lge broad beans in the
  pod
2 medium sweet onions
4 tbsp olive oil

a lge bunch of very fresh chervil
salt, pepper
optional: small croûtons fried in
  olive oil

Shell the beans and peel off their outer skin.

Chop the onions, and sweat them slowly in a covered saucepan with 2 tablespoons of oil for 7–8 minutes, shaking the pan occasionally.

Add the beans, the chopped chervil, and 2 lt (3½ pt) of water, and simmer for 15 minutes. Season with salt and pepper.

Put through a food-mill or blender and reheat if necessary (it should be very hot). Pour into a tureen and stir in the rest of the oil.

Serve the croûtons separately.

Recommended wine: Picpoul de Pinet or Blanc de Blancs de la Clape.

Escargots Sommiéroise
· SNAILS WITH BACON, WALNUTS, AND ANCHOVIES ·

Languedoc is snail country – almost every town has its own recipe, and even ritual. At Saint-Guilhem-le-Désert in the Hérault, on 3 May, the village is illuminated by snail shells, each filled with oil and a wick and perched on a ledge or cranny in the stonework, for a snail-lit procession, headed by the priest, to make its way through the streets, in medieval tradition.

--------------- *Ingredients for 4–8 (depending on appetite)* ---------------

16 doz cleaned snails (see p. 134)
a bouquet garni: 2 sprigs of thyme,
  a bay leaf, 1 piece of dried orange
  peel, 1 sprig of basil
salt, pepper

200 g · 7 oz lean, green streaky
  bacon
100 ml · 3½ fl oz olive oil
250 g · 8 oz walnut kernels
1 doz anchovy fillets
6 cloves of garlic

Wash the snails well and drop them into water boiling fast enough that it does not go off the boil. Drain after 10 minutes. Detach and set aside the shells.

Return the snails themselves to the pan, pour boiling water over them, and simmer, covered, with the bouquet, salt and pepper, for 1 hr.

Blanch the bacon (see p. 221). Dice it into a pan with the oil, roughly chopped walnuts, pounded anchovies, crushed garlic, and the snails, drained and restored to their shells; cover and simmer 30 minutes, shaking regularly.

Recommended wine: Livac or Tavel rosé.

Feuilleté de Collioure
· TOMATO, ANCHOVY, AND OLIVE TART ·

The little port of Collioure is a centre for tinning anchovies. These *feuilletés* are very similar to the pizza in its Italian and Provençal versions (*la pissaladière niçoise*, p. 194), though the latter are based on bread dough.

--------------------- *Ingredients for 4* ---------------------

300 g · 10 oz puff pastry (see p. 224)
3 tbsp olive oil
5 eggs
2 doz anchovies in oil
1 kg · 2 lb very firm tomatoes

salt, pepper
1 tiny pinch of cayenne
1 sml tsp castor sugar
50 g · 2 oz stoned olives, black or
    green

Roll out the pastry to 2 mm (¹/₁₀″) and line an oiled tart tin. Brush the pastry with a beaten egg.

Drain the anchovies carefully. Hardboil the remaining 4 eggs.

Set aside the 2 or 3 firmest tomatoes and chop up the others into a saucepan with the rest of the olive oil, salt, pepper, cayenne, and sugar. Let the tomatoes soften slowly, giving them a regular stir, until all the liquid has evaporated and the mixture is like a light purée. Leave to cool.

Spread the tomato on the tart shell, arrange the sliced hardboiled eggs on top along with the reserved tomatoes, skinned, seeded, if you wish, and sliced. Garnish with the anchovies and olives.

Bake in a medium oven for 20 minutes. Serve hot, warm or cold.

Recommended wine: a white Catalan Taïchat.

Rouille de Supions
· CUTTLEFISH OR SQUID WITH A ROUILLE ·

Traditionally, prepared by the men of Aigue-Mortes for the town's festival. First they must catch these tiny cuttlefish (3–4 cm long), then make the *rouille* over a camp fire (drinking *pastis* and enjoying a few mussels and wedge shells (*tellines*) cooked in butter, parsley, and garlic), before performing the delicate task of removing the cuttlefish beaks, leaving the eyes intact . . .

--------------------- *Ingredients for 8* ---------------------

3 onions
3 leeks
3 green peppers
100 ml · 3½ fl oz olive oil
2 kg · 4 lb little cuttlefish or squid
a bouquet garni: 1 sprig of thyme, 1
    bay leaf, 3 grains of star anise, 1
    piece of orange peel
1 bottle white wine
salt, pepper
3 kg · 6 lb potatoes

FOR THE SAUCE
3 very hot chillis – can be dried
2 heads of garlic
4 anchovy fillets
2 slices of stale bread
milk
cayenne – or a little *harissa* (North
    African chilli paste)
4 egg yolks
250 ml · 8 fl oz olive oil
parsley
slices of bread

Peel the onions, clean the leeks, and tail and seed the peppers; slice them all and stew, covered, in the oil in a thick pan, for 15 minutes, shaking occasionally.

Clean the cuttlefish: pull the heads off carefully so as to bring the entrails with them and discard the ink pockets; with your fingers, remove everything inside the mantle (the body), including the back bone. Take off the thin skin covering the mantle, thereby detaching the fins. Rub the tentacles to remove the skin (and if cooking tiny cuttlefish, cut up the beak and eyes). Wash well.

Add the roughly chopped cuttlefish to the onions, leeks, and peppers along with the bouquet, wine, 1 lt (1¾ pt) of water, and salt and pepper, for 1 hr.

Meanwhile, cook the potatoes in their skins and peel and slice them thickly when they are ready. Add to the cuttlefish at the end of the hour and continue boiling, more gently, for 15 minutes.

To prepare the *rouille*: pound the tailed and seeded chillis in a mortar with the garlic and as it all reduces to a purée add the anchovies, the bread, previously soaked in milk, and the cayenne or chilli paste (or put all the ingredients through a blender). When the purée is smooth and evenly mixed, fold in the egg yolks and beat in the olive oil very gradually as for mayonnaise.

To serve, mix the *rouille* off the heat into the cuttlefish and potato ragout, and arrange on a dish. Sprinkle with parsley and encircle with toast, if you wish.

Recommended wine: a white or rosé vin des sables *such as Clairette du Languedoc, otherwise Listel.*

Cassoulet de Seiches
· CUTTLEFISH CASSOULET ·

Dried haricot beans play a large part in the local cooking, rich or modest. With stuffed cuttlefish they make a surprising – and delicious – meal.

———————————————— *Ingredients for 8* ————————————————

600 g · 1¼ lb dried white haricot
   beans
a bouquet garni: 1 sprig of thyme, 1
   bay leaf, 2 sprigs of parsley
1.5 kg · 3 lb medium-sized cuttlefish
175 g · 6 oz bread
milk
2 onions
2 cloves of garlic

6 sprigs of parsley
250 g · 8 oz minced pork
2 eggs
salt, pepper
100 ml · 3½ fl oz olive oil
100 g · 3½ oz carrots
200 g · 7 oz fresh tomato purée
500 ml · 17 fl oz white wine

Put the beans to soak in cold water overnight.

Next day, cook them slowly in fresh water with the bouquet for 1 hr after they reach boiling point, and then drain. Do not salt them till the end or they will go hard.

Prepare the cuttlefish as in the previous recipe. For the stuffing: soak 100 g (3½ oz) of crumbled bread in a little milk; chop an onion, a clove of garlic, and all the parsley finely; mix this into the minced pork along with the bread, squeezed dry, eggs, and salt and pepper. You can add the tentacles and the fins to the stuffing if you like. Stuff the cuttlefish and sew them up.

In a thick pan, sauté them in the oil, on a medium heat, and set aside.

Reduce the heat and in the same pan toss the sliced carrots and the remaining onion and garlic, chopped, for 10 minutes. Mix in the tomato purée and the wine and let bubble a moment.

Return the cuttlefish and just cover with water. Stew, with a lid on, for 1 hr, turning the fish over at halftime.

Add the beans to the cuttlefish. Simmer for 15 minutes. Check the seasoning.

Transfer to an oven dish, strew over the rest of the bread, crumbled up, and put in a medium oven to brown the top. Serve in the same dish, having removed the stitching.

Recommended wine: red Minervois, chilled, or a Faugères rosé.

Loup en Gibelotte
· SEA-BASS WITH CRAB, TOMATO, AND VERMOUTH · SAUCE

For a Languedocien, *le loup* is a Mediterranean fish and not the same as *le bar* (sea-bass) from the Atlantic.

─────────────── *Ingredients for 8* ───────────────

2 onions
150 ml · ¼ pt olive oil
1 kg · 2 lb tomatoes
1 head of garlic
1 kg · 2 lb small crabs, if you can get
  them, or prawn shells
1 bouquet garni: 1 sprig of thyme,
  ½ bay leaf, 2 sprigs of parsley
200 ml · 7 fl oz white wine

50 ml · 2 fl oz Noilly-Prat – or other
  dry white vermouth
1 sea-bass, 2–2.5 kg · 4–5 lb
200 ml · 7 fl oz stock
salt, pepper
100 g · 3½ oz anchovy purée or
  mashed anchovies
optional: croûtons fried in olive oil

Slice the onions and soften gently without colouring in a third of the oil in a saucepan for 7–8 minutes. Skin the tomatoes and chop with the garlic and add to the pan; stir to let the liquid evaporate before mixing in the crabs, bouquet, wine, and vermouth. Cook with an occasional stir, until the tomatoes have become a light purée.

Meanwhile, scale and gut the bass and cut off the head (if the fishmonger has not done so). Wash the fish well and cut into 8 steaks.

Press the tomato sauce through a sieve into a frying pan. Arrange the steaks in a single layer on top and pour over the stock; season, taking account of the latter. Cover and simmer for 10–12 minutes or until the steaks are cooked through.

Gradually work the rest of the oil into the anchovy purée.

Transfer the bass to a hot serving dish. Away from the heat, beat the anchovy purée into the sauce. Pour over the fish.

Garnish with the croûtons.

Recommended wine: Picpoul de Pinet or Blanc de Blancs de la Clape.

Civet de Langouste à la Catalane
· LANGOUSTES IN MUSCAT WINE ·

―――――――――――― *Ingredients for 4* ――――――――――――

2 small langoustes, about
   700 g · 1½ lb each
100 ml · 3½ fl oz olive oil
100 g · 3½ oz onions
100 g · 3½ oz shallots
4 cloves of garlic
4 firm tomatoes
2 tbsp cognac

½ bottle Banyuls Rancio or Muscat
   de Beaumes-de-Venise
a bouquet garni: 1 sprig of thyme, 1
   bay leaf, 2 sprigs of parsley
salt, pepper
100 g · 3½ oz butter
a pinch of cayenne

Working over a bowl to catch the lymph, detach the legs and the chest, cut the tail into sections along the articulation marks of the shell, and save any roes. (If you can't face this, try to get a fishmonger to give you some langouste or, more likely, lobster tails.)

Sauté the tail slices and the legs, straightaway, in the oil, over a medium heat, turning them over until the shells are red. Remove from the pan.

Split the chests in two lengthways, throw away the stomachs, save the corals and the creamy parts. Sauté the chests and set aside.

Reduce the heat and soften the chopped onions and shallots for 7–8 minutes; stir in the garlic and the skinned tomatoes, all chopped. Leave to cook for 10 minutes.

Return the sautéed langoustes to the pan, pour in the cognac and set it alight; when it goes out, add the Muscat and the bouquet. Season with salt and pepper and simmer for 10 minutes.

Remove the langoustes to a serving dish while, away from the heat, you sieve the coral, creamy parts, roe, and juices into the sauce, and gradually beat in the butter and cayenne.

Pour the sauce over the langoustes.

Recommended wine: white Côtes du Roussillon, a very dry Banyuls, or a Catalan Blanc de Blancs.

Bourride Sétoise

A Provençal *bourride* is made with various white fish, but in Sète only monkfish is acceptable; a further refinement, for some, is to add the crushed fish's liver to the final liaison.

―――――――――――― *Ingredients for 6* ――――――――――――

4 good white leeks
2 onions
150 g · 5 oz chard leaf (about half a
   bunch) or spinach
2 tbsp groundnut oil
1.5 kg · 3 lb monkfish

400 ml · ¾ pt white wine
salt, pepper
7 cloves of garlic
5 egg yolks
400 ml · ¾ pt olive oil

Clean and slice the leeks, keeping not more than 2 cm ($^3/_4$") of the green. Slice the onions thinly. Wash and snip the chard (or spinach).

Heat the groundnut oil in a large frying pan. When it's hot, stir in the onion, then the leeks and chard. Cover and sweat for 5 minutes.

Put in the monkfish, cut into 12 thin steaks, and let the liquid given off evaporate before pouring in the wine. Increase the heat and add enough water to cover the fish. Season with salt and pepper and cook hard for 15 minutes so the fish is cooked but still firm.

Remove the fish and keep hot. Continue cooking the vegetables more gently while you prepare the liaison.

Crush the garlic. Mix the egg yolks (the purpose of so many is to thicken the cooking juices) into it and beat in the olive oil, a drop at a time as for a mayonnaise, increasing latterly to a trickle, then a little of the cooking liquid. When the liaison is of a pouring consistency, beat it gradually into the cooking vegetables, on a very low heat, until the sauce thickens. Check the seasoning.

Pour over the fish and serve.

Recommended wine: white Listel (Château de Villeroy) or Clairette du Languedoc.

Brandade Nîmoise

A true *brandade* consists of salt cod, olive oil, and milk. Although garlic is often added it was not present in the recipe recorded by Durand, chef at the Hôtel du Midi in Nîmes, in 1830. It may be eaten hot or cold. When potatoes are included, it is no longer *brandade* but *morue bénédictine*. (This is worth trying with smoked mackerel, using slightly less oil.)

———————————————— *Ingredients for 8–12* ————————————————

500 g · 1 lb salt cod   200 ml · 7 fl oz milk
200 ml · 7 fl oz olive oil   salt, pepper

Soak the cod for 12 hr if in fillets, for 24 hr if in the piece (see p. 222). Poach in simmering water for 5–6 minutes. Drain.

Flake it into a thick pot (not aluminium or unlined cast-iron which will discolour the mixture) on a low flame; mash it with a spatula as you beat in the olive oil, drop by drop.

When the fish has absorbed about 150 ml ($^1/_4$ pt) of oil, trickle in an equal amount of milk, previously boiled and allowed to cool, still beating.

Continue adding oil and milk until the mixture can take no more. Add salt and pepper to taste.

Recommended wine: white: Costières du Gard or Laudun.

Cassoulet de Castelnaudary

The cassoulet de Castelnaudary, said Anatole France, was 'God the Father' of cassoulets, that of Carcassonne 'the Son', and that of Toulouse (see p. 136), 'the Holy Ghost' – a statement that signally failed to settle the disputed history of the dish. The cassoulet appears originally to have been made with broad beans (*fèves*), but, when first introduced from the New World, haricot beans were called '*sortes de 'fèves'*, then '*fèves de haricots'*, and could therefore have always been the proper bean. And was it called a cassoulet from a certain glazed clay pot, called a *cassole*, produced in Issel, not far from Castelnaudary? If so, does that make Issel the true birthplace of the cassoulet? Whatever its origins (and they are all Languedocien), what counts in a cassoulet is the choice of beans (*le petit coco de Pamiers*, *le haricot de Mazères*, or *le haricot de Lavelanet* in Toulousain Languedoc; *le lingot* in Bas-Languedoc), and the long slow simmering in the oven, uncovered so that a skin forms on top, this skin to be broken and stirred back into the pot seven times before the cassoulet is ready. Usually, a cassoulet de Castelnaudary has only the meat given in this recipe, while that of Carcassonne has roast shoulder of mutton instead of roast loin of pork, plus, sometimes, chicken or partridge livers. Neither would have included *confit* or fresh sausage, but the Toulouse cassoulet, the most influential, has encouraged inclusion of the latter.

──────────── *Ingredients for 8* ────────────

2 kg · 4 lb sml dried haricot beans (*lingots*)	120 g · 4 oz lard
a bouquet garni: 2 sprigs of thyme, 3 sprigs of parsley	2 cloves of garlic
	400 g · 14 oz fresh pork rinds
1 lge onion	1 salted knuckle of pork (see p. 226)
2 cloves	800 g · 1¾ lb salted barbecue or Chinese spare-ribs
2 large carrots	
2 very white leeks	1 garlic-flavoured boiling sausage
800 g · 1¾ lb loin of pork	4 tomatoes
salt, pepper	100 g · 3 oz homemade breadcrumbs

Put the beans to soak in cold water overnight.

Drain them the next day, and put them to cook gently for 20 minutes in a large saucepan or stewpot with the bouquet, the peeled and quartered onions, stuck with the cloves, the carrots, cut into 4 longways, the leeks, cleaned and cut into sections, and cold water to cover.

Season the pork loin with salt and pepper and roast in a tin greased with a little lard for 40 minutes, turning it over halfway through.

Rub the inside of a large pot (unglazed clay if possible) with the peeled cloves of garlic until they are used up, and line the pot with the rinds, fat side down.

Blanch the knuckle and spare-ribs (see p. 221). Drain and add to the cooking beans with additional boiling water, if necessary, to cover. Simmer a further 20 minutes before putting in the boiling sausage and cooking another 30 minutes.

Transfer half the beans, using a draining spoon, to the lined pot, along with the knuckle and the roast loin, both sliced thickly, the spare ribs, cut up along the bones, the boiling sausage, skinned and sliced, and the tomatoes, skinned, seeded, and quartered; season with salt and pepper after tasting the beans. Cover with the rest of the beans, drained, and dot with the remaining lard.

Cook very slowly in the oven, uncovered, and, approximately every 30–40 minutes, break the skin back into the beans. After this procedure has been followed 7 times, and it has been cooking for 4–5 hr, sprinkle with the breadcrumbs and leave, untouched, a further 40–60 minutes or until the bread is golden without being burnt. Serve from the pot.

Recommended wine: red Minervois, Coteaux du Languedoc, or mature Corbières.

Broufade Nîmoise
· NÎMOIS BEEF CASSEROLE ·

─────────────────────── Ingredients for 4 ───────────────────────

8 thin pieces of beef, cut across the
  grain, from a tender part, e.g.
  chuck, rump, or silverside, that
  needs slow cooking – expensive
  cuts will be too dry
150 ml · ¹/₄ pt olive oil
8 cloves of garlic
¹/₂ tbsp crushed peppercorns
a bouquet garni: 1 sprig of thyme, 1
  bay leaf, 2 cloves, 2 sprigs of
  parsley

250 g · 9 oz onions
salt
150 ml · ¹/₄ pt good wine vinegar (7°
  if possible)
1 tbsp flour, cornflour, or potato
  flour
2 tbsp capers
4 anchovy fillets

Marinate the beef with 100 ml (3¹/₂ fl oz) of oil, 2 chopped cloves of garlic,
pepper, and the bouquet, for 10 hr in a cool place, turning the meat over several
times. Thinly slice the onions and remaining garlic.

Put a tablespoon of oil in a casserole with a cavity in the lid (if you don't have
such a thing you can improvise, for instance by turning the lid upside down).
Arrange a layer of onion and garlic in the bottom, and alternate with the beef,
finishing with onion. Season with salt. Pour in the vinegar and marinade. Seal
tightly and fill the lid with water. Cook in a slow oven for 2 hr, refilling the lid
when the water evaporates.

Take the casserole out of the oven, transfer the meat to a serving dish and
keep it hot. In a cup, blend 100 ml (3¹/₂ fl oz) of warm water into the flour and
stir into the cooking liquid. Heat gently on top of the stove to cook the flour,
stirring almost continually for 10 minutes.

Mash the anchovies and beat in the oil.

Away from the heat, mix the well-drained capers and the anchovy purée into
the sauce and pour over the meat.

Recommended wine: Chusclan, Côtes du Rhône-Villages, or Corbières.

Pigeon à la Catalane

Bitter oranges impart a subtle flavour to pigeon and other game. When bitter
oranges are unavailable, use half a sweet orange and half a lemon.

─────────────────────── Ingredients for 4 ───────────────────────

12 cloves of garlic
4 wood-pigeons (or 2 French
  pigeons)
salt, pepper
thin bacon rashers
50 g · 1³/₄ oz butter
2 tbsp olive oil
80 g · 2¹/₂ oz uncooked ham or

gammon, lean only
2 bitter oranges (or ¹/₂ a sweet
  orange and ¹/₂ a lemon)
200 ml · 7 fl oz white wine
200 ml · 7 fl oz chicken stock
1 tbsp flour, cornflour, or potato
  flour
2 tbsp wine vinegar

Peel the garlic and boil for 10 minutes in a little water.

Salt and pepper the pigeons inside and tie them in the bacon.

Sauté them all over in the butter and oil in a casserole, on a medium flame. Reduce the heat, add the ham, finely diced, the garlic, drained and crushed, and the fruit, pared of peel and pith, sliced, and the pips removed. Pour in the wine and stock, season lightly, taking account of the strength of the stock and the earlier seasoning of the birds. Cover and simmer for ½–1 hr turning the pigeons over when they seem half-cooked.

Take out the pigeons and the orange; blend the vinegar into the flour and pour slowly into the sauce, stirring constantly for several minutes. Leave to cook very gently, with the odd stir to stop it sticking, while you take off the bacon and carve the pigeons in two.

Coat them in the strained sauce and garnish with the orange.

Recommended wine: Côtes du Roussillon-Villages or Fitou.

Oreillettes de Montpellier
· SWEET FRITTERS ·

Oreillettes are eaten from Epiphany to Shrove Tuesday, and they owe their name to the Cévennes Protestants who made them to commemorate Jesus healing the centurion's ear. The dough, once rolled out, should be further stretched across one's knees. *Oreillettes* keep for several days in an airtight container.

—————————————— *Ingredients for 8* ——————————————

2 lemons
10–15 g · ¼–½ oz fresh baker's yeast
500 g · 1 lb flour
10 g · ¼ oz salt
125 g · 4 oz castor sugar
5 eggs
75 g · 2½ oz butter

50 ml · 1½ fl oz dark rum
1 tbsp orange flower water
50 ml · 1½ fl oz milk or water
flour for working the dough
oil for deep frying
icing sugar to taste

Wash the lemons and grate the peel without taking the pith. Dissolve the yeast in warm water with 100 g (3 oz) of flour, the salt, and a pinch of sugar.

In a bowl, make a well in the rest of the flour. Using a spatula, blend together the sugar and the egg yolks in the well, then slowly incorporate the flour into this mixture, simultaneously adding the melted butter, rum, orange flower water, lemon peel, and, lastly, the yeast. Roll into a ball, working in a little milk or water if the dough is too stiff.

On a lightly floured board, flatten out the dough, a spoonful at a time, with the heel of your hand, to give it body. Make back into a ball and leave in a bowl, under a damp cloth, for at least 3 hr.

Divide the dough into about 40 round portions and leave on a floured dish for 15–20 minutes.

Roll out each little ball as thin as possible to the size of a small plate.

Deep fry in hot oil until both sides are golden brown. Drain on absorbent paper and dust with icing sugar.

Recommended wine: a Muscat: Rancio or Banyuls.

17

LANGUEDOC: *The Toulouse Region*

Albigeois · Comminges · Couserans

Lauragais

THE COMTÉ DE FOIX

Toulousain or Pyrenean Languedoc, according to point of view, is blessed with two culinary capitals, both in pink brick: Toulouse and Albi. Neither has ever gained supremacy over the mountainous southern regions, but Toulouse can claim to be the seat of the first gastronomic society, the Confrérie de la Jubilation, founded in the eighteenth century, and is, of course, the home of the Toulouse sausage.

The cookery here is less colourful than in Bas-Languedoc, but slow and savoury. The range of soups is small, surprisingly, and there was little fish, except from the fast-flowing mountain streams and lakes which yielded trout and crayfish (prepared with saffron), gudgeon, barbel, and other small fry; and there was salt cod, from the distant sea, for which the Toulousains had numerous recipes.

More important was the charcuterie, a long tradition in the Tarn where the old houses of Albi had built-n drying places for grain and cured meat. When the Christmas pig was killed, the liver would be salted immediately and left for two months; the *fetze*, as it was called, was then rolled up and dried in the fireplace until Easter when it would be eaten grilled, fried, or baked in the oven, with little onions, young artichokes, radishes, and vinegar. Pig's liver is still made into sausages which are dried, and eaten grilled with eggs and tomato sauce. Ham is served in many ways, notably with fresh figs.

The Montagne Noire, so called because of the dark appearance given by its covering forest, sheltered wild boar, and hams and sausages were made from the meat. If these are now a thing of the past, game (partridge, woodcock, hare) pâtés and fricandeaux are still available. Izard and bears are a dim memory, as are the recipes for little birds, casseroled with bacon and croûtons. But the Haute-Garonne has its veal, the marbled meat of Montrejeau being particularly prized.

Throughout Haut-Languedoc, however, it is the slow cooked *daubes* and *estouffats* that are most enjoyed, the richest and most slowly cooked being the *cassoulet toulousain* (see p. 136). Geese and boiling fowl are also cooked thus, *la poule farcie du Comminges* providing two courses: first, the broth which is served with vermicelli, then the chicken which each person turns over in a mixture of coarse sea-salt and pepper in his empty bowl, and eats with gherkins and mustard.

Despite a large population of geese, and a good deal of *confit* and goose fat in Toulousain cooking, there is little foie gras production, although there is a well-known Toulouse dish which calls for a capon to be stuffed with foie gras and truffles (from the Montagne Noire forests), and braised with mushrooms and olives. In Albigeois, duck was cooked in stock with leeks and celery and served on slices of *pain de campagne* spread with a pear compote.

Beans are as plentiful as their various names (*mounjetos, fabols, favots*) suggest. The *petits cocos de Pamiers* are sought after for *estouffats*. White maize had a place, apart from fattening geese (for which it was preferred to yellow), in *millias*, which were eaten instead of bread and which can still be bought in slabs in the markets of Toulouse.

In Foix, *millias* were also eaten as a dessert, either grilled with sweetened hot milk poured over, or fried and spread with jam or honey. Honey was so important hereabouts that when the head of the house died, the hives were covered in crêpe to stop the bees escaping. Pancakes, incidentally, were not eaten in the Ariège during a period of mourning because they were regarded as a symbol of abundance and joy.

As for cheese, there is Engordany, a sheep's cheese from Andorra, and Bethmale, a cow's cheese, also known as Oustet in winter, and Les Orrys in summer, reflecting the change of pastures. The so-called Pyrenean cheeses are imitations of Bethmale and of Montségur, a black-rinded cow's cheese produced by co-operative.

Gaillac is the chief wine. The whites are notable, and may be dry or sweet, or sparkling (*blanc perlé* or *mousseux*). Locally, the *appellation* Côtes du Frontonnais (divided into Fronton and Villaudric) and the Côtes du Tarn (a *vin de pays*), and the red Lavilledieu are appreciated.

Soupe Ariégeoise à la Rousolle

Roussolle, rousole, from the local word rosola, to brown.

―――――――――――――――― *Ingredients for 4* ――――――――――――――――

150 g · 5 oz lean uncooked ham or
  gammon
150 g · 5 oz uncooked ham or
  gammon fat
6 sprigs of parsley
2 cloves of garlic
75 g · 2½ oz homemade
  breadcrumbs

3 eggs
salt, pepper
2 tbsp goose fat, oil, or dripping
1 lt · 1¾ pt clear vegetable stock, or
  well-skimmed chicken or beef
  stock, or even cabbage soup

Chop up all the ham with the parsley and garlic and, if you like, other herbs, a tiny piece of mint, for instance; mix in the breadcrumbs, eggs, and salt and pepper. Leave, wrapped up, in the fridge, for 1–2 hr.

Press the mixture into a large flat cake and sauté it for 10–12 minutes on each side in the hot fat, keeping it together with a spatula, until it is well browned and cooked right through.

Bring the stock to the boil on a medium heat, add the *rousolle*, cut into small pieces, and simmer for 10–12 minutes.

Pour into individual bowls.

Aillade Toulousaine
· GARLIC AND WALNUT SAUCE ·

Two dishes go under this name: a rough soup made with pieces of toast, rubbed with garlic, sprinkled with olive oil, and dunked in boiling water seasoned with salt and pepper; and this sauce, which is served with veal or slices of grilled goose.

———————————————— *Ingredients for 4* ————————————————

50 g · 2 oz garlic   250 ml · 9 fl oz walnut oil
75 g · 3 oz shelled walnuts   pepper
salt   4–5 sprigs of parsley

Pound the chopped garlic together with the walnuts and salt, using a pestle
and mortar, and adding, now and then, a small teaspoonful of iced water (up
to 50 ml / 1³/₄ fl oz), until the mixture is smooth and creamy.

Beat in the oil, drop by drop, as for mayonnaise; season with pepper and
work in the finely chopped parsely.

Recommended wine: a red Gaillac.

Escargouillade du Comminges

In Languedoc, this is reserved for a special kind of snail, collected only in wet
weather, from the herbs and wild raspberry plants that grow high on certain
Pyrenean slopes, but it can be made with other kinds. The snails are served in
the sauce, in the cooking pot. Everyone is armed with a pin (an acacia needle)
to extract the snails, each one being eaten with a square of bread dipped in the
sauce.

———————————————— *Ingredients for 4* ————————————————

8 doz sml snails   100 ml · 3¹/₂ fl oz oil
coarse salt   100 g · 3¹/₂ oz flour
3 tbsp vinegar   500 ml · 17 fl oz white wine
2 sprigs of thyme   6 cloves of garlic
1 bay leaf   8 sprigs of parsley
300 g · 10 oz raw ham or unsmoked   salt, pepper
   gammon   150 g · 5 oz homemade breadcrumbs
200 g · 7 oz onions   small squares of bread
70 g · 2 oz shallots

If the snails are not prepared, starve them for 3–4 days, then leave for 24 hr in
a container with a large handful of coarse salt (the snails must be able to breathe
but not, of course, escape), and finally wash under running water until the
water is clear.

Leave them in a casserole or large saucepan, with the vinegar, thyme, and
bay leaf, and covered with cold water, until they start to show their horns.

Encourage this process by heating them gently until they all seem to show,
increase the heat and bring to the boil. Simmer for 1 hr and drain.

Meanwhile, make the sauce: toss the diced ham (there should be at least one
bit per snail) and the roughly chopped onions and shallots in the oil, for 5–7
minutes, in a thick pan. Sprinkle in the flour and stir for 3–4 minutes until it
begins to pale. Add the wine, the snails, with hot water to cover, the finely
chopped garlic and parsley, and salt and pepper. Cover and cook for 1 hr.

Mix in the breadcrumbs and leave another 15–20 minutes on the heat before
serving in the cooking pot (so it doesn't cool too quickly).

*Recommended wine: the wine used in the cooking, from a better year, or a dry white
Gaillac Premières Côtes, or a Pacherenc du Vic-Bilh.*

Melsat de Dourgne
· A PORK BOILING SAUSAGE ·

A sort of large white pork, bread, and egg *boudin*. As Christmas fare which has the advantage of keeping for several weeks, it is a traditional present for absent relatives. The sausage is eaten hot, fried in lard, or cold.

--------------------------- *Ingredients for 10–12* ---------------------------

500 g · 1 lb good stale bread
  (including crust)
12 eggs
salt, pepper

1 kg · 2 lb pork loin
500 g · 1 lb cold lean pork belly
lge sausage skins

Crumble the bread, moisten it with water, and add the beaten eggs and salt and pepper. Work the mixture well. Cover and refrigerate for 12–24 hr.

Dice half the pork into 1–2 cm (½–¾") cubes. Mince the rest coarsely. Mix it all into the bread and egg mixture and taste for seasoning.

Fill the skins using a large funnel or a mincer attachment, but without overfilling as the bread will swell in the cooking. Tie up the ends of the sausages leaving a long string.

Immerse the sausages in just-bubbling water, attaching the string at each end to the pan handles, so that the sausages are entirely submerged in the water but not touching the bottom. Leave to simmer for 5–6 hr at 90°C.

Drain the sausages on a thick cloth, quickly covering them with a second cloth so that they don't cool too quickly and burst.

When they are quite cold, wrap individually in foil and store in the fridge.

Gras-Double Tarnais au Safran
· TRIPE WITH SAFFRON ·

A dish reminiscent of the time when saffron was cultivated locally. Tripe is sold ready cleaned and blanched. This recipe requires long cooking, and cannot be made in small quantities, but it reheats well.

--------------------------- *Ingredients for 8* ---------------------------

1.5 kg · 3 lb tripe
a ham bone, a lamb bone, and a veal
  knuckle
300 g · 10 oz carrots
150 g · 5 oz onions
3 cloves
a head of garlic
2 sprigs of thyme
1 bay leaf

12 peppercorns
flour
300 g · 10 oz uncooked ham or
  gammon
30 g · 1 oz lard
4 sprigs of parsley
2 good pinches of saffron
salt, pepper
2 tbsp capers

Put the uncut tripe, the bones, the sliced carrots, the onions, peeled and quartered, and stuck with cloves, the head of garlic, whole and peeled only of the outer layers, and the thyme, bay leaf, and peppercorns in a large oven-proof pot with enough water just to cover. Seal the lid tightly with a strip of dough – flour worked with a little water. Place in a very slow oven for 10 hr.

Fifteen to twenty minutes before the end of the cooking time, gently sauté the diced ham, including the fat, in the lard, for 5 minutes before sprinkling in a good tablespoon of flour and stirring for 2–3 minutes. Pour in 750 ml (1¼ pt) of the tripe's cooking liquid; continue stirring another minute or two.

Take out the tripe and garlic. Crush the garlic into the sauce and mix in the saffron and the tripe, cut up into 4–5 cm (1½–2″) cubes. Simmer for 25 minutes.

Stir in the capers, off the heat, just before serving.

Recommended wine: red: Gaillac or Lavilledieu.

Bougnettes Albigeoises
· POTTED FAGGOTS ·

These are conserved in stone jars under a coating of lard and are eaten either cold or reheated in the lard or poached in soup, the fat carefully removed. Nowadays, minced pork is often substituted for the pig's head.

———————————————— *Ingredients for 8* ————————————————

300 g · 10 oz homemade
  breadcrumbs
milk
6 eggs
1.5 kg · 3 lb fat and lean meat from
  a pig's head, cooked in stock,
  or minced pork

4 cloves of garlic
4–6 sprigs of parsley
salt, pepper
quatre-épices or allspice
pieces of caul fat
lard

Soak the breadcrumbs in a little milk, and mix in the beaten eggs; leave in a cool place for 12 hr.

Dice the pork (if necessary).

Mix the bread with the pork and the finely chopped garlic and parsley; season with salt and pepper and a good pinch of *quatre-épices*.

Soak the caul fat in warm water to soften it, stretch it out and cut into 12 equal squares. Place a portion of the filling on each, flatten it, and wrap the caul round.

Melt 50 g (2 oz) of lard in a gratin dish and arrange the faggots side by side; dot with lard and bake in a moderate oven for 40 minutes, turning them over at halftime. Leave to cool.

To store: pack into stone jars and pour over enough of the cooking fat and additional melted lard to cover entirely. Store in a cool place.

Recommended wine: Côtes du Frontonnais, Fronton, or a neighbouring Cahors or Madiran.

Cassoulet Toulousain

The composition of a Toulousain cassoulet is as controversial as that of a Castelnaudary one (see p. 128): should it include mutton, should the beans be *petits cocos de Pamiers* which break up, or *demi-lingots* which remain intact even when soft? . . . Cassoulets improve with reheating, so do not be deterred by the quantities.

———————————————— *Ingredients for 12* ————————————————

c. 1.2 kg · 2¾ lb dried white haricot
  beans
1 salted ham knuckle (see p. 226)
600 g · 1¼ lb salted barbecue pork
  spare-ribs
pork boiling sausage
2 sprigs of thyme
1 lge onion
2 cloves
2 carrots

2 cloves of garlic
400 g · 14 oz fresh pork rind
3–4 good firm tomatoes
salt, pepper
1–2 pieces of goose *confit*
800 g · 1¾ lb (12) Toulouse or other
  good pork sausages
100 g · 3½ oz homemade
  breadcrumbs

Soak the beans overnight in plenty of cold water, changing the water if they are left more than 12 hr to avoid fermentation.

Blanch the ham knuckle and spare-ribs (see p. 221). (If you use salted meat it will retain its pink colour, unlike fresh meat.)

Put the drained beans, ham knuckle, and spare-ribs in a casserole, along with the boiling sausage, thyme, onion, peeled, quartered, and stuck with the cloves, and carrots, sliced into four lengthways. Cover with cold water but do not add salt which will harden the beans. Leave to bubble gently for 1 hr.

Rub the inside of a large clay (if possible) casserole or terrine dish with the peeled garlic, until it is worn to nothing. Line with the pork rinds, fat side down.

Drain the beans, reserving 2 ladlesful of their cooking liquid and discarding the flavourings. Put half the beans in the casserole, with the ham knuckle, sliced and boned, the spare ribs cut along the bones, the peeled, seeded, and chopped tomatoes, and the boiling sausage, skinned and sliced, on top; season with salt and pepper, taking account of the saltiness of the ham and pork. Cover with the rest of the beans and the reserved liquid. Leave in a very low oven uncovered for 30 minutes.

Break the skin that will have formed and stir it into the cassoulet. Return to the oven. Break up and mix in the skin a further 6 times at 20 minute intervals (total oven time is therefore 2½ hr).

Having stirred in the skin for the last time, add the goose, cut into 12, and the grilled sausages, sprinkle with the breadcrumbs and return to the oven for another 30 minutes.

Serve immediately, in the cooking pot.

Recommended wine: red Gaillac, Madiran, or Cahors.

Oie en Daube
· CASSEROLED GOOSE ·

'A goose always needs a drink . . . alive, it wants water, dead, it wants wine,' observed the medieval School of Medicine at Salerno. This recipe for a mature bird (don't use a roaster) respects the good doctors' tenet.

1 medium goose, c. 3 kg · 6 lb, fleshy
   but not too fat, cut into pieces
2 sprigs of thyme
1/2 bay leaf
2 cloves
pepper
100 g · 3 oz lean green streaky bacon

100 g · 3 oz onions
3 cloves of garlic
3 sprigs of parsley
1 bottle red wine
flour
salt

Take the fat off the goose pieces and break it up into a thick pan or casserole. Add 100 ml (3 fl oz) of water and let it melt very slowly until it has virtually stopped steaming. Pour all but 2 tablespoons' worth into a storage jar for later use.

Mix the thyme leaves from one of the stalks with the bay leaf, broken up, the cloves, pounded, and plenty of freshly milled pepper. Cut the bacon into matchsticks, roll in the herbs, and lard the goose pieces using a small knife or larding needle.

Marinate these for 12 hr, covered, in a cool place, with the other thyme stalk, half the onions and a clove of garlic, finely chopped with the parsley, and enough wine to immerse everything.

Wipe the goose and rub in flour to dry. Reserve the marinade. Brown the pieces all over in the 2 tablespoons of goose fat, on a medium heat, in a casserole; remove them and pour away excess fat.

Reduce the heat and soften the remaining onions, chopped, for 4–5 minutes. Return the goose to the pan with the thyme from the marinade, the other two cloves of garlic, chopped, the marinade, strained, and salt.

Seal the casserole tightly, using a little flour and water paste, and cook very slowly in the oven for 3 hr.

Transfer the goose pieces to a serving dish and keep hot while leaving the sauce to stand for 5 minutes before skimming it. Check the seasoning and pour over the meat.

Recommended wine: Madiran or Côtes de Frontonnais-Villaudric.

Petites Galettes Lauragaises
· APPLE GALETTES ·

Also known as a *patrouillard*. It would have been made with too much pastry for modern tastes – and as one large *galette*.

170–210 g · 6–71/2 oz castor sugar
125 g · 4 oz butter
salt
1 lemon
7 g · 1/4 oz fresh baker's yeast
1 sml tsp orange flower water

3 eggs
175 g · 6 oz flour
1 sml tsp oil
4 Bramleys, or other apples which
   soften well
4 sml tsp granulated sugar

Put 70 ml (⅛ pt) of water, 50 g (1¾ oz) of sugar, an equal quantity of butter, and a pinch of salt in a bowl in a bain-marie of boiling water, and work until the butter has melted and the sugar dissolved. Remove the bowl from the bain-marie.

Blanch a quarter of the lemon peel for 3 minutes in boiling water; drain and chop finely. Dissolve the yeast in the orange flower water and fold it into the butter and sugar, along with the blanched peel, a whole egg, and a white. Beat till the mixture is smooth.

Continue beating as you sift in the flour gradually; when the dough gets too stiff to beat, work it by hand.

Roll it into a ball, cover with a damp cloth, and leave to rise for 2 hr.

Divide the dough into 8 portions. Stretch each piece of dough by hand until you have 8 equal discs. Space 4 of them out on an oiled baking tray, hollowing them out slightly to hold the filling.

Melt 75 g (2½ oz) of butter and brush them with a little of it, put a peeled, cored, and shredded apple on top, and sprinkle each one with 30–40 g (1–1½ oz) of sugar, according to the sweetness of the apples. Pour over the remaining melted butter.

Seal the lids to the bases, pressing them together with your fingers; make a criss-cross pattern on the crust with a sharp knife and brush with beaten egg. Scatter a small teaspoon of granulated sugar over each one.

Bake in a medium oven for 25 minutes. Serve warm if possible.

Recommended wine: a Pacherenc du Vic-Bilh or a Gaillac Perlé.

18
LIMOUSIN · MARCHE

The Limousin was turned into the departments of Corrèze and Haute-Vienne, the Marche into the Creuse. Although the two provinces were politically divided, since Limousin was long under English rule, their gastronomy was closely united, as it was based on the same produce. And their dishes could, after kaolin was discovered at Saint-Yriex in 1768, all be presented on fine Limoges china.

The ingredients the Limousin cook had most to hand were pork, lamb, beef, and veal (though the Plateau de Millevaches is covered not with cattle, but with springs, for which '*vaches*' is patois), poultry and game, freshwater fish, chestnuts, walnuts, and hazelnuts, fresh herbs, strawberries, and raspberries, and bilberries from both the Plateau de Millevaches and Basse-Corrèze. It was these bilberries that went, along with the must, to make the purple mustard of Brive.

Among local soups were the *potée creusoise* which included chitterling sausage and brown bread, and *la bréjaude limousine* (from *bréger*, to mash in Limousin) which is a bacon and vegetable soup: the bacon is boiled in the piece until the rind comes away; it is then mashed and returned to the pot with the rind, still whole, and the raw vegetables (cabbage, potatoes, turnips, carrots, and leeks) until the latter are cooked, when the head of house (who would have been served first) would have the privilege of eating the rind (*le bréjou*).

The fisherman can still hope to bring home a few crayfish or a trout to be cooked with lots of chopped herbs. Or he might catch eel and carp for a *matelote corrézienne*, nowadays increasingly made with a red Cahors or Bergerac rather than white wine. If he only managed roach, they would go into an omelette. Otherwise, omelettes might be potato, bacon or ham, or wild mushroom. Eggs (*oeufs mollets*) also go into dandelion salad, along with either bacon or croûtons, fried in goose or duck fat.

A *daube* here demanded exceptional patience as it required forty-eight hours' cooking and had to be watched over all night to ensure the fire didn't go out or the stew run dry. Quicker to prepare was the poultry: though chickens from the Creuse were rather lean, those from Limousin were weightier and went well with mushrooms and cream, or ceps, or chestnuts – which underlie much of Limousin cooking – in which case the chicken would be roast in an open tin and the pre-cooked chestnuts added, with their cooking liquid, just before the end. The tin was then covered and the flavour sealed in until the bird was quite done. Chestnuts came too in *boudin* and *gogue d'Uzerches* (a large blood sausage), and with turkey, brussel sprouts, or cabbage. Blanched chestnuts, *châtaignes blanchies*, i.e. peeled but not cooked, are still sold in the street.

Perhaps to make up for a modest array of cheeses, there being only Creusois (or Creusot), a cow's cheese served with potatoes, and Tomme Bleue de Brach, a ewe's cheese, there are plenty of desserts and puddings, tarts and cakes, *clafoutis* (see p. 145), *flognardes* or *flaugnardes* (apple or pear flans), walnut, chestnut, hazelnut, and other cakes (see p. 145), a *pâté de fromage sucré* (*fromage blanc* and cream), *crème de marrons*, from Tulle, and madeleines from Saint-Yriex. *Creusois*, fourteenth-century cakes, long-forgotten, were revived by a local *pâtissier* in the 1960s.

The Marche has no wine, but the Limousin has *vin gris* in the Haute-Vienne, red Clos de Vertoujit in Corrèze, and, more important, its *vin paillé*, drunk as an apéritif or dessert wine and produced around Queyssac, Nonards, St-Julien, and Maumont. It is an uneconomic wine, since the grapes must be left in bunches on slatted wooden trays on beds of rye straw until Christmas by which time the level of dehydration is such that for every five litres of juice the grapes would have yielded initially, one litre is extracted. Plums, walnuts, and hazelnuts are made into *eaux-de-vie*, while mineral water is available in the Creuse at Évaux-les-Bains.

Fricassée au Tourain
· SORREL AND BACON SOUP ·

―――――――――――――― *Ingredients for 8* ――――――――――――――

100 g · 3 oz lean streaky bacon
125 g · 4 oz onions
20 g · ½ oz lard or goose fat

1 tbsp flour
300 g · 10 oz sorrel (fresh or bottled)
salt, pepper

Dice the bacon finely. Chop the onions small and toss them with the bacon in the fat for 8–10 minutes, on a medium heat.

Sprinkle in the flour and stir until the roux is almost brown, but not burnt.

Continue stirring, gradually adding 1.5 lt (2 pt) of boiling water.

Mix in the sorrel, stalks discarded, washed, and finely snipped, and simmer the soup for 30 minutes. Season with salt, taking account of the saltiness of the bacon, and plenty of pepper.

Pour into individual soup bowls.

Soupe de Marrons
· CHESTNUT SOUP ·

A close relation of the Auvergne chestnut soup, but made with stock and cream instead of milk.

―――――――――――――― *Ingredients for 4* ――――――――――――――

2 leeks, with plenty of white
1 onion
20 g · ¾ oz butter
2 dozen fully peeled chestnuts (the whole tinned ones will do)
1 lt · 1¾ pt stock

a bouquet garni: 1 sml sprig of thyme, 1 good celery stalk
salt, pepper
200 ml · 7 fl oz thick cream
toast

Trim and wash the leeks, keeping only the white. Slice them with the onion, and soften gently in the butter in a saucepan for 7–8 minutes, without letting them brown.

Add the chestnuts and the bouquet, pour in the stock, and season according to the strength of this last. Simmer for 45 minutes.

Remove the bouquet and put the soap through a food mill. Return to the saucepan, add the cream, and cook gently for another 10–15 minutes.

Pour over the toast to serve.

Recommended wine: red Côtes de Bergerac.

Tourte Limousine
· LIMOUSIN VEAL AND PORK PIE ·

A pie with numerous variations both in name and composition. *Pâté de Roche-chouart* has a brioche pastry and a pure pork filling; *broccana*, from Tulle, is puff pastry filled with veal and sausagemeat; *tourtière* is brioche pastry with minced pork, potato, garlic, and herbs; while *pâté de boulettes*, from Aubusson, where it was traditional for the carpetmakers' festival, is very close to this one, which is found throughout the region. After cooking, a *tourte limousine* was usually tucked under an eiderdown, to encourage the crust to absorb the fat – hence its nickname, *la malade*.

―――――――――――― Ingredients for 8 ――――――――――――

350 g · 12 oz shoulder veal	3 eggs
150 g · 5 oz pork loin	salt, pepper
150 g · 5 oz green fat bacon	400 g · 14 oz puff pastry (see p. 224)
100 g · 3½ oz onions	40 g · 1½ oz butter
20 g · ¾ oz lard	1 shallot
4 sprigs of parsley	150 ml · ¼ pt white wine
8 sprigs of chervil	150 ml · ¼ pt stock
12–20 chives	100 g · 3 oz rye breadcrumbs

Mince the shoulder veal, pork, and bacon fairly coarsely. Chop the onions and toss in the lard, for 7–8 minutes. Mix them into the mince, along with half the parsley, chervil, and chives, finely chopped or snipped, 2 eggs, and salt and pepper.

Roll out two-thirds of the pastry to 2 mm (¹/₁₀″) and line a tart tin or pie dish, greased with half the butter, leaving a 2 cm (¾″) border all round.

Divide the mince into tiny balls, about a dessertspoon's worth, and arrange on the pie base. Put in a pie funnel if you wish.

Fold in the pastry over the filling and brush the upper side with beaten egg; roll out the second piece of pastry to the same thickness, make a pie lid and ensure that it's firmly sealed to the base all round. Brush with egg, make a small hole in the middle for the pie funnel or to insert a pastry (or cardboard) chimney, and place the pie in a hot oven. After 10 minutes, reduce the heat to medium and continue baking for 15 minutes.

Meanwhile, soften the chopped shallots gently in the remaining butter in a saucepan for 3–4 minutes. Pour in the wine and stock and after about 5 minutes, add the breadcrumbs, and simmer until it has the consistency of a light purée. Away from the heat, add the rest of the herbs, chopped or snipped.

Remove the pie from the oven, pour in the sauce through the hole, and tilt the pie to ensure it reaches the furthest corners.

Serve very hot.

Recommended wine: red Bergerac, Pécharmant, or Cahors.

Lièvre en Cabessal

Argument has long raged over this dish and its probable offspring *le lièvre à la royale*. In the latter part of the last century, when the affluent really ate well, professional men, writers, doctors, lawyers, did not hesitate to address long diatribes to the papers, relating the finer reactions of their tastebuds, thereby sparking off rich controversies. Looking back over the correspondence, it appears that although *le lièvre à la royale* came from the Périgord, it certainly derived from *le lièvre en cabessal*, a country dish, originating in either neighbouring Limousin or Poitou. (The lengthy recipe given by Senator Couteaux in *Le Temps* on 28 November 1898, and found in translation in E. David's *A Book of Mediterranean Food* (London, 1950) shows that *le lièvre à la royale* began as a relatively simple dish; for all the 7½ hours' preparation, it had none of the foie gras, stuffings, and trimmings of later versions.)

As for the *cabessal* (or *chabessal*), that is possibly a reference to the shape of the hare lying in the casserole, a *cabessal* being the curved headpiece worn by women when they had to carry buckets on their heads.

--------------------------------- *Ingredients for 8* ---------------------------------

1 good hare + the blood
wine vinegar
thin bacon rashers
150 g · 5 oz carrots
200 g · 7 oz onions
2 cloves
16 cloves of garlic
100 g · 4 oz goose fat or lard
a bouquet garni: 2 sprigs of thyme,
   1 bay leaf, 2 sprigs of parsley

salt, pepper
200 g · 7 oz green fat bacon
125 g · 4 oz mushrooms (ideally field
   mushrooms)
10 shallots
stale bread, without crust
200 ml · 7 fl oz red wine, preferably
   a Bordeaux
1 lt · 1¾ pt stock
2 tbsp cognac

Beat the blood with about 50 ml (2 fl oz) of wine vinegar to stop coagulation. Set aside the liver, heart, and kidneys, and cut the head off at the bottom of the neck. Extract as many of the ribs as possible and 'break' the back so as to fit the hare into a round casserole. Wrap and tie it in the thin bacon rashers.

Slice the carrots, cut two peeled onions into eighths and stud with the cloves, and peel four cloves of garlic.

Paint the bottom and sides of a broad, shallow, casserole with the fat. Strew the bottom with the carrots, onions, peeled garlic, and bouquet, and put in the hare. Season with salt and pepper, cover, and sweat gently for 40 minutes.

Meanwhile, chop up the fat bacon, offal, cleaned mushrooms, remaining garlic and onions, and shallots. Mix them together, incorporating the bread, crumbled, to stiffen the mixture, then stir in the blood.

Pour over the hare, at the end of the 40 minutes, and add the wine, stock to cover, and a spoonful or so of vinegar to make the sauce strong and piquant. Seal tightly and cook very slowly (best in the oven) for 5 hr.

Delicately transfer the hare, which will be extremely fragile, to a deep round serving dish.

Skim the sauce and take out the bouquet and cloves. Mash the vegetables in the bottom of the casserole carefully, add the cognac, check the seasoning, and simmer 5–6 minutes.

Untie the hare and discard any bacon still attached and any bones which come away easily and have no meat on them.

Pour the sauce over the hare and serve – only spoons should be laid, as this is never eaten with a knife and fork.

Recommended wine: red Bergerac, Pécharmant, or St-Estèphe.

Farcidures à l'Oseille
· POTATO AND SORREL DUMPLINGS ·

These are similar to *miques* (see p. 114) and are also usually poached in a cabbage or bacon soup. They may be yeast dough, or potato plus bacon, or potato plus bacon and a vegetable, such as leeks or chard – or sorrel.

———————————— Ingredients for 4 ————————————

1 kg · 2 lb potatoes
1 sml tsp coarse salt
200 g · 7 oz sorrel
100 g · 3½ oz onions
3 cloves of garlic

5–6 sprigs of parsley
flour
2 eggs
250 g · 9 oz fat bacon
12 good cabbage leaves

Peel, grate, and rinse the potato, and drain in a colander, covered with a damp cloth to stop it going black, for at least 1 hr.

Mix the drained potato with the salt, the washed and shredded sorrel, and the onions and garlic, chopped with the parsley. Incorporate a little flour and work the mixture until it no longer feels damp and holds together (in a good handful). Stir in the eggs.

Dice the bacon finely. Cut out the main stalk of the cabbage leaves and wash and blanch these for a few minutes in boiling water to soften them.

Divide the dough into small portions and roll each into a ball, working in a little bacon at the same time. Tie each ball in a cabbage leaf.

Simmer fairly hard in stock or in a soup you are cooking, without turning them over, for 30 minutes.

Tarte à la Caillade
· CURDLED MILK CAKE ·

Curdled milk is found in cakes and pastries in many dairy regions. For this one (baked in a tart tin, hence its name), you need equal measures of eggs, flour, sugar, milk, cream, and curdled milk.

———————————— Ingredients for 8 ————————————

5 eggs of 55 g · 2 oz each
250 g · 9 oz flour
1 sml tsp salt
250 g · 9 oz castor sugar
250 ml · 9 fl oz milk

250 ml · 9 fl oz cream
½ sachet dried yeast
250 g · 9 oz curdled milk, well
    drained, almost dry
25 g · ¾ oz butter

Beat the eggs together in a bowl, gradually folding in the flour, salt, sugar, milk, cream, and, lastly, the yeast and curdled milk. Continue beating until the mixture is well blended.

Pour into a buttered tart tin and bake in a medium oven for 40 minutes.

Leave to cool before unmoulding. Serve warm or cold.

Clafoutis

In the Limousin, *clafoutis* can only be made with small black unstoned cherries.

———————————————— *Ingredients for 4* ————————————————

250 ml · 9 fl oz milk
750 g · 1¹/₂ lb small black cherries
100 g · 3¹/₂ oz butter
200 g · 7 oz flour

125 g · 4 oz castor sugar
¹/₂ sml tsp salt
4 eggs

Boil the milk and leave to cool; wash, drain, and tail the cherries.

Grease an oven dish with half the butter and arrange the cherries, unstoned, in the bottom.

In a bowl, mix the sugar and salt into the flour and make a well in the centre. Work in the eggs, one by one, the rest of the butter, melted, and the lukewarm milk.

Pour the mixture over the cherries, being careful not to disarrange them, and bake in a slow oven for 45 minutes, opening the door slightly after 30 minutes.

Recommended wine: vin paillé *or a Muscat.*

Gâteau aux Noisettes
· HAZELNUT CAKE ·

———————————————— *Ingredients for 4* ————————————————

200 g · 7 oz hazelnuts, hulled and
   skinned
100 g · 3¹/₂ oz flour
50 g · 2 oz castor sugar

4 eggs
100 g · 3¹/₂ oz honey
70 g · 2¹/₂ oz butter

In a blender, chop up the nuts fairly finely without pulverising them. Mix them with the flour and sugar and make a well in the centre.

Gradually add two whole eggs and two yolks, the honey, and 50 g (2 oz) of melted butter, beating hard.

Pour into a buttered sandwich tin and bake in a moderate oven for 35 minutes. Cool before unmoulding.

Recommended wine: vin paillé, *Muscat, or Sauternes.*

Gâteau de Châtaignes
· CHESTNUT PUDDING ·

A winter pudding, it can be flavoured with vanilla, or with rum as here, or with the addition of a bar of bitter chocolate, softened first over a pan of hot water. It is always eaten next day, accompanied by whipped cream. It can be made with tinned whole chestnuts.

———————————————— *Ingredients for 4* ————————————————

700 g · 1½ lb chestnuts, cooked, and   120 g · 4 oz butter
  still hot   1 tbsp rum
100 g · 3½ oz castor sugar   whipped cream
2 egg yolks

Put the chestnuts through the fine mesh of a food mill into a bowl in a bain-marie. Add the sugar, egg yolks, 100 g (3½ oz) of butter, softened but not melted, and the rum, beating hard until it thickens, but without overdoing it.

Pour the mixture into a buttered sandwich tin and leave to cool before putting it in the fridge for 24 hr.

Unmould and serve with whipped cream.

Recommended wine: vin paillé, *Muscat, or Sauternes.*

19
LORRAINE

Quiche Lorraine *is* a typical local dish in its combination of butter, cream, bacon, and eggs. Closely related but less well-travelled are *sauce messine*, made with cream, *beurre manié*, mustard, egg yolks, shallot, lemon, and herbs, and inseparable from pike; *omelette messine*, with bacon, Gruyère, cream, and *fines herbes*; *la meurotte* and *la migaine* (see below); and *soupe lorraine*, an onion and bacon soup served with toast, cream, and grated cheese.

Other tarts and pies include *la fiousse*, a savoury cream cheese tart; *tarte à la purée*, filled with potato, cream, and butter; and onion, spinach, or meat (notably, marinated veal and port) pies. Pancakes (*kneppes*), are rolled in ham, coated with *fromage blanc*, and browned in the oven. Eggs appear frequently, for instance, *à l'escargot*, when they are hardboiled, cut in half, and served with snails, parsley, shallots, more eggs, and a béchamel sauce.

Freshwater fish were once the glory of Lorraine cookery. But if there are no longer crayfish to accompany the Twelfth Night ham (which was marinated for two days before being roasted), there are always eels, barbel, bream, pike, gudgeon, perch, and carp (which are stuffed with soft roes), and trout, which are made into pâté at Remiremont. Fish stews are slightly different here: *matelote lorraine* is made with *vin gris* and bound with onions softened in butter, and a *matelote messine* is highly seasoned and cooked in stock rather than wine.

An area of pig-breeding, Lorraine has a full range of *charcuterie* products, while milk-fed pork, grilled or in aspic, is a speciality of Metz. The inevitable *choucroute* is served with pig's cheek. Other meat dishes are much as elsewhere, though two veal dishes are worth mentioning: *côtelettes au petit lard*, where the veal is cooked with bacon rashers, deglazed with white wine and stock, and the reduced liquid is bound with egg yolk and a drop of vinegar; and *veau à la couenne*, a casserole of layers of shoulder veal, pork rind, and fat bacon, requiring some five hours' cooking.

Pheasant and grouse shooting is no longer permitted, but goose is made into a *daube* with *vin gris* and ceps, and small turkeys are roast and served *en ravigote*, i.e. the liver is mashed up with mustard, lemon juice, shallots, gherkins, egg yolk, and parsley. Cockerel is also cooked in *vin gris*, with little onions and tomato purée.

The cheeses are Géromé, a Munster-like cheese from the Vosges, Voïd, from the Meuse, and Matton, a skimmed milk cheese.

In the land of quiches there are plenty of sweet tarts as well: mirabelle; quetsch; apple, raisin, and cinnamon; carrot; cherry; rhubarb; poppy seed (see p. 149). Stanislas Leczinski, the dethroned king of Poland, who was given the duchies of Lorraine and Bar in 1738, was reputedly influential in the matter of cakes, changing *kougelhopf*, for which he had a passion, by adding Malaga wine and calling it Ali-Baba; and naming certain little cakes from Commercy after the cook – Madeleine. Macaroons were made in Nancy some three hundred years ago by the nuns of the rue de la Hache, the '*soeurs macarons*', while the town's bergamots are said to have originated around the same time with a *pâtissier* adding Eau de Cologne (which is scented with bergamot) to his cakes as a joke. Jam is a speciality of Bar-le-Duc, where the fruit used to be seeded with the aid of a goose feather, then left whole in a clear syrup.

Moselle wines are red, white, and rosé, as are the Côtes de Toul, but the Côtes de Toul rosé is so colourless it is known as *vin gris*. Hedgerow fruit, including hops and sloes, are picked for *eaux-de-vie* and ratafias, and from the high stubble fields of the Vosges comes a gentian liqueur, served in the mountain inns. Contrexéville and Vittel water are also from Lorraine.

Salade de Pissenlits à la Chaude Meurotte
· HOT POTATO AND DANDELION SALAD ·

La meurotte is the bacon and shallot dressing. The order in which this salad is prepared is important.

─────────────────── *Ingredients for 8* ───────────────────

600 g · 1¼ lb potatoes
400 g · 14 oz small dandelion leaves
  (or chicory or watercress)
150 g · 5 oz smoked lean streaky
  bacon

3 tbsp oil
4 tbsp wine vinegar
salt, pepper
2 shallots
8–10 chives

Boil the potatoes in their skins for 20–30 minutes according to size.

Discarding any dead leaves, wash the dandelion and dry well; halve or quarter the bigger roots and put them all in the salad bowl.

When the potatoes are almost cooked, cut the bacon into small lardons and soften gently until they have rendered their fat and are very crisp.

Peel the potatoes while they are still hot, and slice into a second salad bowl. Immediately pour over the oil beaten with 1 tablespoonful of vinegar in which the salt has been dissolved. Season with pepper and the finely chopped shallots and the chives, snipped. Mix well.

When the bacon is ready, pour it over the dandelion, along with the rendered fat. Let the remaining vinegar bubble once or twice in the same pan, then mix into the dandelion.

Add the potato salad, which must still be hot, to the dandelion salad. Serve at once.

Recommended wine: Riesling.

Quiche Lorraine

The word 'quiche', relatively recent in the long history of this savoury tart, seems to come from the German *kuchen*, cake. Whether or not a quiche should contain cheese, as in this recipe, is not easily answered. Quiches figured in all the popular festivities, each village having its own version. They seem originally to have been made with bread dough, smoked bacon, and *la migaine* (a mixture of eggs and cream, predominantly the latter). But the word '*migaine*' is believed to come from '*fremeye*', meaning drained *fromage blanc*. . . .

─────────────────── *Ingredients for 4* ───────────────────

250 g · 9 oz shortcrust pastry (see
  p. 224)
20 g · ¾ oz butter
8 eggs

200 g · 7 oz smoked streaky bacon
  – lean but well streaked with fat
175 g · 6 oz Gruyère cheese
500 ml · 17 fl oz thick cream
salt, pepper, nutmeg

Roll out the pastry to 3 mm (⅛″) and prick it with a fork. Turning it the other way up, line a buttered tart ring or tin, making sure the sides are deep and firm. Brush with beaten egg.

Blanch the bacon (see p. 221), and cut into matchsticks. Sauté gently without letting it go crisp and scatter on the tart base with the finely diced Gruyère cheese.

Beat the remaining (7) egg yolks with the cream; season with salt, bearing in mind the saltiness of the bacon and cheese, and pepper, and a little grated nutmeg.

Pour into the tart shell, which should not be more than three-quarters full (because the filling will puff out during cooking). Bake in a pre-heated oven, mark 9/240°C, reduce to a medium heat after 20 minutes, and cook for a further 25 minutes. Serve hot.

Recommended wine: Riesling, Chablis, or Sancerre.

Tarte au Pavot
· POPPYSEED TART ·

A pie from Toul, where it is called *tarte au seme-z-en*, after the local name for white poppyseeds. It is very good cold.

———————————————— *Ingredients for 4* ————————————————

120 g · 4 oz white poppyseeds
milk
4 eggs
200 ml · 7 fl oz thick cream
1 onion

30 g · 1 oz butter
salt, pepper
250 g · 9 oz shortcrust pastry (see p. 224)
250 g · 9 oz puff pastry (see p. 224)

Put the seeds through a blender (in the past the seeds would have been ground in a mortar – a lengthy business), and cover with milk previously brought to the boil and cooled. Leave 3–4 hr to swell.

When they are ready, beat in 3 eggs, one at a time, and the cream.

Chop the onion and toss in 10 g (1/3 oz) of butter, on a low heat, until they are quite soft. Add to the poppyseed mixture and season with salt and pepper.

Roll out the shortcrust pastry to 3 mm (1/8") and prick it with a fork. Line a buttered tart tin, turning the pastry the other way up, and leaving a 3 cm (1") border all round.

Roll out the puff pastry to 2 mm (1/10"), cut to the exact size of the tin and set aside.

Pour the filling into the tart shell, fold in the border, and brush the upper surface with beaten egg. Put the puff pastry lid in place, sealing the edge tightly to the base, and brushing the top with egg.

Make a criss-cross pattern with a knife and cut a small hole in the middle for a pastry (or cardboard) chimney.

Bake in a hot oven, turning it down to medium after 15 minutes. Cook a further 20 minutes. Leave to cool.

Recommended wine: white Moselle or champagne.

Fromage de Porc à l'Ancienne
· PIG'S HEAD BRAWN ·

An ancient recipe from the Vaucouleurs region. It keeps ten days in a fridge, provided it is always wrapped in foil.

———————————— *Ingredients for a large terrine dish or salad bowl* ————————————

1 pig's head, cut in 2, + the tongue
2 pig's trotters
4 cloves of garlic
3 onions
4 shallots

4 sprigs of parsley
1 tbsp peppercorns
2 sprigs of thyme
salt
1 bottle white wine

Put the head and trotters in a deep cooking pot and cover with cold water.

Slice the garlic, onions, and shallots roughly; chop the parsley and tie all these seasonings, along with the peppercorns and thyme, in a piece of muslin. Drop this bouquet in the cooking pot, looping the string over the handle so you can fish it out easily. Salt the water.

Put the pot on a low flame, and skim as soon as it boils. Simmer quite hard for 7 hr, adding the tongue for the last 20 minutes.

When cooked, take out all the meat. Strain the cooking liquid and return to the pot, pour in the wine, and continue simmering (the bouquet still anchored in place) while the meat is prepared.

Skin and bone the tongue leaving it whole. Bone the rest of the pork and cut into 5 cm (2") cubes.

Return all the meat to the pot, discard the bouquet, adjust the seasoning, and simmer a further 30 minutes.

Pour 2 ladlesful of the cooking liquid into a terrine dish or salad bowl large enough to hold everything, and tilt it to ensure the bowl is entirely coated with the liquid. Leave to set in a cool place.

Extract the meat with a draining spoon and slice the tongue. Arrange pieces of fat and lean meat and tongue alternately in the aspic-lined bowl. Pour in enough cooking liquid to cover, and let cool a little before pressing under a small board or plate and a weight. Leave to get quite cold.

Refrigerate for 24 hr, unmould, and cut in slices or wedges according to its shape.

Recommended wine: Sylvaner, Chablis, Sancerre, Gris de Toul, red or white Mâcon, or Beaujolais.

Jambon au Foin
· HAM COOKED IN HAY ·

This requires a ham that has been smoked for no more than 3 days. The flavour of the hay should not be spoilt by adding other herbs. In the past, the ham would have been sewn into a linen cloth and placed on a bed of hay in water throughout the cooking, thereby acquiring a more pronounced taste. The sauce will go well with any good cooked ham.

―――――――――――― *Ingredients for 8* ――――――――――――

a lightly smoked ham joint,
   c. 4 kg · 8 lb
a large handful of healthy hay

FOR THE SAUCE
1 lt · 1³/₄ pt thick cream
8 shallots

2 tbsp strong smooth Dijon mustard
100 g · 3¹/₂ oz butter
20 g · ¹/₂ oz flour
salt, pepper
3 egg yolks
12 fresh tarragon leaves
12 chives

Leave the ham for 12 hr under a trickle of running water, or soak with frequent changes of water.

Attach a piece of string to the knuckle, and immerse the ham in a large two-handled pot of cold unsalted water, tying the string to the handles to stop the ham touching the bottom. Put on a low heat. When it reaches boiling point, drain, and replace with boiling water (still unsalted). Cover and simmer very slowly for 3 hr.

At the end of this time, add the hay, pushing it in with a spatula so it encircles the ham. Cover and continue simmering for 15–25 minutes.

In the meantime, prepare the sauce: let the cream, the very finely chopped shallots, and the mustard bubble gently on a low heat for 10 minutes. Mix in the butter worked with the flour, and stir constantly for 10 minutes, to cook the flour, without letting it boil.

Beat the egg yolks in a sauceboat as you very gradually pour in the sauce. Season with salt and pepper and the finely snipped herbs.

Take the ham out of the pot, drain the hay and strew it on the serving dish with the ham on top. Serve still steaming, with the sauce on the side. Whatever is left over can be eaten cold.

Recommended wine: Gris de Toul.

Grenouilles à la Vitelloise
· FROGS' LEGS WITH MUSHROOMS ·

Simple and delicious and, unusually for the region, without cream.

―――――――――――― *Ingredients for 4* ――――――――――――

4 dozen frogs' legs
milk
flour
100 g · 4 oz stale bread, without
   crust
100 g · 4 oz mushrooms

50 g · 2 oz butter
2 tbsp oil
salt, pepper
fresh herbs to taste (e.g. chives,
   chervil, parsley)

Soak the prepared legs in milk for 1 hr. Drain and wipe and roll in flour.

Dice the bread and cleaned mushrooms very small.

Heat the butter and oil in a large frying pan and brown the legs all over on a medium heat, cover and cook a further 5–6 minutes.

Remove the lid, turn the legs over, season with salt and pepper, and stir in the diced bread and mushrooms. Cook, uncovered, for 7–8 minutes, shaking

the pan frequently, to let the liquid from the mushrooms evaporate.
Snip the herbs in and serve.

Recommended wine: Riesling, Muscadet, or white Graves.

Roncin
· FROMAGE BLANC WITH EGG AND POTATOES ·

From the Vosges, where it is eaten with potatoes boiled in their skins.

———————————— *Ingredients for 4* ————————————

400 g · 14 oz well-drained *fromage*
  blanc, preferably salted
2 eggs

1 tbsp flour
salt, if cheese unsalted

Melt the cheese on a low heat, stirring occasionally.
Beat the eggs and fold in the flour.
Trickle this mixture into the melted cheese, stirring constantly, and continue
stirring for 10 minutes while the flour cooks and thickens the mixture.
Serve hot.

Recommended drink: red or white wine, or beer.

Tarte aux Brimbelles
· BILBERRY TART ·

Brimbelles, a familiar word to our ears (if not eyes), but in Lorraine, and in the
neighbouring Ardennes, it means bilberries. This recipe from Gérardmer makes
a particularly good tart.

———————————— *Ingredients for 8* ————————————

400 g · 14 oz fine shortcrust pastry
  (see p. 224)
25 g · ³/₄ oz butter
1 egg
250 g · 9 oz boudoir biscuits

750 g · 1¹/₂ lb bilberries (or
  blackberries, red or black
  currants, etc.)
icing sugar

Roll out the pastry to 3 mm (¹/₈″), prick it with a fork, and turning it the other
way up, line a buttered tart tin. Make a rolled edge, curving it inwards slightly
so it is easier to unmould. Brush with beaten egg.
Crumble up the biscuits and sprinkle them on the tart base (this stops the
pastry going soggy).
Wash, drain, and tail the bilberries. Set aside about 100 g (4 oz) of them. Fill
the tart, which should not be more than three-quarters full, with the rest. Bake
in a medium oven for 25 minutes.
Leave to cool, then scatter with the reserved fruit, pressing it into the tart.
Dust with icing sugar.

20
LYONNAIS

The Roman town of Lugdunum was founded in 43 BC on the hill which now forms the Fourvière district of Lyon. Strategically placed on the route north, it inevitably became a stopping place for travellers and attracted those whose profession it was to provide food and shelter. As the town prospered, so it became the heart of a huge farming area – and of good eating. One of the strengths of modern Lyonnais cookery has been its imperviousness to fads, its loyalty to the old recipes devised by the Lyonnaises at home, in other words, true *cuisine du terroir*.

Onions rule the Lyonnais pot, starting with *soupe à l'oignon* (or *soupe lyonnaise*), a simple onion and stock preparation, the onions first cooked in butter, then bound with flour, the stock poured in, and, after an hour's slow cooking, the soup added to beaten eggs in the tureen. *Soupe au riz* is also onion, browned in pork fat, water added, and a handful of rice per person. A *pot-au-feu* is strengthened by the inclusion of plenty of bones: it is flavoured with leeks, carrots, turnips, parsnips, onions, chervil, and tarragon, and coloured with dried pea pods. The broth is eaten first, poured on to bread, with just the leeks left in; this is followed by toast spread with the bone marrow and sprinkled with coarse salt; finally the meat and remaining vegetables are served with red cabbage, cooked separately.

The other facet of Lyonnais cooking is its *charcuterie*, centred on Lyon, where *saucisson de Lyon*, a pork, beef, and bacon sausage, and *cervelas lyonnais*, a boiling sausage, flavoured with truffles and pistachio nuts, and sometimes encased in brioche, hold pride of place. *Rosette*, a more widely travelled, pure pork *saucisson*, is also from Lyon. Lyon's *charcuterie* and *triperie* (offal dishes such as *boudin à la crème aux herbes fraîches*) provide mid-morning refreshment, as well as being the stock-in-trade of the bistros, with their warm atmosphere of good wine and country cooking, that are typical of Lyon. Such bistros also serve carefully composed salads, lentil, fresh white bean, dandelion (*groin d'âne*), or leek, for instance, often with a helping of potato at the same time.

Lyonnais butchers used to cut differently from Parisian ones, and this has left a legacy of different terms even though the cuts are now standardised. There is a preference for young meat, such as milk-fed pork (boned, stuffed and cooked with white wine and herbs), and veal, whose predominance is reflected in the number of preparations, such as *andouille de Lyon* (calf's mesentery, calf's liver, and onions) using calf's offal. So close to La Bresse, home of France's best poultry, the Lyonnais eat a considerable amount of chicken and share recipes with Franche-Comté and Dauphiny (but its own *poulet à la Célestine*, often described as a *terroir* dish, was the creation of a nineteenth-century chef in love).

Aside from onion, and its ally, potato, favoured vegetables include squash and pumpkin, cardoons, chard, globe artichokes, green beans, spinach (which used to be blanched with equal quantities of dandelion, endive, and cress, then all chopped and gratinéed), chestnuts, scorzonera (*doigts-de-mort*), and lamb's lettuce. Chestnuts and pumpkin also appear in puddings.

Whilst enjoying cheeses from all the surrounding areas, the Lyonnais make a special *fromage fort* themselves. They take a mature blue cheese, from which they strip the rind before soaking it in white wine for a couple of days. They then stir in grated goat's cheese and leave it another two or three days before it is ready for eating, each scoop that is taken being replaced by more goat's cheese and wine. Plenty of little goat's cheeses are made in the region, and *fromage blanc* is popular, particularly in *cervelle de canut* (see below).

The French never tire of Léon Daudet's remark that Lyon is watered by three rivers, the Saône, the Rhône (both home of the pike for the famous *quenelles*, see below), and Beaujolais, so plentifully does the wine flow here, in *pots* of 46 cl, these *pots de l'Archevêque* being the measure used by the Augustinian monks for the wine they grew on Fourvière. A good drinker can apparently down a metre's worth of them, lined up shoulder to shoulder along the bar.

Quenelles de Brochet

Not so much a speciality as an institution, a subject of debate, and a matter for rebellion, when food manufacturers trade on reputation to market products that are neither *quenelles* nor pike in anything but name. Whatever the recipe, *quenelles* require care and attention to detail.

─────────── *Ingredients for 10 quenelles of 100 g · 4 oz* ───────────

FOR THE PANADE
250 ml · 8½ fl oz milk
25 g · ¾ oz butter
85 g · 3 oz flour
1 egg

FOR THE STUFFING
300 g · 10 oz pike meat
200 g · 7 oz clarified butter
7 eggs

100 ml · 3½ fl oz thick cream
salt, pepper, nutmeg
flour

FOR THE SAUCE
1 lt · 1¾ pt creamy béchamel sauce
 (see p. 220)
100 g · 3½ oz crayfish butter (see
 p. 220)

To make the panade: bring the milk and butter to the boil and beat in the flour very gradually; continue beating hard until the mixture is smooth and creamy with no lumps. Remove from the heat to work in the egg, then return to a medium flame to dry out the panade, making sure that it doesn't stick. For the proportions given you should end up with 220 g (7¾ oz) of panade, not more (you may want to weigh it the first time you make it).

For the stuffing: sieve the fish twice through the fine mesh of a food mill, and mix to a smooth consistency with a spatula. Sieve the panade twice similarly and, when it is quite cold, blend it well into the fish. Work the clarified butter, softened but not hot, slowly into the fish mixture, followed by 4 eggs, one at a time, 3 lightly beaten whites, and the cream; the final 'dough' should be fine and smooth. Season with salt, pepper, and a touch of grated nutmeg. Leave in the fridge for several hours to become firmer.

Prepare the cream béchamel and add the crayfish butter to it. Pour into an oven dish.

Divide the *quenelle* mixture into 10 portions of 100 g (3½ oz) each. Roll each into a 10 cm (4″) long sausage-shape, on a very sparingly floured board (too much flour will alter the careful composition of the mixture).

Bring a wide pan of salted water to simmering point. Drop in the *quenelles*, a few at a time as they need plenty of room to puff out, and poach at a simmer, not more, for 8–10 minutes, shaking the pan occasionally to turn them over. Drain well.

Arrange them in the sauce and bake for 15 minutes at mark 4 / 180°C, when they will puff up another third. Serve very hot.

Recommended wine: St-Véran, Pouilly-Fuissé, or Viré-Mâcon.

Cervelle de Canut

· FROMAGE BLANC WITH WINE AND FRESH HERBS ·

Canut was the name given to the silk-workers who were an all-important part of Lyon's population and economy. *Cervelle* (brains) is no more than a reference to the dish's appearance – it is also called *claqueret*, because the cheese (which should be 'male', i.e. firm) has been well beaten (*claqué*).

―――――――――――――――― *Ingredients for 4* ――――――――――――――――

400 g · 14 oz well-drained *fromage*
  blanc
20 g · ³/₄ oz shallots
4 sprigs of parsley (the flat-leaved
  variety, if possible, it's more
  aromatic)
6 sprigs of chervil

6 chives
100 ml · 3¹/₂ fl oz olive oil
50 ml · 1³/₄ fl oz wine vinegar
50 ml · 1³/₄ fl oz white wine
salt, pepper
100 ml 3¹/₂ fl oz whipping cream

Beat the cheese hard with a spatula (not with a whisk, as the purpose is to lighten the cheese, not to make it smooth).
  Chop the shallots and parsley very finely. Snip the chervil and chives, and beat all these into the cheese, adding the oil, vinegar, wine, and salt and pepper.
  Whip the cream (which must be very cold) to aerate it but without making it too stiff. Fold it into the cheese.
  Refrigerate and serve cold.

Recommended wine: Beaujolais Primeur (Nouveau) or a young St-Joseph.

Saladier Lyonnais

A composed salad, typical of the Lyonnais. Based on sheep's feet, it used to be served in a vinaigrette, accompanied by *melettes*, i.e. sheep's testicles.

―――――――――――――――― *Ingredients for 4* ――――――――――――――――

1 tbsp vinegar
salt, pepper
4 tbsp oil
2 chicken livers
2–4 eggs
2–4 sheep's feet, cooked and boned,
  preferably still warm

2 herring fillets, soused in vinegar
2 sprigs of parsley
3–4 tarragon leaves
2–3 sprigs of chervil
3–4 chives

In a salad bowl, dissolve a little salt and some freshly milled pepper in the vinegar and beat in 3 tablespoons of oil until the dressing emulsifies.
  Brown the chicken livers quickly all over, on a medium flame, in the last spoonful of oil. Don't let them harden and shrivel up. Hardboil the eggs at the same time.
  Dice the sheep's feet, chicken livers, and well-drained herrings into the

vinaigrette. Snip in the herbs and mix everything well.
  Garnish with the eggs, quartered, and serve.

Recommended wine: white Bugey, Rully, or a Bourgogne Aligoté.

Sabodet Lyonnais
· LYONNAIS BOILING SAUSAGE WITH HOT · POTATO SALAD

A pig's head and pork rind sausage, the *sabodet* owes its name to the clog-like shape in which it used to be tied. It is eaten with hot potato salad – and heartily, not picked at.

———————————————— *Ingredients for 4* ————————————————

1 boiling sausage
1 kg · 2 lb firm waxy potatoes
1 tbsp wine vinegar
salt, pepper

optional: a tbsp dry white wine
3 tbsp oil
1 medium onion

Prick the sausage in several places and poach it, making sure the water never boils, for 1½–2 hr, according to size.
  Boil the potatoes in their skins for 20–30 minutes, as necessary; but don't put them to cook too soon as they need to be hot when the salad is made.
  Make a vinaigrette in a salad bowl: dissolve the salt, plenty of milled pepper (and the wine) in the vinegar and beat with the oil. Add the onion, finely chopped.
  Peel the potatoes, slice them into the salad bowl, and toss them in the vinaigrette.
  Skin and slice the sausage, still hot, and arrange it on the warm salad.

Recommended wine: Brouilly, Côtes de Brouilly, or a young Chiroubles.

Gras-Double Lyonnais
· LYONNAIS TRIPE ·

Around Lyon, *gras-double* means everything covered by the English (and French) word 'tripe' (see p. 169). In this area, as in the United Kingdom, it is usually ox. A Lyonnais would not, incidentally, feel outfaced by nearly a pound of tripe to himself.

———————————————— *Ingredients for 4* ————————————————

1.5 kg · 3 lb blanched tripe
50 g · 1½ oz butter
50 ml · 1½ fl oz oil
2 onions

3 shallots
12 sprigs of parsley
salt, pepper
wine vinegar

Cut the tripe into thin strips or small squares.

Heat the oil and butter in a large frying pan. When the fat is hot, put in the tripe and keep turning it over until it is well browned. Add the onions, shallots, and parsley, all chopped up finely, and salt and pepper. Reduce the heat, cover, and continue cooking for about 20 minutes, or until the tripe is tender and the onion and shallot quite soft.

At the last minute, remove the lid, turn the heat right up, and pour in a dribble of vinegar. Shake the pan over the heat for a minute or two, to turn the contents over, and serve very hot.

Recommended wine: white Mâcon – something robust like a Viré-Mâcon; or red Beaujolais, even a Beaujolais Cru, e.g. Moulin-à-Vent.

Poularde Demi-Deuil
· CHICKEN WITH TRUFFLES ·

The dish that made the reputation of one of Lyon's several great female restaurateurs, la Mére Fillioux. It had long been part of Lyonnais bourgeois cuisine (as *poularde petit-deuil*), and is a reminder that Lyon was once a centre for truffles.

——————————— *Ingredients for 8* ———————————

a very good chicken, 1.8 kg · 4 lb
2 or 3 truffles
5–6 lt · 8–10 pt chicken or shin of
  veal stock, fairly concentrated
carrots and turnips, to be cooked in

the stock with the chicken and
  served as a garnish
potatoes, steamed separately over
  stock
coarse sea salt

Slice the truffles very finely. Make a tiny incision in the chicken's skin, without penetrating the flesh, insert the knife blade between the skin and flesh to loosen the skin in an area the size of a truffle slice, and slip one in.

Proceeding thus, dot the legs and breast of the bird with the truffles until you run out. Wrap the chicken in a muslin or linen cloth, and tie up the ends.

Immerse the parcel in the stock (use a two-handled pot so you can tie the string to the handles and the chicken is suspended in the liquid without touching the bottom). Boil briskly for 15 minutes and simmer a further 20–30 minutes, having added the carrots and turnips. Steam the potatoes.

Unwrap the chicken and arrange it on a serving dish, surrounded by the vegetables, and with the salt which is essential on the side.

Recommended wine: Juliénas, Chenas, Moulin-à-Vent, or Hermitage.

Poulet au Vinaigre

Not of proven Lyonnais origin, but possibly a descendant of the local chicken with verjuice and very much a part of current Lyonnais cuisine.

——————————— *Ingredients for 4* ———————————

1 chicken, cut into pieces
75 g · 2½ oz butter
salt, pepper

150 ml · ¼ pt wine vinegar
50 ml · 1¾ fl oz white wine
1 sml tsp flour

Brown the chicken pieces in a large frying pan or sauteuse in 50 g (1¾ oz) of butter, on a medium heat; season with salt and pepper.

Pour in two-thirds of the vinegar and cover at once (this is very important, otherwise it evaporates immediately). Reduce the heat, and cook for 25–30 minutes, according to the size of the chicken pieces.

Transfer the chicken pieces to a serving dish and keep hot.

Pour the remaining vinegar and all the wine into the pan and boil for 3–4 minutes. Turn the heat down low and add the last of the butter, worked with the flour, and whisk until the sauce thickens. Taste for seasoning.

Pour the sauce over the chicken.

Recommended wine: red Hermitage or Crozes-Hermitage.

Bugnes Lyonnaises
· LYONNAIS LEMON FRITTERS ·

As much an institution and just as contentious as *quenelles*. They were eaten unfailingly on the first Sunday in Lent (*dimanche des bugnes*), but if the rigours of Lent have disappeared, the taste for *bugnes* remains.

———————————————— *Ingredients for 8* ————————————————

½ lemon
500 g · 17 oz flour
6 eggs
90 g · 3 oz castor sugar
10 g · ⅓ oz salt

100 g · 3½ oz butter
2 tbsp dark rum
flour for working the dough
oil for deep-frying
castor sugar to taste

Pare the lemon with a peeler and put the zest into boiling water for 3 minutes. Drain and chop.

Make a well in the flour and break in the eggs. Add the sugar, salt, softened butter, chopped peel, and rum. Mix together, working outwards gradually to incorporate the flour. Gather into a ball.

On a lightly floured board, flatten the dough, a spoonful at a time, with the heel of your hand, pushing it away from you; this will give it body and a final blending. Reshape into a ball, wrap it, and refrigerate for 2 hr.

Roll it out, as thinly as possible, on a floured board, in big enough portions to cut out 15 × 7 cm (6 × 2½″) pieces.

Drop these into hot oil, a few at a time, so as not to cool the oil thereby impregnating the fritters with fat, and so that they have room to puff out.

Turn them over with a draining spoon. When they are nicely gilded transfer them to absorbent paper.

Dust with sugar and serve.

Recommended wine: a Condrieu Doux or a Crémant de Bourgogne.

Tarte à la Mie de Pain
· BREAD TART ·

There is a modern tendency to use brioche for this instead of bread and it gives quite a different flavour. It is essential, however, to use excellent bread.

———————————————— *Ingredients for 4* ————————————————

250 ml · 8 fl oz milk
100 g · 3 oz good, stale bread,
   without crust (in France, *pain de*
   campagne)
25 g · ³/₄ oz almonds
100 g · 3 oz castor sugar

1 tbsp orange flower water or Kirsch
6 eggs
250 g · 8 oz fine shortcrust pastry
   (see p. 224)
20 g · ½ oz butter

Bring the milk to the boil and let it cool; pour it over the crumbled bread and leave to soak for 5–6 minutes. Meanwhile, mix the almonds, hulled and ground (or put through the blender), with the sugar. Add to the bread and beat in very gradually the orange flower water or Kirsch, 4 eggs, one by one, and two stiffly beaten whites.

Roll out the pastry to 3 mm (¹/₈″), prick it with a fork, and, turning it the other way up, line a buttered tart tin. Make the sides high and firm. Brush with the remaining egg yolks, diluted with a little water.

Turn the filling into the tart shell and bake in a medium oven for 30 minutes or until the pastry is cooked.

Let it cool before serving.

Recommended wine: Crémant de Bourgogne.

21

NIVERNAIS
BOURBONNAIS
Forez · Morvan

These two central provinces with their tradition of good eating, have contributed several recipes to the classic repertoire of French cuisine without their *terroir* origins being suspected.

The Bourbonnais used to eat quantities of soup, beginning, after coffee in the morning, with onion soup, accompanied by baked potatoes, fat bacon, and bread. This was followed by a meat soup at lunchtime and a slow cooked milk and bread soup or simply bread dunked in milk straight from the cow for supper. In neighbouring Nivernais, they make a *potée*, with salt pork and *saucisson*, which should not be confused with *soupe de Nevers*, made with carrots, Brussels sprouts, and vermicelli, or the vegetable *soupe nivernaise*.

When the region's waterways were fully navigable, salted herrings were often available for the evening meal, while salmon still came this far up the Loire to enliven the diet. As a taste for the old salmon dishes lingers on, sander or pike sometimes stand in. Crayfish are still caught and are cooked in red Saint-Pourçain in Bourbonnais and white Pouilly in Nivernais.

Eggs often make up the first course, possibly stuffed, or hardboiled, and accompanied by bacon and hot vinegar. Alternatively, there is *charcuterie*, with local specialities such as *beursaudes nivernaises*, diced belly pork, conserved in sandstone jars with garlic, onion, thyme, parsley, and other available herbs, or *jambon du Morvan*, another ham dried at high altitude and eaten raw, with rye bread, or *boudin nivernais*, flavoured with wild thyme. Bacon was put into thick pancakes (*crapiaux*) which were either broken up into a bowl and moistened with a little watered-down *fromage blanc* or were eaten with the beef from the soup, with a good sprinkling of salt.

The Nivernais and Bourbonnais have their meat dishes, such as calf's kidneys, previously cooked, rolled in veal escalopes, braised, and served in a red wine sauce, but the Nivernais's reputation is based on its vegetables: turnips from Jarnoy (cooked locally with duck to excellent effect); peas, prepared with onions, carrots, lettuce, and cream; lettuce, braised on a bed of carrots with pork rinds, onions, and cream; cabbage and kohlrabi (made into a cake); and chestnuts which, around Roanne, were hung up with potatoes to cook over the fire. The garnish which is known as 'nivernais', consists of carrots, glazed turnips, onions coated in a white sauce, braised lettuce, and potatoes.

Cheeses are goat's milk for the most part (Bitry, Brique du Forez, Chaucetier du Bourbonnais). Roujadoux, from the Allier, is a cow's cheese which reddens as it matures, hence its name. Montbrison and Coulandon are also cow's cheeses from around Moulins. Sarasson is a *fromage frais*.

There are few puddings or cakes specific to the region, though there is a potato *galette de plomb*, a cheese brioche from Gannat, curd fritters from Nivernais, and a sort of apple or pear flan (*gargouillou*). Chestnuts and walnuts also appear frequently in sweet dishes.

In the Loire, in the days when walnut oil was made at home, a kind of party (a *madée*) would be held, as a way, no doubt, of making a tedious job pleasant: friends, neighbours, relatives, were all invited to shell and break up the nuts (which took till ten or eleven at night), consuming a huge *galette*, some half a yard across, the while, and being entertained, each time a four-lobed rather than a three-lobed walnut was found, by hearing a younger participant declare his or her love for someone. All this may have died out, but there is small-scale commercial production of walnut – and hazelnut – oil.

Bourbonnais vineyards are believed to have been planted by the Phoenicians, and Portianas, the Abbé de Mirande who achieved sainthood, may be the origin of the name of the town and the wine, Saint-Pourçain. The vineyards of Nivernais, on the right bank of the Loire, opposite those of Sancerre, have two famous white wines: Pouilly-sur-Loire and Pouilly Fumé. From here too come the Loire Sauvignons – and Vichy water.

Soupe Nivernaise
· NIVERNAIS VEGETABLE SOUP ·

A kitchen-garden soup, thin and clear, made with whatever's in season: cabbage, carrots, leeks, and turnips in winter; and much as in this recipe in summer. No bacon or pork is added, and the soup is never milled or blended. The sorrel is very important.

------------------------------ *Ingredients for 4* ------------------------------

400 g · 14 oz carrots
200 g · 7 oz turnips
40 g · 1½ oz butter
1 spring cabbage

1 lettuce
100 g · 4 oz sorrel
salt, pepper

Dice the cleaned carrots and turnips. Put them in a saucepan with half the butter and soften gently for 10 minutes.

Cover with 1.5 lt (2½ pt) of water and simmer for 30 minutes.

Trim, wash, and shred the cabbage and lettuce. Cut off the sorrel stalks, unless they are very tender, in which case leave about 2 cm (¾"); wash and shred the leaves. Soften these vegetables in another saucepan with the remaining butter for 7–8 minutes, stirring almost constantly. Add to the carrots and turnips and season with salt and pepper. Cook slowly for another 15 minutes.

Pompe aux Grattons
· BACON BRIOCHE ·

Pompe would have been made with a handful of bread dough, but nowadays, it is made with brioche dough, with lard replacing the butter. *Grattons* (or *frittons*) are the crispy pieces left at the bottom of the pot after rendering fat or preparing a *confit*. Bacon can be substituted. *Pompe* is eaten fresh or stale, hot or cold, and, with or instead of bread, as an accompaniment to meat.

------------------------------ *Ingredients for 8* ------------------------------

500 g · 17 oz well-risen brioche
   dough, made with lard (see
   p. 223)
a little flour

500 g · 17 oz crisp lardons of green
   bacon – or *grattons*
1 sml tsp oil
1 egg

Rework the dough with floured hands, incorporating the bacon or *grattons*.

Form the dough into a ring and leave it for 20–30 minutes on an oiled baking tray before brushing it with beaten egg.

Bake in a medium oven for 40 minutes.

Recommended wine: depends on what the pompe *is to accompany. However, it goes rather well with wine, particularly young local wine, on its own.*

Pâté Bourbonnais
· POTATO PIES ·

Often made with puff pastry, but much better with the traditional shortcrust which takes the flavour of the filling without soaking up the liquid.

——————————— *Ingredients for 4* ———————————

800 g · 1¾ lb firm waxy potatoes
  (e.g. new Egyptian potatoes)
100 g · 3½ oz butter
100 ml · 3½ fl oz white St-Pourçain
  or other dry white wine

salt, pepper, nutmeg
500 g · 17 oz fine shortcrust pastry
  (see p. 224)
1 egg
200 ml · 7 fl oz thick cream

Clean and boil the potatoes in their skins until not more than two-thirds cooked (skinned after rather than before cooking, they will absorb the butter and wine much better).

Peel and slice them thickly (2 cm / ¾″) into a salad bowl before they cool. Dot with 80 g (3 oz) of butter, pour in the wine, and season with salt, pepper, and a little grated nutmeg. Turn the potatoes over in the wine and butter without breaking them.

Divide the dough into two: two-thirds, one-third. Roll out each piece to 2 mm (¹/₁₀″), prick the larger piece all over, and turning it the other way up, line a buttered tart tin, leaving an extra 2 cm (¾″) border all round. Cut the second piece 2 cm (¾″) larger in diameter than the tin.

Fill the pie shell with the potato, keeping the slices flat. Centre the crust carefully over the tin and seal the top of the pie to the bottom, rolling the edges together into a thin sausage. Brush the top with beaten egg and cut out a 2 cm (¾″) hole in the middle.

Bake in a medium oven for 20 minutes, fill with cream through the hole in the crust, and cook another 5 minutes.

Recommended wine: what was used in the cooking.

Sandre de Loire au Pouilly
· SANDER WITH POUILLY FUMÉ ·

The sander was a common fish in Central Europe and its name probably comes from the German *zahn*, a tooth. In France it was once abundant in the Saône and Doubs rivers and modern restocking policies have been successful in the Loire. With its fine white flesh, it is well suited to this traditional recipe. Sander can be found in some parts of England.

———————————————— *Ingredients for 8* ————————————————

c. 1 kg · 2 lb sander or other
   freshwater fish, scaled, and
   gutted through the gills
salt, pepper
120 g · 4 oz butter
100 g · 3 oz shallots

6 chives
6 tarragon leaves
3 sprigs of parsley
250 ml · 8 fl oz Pouilly Fumé or other
   dry white wine
400 ml · 14 fl oz thick cream

Wash the fish, and season it inside (via the mouth) with salt and pepper, plus 25 g (1 oz) of butter.

Butter an oven dish, strew with the chopped shallots and the herbs, snipped or chopped, and pour in the wine.

Put the fish on top, season with salt and pepper, and dot with 25 g (1 oz) of butter. Cook in a medium oven for 18–22 minutes, according to the size of the fish, turning it over at halftime.

Transfer the fish to a long serving dish and keep hot. Strain the wine and shallot mixture, pressing it through the sieve with a pestle, into a saucepan on a low heat; add the cream and reduce by a third. Check the seasoning and beat in the rest of the butter, little by little, away from the heat. Serve the sauce separately.

Recommended wine: what was used in the cooking.

Langues de Mouton aux Navets
· LAMBS' TONGUES WITH TURNIPS ·

———————————————— *Ingredients for 8* ————————————————

12–16 lambs' tongues, depending on
   their size
a *blanc* (see p. 220) – enough to
   immerse all the tongues
200 g · 7 oz green fat bacon
1/2 bay leaf
3 sprigs of thyme
2 cloves, ground
salt, pepper
thin rashers of bacon

200 g · 7 oz onions
300 ml · 10 fl oz Sauvignon de Loire
   or other white Loire wine
beef or chicken stock
100 g · 3½ oz shallots
50 g · 1¾ oz butter
1 tbsp oil (walnut if you like)
1.5 kg · 3 lb small turnips
3 sprigs of parsley
1 sml tsp of castor sugar

Brush the lambs' tongues under running water, drop them into the boiling *blanc*, and simmer very gently for 20 minutes. Drain.

Skin and bone the meat and remove the fatty parts. Cut up the fat bacon into short matchsticks, and roll in a mixture of broken-up bay leaf, thyme leaves (from one of the sprigs), ground cloves, and salt and pepper. With the aid of a larding needle, embed a couple of pieces in each tongue.

Line a wide shallow pan or cocotte with the bacon rashers, and arrange a bed of thinly sliced onions with any of the herb mixture remaining, sprinkled on top. Put in the tongues, side by side, head to tail, pour over two-thirds of the wine and stock to cover, and season with salt and pepper, bearing in mind the strength of the stock and the seasoning of the lardons. Seal the pan tightly and cook in a low oven for 1¼ hr.

Meanwhile, chop the shallots roughly, soften them slowly for 7–8 minutes in the butter and oil, and add the peeled and washed turnips, the rest of the thyme, the parsley, the remaining wine, and salt and pepper. Cover and cook gently for 35 minutes, shaking the pan at intervals to roll the turnips around.

Taste for seasoning, sprinkle the sugar over the turnips, and cook another 10 minutes, uncovered, to glaze them, turning them over occasionally.

Cut each of the tongues in two lengthways and put on a serving dish, surrounded by the turnips, transferred with a draining spoon. Keep hot while you strain the tongues' cooking liquid into the turnip pan, let it reduce by half, and pour over the tongues.

Recommended wine: a Côte Roannaise or a red Côte du Forez.

Saupiquet des Amognes
· HAM WITH CREAM AND JUNIPER SAUCE ·

Les Amognes are to the east of Nevers. *Saupiquet* means salt + piquant, but this recipe has no connection other than etymological with the *saupiquet* (a spicy wine sauce for hare and rabbit) of south-western French cookery. The Nivernais eat this with chestnuts sautéed in butter.

———————————— *Ingredients for 4* ————————————

8 fairly thick slices of raw ham or
  gammon
milk
5 shallots
200 ml · 7 fl oz wine vinegar
2 peppercorns
2 juniper berries
40 g · 1½ oz butter
30 g · 1 oz flour

200 ml · 7 fl oz Pouilly Fumé or other
  dry white wine
200 ml · 7 fl oz strong beef stock,
  very well degreased
20 g · ¾ oz lard
100 ml · 3½ fl oz very thick cream
salt, pepper
parsley sprigs

Soak the raw ham or gammon in milk to remove the salt.

Chop the shallots and heat gently in a saucepan with the vinegar, peppercorns, and juniper berries, for 10 minutes, to reduce the vinegar.

Meanwhile, in another saucepan, make a roux with 30 g (1 oz) of butter and the flour, without it browning, and pour in the wine and stock, previously warmed, and cook, stirring frequently to ensure nothing is stuck to the bottom, for 10 minutes.

At the same time, let the lard melt in a frying pan, and brown the drained and wiped ham or gammon for 4–6 minutes on each side.

Strain the contents of both saucepans and mix together. Add the cream and the rest of the butter, in tiny pieces; reduce on a low heat for 4–5 minutes.

Transfer the ham to a serving dish with a draining spoon, coat with the sauce and sprinkle with finely chopped parsley.

Recommended wine: Pouilly-sur-Loire.

Poulet au Fromage

This was not always a domestic dish, but it has now long been part of the Bourbon household repertoire. What *poulet au fromage* has never been, here-abouts, is a roast chicken, gratinéed, or cut into pieces and covered with a Mornay sauce. It is rather a chicken poached first, then covered in its sauce, sprinkled with cheese, and grilled. Locals sometimes add a touch of Fourme d'Ambert, blue cheese from the neighbouring Auvergne.

─────────── *Ingredients for 4* ───────────

2 good leeks
2 carrots
50 g · 2 oz onions
2 cloves
1 plump chicken
a bouquet garni: 1 sprig of thyme,
   1/4 bay leaf, 1 sml celery stalk, 2
   sprigs of parsley

1 clove of garlic
chicken stock
salt, pepper
250 ml · 9 fl oz milk
2 eggs
200 ml · 7 fl oz thick cream
20 g · 3/4 oz butter
100 g · 3 1/2 oz grated Gruyère

Trim off the green part of the leeks; wash and slice the rest thinly. Slice the carrots; peel the onions and cut into eighths, and stud with the cloves. Poach the chicken in a deep, covered pan with all these vegetables, the bouquet, the peeled garlic, enough stock to immerse the bird, and salt and pepper, for 45 minutes.

Take out the chicken and set aside. Add the milk to the stock and reduce by at least half.

Mix the egg yolks with the cream, diluting it with a little stock, and trickle slowly into the cooking pot, stirring constantly. Set aside.

Cut the chicken into 4 and arrange on a buttered gratin dish, coat with the strained sauce, and sprinkle with the cheese.

Put under a hot grill for 10–15 minutes.

Serve at once.

Recommended wine: Pouilly-sur-Loire or Meursault.

Rapée
· POTATO CAKE ·

A speciality of the Forez, especially around Saint-Étienne, where it is often eaten with a roast.

─────────── *Ingredients for 4* ───────────

600 g · 1 lb medium-sized floury
   potatoes
1 egg per potato

salt
50 g · 1 1/2 oz butter

Peel and wash the potatoes and grate fairly coarsely.

Beat the grated potato and eggs together hard, adding salt.

Heat half the butter in a pancake pan (i.e. a very shallow frying pan). When it is very hot, but not burning, put in the potato mixture and spread evenly over the pan. Cook until the bottom begins to brown at the edge.

Turn the cake over, buttering the pan again. Cook until the underside is brown and crispy.

Piquenchâgne
· PEAR PIE ·

─────────────── *Ingredients for 8* ───────────────

750 g · 1³/₄ lb cooking pears
70 g · 2¹/₂ oz butter
500 g · 17 oz puff pastry (see p. 224)
3 eggs
75 g · 2¹/₂ oz castor sugar

100 ml · 3¹/₂ fl oz thick cream
500 g · 17 oz *crème pâtissière* (see p. 222)
optional: 8 whole pears, bottled in syrup + 8 tbsp redcurrant jelly

Split the cooking pears in two and core. Slice them roughly and sweat gently, covered, for 5–6 minutes in 50 g (1³/₄ oz) of butter, shaking the pan occasionally.

Divide the pastry into two: two-thirds, one-third. Roll out the larger piece to 3 mm (¹/₈″), the smaller to 2 mm (¹/₁₀″). Line a deep buttered tart tin with the bigger piece, leaving an extra 3 cm (1″) border all round.

Beat 2 eggs, the sugar, cream, and cooked pears into the *crème pâtissière*, and fill the tart case.

Fold the border over the filling and paint it with beaten egg. Cut the second piece of pastry to the diameter of the tin and put it in place, pressing lightly all round the edge to seal it. Brush with egg. Make a hole in the centre for a little pastry (or cardboard) chimney. Bake in a hot oven for 15 minutes, reduce the heat to medium, and cook a further 25 minutes.

Let the pie cool, then, if you wish, drain the bottled pears, and, with a serrated knife, cut out 8 notches round the edge, deep enough to seat these pears, stalks uppermost, in the *crème pâtissière*. Put the pears in position, and pour a spoonful of redcurrant jelly over each.

Recommended wine: a Côte Roannaise or a red Côte du Forez.

22
NORMANDY

In 911 AD, Charles III (the Simple) gave up this area to the Vikings and these *hommes du Nord* or Norsemen gave their name to the province.

Normandy is of course famous for its milk products (butter, cream, cheeses, including Camembert, now protected from imitation by labelling laws, Pont l'Évêque, and Petits Suisses), its pretty apple orchards, and its cider and Calvados; all this, together with the fish along the length of its coastline from Le Tréport to Mont-Saint-Michel, gives the cooking its flavour.

Soup was a morning dish, made in Haute-Normandie with milk, and in Basse-Normandie with *graisse de Cherbourg* (half pig's kidney fat, half beef and mutton kidney fat, rendered slowly with vegetables and herbs, strained, and stored in stone jars), while the fish soups or *marmites* were closer to the fish dishes of the south of France, such as bouillabaisse, than to soups proper.

The range of fish and shellfish is familiar enough to the English, though the Normans are more inclined to cook little crabs and spider crabs, and have a higher regard for plaice than their northern neighbours. Restaurateurs have concentrated their inventiveness on ways of presenting the Dover sole, but in the domestic kitchen, sole would simply have been fried or grilled (on a bed of straw) and served with a shallot and cream sauce. Conger-eel is made into a *matelote*, Normandy being the only part of France where these stews are made with sea fish. The Normans, with their little farmyards dotted everywhere, also have numerous dishes combining fish and eggs.

Inland, *boudins* or black puddings assume a great importance, mirrored in the international competition held each year at Montagne. In the Contentin, they are prepared by cooking the pig's blood in an open pan with little onions and strips of fat bacon, but in other areas, they are baked in the oven with milk, diced pork kidney fat, and herbs. White *boudins* are made in the Orne, although production appears to be dying out. Of the various *andouilles* and *andouillettes*, the best known come from Vire, a town whose architectural history was abruptly altered by the Second World War, but which held on to its sausage-making traditions.

Meat recipes specific to the region are few, despite cattle farming in the Pays d'Auge, Contentin, and the Pays d'Ouche, and the salt-marsh lamb shared with Brittany. Two dishes worth noting are shin of veal poached with vegetables and eaten with braised lettuce, and *gigot à la mode d'Yvetot*, a leg of lamb similarly poached and accompanied by a sauce velouté made from the cooking liquid plus cream and capers.

Duck has inspired several recipes, including one for duckling, from the village of Duclair, which requires a special crossbreed of duck, half wild, half domestic (the latter a fleshy bird with a good amount of blood). Turkey and game (young partridge, pheasant, lark, when available), are usually served with apple.

Watercress figures in the coat-of-arms of Vernon, in memory of a visit paid to the town on a very hot day in the thirteenth century by Louis IX and of the refreshing watercress salad he was given by an innkeeper. Vegetables are frequently prepared with cream, and a salad *à la normande* is dressed with cream and cider vinegar. There was no shortage of mushrooms in the horse-breeding areas of Avranchin and in the Orne forest, though they were not as popular here as in other regions.

Predictably, puddings and cakes are often with apple – *bourdelots* (or *douillons*) and *rabottes* (apples in pastry) at the Picardy end, *pâtés aux pommes* in Upper Normandy, *pommes à la grivettes* (grated apple with curdled milk) and *sucre de pommes* from Rouen. At Duclair, they make a cherry and *fromage blanc* tart.

Aside from the cider, drunk from the cask or from corked bottles, dry or sweet, and Calvados (the latter taken between courses, the true *trou normand*), there is perry (*poiré*) and Bénédictine. No wine or beer is made here.

Potage aux Meuniers
· FIELD-MUSHROOM SOUP ·

This can also be made with cultivated mushrooms, but it won't have the same flavour. It needs a poached chicken breast.

─────────────── *Ingredients for 4* ───────────────

250 g · 8 oz chicken breast, poached
   in stock
350 g · 10 oz mushrooms, field, if
   possible
25 g · ³/₄ oz butter
¹/₂ lemon

1 lt · 1³/₄ pt milk
salt, pepper, nutmeg
4 egg yolks
200 ml · 7 fl oz thick cream
3 sprigs of parsley

Skin and dice the chicken breast.

Clean and dice the mushrooms, and stew very gently, covered, in a saucepan with the butter and lemon juice, for 5–6 minutes, shaking the pan occasionally. Remove the lid and let the liquid evaporate.

Add a quarter of the milk, and the chicken, and cook, stirring almost constantly, for 10 minutes.

Put through a food mill or blender, return to the saucepan and pour in the remaining milk, heated. Season with salt, pepper, and a little grated nutmeg, and simmer a further 5–6 minutes, stirring now and then.

Mix the egg yolks with the cream, diluting it gradually with a little soup, then pour very slowly into the saucepan, stirring continuously and not allowing it to boil.

Sprinkle with finely chopped parsley before serving.

Recommended wine: Pouilly-sur-Loire or Meursault.

Barbue Cauchoise
· BRILL WITH CIDER ·

Brill is a cousin of the turbot, but easily distinguishable by its scales (turbot has no scales, only tubercles – the bony bits that stick out). If you've got a large brill, cut it on the dark side down the backbone and break it before cooking; this helps the fish keep its shape.

─────────────── *Ingredients for 4* ───────────────

a brill c. 1.5 kg · 3 lb
80 g · 3 oz shallots
75 g · 2¹/₂ oz butter
200 g · 7 oz mushrooms
salt, pepper

¹/₂ bottle dry cider
100 ml · 3¹/₂ fl oz thick cream
50 g · 1¹/₂ oz homemade
   breadcrumbs

Scale, gut, and wash the brill.

Soften the finely chopped shallots, slowly, in a saucepan, with 25 g (³/₄ oz) of butter, for 3–4 minutes. Add the cleaned and diced mushrooms, cover, and stew, shaking the pan occasionally. Season generously with salt and pepper.

Grease a non-metal, oven dish, large enough to hold the fish, with 25 g (³/₄ oz) of butter. Strew half the mushrooms and shallots in the bottom, put the fish on top, and pour over the cider. Cover with the remaining mushrooms and shallots, the cream, and breadcrumbs, and dot with the last of the butter.

Bake for 20 minutes in a medium oven, basting once or twice.

Recommended drink: a white Chasselas (e.g. Pouilly-sur-Loire), Muscadet-sur-Lie, Coteaux Champenois, or a good dry cider.

Morue de Honfleur
· SALT COD WITH POTATOES AND CALVADOS ·

Never buy salt cod that looks yellow or grey – it is either oversalted or old. It should be a clear slightly creamy colour, with firm flesh and, whether bought in the piece, or as fillets, thick. A well-soaked salt cod will need salting during the cooking.

──────────────── *Ingredients for 4* ────────────────

750 g · 1¹/₂ lb salt cod, previously
   soaked, see p. 222
80 g · 2¹/₂ oz butter
750 g · 1¹/₂ lb potatoes
100 g · 3¹/₂ oz onions

8 sprigs of parsley
salt, pepper
white wine
2 tbsp Calvados

Flake the fish. Butter an oven-proof dish. Peel, wash, and cut up the potatoes roughly. Chop the onions and parsley.

In the buttered dish, arrange alternate layers of cod, potatoes, and onions and parsley seasoned with salt and pepper.

Pour in enough wine just to cover. Dot with the rest of the butter and cook in a medium oven for 1 hr. Pour in the Calvados 15 minutes before the end, taking the dish out of the oven to ensure it does not catch fire.

Recommended drink: a Pouilly-sur-Loire, a Meursault, a rosé, or a good dry cider.

Tripes à la Mode de Caen

This would have been prepared in a *tripière*, a large round pot, some 70 cm (28″) in diameter, with only a small opening (20 cm / 8″). Once filled with the appropriate ingredients, it would require four bearers and a stretcher to carry it round to the baker's where it was left to simmer long hours buried in the hot cinders. The baker, in hallowed tradition, was then entitled to a third of it.

For cooking at home, a broad, shallow glazed earthenware terrine dish or casserole, with a lid, is best. *A la mode de Caen* is a precise formula. It means that all the ox tripe is included, the paunch, the honeycomb or reticulum, the psalterium, and the fourth or 'true' stomach, also called the reed or maw; that a cow heel (never a calf's foot), not more than 30% of the weight of the tripe, is added; and that the only vegetable is carrot (the onion is only there as flavouring). The cider can be strengthened with a drop of Calvados. The tripe should not be semi-cooked, just cleaned and blanched. The cow heel, on the other hand, needs to have been previously boiled for 3 hr in a vegetable stock.

―――――――――*Ingredients for 10–12*―――――――――

1 lge fresh pork rind
3–4 kg · 6–8 lb blanched ox tripe
1 kg · 2 lb carrots
2 lge onions
a bouquet: 1 leek, 1 head of garlic,
  3 cloves, 1 tbsp crushed
  peppercorns, 2 sprigs of thyme,

1 bay leaf, 2 sprigs of parsley
1–1½ cow heels, cooked (see above)
  and split in 2
1 bottle dry cider
2–3 tbsp Calvados
salt, flour

Line the terrine dish with the pork rinds, fat side down (the Normandy cook often puts an upturned bowl under the rinds to stop the tripe sticking). Cut the tripe into 5–6 cm (2–2½") pieces. Slice the carrots. Peel and quarter the onions. Tie the washed and sliced leek with the bouquet in a muslin bag.

Arrange the tripe, cow heel, carrots, and onions in alternate layers in the terrine dish, with the bouquet in the middle. Pour over the cider and enough water to fill the dish.

Seal the lid with a strip of dough (flour worked with a little water), and cook in a very low oven, for 15–16 hr, audibly simmering, but never boiling.

Break the seal, remove the lid, leave for a few minutes for the excess fat to rise to the surface, and skim with a small ladle. Bone the cow heels, discard the bouquet and onions, and mix in the Calvados. Serve from the terrine dish on to heated plates and eat with a spoon.

Recommended drink: very good cider or very dry white wine, e.g. Graves.

Poulet Vallée d'Auge
· CHICKEN FROM THE AUGE VALLEY ·

This was a recipe for a good spring chicken, nowadays a white-fleshed, free-range bird is the nearest equivalent. It is important to reduce the sauce properly so that the meat is coated but not swimming in it. You can add a little chopped white of leek to the shallot.

―――――――――― *Ingredients for 6* ――――――――――

1 good chicken, 2 kg · 4 lb
salt, pepper
75 g · 2½ oz butter
2 tbsp Calvados
50 g · 2 oz shallots

500 ml · 17 fl oz cider
200 g · 7 oz small mushrooms (field
  mushrooms if possible)
200 ml · 7 fl oz fresh cream

Cut the chicken into 12 pieces, and rub with salt and pepper.

Sauté all over in a casserole or frying pan (ideally, a sauteuse) in a third of the butter, on a medium flame. When the chicken is lightly browned, pour away the excess fat, pour in the Calvados and set it alight.

When the flames die down, add the shallots, cut into three, and the cider. Cover and cook for about 30 minutes, turning the chicken over at halftime.

Meanwhile, clean and slice the mushrooms finely, and sweat in a covered pan in another third of the butter for 3–4 minutes, shaking occasionally. Uncover and let the liquid evaporate without the mushrooms sticking.

Add the mushrooms and cream to the chicken 5 minutes before the end of the cooking time.

Take the chicken out and keep hot. Reduce the juices gently, stirring occasionally, until you have a sauce thick enough to coat a wooden spoon. Taste for seasoning and, away from the heat, beat in the last of the butter.

Return the chicken to the sauce and on a low heat turn it over two or three times until it is well covered with the sauce and warmed through.

Arrange the chicken on a serving dish with all the sauce poured over.

Recommended wine: either, to take account of the cream, a slightly rounded white like a Meursault or a Gewürztraminer, or, conversely, a very dry white – e.g. an Arbois or a Château d'Arley.

Lapin à la Havraise

──────────────── *Ingredients for 4* ────────────────

1 meaty rabbit, the kidneys well
  covered in very white fat – a sign
  of good quality
salt, pepper
200 g · 7 oz butter

1 pig's trotter, poached in stock for
  2 hr and split in 2
2 sprigs of thyme
flour

Take off the rabbit's head and neck, and salt and pepper inside.

Cut out a piece of greaseproof paper large enough to wrap up the rabbit completely and butter it (use *all* the butter) on one side.

Press the pig's trotter and thyme right down into the rabbit haunches, and tuck the rabbit's legs in so that you can curl it round enough to fit in a casserole (of glazed clay, ideally). Wrap it in the paper and tie it up tightly.

Put the parcel in the casserole with absolutely nothing else (there shouldn't be room for much). Seal the lid with a strip of dough (flour worked with a little water) and cook in a slow oven for 3 hr.

Leave to cool. Take out the parcel and open the wrapping without removing it. Bone the trotter. Spoon the jelly from the bottom of the pot over the rabbit and serve from the paper.

Recommended wine: Bourgueil or Chinon.

Haricots Verts à la Crème

──────────────── *Ingredients for 4* ────────────────

600–800 g · 1–1½ lb very fine French
  beans, freshly picked
salt

20 g · ¾ oz butter
200 ml · 7 fl oz cream
salt, pepper

String and wash the beans and immerse in boiling salted water to cook for 10 minutes, uncovered; drain and run under cold water to revive their colour.

Butter an oven dish, put in the beans, pour over the cream, season with salt, taking account of the previous salting, and pepper.

Cook in a medium oven until the cream is reduced by about a third, and serve.

Beurré Normand
· APPLE AND CALVADOS CAKE ·

A large light cake. The secret is to give the diced apple a preliminary cooking in butter to stop it giving off so much juice when the cake is baked.

─────────────── *Ingredients for 4* ───────────────

50 g · 2 oz sultanas or currants
2 tbsp Calvados
4 good eating apples, e.g. Coxes
50 g · 2 oz butter

4 eggs
150 g · 5 oz castor sugar
salt
150–200 g · 5–7 oz flour

Tail the sultanas, if necessary, and soak in the Calvados, diluted with 1 tablespoon of water.

Peel and core the apples, and cut into roughly 1 cm (½″) dice. Cook immediately, before they have time to harden, in 20 g (¾ oz) of butter, on a low flame, tossing to coat them in the butter for a minute or so; continue cooking, shaking the pan occasionally, until the apples are very lightly browned on the edge but have not collapsed. Leave to cool.

Cream the egg yolks and sugar, plus a pinch of salt, until the mixture is smooth and creamy – if a single grain of sugar is left undissolved it will melt during cooking and prevent the cake rising fully. Sift in the flour gradually, until the mixture is of a softish, fruit cake consistency.

Butter a sandwich tin which the mixture will not fill by more than two-thirds.

Stir the drained sultanas and apple very carefully into the sponge mixture and fold in the stiffly beaten egg whites. Spoon into the tin straightaway and bake in a moderate oven for 50 minutes. If a skewer does not come out clean, continue cooking as long as necessary, covering the cake with buttered greaseproof paper if it is browning too much.

Recommended wine: Pouilly-sur-Loire, Meursault, or a rosé, or good cider.

Terrinée, Tordgoule, Teurgoule, or Bourgoule
· NORMAN RICE PUDDING ·

Rice puddings, under any other name, were household fare all over France. This one from Rouen would have spent hours in the baker's oven. The skin was appreciated by some, removed by others. The type of rice is important.

Ingredients for 4

1½ lt · 2½ pt milk
150 g · 5 oz short-grain, unglazed
    rice
100 g · 3½ oz castor sugar

a pinch of salt
1 sml tsp cinnamon
50 g · 1¾ oz butter

Bring the milk to the boil; leave to cool completely.
    Wash the rice and mix in the sugar, salt, and cinnamon. Stir in the milk.
    Butter an oven dish, pour in the rice, and stand in a tin of water. Cook in a
very low oven for 2½ hr.

Recommended wine: a Crémant de Loire or d'Alsace.

23

PICARDY · ARTOIS
Thiérache

A difficult region, from a gastronomic point of view, to distinguish firmly from its neighbours. Almost no one could differentiate between the cooking of the Avenois (which has been included with Flanders) and Thiérache cookery (included here), while Boulonnais and Artois were also once part of Flanders.

Like Flanders, Picardy has a full calendar of *fêtes* marking out the year: a *foire de crabes* at Audresselles in May; a strawberry festival at Samer and a pancake and cider *kermesse* at Gouves in August; garlic fairs at Bapaume, Feignies, and Palluel and an *andouille* festival at Aire-sur-la-Lys in September, and a turkey fair at Licques in December (also on the Flemish agenda).

The wetlands of the Somme offer rich pickings for the huntsman-fisherman-cook. The ponds and streams shelter pike, bream, roach, tench, carp, trout, frogs, and eels, these last now bred for the Dutch who smoke them for exportation. Locally, they are cooked with onions and beer. Above water, there are duck, teal, snipe, pintail duck, and mallard, while the alluvial lands between the ponds are a market-gardener's haven. Leeks, cucumbers, cabbage, sprouts, cauliflowers, broad beans, pumpkins, salsifis, garlic, white haricot beans (*soissons*), as well as the onions which are omnipresent in Picard cookery (usually cooked right down to make a garnish known familiarly as *soubise picarde*), all benefit from the rich soil. Elsewhere, the enormous quantity of potatoes grown for crisps and packet mashed potato would doubtless have cheered Parmentier, the Picard who introduced the potato to France.

All these vegetables are destined for the soup pot. There are fish soups too, unsurprisingly, since Boulogne-sur-Mer is France's largest fishing port. Herring was once the prize catch and the virtues of Boulogne's salted and smoked herring (*sorret*) were extolled by Villon in the fourteenth century. Today's fishermen bring in bream, monkfish, skate, mackerel, gurnard, whiting, hake, John Dory (*Saint-Pierre* elsewhere in France, but here *John Doré*), brill, sole, and turbot. Many of the local fish recipes are based on cream and herbs. Shellfish are cooked similarly.

Pâtés, tarts, and pies are made in great number. In the past, the lady of the house was said always to have her hands in the dough (often made with yeast) or batter, making large pancakes, filled with ham, onions, mushrooms, perhaps, and coated with cream sauce and grated cheese, *ficelles picardes*.

Among meat dishes, there is: *la caqhuse*, a thick slice of leg pork (a *rouelle*) stewed with a large quantity of onions and eaten hot or cold; veal chops *bellovaque* (i.e. from Beauvais) sautéed with wild mushrooms, deglazed with cider, and thickened with cream; *bifteck à la boulonnaise*, *paupiettes* filled with pork sausagemeat and herbs and spices, including juniper berries, and braised with onions, tomatoes, and beer. As in England, roast pork is eaten with apple; leg of lamb is roasted *à la française* or poached *à l'anglaise*. Chops from the lamb on the salt-marshes of the Somme estuary are simmered with pork rinds, bacon, white wine, and *soissons* beans. Larks, quail, and other little birds used to be cooked whole with potatoes, a dish known affectionately as *pommes de terre à moineaux* (potatoes with sparrows); bigger game, pheasant, partridge, hare, venison, and wild boar, are still available from the forests – where wild mushrooms flourish too.

Cheeses are few. There is Maroilles which comes in various sizes: Sorbais (600 g), Mignon (400 g), and Quart (200 g), and is best when farm-produced from around La Capelle. A cylindrical cow's cheese is made at Montdidier,

Rigolot – the same cheese is sometimes in a heart shape when it becomes Guerbigny or Cœur d'Arras – and there is a strong cheese made at Béthune, a sort of Puant Macéré.

And to finish, there are sweet tarts and pancakes. *Tarte au sucre* has a layer of castor sugar sprinkled with water or beaten egg and milk and closely dotted with butter. *La tarte à l'ancienne*, a mixture of *fromage blanc*, eggs, and cream, is eaten in Boulogne for Twelfth Night. There is a sort of apple flan, flavoured with rum, called *gâteau de pommes de Mers*, and there are apricot jam-filled macaroons from Amiens, and *tuiles au chocolat* from Péronne.

If there is no wine, it is nonetheless enjoyed, along with cider and beer, and, in the past, perry and *frénette* – an extremely economical, extremely alcoholic drink made from ash leaves.

Caudière de Berck
· BERCK CHOWDER ·

A fishermen's soup eaten all along the Picardy coast.

──────────────── *Ingredients for 4* ────────────────

3–4 onions
2–3 cloves of garlic
3 sprigs of parsley
1 sprig of thyme
1 bay leaf
800 g–1 kg · 1½–2 lb potatoes
salt, pepper

1.5 kg · 3 lb assorted fish (e.g. sml turbot, slip soles, dabs lemon sole, gurnard, conger eel, John Dory)
2 lt · 3 pt cleaned mussels
4 egg yolks
200 ml · 7 fl oz thick cream

Slice the onions finely and put them in a layer in the bottom of a shallow pan or sauteuse. Add the chopped garlic, the parsley, snipped, the thyme and bay leaf, and the peeled, washed, and quartered potatoes. Pour in 3 lt (4–5 pt) of water and season with salt and pepper. Boil for 5–10 minutes.

Scale or skin the fish and gut, wash, and cut it up. Immerse in the liquid; if there is not enough to cover, add boiling water. Simmer for 15 minutes.

Cook the mussels with a small ladle's worth of soup in a covered pan, on a fairly strong flame; when steam starts to escape, stir them round with a spatula, and take them out as they open. Discard the shells, and put the mussels in a tureen. Reserve the liquid.

Transfer the fish and potatoes to the tureen with a draining spoon. Remove the thyme and bay leaf and leave the soup on a gentle heat.

Mix the egg yolks and cream together in a large bowl, adding gradually a few spoonfuls of the soup. Pour the well-strained mussel liquid into the soup, and trickle in the egg yolk and cream mixture very slowly, stirring constantly, and without letting the soup boil. Pour into the tureen.

Recommended wine: a very dry white, e.g. Chablis or Muscadet.

Soupe des Hortillonnages
· SPRING VEGETABLE SOUP ·

The *hortillonnages*, the drained marshlands of the Somme, are furrowed with canals, which serve as access to the market-gardeners in their flat-bottomed boats. This soup is sometimes called after them – *soupe des maraîcheurs*.

──────────── *Ingredients for 4* ────────────

1 spring cabbage
120 g · 4 oz butter
6 leeks
optional: 2 lt · 3½ pt stock
salt, pepper

4 potatoes
1 sml hearty lettuce
80 g · 3 oz sorrel
500 g · 1 lb peas, unshelled
7–8 sprigs of chervil

Trim and cut the cabbage into eight; wash it and cook, slowly, covered, in 100 g (3 oz) of butter, for 10 minutes.

Add the cleaned and sliced leeks and stew a further 10 minutes.

Pour over 2 lt (3½ pt) of water or stock, season with salt and pepper as necessary. Add the peeled, washed, and diced potatoes and cook gently for another 10 minutes.

Meanwhile, wash and shred the lettuce and sorrel, and stew separately, covered, in the rest of the butter. Shell the peas.

Add the peas, lettuce, and sorrel to the soup, simmer a last 10 minutes, scattering in the chervil leaves just before the end.

Serve piping hot.

Soupe de Grenouille
· PICARD FROG'S LEG SOUP ·

This soup used to be made with veal and vegetable stock, but nowadays is more likely to be prepared as follows.

──────────── *Ingredients for 4* ────────────

2 onions
50 g · 2 oz butter
2 doz frogs' legs
250 ml · 9 fl oz white wine
a bouquet garni: 1 sprig of thyme, 1
    bay leaf, 2 sprigs of parsley, 1
    celery stalk, 1 clove

salt, pepper
50 g · 2 oz bread, without crust
2 egg yolks
200 ml · 7 fl oz thick cream
6 chives
toast as required

Slice the onions finely, and stew in a covered saucepan in the butter, for 15 minutes, shaking frequently.

Add the frogs' legs (which should previously have been strung on skewers and soaked for several hours in very cold water, changed every 2 hr, to whiten and puff them out), the wine, an equal quantity of water, the bouquet, and salt and pepper. Simmer for 15 minutes.

Moisten the crumbled bread with a little soup. Discard the bouquet and bone the legs. Put the bread and a third of the legs through a blender, and return to the saucepan with the soup, which should, meanwhile, have been strained. Heat slowly.

Mix the egg yolks and cream together, dilute with a drop of soup, and, stirring constantly, trickle this into the saucepan, making sure the soup doesn't boil. Taste for seasoning.

Put the remaining frogs' legs in a tureen with the finely snipped chives and pour over the hot soup. Serve on to the toast.

Recommended wine: Pouilly Fumé, Meursault.

Flamiche ou Flamique aux Poireaux
· LEEK PIE ·

A dish common to Picardy, Artois, and parts of Belgium. Onions or pumpkin can be used instead of leeks. The name may come from *flambiche*, meaning 'cooked on an open fire' (*à la flambe*), rather than indicating Flemish origins. Though a pie, the top is often made simply by giving a big extra border to the base and folding it over the filling in pleats (*'eun flamique à plos'*).

———————— *Ingredients for 4* ————————

400 g · 14 oz enriched shortcrust pastry (see p. 224)	70 g · 2¹/₂ oz butter
12 good white leeks	4 eggs
salt	100 ml · 4 fl oz thick cream
	pepper, nutmeg

Divide the pastry into two, two-thirds, one-third. Roll out the larger piece to 2 mm (¹/₁₀″), prick it, and turning it the other way up, line a buttered tart tin, leaving an extra 2 cm (³/₄″) border all round.

Trim the leeks, discarding the green; wash and split into two lengthways, and slice into 1 cm (¹/₃″) pieces. Drop them into boiling salted water and let bubble gently for 5 minutes. Drain and run under cold water.

Stew them, covered, with the remaining butter in a saucepan, until they are soft, shaking occasionally, so they don't stick. Don't let them brown.

Beat the egg yolks with the cream and, away from the heat, pour slowly into the leeks, stirring at the same time. Season with pepper and a pinch of grated nutmeg. Pour into the pastry case. Fold the edge in over the filling and brush the upper surface with egg white.

Cover with the other piece of pastry, rolled out to the size of the tart tin, and seal top and bottom well together. Make a small hole in the centre and insert a pastry (or cardboard) chimney. Bake for 35–40 minutes in a medium oven.

Serve hot.

Recommended wine: white Coteaux Champenois or Gros-Plant.

Pâté de Canard d'Amiens
· STUFFED DUCK EN CROÛTE ·

Traces of this recipe can be found in sixteenth-century records under the name *annates* (from the Latin for duck, *anas*), a word which lives on in the Picard patois for duckling, *énette*. it was made with wild duck which was left on its carcass and stuffed with chicken livers; there was no other meat nor mushrooms. The pastry wasn't eaten. Except that the duck is boned, it is the old method given here.

―――――――――――― *Ingredients for 8* ――――――――――――

1 plump duck, 2–2½ kg · 4–5 lb +
    liver
salt, pepper
a pinch of *quatre-épices* or allspice
150 g · 5 oz fat green bacon
2 shallots
1 onion
1 sprig of thyme
1 bay leaf
500 g · 1 lb chicken livers

3 eggs
20 g · ¾ oz lard
1 kg · 2 lb hot crust pastry (see
    p. 225)
1 calf's foot, blanched (see p. 221)
    and boned (but keep the bones)
a bouquet garni: 2 sprigs of thyme,
    1 bay leaf, 2 sprigs of parsley
gelatine

Reserve the liver, and singe the duck to ensure it is completely plucked. Put the duck on a board breast downwards and split it along the back. Using a knife, and your fingers, take the bones very carefully out of the meat, making sure that the blade is always directed towards the bones rather than the meat so that you don't hole the skin. Remove the parson's nose which is bitter and cut off the wing tips. Season inside with salt, pepper, and *quatre-épices*. Set aside.

To prepare the stuffing: cut the bacon as finely as possible and melt it slowly in a frying pan. When it is soft, add the chopped shallots and onion, the thyme, and the bay leaf, and toss for 4–5 minutes, on a low heat. Trim and dice the duck and chicken livers and sauté with the shallots, increasing the heat slightly, just to seal the livers and no more. Away from the heat, remove the herbs and mix in 2 eggs, salt, and pepper.

Stuff the duck, sew it back into shape, and brown it all over on a medium heat in the lard; drain. Leave to cool.

Divide the pastry in half, roll out each piece to an oval shape, longer and wider than the duck; the piece destined to go under the duck should be slightly thicker than the other piece. Grease a baking tray and place this piece on it. Put the duck on top, on its back, well centred, and brush the exposed pastry with beaten egg. Cover the bird with the other pastry, and pinch the two pieces together hard to seal them. Nick all round the edge with a knife. Brush the outside with beaten egg. Cut some decorations out of the pastry trimmings, and attach and brush them with egg. Make a hole on top at each end and insert little pastry chimneys to let the steam escape.

Bake in a moderate oven for 1 hr.

Break the duck bones up into a saucepan, add the wing tips, but not the parson's nose, the calf's foot meat, cut up, and bones, the bouquet, and a little gelatine (as insurance). Cover generously with water and leave to simmer while the duck cooks.

When the duck is ready, strain the stock and season it with salt and pepper, then pour a little through the holes on to the duck, and leave to cool for this to set.

Slice to serve.

Recommended wine: St-Émilion or St-Esthèphe.

Col-Vert aux Pruneaux
· MALLARD OR WILD DUCK WITH PRUNES ·

Along the river Somme, there stretch some sixty kilometres of ponds, believed to have been the work of beavers. Whatever their origins, they are ideal water-lands for duck.

──────────────── *Ingredients for 4* ────────────────

2 dozen prunes
2 wild duck + livers
salt, pepper
thin rashers of bacon
100 g · 3½ oz butter
200 ml · 7 fl oz white wine

optional: 200 g · 7 oz chicken livers
2 shallots
50 ml · 2 fl oz Dutch gin or gin + 6
    crushed juniper berries
1 tbsp redcurrant jelly

Put the prunes to soak in water for several hours in advance.

Salt and pepper the inside of the duck and wrap in the bacon. Brown in a casserole in 20 g (¾ oz) of butter, on a medium heat, reduce the flame, season again, lightly, and cook, covered, turning them over halfway through, for 40 minutes, so that the meat is still pink. If when you turn them they seem to be sticking pour in 2–3 tablespoons of hot water.

Meanwhile, simmer the prunes in their soaking water until quite soft.

When the duck are ready, cut off the legs and breasts and keep hot. Break up and return the carcasses to the casserole with the wine, the livers, diced, the chopped shallots, and the juniper berries. Cover and cook at a medium pace for 10 minutes, shaking occasionally. Remove the lid and continue cooking for a few minutes to let the excess liquid evaporate.

Take out the prunes with a draining spoon and stone them, leaving the juice to reduce to about 150 ml (¼ pt). Pour the gin into the casserole to deglaze the cooking liquid, add the prune juice, and leave to reduce another 4–5 minutes.

In the meantime, give the duck legs a final cooking under the grill but leave them pinkish.

Strain the sauce, pressing it through the sieve to extract all the juices. Back on a low heat, incorporate the rest of the butter and the redcurrant jelly.

Sliver the breasts, arrange the prunes on top, and coat with the sauce. Serve the legs separately, with a salad.

Recommended wine: red Graves, St-Émilion, or Médoc Cru.

Harengs Calaisienne
· STUFFED HERRINGS ·

In the fourteenth century, the herring ruled supreme in both France and

England. Festivals and processions were devoted to it, even deep inland, and it was an acceptable form of currency. These stuffed herrings are eaten with boiled potatoes either strewn with parsley or coated in soured cream.

———————————————— *Ingredients for 8* ————————————————

8 fresh herrings, approximately
   250 g · ½ lb each, with roes if
   possible
50 g · 2 oz shallots
50 g · 2 oz mushrooms

50 g · 2 oz parsley
100 g · 3½ oz butter
salt, pepper
1 tbsp oil

Scale the fish, then split them down the back, cut the backbone just behind the head and in front of the tail, and pull it out. Gut the fish as cleanly as possible, saving any roes, and wash and wipe.

Put the shallots, mushrooms, parsley, soft roes, butter, and salt and pepper through a blender. Dice any hard roes and add to the mixture.

Stuff the herrings with this, rub the outside with salt and pepper, and wrap each one in oiled foil.

Cook in a very hot oven for 15 minutes.

Recommended drink: strong beer, stout, or dry cider.

Gâteau Battu de la Somme
· A HAND-BEATEN SWEET BRIOCHE ·

A light cake, delicious with a creamy pudding.

———————————————— *Ingredients for 4* ————————————————

2 tbsp milk
7 g · ¼ oz salt
20 g · ¾ oz fresh baker's yeast
250 g · 9 oz flour

195 g · 7 oz butter
50 g · 2 oz castor sugar
1 tbsp cognac
6 eggs

Bring the milk to the boil, let it cool, and dissolve the salt in it. Mix in the yeast.

Make a well in the flour, and work in 175 g (6 oz) of butter, just melted and warm, then the sugar, cognac, and yeast mixture. Now, by hand, beat in the egg yolks, one by one, and two stiffly whisked whites; continue beating until the mixture comes away from the sides of the bowl.

Cover with a damp cloth, and leave to rise for 3 hr in a warm place.

Beat the dough again with lightly floured hands, and pour into a large ribbed brioche mould, well-buttered, in which the dough comes not more than half way up. Leave to rise until the dough fills the mould.

Bake in a medium oven for 30 minutes. Let it cool for 10–15 minutes before unmoulding.

Recommended drink: Monbazillac, champagne, or coffee.

Tarte à la Rhubarbe
· RHUBARB TART ·

This is eaten all over the north and east of France, often with coffee rather than as a pudding. The rhubarb is not pre-cooked.

———————————————— *Ingredients for 4* ————————————————

300 g · 10 oz enriched shortcrust
   pastry (see p. 224)
1 kg · 2 lb rhubarb

20 g · ³/₄ oz butter
1 egg
200 g · 7 oz granulated sugar

Roll out the pastry to 3 mm (¹/₈″) and prick it all over. Turn it over to line a buttered tart tin. Make sure the sides are solid and brush them with beaten egg.

Trim and wash the rhubarb, discarding any leaves, and peel the film of skin off the stalks. Slice into 2 cm (³/₄″) sections.

Spread half the sugar over the pastry, arrange the rhubarb on top, and sprinkle with the rest. Bake for 45 minutes in a medium oven.

Serve warm or cold.

Recommended wine: Monbazillac.

24
POITOU
The Vendée

Separated from Brittany by the Loire, Poitou takes in the sandy reaches of the Marais Breton in the north west and the marshes, ponds, and canals of the Marais Poitevin, which was reclaimed with Dutch assistance, in the south. In between is the fertile bocage, undulating countryside, interspersed with woodland, and given over to cattle and arable farming. Crops include hemp, flax, and tobacco.

Soup was an everyday affair, the selection enriched with fish soups in the Vendée – shad soup was a speciality of Aiguillon-sur-Mer – but also reflecting a certain amount of poverty: *soupe 'de vie'* was merely water with garlic, thyme, bay, rosemary, and oil, the mixture poured boiling over slices of bread; and *soupe à la grolle* was a crow broth.

The Marais Poitevin is the home of crayfish, eels, and elvers (known here as *anguillettes* or *viots*). From the sea come mussels, much appreciated, clams, oysters, mackerel (mackerel prepared with rice is part of culinary folklore hereabouts), and sardines. Port Joinville on the Ile d'Yeu was France's main fishing port for tuna.

Further evidence of endemic poverty is found in a strong liking for offal, while, traditionally, the totally destitute were given veal pluck by the butchers. Recipes for minnow omelettes also suggest low levels of subsistence, as do a range of puddings to make stale bread palatable, for instance, dunking it in sugared water and red wine (*le miget*).

Those able to take a greater pleasure in cooking and eating, but without throwing economy to the wind, elaborated dishes for calf's ears (filled with mushrooms), pig's trotters (in wine), pig's liver (roast), and tongue (in a piquant sauce reflecting the Poitevin appreciation of sauces); they also enjoyed a wide selection of poultry, game, and water fowl. Chicken was pot-roast with garlic, spices, and croûtons, *à la montmorillonnaise*, or sautéed with potatoes and onions, *à la niortaise*. White geese were spit-roasted or casseroled with cabbage. Rabbit was cooked like hare in a *sauce rousse* – hare itself was cooked as in the Limousin (see p. 142) or roast with garlic. Wild rabbit was stuffed with apple. Eggs were poached in red wine and eaten with croûtons. But, although known as *oeufs 'à la huguenote'*, some Catholics preferred to relate them to the Burgundian *oeufs pochés meurette* (see p. 61), calling them *la meurotte*.

The range of pâtés was large, and pork was made into *grillons* (similar to rillettes, p. 19) and eaten with pickled green walnuts. Cut into tiny pieces and heavily seasoned with herbs, pork was also the main ingredient of a huge ragoût for carnival days when so much was made it had to be stirred with a hayfork or *tribalée*, which gave its name to the stew.

Cabbage occupied such an important place on the menu that the Royalist insurgents of the Vendée, and later all the counter-revolutionaries of the 1790s, were dubbed Chouans. Young it was eaten with a vinaigrette or cream, or the tender leaves were buttered, filled with potato, and covered with a kind of pancake batter. Older, it was stuffed (see below). The flat beans known as *mojhettes* (see p. 15) and broad beans were also very popular. Purslane went into salads, and dandelion was eaten with hardboiled eggs on Ash Wednesday.

In 732, Charles Martel defeated the Saracens in the Montbernage hills, but those who escaped, it is said, took the beautiful women with them, instead of their goats. They also, it seems, left a word, *chabli*, the Arabic for goat, since the local generic name for goat's cheese, of which there is a great deal (all found at an annual cheese fair at Civray), is Chabichou or Chabi. There is a solitary sheep's cheese too, Trébèche or Trois-Cornes.

As elsewhere, fruit, particularly apples and plums, goes into flans and tarts. Table grapes are grown south of Poitiers; and there are melons, but with skins so tough they are called *'culs de singe'*. Angelica comes from Niort, where a liqueur is made. As for the wine, it has improved since the days when it was simply poured down the throat from the bottle (*à la régalade*).

Soupe à l'Ouzille
· SORREL SOUP ·

Ouzille = *oseille*. Nowadays, the bread in the recipe is often replaced by a pound or so of sliced potatoes.

──────────────── *Ingredients for 4* ────────────────

200 g · 7 oz sorrel	200 g · 7 oz stale bread
20 g · 3/4 oz butter	2 eggs
salt, pepper	200 ml · 7 fl oz thick cream

Trim the sorrel, leaving no more than 2 cm (3/4") of stalk, and wash well.

In a saucepan, on a low heat, toss the shredded sorrel in the melted butter for 5–6 minutes.

Add 1.5 lt (2½ pt) of water, and salt and pepper, and bring to the boil.

Drop in the bread, cut into thin strips. Cover and leave to simmer very gently (without bubbling) for 15 minutes.

Mix the egg yolks with the cream, diluting it with a ladle of soup. Pour into a tureen, followed by the contents of the saucepan. When serving, plunge the ladle deep into the soup to ensure everyone gets some bread.

Recommended wine: possibly Gros-Plant.

Pain de Porée
· LEEKS AND CREAM ·

Porée means *poireau*. This dish is not bread, but a thick, well-drained mixture of leeks, cream, and egg yolks, another example of the Poitevin appreciation of vegetables.

──────────────── *Ingredients for 4* ────────────────

2 kg · 4 lb lge white leeks	salt, pepper
100 g · 3½ oz butter	2 eggs
20 g · 3/4 oz flour	100 ml· 3½ fl oz thick cream

Trim the leeks, discarding all but 2 cm (3/4") of the green. Wash and slice them, and put into a pan of boiling salted water. Boil for 10 minutes and drain.

Return the leeks to a dry saucepan with the butter and heat gently for 10 minutes for all the liquid to evaporate, turning them over frequently so as not to let them brown. Mix in the flour and season with salt and pepper. Cook a further 10 minutes, stirring almost constantly.

Mix the egg yolks with the cream and pour very slowly on to the leeks, away from the heat, still stirring.

Recommended wine: Muscadet or a white Saumur.

Farci Poitevin
· POITEVIN STUFFED CABBAGE ·

A delicious dish from the Civray region. Cheesecloth or butter muslin can be used in place of the traditional stuffing bag.

Ingredients for 8
---

a firm cabbage c. 2 kg · 4 lb
500 g · 1 lb lean green streaky bacon
2 or 3 chard stalks
  or 2 lge white leeks
250 g · 8 oz sorrel
2 lettuces
100 g · 3 oz onions
4 cloves of garlic
12 sprigs of parsley

12 chives
200 g · 7 oz homemade breadcrumbs
6 eggs
salt, pepper
a lge fresh pork rind
bones, veal if possible
2 sprigs of thyme
1 bay leaf

Separate the outer leaves of the cabbage, cut out the main stalk, and plunge leaves and heart into boiling water. Drain after 5 minutes' cooking, being careful not to damage the leaves. Reserve the heart.

Blanch the bacon (see p. 221). Drain and dice.

Prepare the chard stalks or leeks, trim the sorrel stalks, and wash the leaves and the lettuces. Chop all these vegetables, together with the onions, garlic, parsley, chives, and cabbage heart.

Line a pudding basin first with a cheesecloth, allowing enough to cover the top, and then with the best cabbage leaves, so that they overlap and there are no gaps through which stuffing can escape; ensure that they also extend well over the rim of the bowl.

Mix the chopped vegetables with the bacon, breadcrumbs, slightly moistened with water, eggs, and salt and pepper. Fill the basin, fold the cabbage leaves over, and tie up the cheesecloth with string.

Put the pork rind and bones in a large saucepan or casserole with enough water to cover the cabbage parcel. Add the thyme and bay leaf, and a very light seasoning of salt and pepper (as the stuffing is already seasoned). Place over moderate heat.

Immerse the cabbage parcel in the pot when the water boils, and keep it under water by pressing with a spatula for about 5 minutes, then cover and leave to simmer gently for 3 hr.

Eat hot or cold, having removed the cheesecloth as you turned the parcel out upsidedown on to a dish; cut it like a melon.

Recommended wine: if the cabbage is hot: a red Haut-Poitou or Saumur; if cold, a white Loire.

Pâté Vendéen
· RABBIT PATE ·

This would have been made with wild rabbit.

──────────────── *Ingredients for 8* ────────────────

1 blanched, boned calf's foot +
  bones (see p. 221)
1 lge carrot
1 lge onion
8 sprigs of parsley
1 clove
1 sprig of thyme
1/4 bay leaf
500 ml · 17 fl oz white wine

2 wild or 1 farm rabbit + liver, heart,
  and kidneys
1 clove of garlic
150 g · 5 oz green fat bacon
salt, pepper
1 sml tsp *quatre-épices* or allspice
2 tbsp cognac
500 g · 1 lb pork fillet
1 lge piece of caul fat
flour

Put the calf's foot and bones in a large saucepan, along with the sliced carrot
and onion, 2 sprigs of parsley, the clove, thyme, and bayleaf, half the wine,
and an equal amount of water. Reduce by half.

Meanwhile, cut the leg and saddle meat of the rabbit in fairly large slices,
and remove all the meat on the bones with a small pointed knife.

Mince these small bits of meat with the livers, heart, and kidneys, the garlic,
the remaining parsley, and the bacon; season with salt, pepper, and *quatre-
épices*; pour in the cognac and the remaining wine. Work the mixture together
well and leave for 1 hr.

Add the pork, in 2 cm (³/₄″) cubes, to the pan with the calf's foot and cook
gently for 30 minutes. Extract the pork with a draining spoon and leave to cool
before mixing into the mince.

Line a terrine dish with the caul fat, pre-soaked and squeezed dry, leaving
a wide border all round. In it, arrange, in alternate layers, the minced and the
sliced rabbit, beginning and ending with the mince.

Fold the caul over the pâté. Seal the terrine lid with a strip of flour-and-water
paste and stand in a container of water in a medium oven for 2¹/₂ hr.

Take out the pâté, break the seal, and drain off the fat. In its place, pour in
the well-strained calf's foot liquid. Cool and refrigerate for 24 hr, for this to set,
before unmoulding and serving.

Recommended wine: Chinon or a Gamay de Loire.

Pigeonneaux aux Herbillettes
· PIGEON WITH HERBS AND TRUFFLES ·

Herbillettes is a local word meaning parsley, chives, spring onions, basil, chervil,
and hyssop, collectively. They figure in green salads and in cooked dishes with
the addition of thyme and rosemary. While this recipe would be made in France
with squab (young reared pigeons – at their best around midsummer when the
herbs are plentiful), given longer cooking it would suit English wood-pigeon,
tasty, underrated birds.

──────────── *Ingredients for 4* ────────────

4 wood-pigeons or squab + giblets
200 g · 7 oz uncooked ham or
  gammon
100 g · 3¹/₂ oz ham or gammon fat
1 clove of garlic
1 sml handful of the herbs listed
  above
100 g · 3¹/₂ oz butter

1 egg yolk
1 sml tin of truffles
salt, pepper
100 g · 3¹/₂ oz shallots
200 g · 7 oz mushrooms, field or
  cultivated
100 ml · 3¹/₂ fl oz white wine
100 ml · 3¹/₂ fl oz chicken stock

Split the pigeons down their backs, and flatten them with a meat cleaver.

Mince together, medium fine, the pigeons' hearts, gizards, and livers, the ham, fat and lean, the garlic, and the herbs. Work in half the butter, the egg yolk, and the diced truffles with their liquid. Season with salt, taking account of the saltiness of the ham and the stock to be added, and pepper. Set aside.

Turn the finely sliced shallots over in the remaining butter in a large shallow pan or sauteuse, on a low heat, for 6–8 minutes, adding the diced mushrooms, after 3 or 4 minutes.

Pour in the wine and stock, bring to the boil, and mix in the mince; taste for seasoning.

Arrange the flattened pigeons on top, cover, and cook, 10 minutes on each side for a squab, about double for a wood-pigeon, depending on size and age.

Recommended wine: Saumur-Champigny.

Tourteau Fromagé
· GOAT'S CHEESE TART ·

A tart that is not found anywhere else in France. It should look burnt. Soft goat's cheese can be bought from better supermarkets and delicatessens.

──────────── *Ingredients for 4* ────────────

250 g · 9 oz shortcrust pastry (see
  p. 224)
20 g · ³/₄ oz butter
250 g · 9 oz soft goat's cheese
175 g · 6 oz castor sugar

50 ml · 1³/₄ fl oz milk
6 eggs
60 g · 2 oz flour
a drop of vanilla essence

Roll out the pastry to 2.5 mm (¹/₁₀″) and line a deep buttered 24 cm (9″) cake tin – in Poitou they have a special mould.

Beat the goat's cheese with 125 g (4 oz) of sugar and the milk, until you have a smooth mixture.

Fold in the separated egg yolks, one by one, then the flour and vanilla essence.

Beat the egg whites stiff, sifting in the rest of the sugar gradually, with the other hand, as they begin to stiffen. Fold into the mixture and pour on to the pastry base. Bake at mark 3 / 170°C for 45 minutes.

Leave to cool but unmould before it is quite cold.

Recommended wine: a red Haut-Poitou or Thouarsais.

Broyé du Poitou
· A HOUSEHOLD GALETTE ·

This cake was not cut into portions but broken up by an incisive punch in the centre! It keeps well in an airtight container.

―――――――――――――――――――― *Ingredients for 4* ――――――――――――――――――――

3 eggs
250 g · 8 oz castor sugar
¹/₂ sml tsp salt
1 tbsp mature cognac

250 g · 8 oz butter
500 g · 1 lb flour
¹/₂ sml tsp oil

Cream 2 eggs, the sugar, and salt, until the mixture is pale and smooth, the grains of sugar completely dissolved.

Fold in the cognac, the butter, softened but not melted, and the flour. Knead the mixture by hand and when it is well blended, pull it apart into small pieces. Make these back into a ball and leave in a bowl, under a damp cloth, for 2 hr.

Flatten into a disc-shape, with a rolling-pin, and place on a lightly oiled baking tray. Brush with beaten egg and bake for 25 minutes in a medium oven.

Recommended wine: a sparkling Saumur or a Crémant de Loire.

25
PROVENCE · *The Camargue*
THE COMTÉ de NICE
THE COMTAT VENAISSIN
CORSICA

Many provinces with a greater gastronomic reputation have a more limited range of dishes than Provence with its colourful aromatic cooking, the antecedents of which lie in the ancient civilisations of Phoenicia and Rome.

The long Mediterranean coastline, the hills and plains where the vine, olive tree, and herbs flourish, the Camargue Delta – these are Provence's geographical attributes. And to it are attached, culinarily speaking, Corsica, and, politically speaking, the Comté de Nice, joined administratively some 125 years ago but fiercely maintaining its own cookery, and its own language, 'Nissart'.

The Mediterranean provides that rich assortment of fish that goes into Provençal soups. But the region has other tasty ways of dealing with a catch that arguably makes up in flavour for what the individual fish lack in size. Thus, anchovies, for instance, are the basis of *tapenade* (a purée of olives, anchovies, capers – *tapènes* – and olive oil), and of *anchoyade* (anchovies softened in olive oil, with finely chopped garlic, and grilled on bread). Martigues, which is capital of the anchovy, is also where *poutargue* is made (hard mullet roes, salted, pressed, dried, and coated in paraffin).

Of the bigger fish, commonest are sardines (stuffed with spinach, *à l'antiboise*), sea-bream, red mullet, sea-bass, monkfish, large scorpion-fish, and cod, which is salted, not only for *brandade* (see p. 128), but also to eat *en rayte* (with onions, tomatoes, red wine, and capers), on Christmas Eve. As for stockfish, a hangover from the salt trade, it is vital to Corsican *pestu* and to Niçois *estoficada*, whose preparation is still governed by a Brotherhood.

From inland, came the pork (*saucisson d'Arles* is the only sausage, because of its long history, not obliged by law to divulge its contents), and the lamb (whose meat is flavoured by a diet richer in herbs – thyme, savory, rosemary, hyssop, marjoram – than in grass). Feast days might call for a piece of Camargue beef, or, in the Camargue itself, for a whole bull, demanding twelve long hours' cooking. For the end of the harvest, though, it was the cock that was killed, beaten to death on the threshing-floor.

The Vaucluse, in the Rhône valley, may be regarded as the garden of France, with almost every variety of fruit and vegetable grown there, in the narrow fields between the dark cypress windbreaks. Here, the tomatoes, peppers, courgettes, aubergines, and onions are not so much cooked as melted in oil and seasonings – one of the secrets of Provençal cooking – while the purple globe artichokes can be eaten raw before the choke has formed. Spring onions, rather forgotten in other parts of France, and somewhat larger than in the British Isles, are still appreciated, as are Jerusalem artichokes, essential to a *grand aïoli* (see below). As well as wild mushrooms, there are truffles around Apt, Carpentras, Richerenches, Riez, and Valréas. And there is olive oil, which, like wine, has its great names: Nice, les Mées, Maussane-les-Alpilles, and Valréas.

Cheeses are mostly small – cow's, sheep's, or goat's, depending on the season – Banon (wrapped in chestnut leaves), Picodons, Bossons. Herbs, like *poivre d'âne* (winter savory), and olive oil are used to enliven them: Cachat, for example, is worked with wine, oil, and herbs to make Fromage Fort du Ventoux. Brousse, a whey cheese, goes into the cooking, as does Brocciu, a Corsican cousin. Corsica also has a blue sheep's cheese to rival Roquefort.

Apricots, cherries, plums, strawberries, figs, melons, pears, and peaches – all are ripened by sun and mistral. As well as being dispatched fresh to the less-fortunate, much of the fruit is preserved, as either jam or crystallised fruit. It also goes into cakes and pastries and other sweet confections of which the Provençals are fond. Indeed, the high point of the Christmas Eve supper, which precedes Midnight Mass, is a spread of thirteen desserts, including nougat, dates, pumpkin and almond pie (see p. 198), and *pompe* or *gibassier*, a yeast cake with brown sugar and orange and lemon peel. This supper is eaten in front not of a Christmas tree but a crib, made from whitewashed brown paper, peopled with little figures called *santons*.

Virtually everywhere there is wine: all the Côtes du Rhône, including Châteauneuf-du-Pape (not forgetting its white); the Côtes de Provence; Côtes du Ventoux; Coteaux d'Aix; Coteaux des Baux; the Muscats: Rasteau, Beaumes-de-Venise. Among Corsican *appellations* are Coteaux d'Ajaccio, Sartène, Calvi, and Patrimonio, and a Muscat, Cap Corse.

Aïgo-Sau
· PROVENÇAL FISH SOUP ·

Aïgo-sau ('salt water' in Provençal) is a white fish soup and the potatoes and tomatoes are optional. It may be accompanied by a *rouille* (see over).

———————————— *Ingredients for 8* ————————————

1 lge onion	1 piece of orange peel
2 sml leeks	4 cloves of garlic
2 tbsp olive oil	2 tomatoes
2 kg · 4 lb assorted white fish (e.g.	1 pinch of saffron
bream, base, conger eel,	1 fennel stalk
monkfish), cleaned and sliced,	1 bay leaf
unless small	salt, pepper
800 g · 1³/₄ lb potatoes	sml slices of good bread

Slice the onion and the cleaned leeks (without the green), and toss in the oil on a low heat in a thick-bottomed pan for 7–8 minutes, without browning.

Add the fish and the peeled, washed, and thinly sliced potatoes.

Mix in the orange peel, the crushed garlic, the skinned and chopped tomatoes, the saffron, fennel, bay leaf, and salt and pepper, and pour in enough boiling water to cover by about 5 cm (2"). Cook hard until the potatoes are done or, if omitting the potatoes, for 18 minutes.

Transfer the fish to a hot serving dish, remove the fennel and bay leaf, and turn the soup and potatoes on to slices of bread arranged either in the bottom of a tureen or in individual soup bowls; serve this first, followed by the fish (with the *rouille*).

Recommended wine: Cassis or Côtes de Provence.

Aïoli

The traditional Provençal cook did not use eggs because they were thought to mask the taste of the garlic; but it is more difficult to make without them, and nowadays they are included as a matter of course. Fewer are used however than in a *bourride* (p. 127).

Aïoli was something of a ritual which enlivened fast days and allowed one to entertain one's friends. Regarded less as a sauce than as an accompaniment it may, in a *grand aïoli* (i.e. *aïoli* plus salt cod, eggs and vegetables), become the main dish. Serve it in the mortar.

─────────────── *Ingredients for 8* ───────────────

12 cloves of garlic   1 tbsp lemon juice
salt   500 ml · 17 fl oz olive oil
2 egg yolks

Crush the garlic in a mortar, using ¹/₂ sml teaspoon of salt for the quantity of garlic given – salt helps break down the garlic.

When the garlic is reduced to a purée, add the eggs yolks and start beating, working in 100 ml (3¹/₂ fl oz) of oil, a drop at a time.

When this oil has been absorbed, add a small teaspoon of hot water, and start beating in the rest of the oil, which can be poured in a thin trickle; at the same time, incorporate the lemon juice. If the *aïoli* is inclined to separate, drip in more hot water, but cautiously, the final mixture should be thick and smooth.

Recommended wine: depends on what the aïoli *is being eaten with: for a* grand aïoli, *a white Côtes de Provence or Crémant de Pierrevert.*

Rouille

The accompaniment to certain Provençal soups (see *aïgo-sau*, above) including the legendary bouillabaisse. The recipe given, the standard homemade one, is a reminder that the modern tendency to make a sort of *aïoli* with chillis is historically incorrect.

─────────────── *Ingredients for 8* ───────────────

2 red chillis   250 ml · 8 fl oz olive oil
2 cloves of garlic   a handful of crustless stale bread
salt   a little homemade stock

Tail and seed the chillis and peel the garlic. Cut both up into a mortar and add salt – approximately ¹/₄ small teaspoon for these quantities – and 1 tablespoon of oil. Grind to a smooth purée.

Dunk the bread briefly in some of the stock and squeeze dry either by hand or in a cloth.

Add a walnut's worth of this bread to the mortar and start beating in the oil, following the same procedure as for *aïoli* (see above), adding a small teaspoon of hot stock if the mixture begins to separate, and more bread as required.

Just before serving, dilute the *rouille* with a little very hot stock to give it the consistency of a sauce.

Bouillabaisse

It is almost impossible to make bouillabaisse away from the coves of the Mediterranean coast between Martigues and Toulon, since the little rock fish that are vital to it do not travel. Hence the wild adaptations that have been made, so that bouillabaisse has become synonymous with 'fish soup'. Correspondingly far-flung theories have been devised to explain its name, which is probably a reference to the method of cooking (hard boiling is required to keep the oil suspended in an emulsion), *bouille* and *abaisse* – boil and reduce (the heat).

If bouillabaisse cannot be attempted outside Provence, it is nonetheless included here as it is easy to prepare should the opportunity arise. It does however call for a large variety of fish which means that it cannot be made in small quantities. The fish to include in the stock, if you can, are wrasse, cuckoo wrasse, and rainbow wrasse (*labres*, *girelles* or *demoiselles*, *roucau* or *rouquier*), comber (*serran*), and tiny scorpion fish (*petites rascasses*). Otherwise, buy what Provençal fishmongers sell as *poissons à soupe*. For the bouillabaisse itself you need four or five different fish, such as monkfish, conger eel, gurnard, John Dory, or rascasse (which should be live).

The cooking is very brief and, like a soufflé, it needs serving as soon as it is ready. In Marseille, bouillabaisse would never have been eaten without a *navette* – special bread rolls (see next recipe) – and a *rouille*.

The Corsican variant, *la zuminu*, also requires little rockfish, but may include mackerel or grey mullet, cuttlefish, crabs, and other shell fish; it has no saffron. Slices of potato or fennel shoots may be added to either.

────────────── *Ingredients for 8* ──────────────

FOR THE STOCK
1 kg · 2 lb assorted rock fish (see above)
head and tail of conger eel, if possible
10–12 little green crabs (unless you have *cigales*, see below)
2 small leeks
50 g · 2 oz onions
2 cloves of garlic
500 g · 1 lb tomatoes
2 tbsp olive oil
1/2 bay leaf
2 sprigs of fennel
1 sprig of parsley

1/3 piece of orange zest
salt, pepper

FOR THE BOUILLABAISSE
2 kg · 2 1/2 lb (not less) assorted fish, whole or in pieces depending on size (see above)
some *cigales* (small flat lobsters) if possible – then omit the crabs in the stock
400 g · 14 oz potatoes
100 ml · 4 fl oz olive oil
2–4 pinches of saffron, to taste
slices of bread (see next recipe)
rouille

Scale, gut, and clean all the fish (whether for the stock or the soup), unless the fishmonger has done so.

Slice the fish destined for the stock into a saucepan with the crabs, previously washed under running water, the white part of the leeks, cleaned and sliced, the roughly chopped onions, garlic, and tomatoes, the oil, bay leaf, fennel, parsley, and orange zest. Soften slowly for 10–15 minutes, stirring occasionally. Pour in 4 lt (7 pt) of boiling water and simmer for 30 minutes. Strain, pressing everything through the sieve lightly. Season with salt and pepper.

Put the potatoes, peeled, washed, and cut into approximately 2–3 mm (1/10–1/8") slices, into a shallow pan or sauteuse, preheated. Arrange all the firm fish on top (rascasse, monkfish, conger, gurnard), cover with the strained stock, previously brought back to the boil. Add the oil and saffron and if the fish is not totally immersed, enough boiling water to cover. Boil hard for 12 minutes.

Add the remaining fish (the John Dory and *cigales*) and leave to bubble hard a further 5–6 minutes.

Transfer the fish and potatoes to separate hot serving dishes, and put them on the table with the soup in its pan, the bread, and the *rouille*. (Very often the soup is eaten first, poured over the bread, the fish and potatoes following afterwards with a little olive oil.)

Recommended wine: white: Cassis, Palette, Côtes de Provence, or even Châteauneuf-du-Pape.

La Navette à Soupe
· BREAD FOR BOUILLABAISSE ·

Best if you can get hold of French flour (*type 55*), otherwise, use good bread flour.

—————————————————— *Ingredients for 8* ——————————————————

500 g · 17 oz plain flour
125 g · 4 oz wholemeal flour
10 g · 1/3 oz salt

18 g · 2/3 oz fresh yeast
a little flour for working the dough

Use a mixer to knead the flour, salt, and yeast (dissolved in 350 ml/12 fl oz of warm water) until the dough comes away clean from the sides of the bowl.

Make into a ball, cut a cross in the top, and leave to rise, in a bowl covered with a damp cloth, for 2 hr at room temperature.

With floured hands, fold the dough in on itself several times to deflate it. Leave to rise again, under a damp cloth.

Divide the dough into eight approximately 250 g (8 oz) portions and form each into an oval roll. Arrange on a greased baking tray with plenty of room in between. Flour lightly, cover with a dry cloth, and leave to rise until they have doubled in volume.

Make diagonal slashes in the top of each roll and bake in a pre-heated oven for 20 minutes at mark 7–8 / 220–230°C.

Leave for 12 hr.

Matelote d'Anguille de la Barthelasse
· EEL MATELOTE FROM LA BARTHELASSE ·

La Barthelasse is the island on the Rhône between Avignon and Villeneuve-lès-Avignon. The banks are wooded, the tree roots disappearing into the water, and it is a fisherman's haven. Eels are the main catch, baited with tiny snails (*mourgettes*) the size of a chick pea.

Ingredients for 6

1.5 kg · 3 lb eels
100 g · 3 oz onions
150 g · 5 oz carrots
3 tbsp olive oil
4 cloves of garlic
4 shallots
1 bottle red Côtes du Rhône
a bouquet garni: 1 sprig of thyme, 1
  bay leaf, 3–4 sprigs of parsley, a

small celery stalk, 2 sprigs of
fennel, 2 sprigs of oregano or
marjoram, 1 clove
salt, pepper
2 tbsp flour
50 g · 1½ oz butter
optional: button mushrooms,
  stewed in butter, little glazed
  onions, and croûtons

Skin and gut the eels, and put to soak overnight in cold water. Drain and slice them thickly, and return, along with the heads and tails, to fresh cold water until required.

Dice the onions and carrots finely and put in a pan or sauteuse with the oil, the crushed garlic, the coarsely chopped shallots, and the heads and tails of the eels. Soften gently, without browning, stirring regularly, until the oil is absorbed, then pour in the wine and let it come to the boil.

Tie up the bouquet with the clove in the middle and add to the pan. Season with salt and pepper and simmer for 20 minutes.

Strain the sauce, returning the bouquet to it, add the sliced eel, and leave to bubble gently for 7 minutes.

Transfer the eel to a serving dish with a draining spoon and keep hot. Skim the sauce if necessary.

Return it to a low heat, discard the bouquet, check the seasoning, and thicken by beating in the flour worked with the butter.

Coat the eel with the sauce, and garnish with the mushrooms, onions, or croûtons fried in butter, if you like.

Recommended wine: the wine used in the cooking, perhaps of a better cru: e.g. Gigondas or Châteauneuf-du-Pape.

Soupe au Pistou

Pistou is the Provençal version of the Genoese *pesto*, but, unlike its Italian forebear, it is much subject to local variation. Thus, around Hyères, for instance, they prefer Gorgonzola to Parmesan, while in Marseille, they like equal quantities of Parmesan, Gruyère, and mature Edam (a cheese found in many traditional Provençal recipes), plus tomato. Everyone, however, agrees about omitting the pine kernels. The basil, incidentally, should be a large-leafed variety, more pungent than the small-leafed plants. In spring the soup would be made with broad beans or peas instead of the haricot beans. Bacon is sometimes added.

──────────────── *Ingredients for 4* ────────────────

300 g · 10 oz dried haricot beans,
   soaked overnight (if lucky enough
   to have fresh haricot beans, this is
   shelled weight)
1 lge onion
1 clove
2 sprigs of thyme
1 lge leek
100 g · 3 oz carrots
50 g · 1½ oz turnip
100 g · 3 oz marrow or pumpkin
c. 50 g · 1½ oz celery stalk
250 g · 8 oz potatoes

250 g · 8 oz green beans
500 g · 1 lb courgettes
250 g · 8 oz firm tomatoes
salt, pepper
100 g · 3 oz macaroni or the thick
   Provençal vermicelli

FOR THE PISTOU
5 cloves of garlic
salt
10–12 lge basil leaves
100 g · 3 oz freshly grated Parmesan
100 ml · 3 fl oz olive oil

Simmer the haricot beans with the onion, peeled and quartered and stuck with the clove, and the thyme, in 3 lt (5 pt) of water for 1 hr (20 minutes if the beans are fresh), without salt as it makes the beans hard.

In the meantime, clean all the vegetables, slice the leek thickly, slice or dice the carrots and turnip, dice the pumpkin and celery, quarter the peeled potatoes, break up the green beans into two or three pieces, top, tail, and cut the courgettes into 2 cm (¾") sections, and skin the tomatoes.

When the haricot beans have simmered for an hour, add the leek, carrots, turnip, pumpkin, and celery; 15 minutes later, put in the potatoes, green beans, courgettes, and tomatoes, and season with salt and pepper.

As the soup comes back to the boil, drop in the macaroni or broken vermicelli and cook a further 15 minutes.

Meanwhile, prepare the *pistou* by crushing the garlic to a purée in a mortar, with a little salt to assist the process; add the basil and continue grinding until the mixture is quite smooth. Grate in the Parmesan and work the oil in very gradually with a fork.

Pour the soup, minus thyme and onion, into a tureen and lightly beat in the *pistou*.

Recommended wine: a Coteaux de Pierrevert rosé, or a Coteaux Varois (vin du pays du Var).

Pissaladière

The Niçoise *pissaladière*, like its sister, the pizza, must be made with bread dough – even if it is sometimes enriched. The *pissalat*, with which the dough was coated before baking, was made from sardines and anchovies, both macerated for a month with salt and herbs. For a homemade approximation of *pissalat*, take some anchovies preserved in salt (not oil), mash them to a purée, bury a bouquet of herbs in the middle, and leave for a fortnight, stirring once or twice a day. Otherwise, replace it, as most modern cooks do, with desalinated anchovies, arranged on top of the onion. The onion itself must be plentiful (2–3 kg for a 25 cm base) and well softened in advance. Should you find *pissalat* for sale, use it sparingly, 4 teaspoonsful to 500 g of dough, and spread it on before the onion.

--- *Ingredients for 4* ---

2.5 kg · 5 lb onions
100 ml · 3 fl oz olive oil
4 cloves of garlic
a small bouquet garni, to include
  oregano

500 g · 17 oz bread dough (see p. 225)
  salt
1 doz anchovy fillets, soaked to
  remove the salt
2 dozen small black olives

Slice the onions and put them with the oil, the whole, unpeeled garlic, and the bouquet, in a thick-bottomed pan or casserole; place on the lowest possible heat, cover, and stew for up to 2 hr, shaking the pan occasionally, to reduce the onions to a purée, without browning.

Stretch the dough (bread dough is not normally rolled) to make a round base, about 3–4 mm (⅛″) thick and 25 cm (10″) in diameter, with a raised edge to hold the filling. Place on an oiled baking tray and leave to rise for 20 minutes, before baking for 10 minutes in a medium to hot oven.

Discard the garlic and bouquet, salt the onions lightly (remembering the anchovies) and spread them on the semi-cooked base, using a draining spoon, so as to leave behind any excess oil. Arrange the anchovies and olives on top.

Return to the oven for 15 minutes. Sprinkle with freshly milled pepper before serving, very hot.

Recommended wine: a red or white Bellet.

Trouchia
· BAKED EGGS WITH PARMESAN AND CHARD ·

Trouchia is sold by the slice in all the grocers' of old Nice. It is not a stuffed omelette, but a careful blend of chard, herbs, cheese, and beaten egg.

--- *Ingredients for 4* ---

the leafy part of 3 bunches, 1 kg ·
  2 lb each, of chard (or spinach)
1 lge bunch of chervil
1 sml bunch of parsley

8 eggs
150 g · 5 oz freshly grated Parmesan
salt, pepper
4 tbsp olive oil

Wash and shred the chard and mix in the chervil leaves and chopped parsley.

Beat the eggs as for an omelette. Stir in the cheese, then the chard and herbs. Season with salt, bearing in mind the strength of the cheese, and pepper.

Pour half the oil into an oven-proof dish on a medium flame. When the oil is hot, pour in the eggs and stir hard until they begin to puff out. Cover immediately and put in a medium oven for 20 minutes.

Turn the *trouchia* upside down on to a large plate, pour the rest of the oil into the dish and slide the *trouchia* back into it, uncooked side uppermost. Return to the oven, covered, for a further 20 minutes.

It can be served hot with a drop of mild wine vinegar; but usually it is left to cool, unmoulded, and sliced.

Recommended wine: white Bellet, Cassis, Côtes de Provence, or Côtes du Lubéron.

Gigot de Broutard à la Crème d'Ail
· LEG OF LAMB WITH GARLIC ·

A *broutard* is a lamb (or calf) old enough to have started grazing. In Provence, the lamb come from the Alpilles, north of Marseille. Dwarf beans, cooked but still crunchy, go well with this dish, where lamb is cooked to French taste, i.e. just. For better done meat, add 15–25 minutes to the cooking, but remember it has been browned.

--------------------------------- *Ingredients for 8* ---------------------------------

a leg of lamb, 1.8 kg · 4 lb, just the knuckle left in, and weighed after boning
1 sprig of thyme
2 needles of rosemary
salt, pepper

70–80 ml · c. 3 fl oz good olive oil
700 g · 1½ lb garlic
750 ml · 1¼ pt thick cream
slightly stale bread
homemade breadcrumbs

Take off any crinkly skin on the joint. In a saucer, mix the thyme leaves and the finely chopped rosemary, and season with salt and pepper. Rub the meat, inside (where the bone was) and out, with this seasoning, pressing it in. Roll the joint into shape, and tie it, not too tightly.

Put all but a tablespoon of the oil into a casserole in which the lamb just fits, and brown the joint all over on a high flame.

Peel the garlic, removing any sprouts, and add to the browned meat. Let the cloves take colour, turning them over as necessary, for 3–4 minutes.

Cover the casserole and cook in a medium oven for 25–35 minutes.

Transfer the joint to another covered pot and keep hot – this procedure makes the meat both pinker and easier to carve. Return the casserole with the garlic to a medium heat, add the cream, and simmer for 5 minutes. Taste for seasoning and strain, pressing the garlic through the sieve. Whip the sauce hard for a few seconds to blend the ingredients and keep hot in a bain-marie.

Cut the bread thinly, at least one slice per person, spread it with the garlic sauce, scatter some breadcrumbs over, and toast under a hot grill. When it's golden-brown, take it out and sprinkle with olive oil (the spoonful reserved earlier).

Carve the lamb and arrange the slices on a dish surrounded by the toast; pour the remaining sauce into a sauceboat. If serving green beans, put them round the meat.

Recommended wine: red: Coteaux d'Aix, Côtes du Ventoux, or Côtes du Rhône-Villages.

Sou-Fassum
· GREEK STUFFED CABBAGE ·

A recipe stemming back to the founding of Antibes by the Greeks in 340 BC. Around Grasse, *sou-fassum* nets can be bought – but a cheesecloth, even a teatowel, will do. It needs a good, rich stock (e.g. chicken plus shins of pork, veal, and mutton), which, well-skimmed, provides a soup to precede the cabbage, itself usually an accompaniment to meat. The cabbage is also eaten cold as an entrée.

————————————— Ingredients for 8 —————————————

1 lge Savoy cabbage c. 3 kg · 6¹/₂ lb
80 g · 3 oz rice
100 g · 4 oz onions
1 tbsp oil
200 g · 8 oz lean streaky bacon
1 clove of garlic
200 g · 8 oz chard leaves (i.e. from
  a 1 kg · 2 lb bunch) or spinach
1 kg · 2 lb minced pork

200 g · 8 oz peas, shelled weight
2 tomatoes
1 sprig of thyme
4 sage leaves
2 sprigs of parsley
2 eggs
salt, pepper
2–3 lt · 4–5 pt stock (see above)

Separate out all the cabbage leaves, removing the large central stalks, and wash. Blanch by covering in cold water, bringing slowly to the boil, and draining immediately.

Dampen a cheesecloth or teatowel, spread it out, and arrange the cabbage leaves on it, biggest ones first, overlapping in a rosette; set aside the inner leaves.

Wash and boil the rice for 15 minutes (or less depending on the rice you are using) in plenty of water; drain well. Slice the onions and fry lightly in the oil for a few minutes. Blanch the bacon (see p. 221) and drain.

Chop up the bacon, garlic, reserved cabbage, and chard finely. Add the pork, rice, onions, and peas, the tomatoes, skinned and chopped, a few thyme leaves, the chopped sage and parsley, and, lastly, the eggs. Season with salt and pepper and work everything together into a smooth mixture. Make into a ball.

Place this in the centre of the rosette, bring the cabbage leaves and the cloth up over it, and tie the cloth tightly.

Immerse the parcel in the stock which should be simmering and leave to cook at the same pace for 3 hr.

Recommended wine: red Côtes du Lubéron or Côtes du Rhône, e.g. a Vacqueyras or Séguret.

Ratatouille

A ratatouille is not a purée of vegetables all cooked together, but a final amalgam of separately prepared ingredients. It thus requires time and several utensils, but is worth the effort as it will do for several meals, keeping well in the fridge, and being quite as good cold as hot.

————————————— Ingredients for 8 —————————————

2 kg · 4¹/₂ lb tomatoes
250 ml · 10 fl oz olive oil
¹/₂ head of garlic
a bouquet garni: 2 sprigs of thyme,
  1 bay leaf, 4 sprigs of parsley

800 g · 1³/₄ lb aubergines
400 g · 14 oz green peppers
800 g · 1³/₄ lb onions
800 g · 1³/₄ lb courgettes
salt, pepper

Cook the skinned, seeded, and chopped tomatoes gently, uncovered for the excess liquid to evaporate, in a saucepan, with 50 ml (2 fl oz) of oil, the crushed garlic, and the bouquet, stirring occasionally, until they are reduced to a purée.

Peel and slice the aubergines, and sprinkle with salt. Leave them in a colander pressed down with a weight for 30–45 minutes.

Split the peppers in two and tail and seed them. Cook slowly, cut side uppermost, in a thick frying pan, with 50 ml (2 fl oz) of oil, for 10 minutes. Remove with a draining spoon and peel off the fine outer skin. Cut the peppers into strips, and return to the pan to soften for about 20 minutes. Leave to drain in a colander.

At the same time, in another 50 ml (2 fl oz) of oil, sauté the finely sliced onions until they are soft, without letting them brown. Drain with the peppers.

Transfer the drained onions and peppers to a dish (kept warm in a bain-marie if you want the ratatouille hot).

Rinse and wipe the aubergines, and cook in one of the pans, with a further 50 ml (2 fl oz) of oil, for 15–20 minutes, turning them over now and then; drain in a colander.

Meanwhile, cook the sliced courgettes in the other pan for 10–15 minutes, with the last of the oil; drain in a colander.

Add the courgettes and aubergines to the onions and peppers. Discard the bouquet; salt and pepper the tomatoes quite heavily. Stir them carefully into the other vegetables so as to coat them without crushing them. Taste for seasoning.

Recommended wine: if eaten cold on its own, a white Bellet, a Bandol rosé, Coteaux d'Aix, Coteaux des Baux, or rosé. Otherwise, depending on what the ratatouille is to be eaten with.

Tarte au Potiron et aux Amandes
· PUMPKIN AND ALMOND TART ·

A traditional Christmas dessert (see p. 189), slightly lightened for modern tastes.

———————————— *Ingredients for 8* ————————————

200 g · 8 oz pumpkin – without the peel
100 g · 4 oz shelled and peeled almonds

100 g · 4 oz castor sugar
sml piece of orange peel
350 g · 12 oz puff pastry (see p. 224)
1 egg

Brush any seeds off the pumpkin and cut into small cubes. Cook gently, covered, with 2 tablespoons of water, watching that it doesn't stick, until soft enough to be crushed with a spatula. Put through a food mill or blender and return to the pan, still on a low heat, but uncovered this time, and, stirring frequently, reduce the pumpkin to a thick purée. Set aside.

Grill the almonds to colour them slightly; mix with the sugar and orange peel and put through the blender.

Stir into the pumpkin.

Roll out the pastry to a maximum of 2 mm (1/10"), make a round tart base, and save the trimmings.

Place it on an oiled baking tray, and, using your thumb and forefinger very lightly, roll the pastry inwards all round to raise the edge sufficiently to hold the mixture. Brush the edge with beaten egg and fill the case with the pumpkin and almond mixture, spreading it evenly.

Use the trimmings to cut 5 mm (¼″) strips the width of the tart, brush them with egg and arrange in a trellis pattern. Bake in a medium oven, mark 4 / 180°C, for 20 minutes.

Recommended wine: Muscat de Beaumes-de-Venise or de Rasteau.

Fiadone
· SHEEP'S CHEESE CAKE ·

A Corsican recipe, which varies from village to village: at Venaco, for example, the eggs are beaten whole with the sugar, milk is added, and orange or lemon peel and a drop of *eau-de-vie* are used to flavour it.

──────────────── *Ingredients for 8* ────────────────

1 lemon
6 eggs
150 g · 5 oz castor sugar
500 g · 1 lb fresh sheep's cheese (in
   Corsica it would be Brocciu;

worth trying with unsalted
Ricotta or other soft sheep's
cheese), sufficiently drained to be
   mashed
1 sml tsp oil

Pare the lemon with a potato-peeler, avoiding the pith. Drop the peel into boiling water, boil for 3 minutes, and drain. Chop finely.

Cream the egg yolks and sugar until the mixture is pale, creamy, and smooth.

Fold in the lemon peel and the cheese, then the stiffly beaten egg whites.

Pour into a deep tart or sandwich tin, oiled, and bake in a medium oven for 30 minutes.

Leave to cool before unmoulding and eat quite cold.

Recommended wine: if eaten as a snack, a white Corsican wine; if the end of a meal, a 'Cap-Corse', i.e. a Muscat or Malvoisie (another sweet wine).

26
SAVOY

The cooking of this mountainous region may be rustic but the flavouring is subtle. The finesse of the freshwater fish from the great lakes of Léman (of which Haute-Savoie enjoys the southern side), Annecy, Le Bourget, and Aigue-belette, sets the tone. If fish stocks are now low, pollution control has helped replenish the supply of char, burbot, bull trout, brown trout, perch, *féra* (from the salmon family), and crayfish.

Otherwise, Savoyard cooking may be characterised as rich in cream, milk, and butter – and eggs – and the wild mushrooms which grow in profusion and which make Savoy the heart of 'mycogastronomy'. With neighbouring Dauphiny, it shares a love of gratins, and, thanks possibly to a period as a province of Sardinia, is a great consumer of polenta, pasta, and risotto. There is also a liking for sweet and sour dishes, often made with raisins. However, the modern Savoyard is not only deprived of his best fish, but his shooting of game and even his gathering of wild plants (such as blue cardoons) are strictly regulated.

If he has a hard day's fishing to get the necessary ingredients for a *soupe de poissons du Léman*, he may still enjoy a good *potée savoyarde* with chestnuts and smoked sausages, or an *omelette haute-savoyarde*, with shallots, cheese, cream, and chervil, chives, and tarragon (known collectively as *herbettes* – a reference to *huit herbettes* meaning basil, parsley, sorrel, spinach, and chard leaf, as well).

Meat tends to be a vehicle for mushrooms: sweetbreads come stewed with sweet chanterelles, a variety peculiar to this area, veal kidneys with royal agaric (*oronges*), beef with ceps, veal escalopes with field mushrooms, kid with morels; chicken, almost needless to say, is cooked with mushrooms and cream. Raw ham, which here, as elsewhere, benefits from the altitude, is also eaten with mushrooms and cream. When rock partridge, hare, or other game is available, it has a distinctive flavour, acquired from a diet rich in aromatic plants.

Other vegetables include cardoons, an important element of the winter diet, potatoes, cabbage, garlic, and chard. These would all appear in gratins or *farçons* (*farcemons* or *farcements*), a kind of pudding made, in the past, when the valleys were cut off by snow, from the resources of the store cupboard: potatoes, bacon, prunes, raisins, eggs, and cheese; or, for a sweet *farçon*, potato, milk, eggs, sugar, vanilla, and chervil. *Matefaims* or *matefams* (*mater*, meaning to kill, thus 'to kill hunger') were water-based pancakes eaten with baked potatoes and *fromage blanc*.

The cheese is plentiful. There is Beaufort, a hard cheese; numerous fresh Tomes; Vacherin, wrapped in birch bark; and Reblochon – a cheese originally obtained by pilfering (the milking was halted before all the milk had been taken, and while what there was was measured, a second milking took place, and from this creamier, underhand draught, the cheese was made). The blue-veined goat's cheeses are no longer made with bread mould, penicillin being used, even domestically.

Puddings and cakes are light and simple, like *brioche aux pralines* and fruit tarts, the fruit raw or cooked, with or without cream. The fruit – apples, pears, peaches (yellow and white), wild strawberries, wild raspberries, bilberries, blackberries – is abundant.

The wine too: reds and rosés (vin de Savoie) and whites (Roussette de Savoie). There are also sparkling wines, notably a Seyssel. There is vermout (never with an 'h') from Chambéry, and *eaux-de-vie* and a *marc de Savoie*. The cellar's contents can be extended with a wild cherry ratafia, a wormwood liqueur from the high glaciers, and some Évian, Thonon, or Saint-Simon water.

Pâté de Fromage de Chèvre

The spoonful of sugar, even in a savoury dish, is typical of Savoy cooking.

―――――――――――――― *Ingredients for 4* ――――――――――――――

250 g · 8 oz vol-au-vent pastry
   dough (see p. 225), using half
   butter instead of lard
50 g · 2 oz butter
4 eggs
30 g · 1 oz flour
500 ml · 17 fl oz milk

200 g · 7 oz lean uncooked ham or
   gammon
200 g · 7 oz fresh goat's cheese
50 g · 2 oz grated Beaufort or
   Gruyère
salt, pepper
1 tbsp castor sugar

Roll out the pastry to 3 mm (⅛″) and prick it with a fork. Turning it the other
way up, line a buttered tart tin, making sure the sides are firm. Brush the edge
with a beaten egg.

   Melt the remaining butter gently in a saucepan without letting it burn, stir
in the flour, to make a roux, and beat in the warmed milk, gradually. Continue
stirring for 10 minutes to cook the flour.

   Away from the heat, work in 3 egg yolks, the diced ham, the crumbled goat's
cheese, and the grated cheese. Season with salt, taking account of the saltiness
of the ham and cheese, and pepper.

   Spread the mixture evenly over the tart base, sprinkle on the sugar, and bake
in a medium oven for 40 minutes.

   Serve hot or cold.

Recommended wine: white, Roussette de Savoie, if eaten cold; if eaten hot as a starter,
whatever wine follows on the menu.

Lavaret à la Gelée de Seyssel
· WHITEFISH OR HOUTING IN WHITE WINE ASPIC ·

Whitefish (which is found under various names in Britain, gwyniad in Wales,
powan in Scotland, skelly in the Lake District) is rare in France, where it is
more or less confined to the lac du Bourget and the lac d'Aiguebelette. It is a
delicate fish which dies almost the moment it is taken out of the water, but it
has a correspondingly delicate flavour. The present recipe is also worth trying
with trout or salmon.

―――――――――――――― *Ingredients for 8* ――――――――――――――

1 bottle still Seyssel or other dry
   white
20 g · ¾ oz coarse sea salt
a bouquet garni: 2 sprigs of thyme,
   3 sprigs of parsley, 1 celery stalk
2 carrots
100 g · 4 oz onions
1 sml tsp peppercorns

2 whitefish, 1.5–1.7 kg · 3–3¾ lb
   each
4 leaves of gelatine
1 lemon
1 sprig of tarragon
2 sprigs of parsley – flat-leaved if
   possible

Prepare a *court-bouillon*: simmer 2 lt (3½ pt) of water and all the wine in a fish-kettle, with the salt, bouquet, sliced carrots, peeled and quartered onions, and the peppercorns, for 20–30 minutes. Leave to cool.

Gut the fish via the gills. Leave the heads on and wash out the fish without cutting them open. There is no need to scale them.

Arrange the fish, head-to-tail, in the cold *court-bouillon*. Put on a medium heat and, as soon as it boils, reduce to a simmer. Cook for 8–10 minutes, depending on the size of the fish. Cool before taking out the fish and the carrots. Soak the gelatine in cold water.

Return the fish-kettle to a medium heat. Break up the softened gelatine into a bowl, mix in a little hot *court-bouillon*, and pour into the fish-kettle. Reduce until there is about 700–800 ml (1¼–1½ pt) of liquid.

Meanwhile, skin both fish and remove the backbone, trying not to spoil the shape of the fish or lose the head.

Strain the reduced *court-bouillon*. Pour half a ladleful into a cold serving dish, and tilt it to coat the bottom with the liquid. Peel the lemon down to the pulp, slice it thinly and remove the pips. Arrange the parsley and tarragon leaves and the rounds of carrots in the dish, pouring in enough of the slowly setting *court-bouillon* to keep everything in place.

Lay the fish in the dish, head to tail, about 2–3 cm (¾–1") apart; pour a coating of *court-bouillon* over each of them, ensuring they are quite covered. Arrange slices of lemon and more parsley and tarragon leaves and slices of carrots in the *court-bouillon* on top of the fish. This is tricky in practice. The vegetables and fish must be quite cold (but not frozen) and the *bouillon* on the point of setting. Refrigerate the fish and the remaining *court-bouillon*, and let set. Before serving, garnish the fish with the extra jelly, roughly chopped up.

Recommended wine: Seyssel (or what was used in the cooking).

Noix de Veau Aixoise
· TOPSIDE OF VEAL WITH CHESTNUTS ·

More economical and tender, if less elegant, than the noix, is the cushion (or sous-noix) or the flank. You can wrap the meat in thin rashers of bacon to stop it drying out during cooking. Accompanying vegetables are not really necessary.

———————————————— *Ingredients for 8* ————————————————

8 tender celery stalks
2 dozen sml young carrots
2 dozen sml turnips
2 dozen sml onions
thin rashers of bacon
1.5–2 kg · 3–4 lb topside of veal (see
    above), cut as a large steak

80 g · 3 oz butter
stock
salt, pepper
30–40 tinned peeled chestnuts
2 tbsp of white (Savoie) wine

Clean the celery, peel and wash the carrots and turnips, and peel the onions; leave them all whole.

Tie the bacon round the veal and brown it all over in half the butter, in a casserole. Take out the meat and pour away the fat.

Return the casserole to a low heat with the remaining butter and sauté all the vegetables in turn, until they are lightly browned all over.

Put the veal back, pour in enough stock to immerse the vegetables, and season, taking account of the stock. Cover and simmer very slowly for 1 hr, turning the meat over at halftime, and adding the drained chestnuts.

Discard the bacon, slice the meat, and arrange it on a serving dish surrounded by the vegetables. Pour the wine into the casserole, let it bubble once or twice, and turn the liquid into a sauceboat.

Recommended wine: red: vin de Savoie (Mondeuse).

Fricassée de Caïon
· PORK FRICASSÉE ·

This was a dish for the day the pig was killed, but can very well be made using pig's liver (as in this recipe) instead of blood for the liaison. It is worth trying for the unusual mixture of red and white wine.

––––––––––––––– *Ingredients for 4* –––––––––––––––

1 kg · 2 lb boned loin of pork, in 4
   cm · 1½" cubes, + the bones
2 tbsp oil
500 ml · 17 fl oz white wine
a bouquet garni: 2 sprigs of thyme,
   1 a bay leaf, 2 sprigs of parsley
2 onions
2 cloves

1 sml tsp of crushed peppercorns
flour
500 ml · 17 fl oz red wine
50 g · 2 oz butter
salt
200 g · 7 oz pig's liver
100 ml · 4 fl oz thick cream

Marinate the pork, for 24 hr, with the oil, the white wine, the bouquet, the peeled onions, cut into eighths and studded with the cloves, and the peppercorns, turning the meat over several times. Keep the bones, wrapped up, in the fridge.

Next day, take the meat out of the marinade, wipe it, and rub with flour. Pour the marinade, without straining, into a saucepan, add the red wine, and simmer for 15 minutes.

In a casserole, brown the pork all over in the butter on a medium flame. Reduce the heat and add the bones, the strained marinade, and salt, and simmer, covered, for 1½ hr, turning the joint over at halftime.

Put the liver through a blender and mix it with the cream.

Transfer the pork to a serving dish, discard the bones, and pour the cream and liver mixture into the sauce. Stir constantly for 5–6 minutes while the sauce simmers, check the seasoning, and strain over the meat.

Recommended wine: a good red Savoie.

Civet de Lièvre

A local dictum has it that 'un bon lièvre se mange au bout de fusil' – in other words, a hare should be eaten the day after it is shot, with just one night in a marinade. Once again there is the liaison of blood and cream dear to these mountain regions. Polenta (see next recipe) is thought to bring out the full flavour of the hare.

─────────────────────── *Ingredients for 8* ───────────────────────

1 hare + blood and liver
red wine vinegar
2 tbsp of oil
1 bottle of red (Mondeuse) wine
120 g · 4 oz onions
2 cloves
100 g · 3 oz carrots
2 cloves of garlic
a bouquet garni: 2 sprigs of winter savory (otherwise, thyme), 2

sprigs of wild thyme (if possible), 1 bay leaf, 2 sprigs of parsley
1 sml tsp of roughly crushed peppercorns
flour
150 g · 5 oz lean green streaky bacon
25 g · ¾ oz lard
salt, pepper
100 ml · 3 fl oz thick cream

Beat a few drops of vinegar into the blood to stop coagulation. Add the liver, cover, and refrigerate.

Cut the hare into pieces and pour over the oil and wine. Add a quarter of an onion, peeled and studded with the cloves, and the remaining three-quarters, chopped; then add the thinly sliced carrots, crushed garlic, bouquet, and peppercorns. Cover and leave in the bottom of the fridge to marinade overnight.

The next day, take the meat out of the marinade, dry it, and rub it in flour. Boil the marinade, with the flavourings, for 10 minutes.

Blanch the bacon (see p. 221), dice it finely, and soften slowly in the lard in a casserole.

Increasing the heat to medium, brown the hare with the rest of the onions, chopped. Reduce the heat and add the strained marinade and the carrots retrieved from the strainer. Cover and cook gently in the oven for 2 hr. Halfway through, turn everything over, and check the seasoning in salt and pepper – if the sauce seems to have reduced too quickly, add boiling water or, better still, stock.

When the hare is ready, put the liver and blood through a blender and mix in the cream. Arrange the hare pieces on a serving dish, and stir the cream mixture very gradually into the cooking juices. Continue stirring for 5–6 minutes, ensuring the sauce does not boil.

Strain over the meat.

Recommended wine: red: Mondeuse, Côtes du Rhône, or Corbières.

Polenta

Polenta is eaten with a *civet de lièvre* or a *fricassée de caïon* (see above), or with sausages (*diots*), cooked in white wine on a bed of vine shoots.

Ingredients for 8
---

400 g · 14 oz coarse polenta
salt
150 g · 5 oz butter

40 g · 1¹/₂ oz homemade
    breadcrumbs
300 g · 10 oz Beaufort or Gruyère

Bring 2 lt (3¹/₂ pt) of salted water to the boil. Sprinkle in the polenta and stir with a spatula until it thickens and the grains of flour soften.

Grease an oven dish with 30 g (1 oz) of butter, coat the bottom with breadcrumbs, and put a quarter of the polenta on top, followed by a quarter of the cheese, in slivers, dotted with 30 g of butter; continue with three further layers of polenta, cheese, and butter.

Bake in a medium oven for 15 minutes. Serve very hot.

Fidés

· VERMICELLI WITH AN ONION AND CHEESE SAUCE ·

Fidés are fat vermicelli, made locally, and owing their name to the method of cooking – *à la fide* – i.e. in a special cast-iron cocotte, made to fit the rings of a wood-burning cooker. They are eaten with a *civet*, roast pork, or sausages.

Ingredients for 4
---

100 g · 4 oz butter or lard, according
    to accompanying dish
80 g · 3 oz onions
400 g · 14 oz thick fresh vermicelli,
    or other fresh pasta

1 clove of garlic
1 lt · 1³/₄ pt stock
salt, pepper
grated Gruyère or Emmenthal

Melt the fat slowly in a thick pan and sauté the sliced onions and the pasta, stirring frequently.

When both pasta and onions have taken colour, add the crushed garlic, the stock, and salt and pepper, taking account of the strength of the stock. Leave to simmer gently, stirring fairly often, for about 20 minutes or until the pasta has absorbed the liquid.

Mix in the cheese and serve at once.

Recommended wine: depending on what the pasta is to accompany.

Biscuit de Savoie

Devised by the cook to Amédée VI, king of Savoy from 1373–83, on the occasion of a reception for the German suzerain, it is made in a special fluted mould, and is thus more of a cake than what we would call a biscuit. It goes well with a cream as a dessert.

4 eggs
100 g · 3½ oz castor sugar
7–8 g · ¼ oz vanilla sugar
50 g · 1¾ oz flour

50 g · 1¾ oz potato flour (*fécule*) or
   cornflour
25 g · ¾ oz butter
30 g · 1 oz granulated sugar

Separate the eggs. Add the castor and vanilla sugar to the yolks and cream until the mixture is pale and smooth.

Sift in all the flour, beating constantly, then fold in the stiffly beaten whites very carefully.

Butter a deep mould heavily, and coat with granulated sugar. Pour in the mixture which should not come more than two-thirds of the way up the tin as it will puff up during cooking.

Bake in a slow oven for 40 minutes. Test with a skewer or knife which should come out quite clean.

Leave until practically cold before unmoulding.

Recommended wine: a sparkling Seyssel.

Rézules de Poires

· PEAR TURNOVERS ·

Rézule is a local word for *rissole*, meaning patty or turnover. Traditional winter fare, from Christmas to mid-Lent, they are either baked or deep fried. The pears used in the past were Blossons, whose wood was highly prized for furniture-making.

2 kg · 4 lb cooking pears
400 g · 14 oz granulated sugar
½ stick of cinnamon
400 g · 14 oz puff pastry (see p. 224)

butter for greasing a baking tray
   or oil for deep frying
icing sugar to taste

Peel, quarter, and core the pears. Cook them very slowly in a casserole with the sugar, 400 ml (14 fl oz) of water, and the cinnamon, for 1½–2 hr, until the fruit is reduced to a thick purée. Uncover and leave to cool.

Roll out the pastry to 5 mm (⅕″), and cut out circles the size of a saucer. Place a spoonful of the purée on each piece so that the pastry can be folded over like a pasty.

Moisten the edges of the pastry with water, and using wet fingers, seal the turnovers carefully.

Cook either by placing the pasties on a greased tray and baking in a hot oven for 15 minutes or by plunging in hot oil, turning them over with a slotted spoon when they surface, and letting them brown for 6–8 minutes; drain.

Sprinkle with icing sugar and serve.

Recommended wine: a sparkling Seyssel or a white Savoie.

Beignets de Fleurs d'Acacia
· ACACIA BLOSSOM FRITTERS ·

Acacias grow on the sunny but arid slopes of Savoy, flowering during May and June.

————————————— *Ingredients for 4* —————————————

big bunches of acacia flowers
100 ml · 4 fl oz brandy or other *eau-de-vie* (e.g. pear, Calvados)

fritter batter using 125 g · 4 oz flour (see p. 223)
oil for deep frying
castor or icing sugar

Separate the flowers, tail them, and soak them in the *eau-de-vie* for 30 minutes.
Drain on absorbent paper.
Heat the oil in a deep fryer.
Coat the flowers lightly in the batter and, using a long-handled fork, take them out of the batter and drop them in the hot oil (watching that it doesn't splash) one by one. As each fritter surfaces, turn it over with a draining spoon, and as they brown, remove, and drain on kitchen roll.
Dust with sugar to serve.

Recommended wine: sparkling Seyssel or Savoie.

27

Sologne
ORLÉANAIS
Gâtinais · Beauce

All four regions brought together here have at some time come under the aegis of the Orléannais family. The town of Orléans, itself, grew up at the point on the Loire where the boatmen unloaded their cargoes of wine for dispatch, by road, to Paris. By this stage in the wine's journey, some had soured and was thus abandoned. This was the basis of Orléans' development as a centre of vinegar production, recognised by Charles VI in 1392 and by Henri III who created the Guild of Master Vinegar-Makers by letters patent in 1580. He also ratified Orléans as a town of mustard-makers, and so it remains, though it is only since 1941 that mustard seed has been grown locally rather than imported.

The cooking here lacks the solidity of regions of harsher climate and less varied resources. There are no *potées* to absorb the contents of the salting-tub. Even the *soupe de cochon beauceronne* is a mixed vegetable soup with just a piece of shoulder pork to earn it its name. When a meat soup is made, it is customary to drop a piece of liver into the broth to absorb the fat.

Although a *pot-au-feu* may include crow, it is not a region which often needs to fall back on such meagre pickings. Rivers, streams, canals, and the ponds of the misty Sologne are a fisherman's paradise with carp, pike, bleak, barbel, tench, black bass, and, in winter, when the ponds are drained, eels – all to be found in a *soupe de pecheurs*, with potatoes, leeks, and a little white wine.

The *charcuterie* is light: thus it is *andouilles* and *andouillettes* that compete at an annual fair at Jargeau; black puddings are made with softened onions and cream or, a speciality of the village of Pruniers, near Romorantin, with chestnuts. A *saucisse beauceronne* is in the shape of a disc so that it just covers the bottom of a frying pan.

The list of pâtés reads like a roll-call of the game that thrives in the woods, on the great Beauce plains (out of which Chartres springs so dramatically), and in the wetlands: the most notable are rabbit (from Beaugency), hare, thrush, lark, this last from Pithiviers, and *pâté de Chartres* which has had a chequered and not undisputed history. It was seemingly first a hare pâté, in the sixth century, though when it next appears in the records around 1763, it is made with a kind of golden plover, which itself disappeared; when the pâté was revived again, it was with partridge, enriched, latterly, with port and foie gras, in far from rustic fashion.

Larks are also served *en cocotte*, quail in vine leaves, and wild rabbit in aspic with prunes or in a gratin. Partridge is braised with cabbage, carrots, smoked bacon, and ham, hare is roasted with mustard, and venison cutlets are fried very quickly and eaten with a purée of vegetables. Almost every town has its own way of stuffing the wild duck taken from the ponds after 14 July.

Vegetables have always been available in profusion. Turnip-nosed chervil and Chinese artichokes (*crosnes* after the town, now near Orly airport, where they were first grown from tubers imported from China) are found among the more familiar plants. Asparagus has been grown here since the 1870s when a Charles Depezay from Sologne, garrisoned at Argenteuil, north west of Paris, found himself crouched for long hours in a sandy asparagus field and noticing the soil closely resembled that at home, took some plants back with him.

The region is rich in goat's cheese – Selles-sur-Cher Cendré, for example, which like Olivet, a blue-rinded cow's cheese, is coated with wood ash; Troo du Vendômois, Gien, Saint-Loup, to cite a few names.

Sweet dishes are based on plentiful honey and fruit, both cultivated and wild. Pithiviers' famous *pain d'épices*, which has been made for some thousand years, needs the honey, while Beaugency's *pâtes de fruits* make the best of the fruit. At Blois, the first greengage was served in the early sixteenth century at Louis XII's daughter's marriage to the future François I, and was named in her honour: *reine-claude*.

The commonest grape is Gris-Meunier, which produces reds, whites, and rosés of the same name. There are also Chevernys (the brief *appellation* replacing, regrettably, the more charming name, Mont-Près-Chambord-Cour-Cheverny), and white Sauvignons, first planted on the plateau of Oisly.

Soupe au Cresson Alénois
· POTATO AND CRESS SOUP ·

Alexandre Dumas called cress 'la plus saine des fines herbes'. In Provence, where it is known as *le nasitor*, it was used to flavour stuffed tomatoes.

───────────────── *Ingredients for 4* ─────────────────

250 g · 1/2 lb cress
75 g · 21/2 oz butter
400 g · 14 oz potatoes

salt, pepper
150 ml · 1/4 pt thick cream
7–8 sprigs of chervil

Wash and snip the cress (using scissors stops the plant oils escaping), and toss for a few seconds in a saucepan with 25 g (3/4 oz) of butter, on a low heat.

Add the peeled, washed, and finely diced potatoes; season with salt and pepper, and pour in 1 lt (13/4 pt) of cold water. Simmer for 20 minutes.

Off the heat, beat in the cream and remaining butter.

Serve directly into individual soup bowls, and sprinkle with the chervil leaves.

Recommended wine: the one to follow on the table.

Coulemelles Grillés
· GRILLED PARASOL MUSHROOMS WITH HERB BUTTER ·

In damp autumn Sologne, parasol mushrooms grow abundantly under the broom – and make a perfect accompaniment to the wild rabbit of the region (see below). Other mushrooms can be treated in the same way.

───────────────── *Ingredients for 4* ─────────────────

12–16 (parasol) mushrooms
1 shallot
8 sprigs of parsley

8 sprigs of chervil
100 g · 4 oz butter
salt, pepper

Discard the mushroom stalks. Wipe the tops with a cloth rough enough to remove the scales, but don't wash.

Work the very finely chopped shallot, parsley, and chervil into the butter, plus a little salt (depending on the saltiness of the butter, French butter is more often unsalted) and pepper.

Put a knob of butter in each mushroom top and place under a hot grill for 4–5 minutes or until lightly browned.

Serve the mushrooms in a hot dish, dotted with the remaining herb butter.

Recommended wine: white Sancerre.

Boulettes des Mariniers
· BEEF AND PORK CROQUETTES ·

This would never have been served at a meal, rather as reviving early morning sustenance for the river boatmen.

──────────────── *Ingredients for 4* ────────────────

350 g · 12 oz good fat pork belly
20 g · ³/₄ oz lard
500 g · 1 lb braising beef, in the piece
4 onions
2 cloves of garlic

5–6 sprigs of parsley
salt, pepper
2 tbsp brandy
100 ml · 3 fl oz red wine
1 egg

Finely dice 100 g (3¹/₂ oz) of the pork belly and soften gently in a thick pan with the lard.

Mince together the beef, onions, garlic, parsley, and remaining pork, medium fine. Season with salt and pepper and add the brandy, wine, and egg. Blend the ingredients together well.

Make the mixture into egg-sized croquettes and cook for 1¹/₂–1³/₄ hr in the pan with the diced pork. The pan must be tightly sealed so that no steam can escape. Shake from time to time.

Serve hot or cold.

Recommended wine: Sauvignon de Loire, red Côtes de Gien, or any Gamay de Loire.

Pot-au-Feu du Braconnier
· POACHER'S RABBIT ·

Should a gamekeeper appear just as the meal was being prepared, he would find nothing to arouse his suspicions since the poacher would have carefully submerged the evidence . . . under a mass of vegetables.

──────────────── *Ingredients for 4* ────────────────

250 g · 9 oz green lean streaky bacon
– in the piece if possible
1 wild rabbit + liver
400 g · 14 oz leeks
200 g · 7 oz carrots
100 g · 4 oz turnips
a bouquet garni: 1 bay leaf,

2 sprigs of thyme, 2 sprigs of
parsley, 1 celery stalk
1 onion
2 cloves
6 cloves of garlic
salt, pepper
200 g · 7 oz slightly stale bread

Blanch the bacon (see p. 221). Set aside the liver.

Bring the rabbit and the blanched bacon slowly to the boil in a casserole, with cold water to cover by about 2 cm (³/₄″), skimming.

When it boils, add the leeks, carrots, and turnips, washed and trimmed or scraped but left whole, the bouquet, the peeled onion studded with the cloves, and the peeled garlic. Season with salt and pepper, cover, and simmer for 40 minutes.

Add the liver and cook the stew another 5 minutes.

Cut the bread in thin strips into a tureen.

Cut up the rabbit and bacon, slice the liver, and arrange on a serving dish, surrounded by the vegetables. Strain the stock, which will not be fatty, into the tureen, and serve as soup.

Recommended wine: a Gris-Meunier.

Pommes de Terres Solognotes

These are eaten locally with rabbit, hare, or a leg of mutton, but they are good on their own with a green salad.

———————————————— *Ingredients for 4* ————————————————

1 lt · 1³/₄ pt milk
1 sprig of tarragon
1 sprig of thyme
¹/₄ bay leaf
1–2 other fresh herbs – whatever is
   to hand
5 peppercorns

1 kg · 2 lb potatoes
1–2 cloves of garlic
30 g · 1 oz butter
250 ml · 8 fl oz thick cream
salt, pepper
75 g · 2¹/₂ oz grated Gruyère

Bring the milk to the boil with the tarragon leaves, 3–4 thyme leaves, the bay leaf, the leaves of the other herbs, and the peppercorns. Reduce the heat immediately it bubbles, and simmer for 10 minutes. Strain the milk into a bowl.

Peel and wash the potatoes and slice thinly. Leave in the milk, covered, for 30 minutes.

Peel and cut the garlic in two, and rub the inside of a charlotte mould with the cut side. Butter it generously. Drain and wipe the potatoes and arrange them slightly overlapping in the mould, each layer alternating with a little cream and salt and pepper. Finish up with the remaining cream, and put the rest of the sprig of thyme on top. Cover.

Bake in a medium oven for 30 minutes.

Remove from the oven, sprinkle with grated cheese, and return to the oven without covering for 15 minutes.

Recommended wine: a Sauvignon de Loire, if eaten on their own or with a salad, otherwise depending on the other dishes.

Tarte Tatin

If this was not originally a dish from the *terroir* (but rather from the kitchen of
Fanny Tatin in her hotel opposite the station in Lamotte-Beuvron towards the
end of the last century), it has certainly become one – not surprisingly as it
ensures lovely crisp pastry underneath the apple. That pastry should not be
puff pastry, a modern affectation. Coxes are the best apples when making this
in the British Isles, Reinettes in France – apples which are both firm and tender.
A *tarte tatin* mould is made of tinned copper and is some 5 cm (2″) deep, but a
sandwich tin or a shallow oven-proof glass dish will do.

--------------------------- *Ingredients for 4* ---------------------------

160 g · 5 oz castor sugar   2 kg · 4 lb eating apples – see above
2 pinches of cinnamon powder   200 g · 8 oz fine shortcrust pastry
160 g · 5 oz butter   (see p. 224)

Mix the sugar and cinnamon together.
   Butter the mould with a quarter of the butter and dust it evenly with a quarter
of the sugar.
   Peel and core the apples and cut them into approximately 3 mm (1/8″) slices,
or just into eighths as the slices shouldn't be too thin. Arrange a third of them
in the base of the mould and sprinkle with a quarter of the sugar and dot with
a quarter of the butter, cover with another third of the apples, and another
quarter of the sugar and butter, finish with the remaining apples, sugar, and
butter.
   Roll out the pastry to 3 mm (1/8″) and cut it to the diameter of the mould *plus*
twice its depth, so that, once centred carefully on the apple, the edge can be
turned down between the apple and the inside of the mould (to form the border
of the eventual tart). Make several small holes in the pastry to allow the steam
to escape.
   Bake in a medium oven for 45 minutes. Wait 5–6 minutes before turning it
over on to the pastry, but don't unmould until it has cooled a little.
   Serve warm for preference.

Recommended wine: a Coteaux de Layon.

Feuilleté aux Amandes ou Pithiviers
· PITHIVIERS PIE ·

An ancient recipe which has become a classic of French *pâtisserie*.

--------------------------- *Ingredients for 8* ---------------------------

250 g · 9 oz ground almonds   200 g · 7 oz butter
4 eggs   2–4 tbsp dark rum (to taste)
250 g · 9 oz castor sugar   800 g · 1 3/4 lb puff pastry (see p. 224)
7–8 g · 1/4 oz vanilla sugar

Mix together the ground almonds and separated egg whites; beat hard, working
in the castor and vanilla sugar, until the mixture is smooth and creamy, every

grain of sugar dissolved. Add the softened (but not melted) butter and the rum.

Divide the puff pastry into two equal portions. Roll one into a round about 3 mm (1/8″) thick and place it on a buttered baking tray; roll out the second portion slightly thinner and therefore larger. Spread the filling evenly over the centre of the base, leaving about 2 cm (3/4″) of pastry uncovered all round. Brush this edge with a beaten yolk.

Quickly position the second piece of pastry on top. Don't press the two pieces together or it will not puff up – if you have worked quickly the egg yolk should hold the top and bottom together.

With the back of a small knife, nick the edge every 2 or 3 cm (1–1½″) round the perimeter, turning it up to make a scalloped border.

Using a pointed knife, make a pattern on the dome, dividing it into eight equal wedges, then crossing these lines with circular lines, parallel to the edge.

Dilute the last three egg yolks with a little water and brush the entire surface of the pie.

Bake in a hot oven for 10 minutes, then reduce to medium for a further 20 minutes.

Let it cool before serving.

Recommended wine: a Crémant de Loire.

28
TOURAINE

Made up of a single department, the Indre-et-Loire, in the shape of a vine leaf, Touraine is the seat of the best-spoken, clearest, most traditional French. It has a gentle climate, propitious to fruit-farming and market gardening. The cooking is clear and gentle too, and the frequent presence of prunes has less to do with a liking for a combination of sweet and sour, than using the local product – now unfortunately just a memory – to enhance the dishes' smoothness.

The province's speciality is rillettes (see also p. 19); here they are made exclusively of pork. Although known as *rillettes de Tours*, it is those from Vouvray that have given them their reputation: supposedly without any addition other than salt, they may, some locals hint, receive a drop or two of Vouvray before they are stirred. Preparing the rillettes was a family affair: a good quarter of a pig was needed, and it had patiently to be separated into fat, bone, and lean, the first to be roughly chopped, the second lightly crushed, and the third cut into long strips along the grain. Everything was then layered in order in a large cast-iron stock-pot with salt, and was left to cook slowly and undisturbed until the meat was tinged with colour when it was stirred once to mix fat and lean together and the bones were removed. Good rillettes are expected to have a very fine texture and a 'singed' pinkish look; and the covering fat must be white as white.

Touraine cookery may be simple but it always uses its wine to effect. Vouvray and prunes give flavour to fish stews; lamprey used to be cooked with prunes and Chinon. Rabbit, after a diet of good grass, pink clover, and dandelion (and *never* cabbage) is semi-roasted and then simmered in Chinon. Hare is also prepared with Chinon.

Vegetables, other than root ones, are particularly enjoyed, cardoons, globe artichokes, green beans, celery, peas, asparagus, cultivated mushrooms. Cos lettuce, like the little hedgerow snails, marries especially well with the walnut oil of Saint-Maure. Also from Saint-Maure come tall moulded goat's cheeses. The moulds are pottery or tin, and are in conical form for Ligueil cheeses and pyramidal for Loches ones. The cheeses of Saint-Maure and Ligueil are distinguished by a piece of straw running through each one; this helps the cheese solidify and eases handling.

Puddings and pastries are often based on bread or brioche dough: *le cordé* is a milk loaf made in the form of 'ropes' which can be detached individually as required; *la rotie* (also found in neighbouring provinces) is bread cut in tiny pieces into hot wine sweetened with honey; *la galette à l'écume de beurre* is made from the foam left by clarifying butter; *la cassemuse* is brioche dough mixed with *fromage frais* and fruit. If *fouaces* or *fougaces* are found elsewhere, it is nonetheless those of the Touraine village of Lerne, where the old ovens were hewn out of the rock some nine hundred years ago, that were, thanks to Rabelais (himself a Tourangeau), the most famous: *fouaces* were the cause of the central quarrel in *Gargantua*. Having almost disappeared earlier this century, these small flat saffron-flavoured loaves are now being made again.

Fruit is plentiful, even if the plums are no longer grown for prunes, for which the St-Catherine and Petit Damas varieties were so well suited. There are still large greengages, and a special kind of peach, the Alberge.

The Touraine wines stored in their cellars cut out of the chalky yellow rock need little introduction. Not so well-known are some of the small *appellations*: the Bourgueils and St-Nicolas de Bourgueil, for instance, whose distinctive taste comes from the gravelly soil; Chinon which is red with a taste of violet; and the Montlouis whites which may be dry, semi-dry, even sweet in the hot years.

Soupe Tourangelle
· SUMMER VEGETABLE SOUP ·

The bacon brings out the flavour of the vegetables.

———————————————— *Ingredients for 8* ————————————————

500 g · 1 lb lean green streaky bacon
    – best in the piece
1 sml cabbage
vinegar
500 g · 1 lb leeks – as white as
    possible (not always easy when
    peas are in season)

350 g · 12 oz turnips
50 g ·1¾ oz butter
3 lt · 5 pt chicken stock
1.5 kg · 3 lb peas – unshelled weight
salt, pepper
thin slices of stale bread

Blanch the bacon (see p. 221).
    Discard the outside cabbage leaves, cut the heart into eight, remove the main stalks, and wash in acidulated water. Cover with cold water, bring slowly to the boil, and drain.
    Cut away all but 2–3 cm (1″) of the green part of the leeks, and wash and slice the white thinly. Clean and dice the turnips. Soften the leeks and turnips in a casserole, in the butter, gently, for 10 minutes, turning them over frequently.
    Add the cabbage, the bacon in 2 cm (¾″) cubes, and the well-skimmed chicken stock. Leave to simmer, covered, for 1 hr.
    Shell the peas meanwhile.
    When the soup is ready, taste for seasoning and add the peas; simmer a further 20 minutes.
    Pour over the bread.

Recommended wine: a mellow Montlouis or Vouvray.

Salade Tourangelle

Not a mixed salad tossed in a single dressing, but an assortment of vegetables, raw and cooked, separately dressed, and served on the same dish.

———————————————— *Ingredients for 4* ————————————————

PROPORTIONS FOR THE VINAIGRETTE
1 tbsp wine vinegar, with a little salt
    dissolved in it, to 3 tbsp of oil,
    including 1 of walnut oil
freshly milled pepper

400 g · 14 oz asparagus tips, cooked
2 sml shallots
3 sprigs of parsley
4 cooked artichoke hearts
½ sml tsp mustard

3–4 tarragon leaves
400 g · 14 oz dwarf green beans,
    cooked
4–5 stalks of celery
1 lemon
400 g · 14 oz sml field or cultivated
    mushrooms
2 tbsp of thick cream
3–4 sprigs of chervil
walnut kernels
bread for toast

Dress the asparagus with one finely chopped shallot and sprig of parsley, and a little vinaigrette.

Slice the artichoke hearts, mix the mustard into an appropriate quantity of vinaigrette, toss the artichokes in it, and snip in the tarragon.

Prepare the beans like the asparagus but with double the amount of parsley.

Slice the celery across, stringing it as necessary, and simply squeeze the juice of a quarter of a lemon over it.

Clean and slice the mushrooms, and quickly pour on the cream; season with salt and pepper, and lemon juice. Sprinkle with chervil leaves.

Arrange each of the salads around the edge of a dish. In the middle make a pyramid of walnuts. Serve with toast.

Recommended drink: water goes better than wine.

Anguilles à la Mode de Chenonceaux

——————————— *Ingredients for 4* ———————————

1 kg · 2 lb sml eels
200 g · 7 oz mixed fresh herbs (e.g.
  chervil, parsley, winter savory,
  lemon balm, mint, sage, sorrel)
100 g · 3½ oz butter

salt, pepper
white wine
6 egg yolks
3 tbsp vinegar or lemon juice

Take off the heads, gut, clean, and skin the eel, and cut into sections.

Put all the herbs, finely chopped, and half the butter in a large frying pan or sauteuse. Arrange the eel on top with salt and pepper. Sweat gently, with a lid on, for 7–8 minutes.

Pour in 125 ml (4 fl oz) of water and enough wine just to cover. Leave to bubble without a lid, on a high flame, for 5–8 minutes.

Meanwhile, beat the egg yolks with the vinegar or lemon juice, plus 3 tablespoons of cold water.

When the eel is ready, remove from the heat, and, shaking the pan hard, add the remaining butter in knobs, then, very slowly, the egg yolk mixture.

Serve hot, warm, or cold.

Recommended wine: Touraine or Montlouis.

Andouillette Vouvrillonne

Andouillettes de Vouvray are long sausages, which, should you ever get hold of any, take better to cooking in the oven – either roasted, braised, or stewed – than to grilling.

——————————— *Ingredients for 4* ———————————

4 *andouillettes de Vouvray*
100 ml · 4 fl oz brandy
100 g · 4 oz onions
200 g · 7 oz field or cultivated
  mushrooms

80 g · 2½ oz butter
dry still Vouvray
salt, pepper

Prick the sausages two or three times and put them with the brandy in a dish in which they fit closely; leave for 24 hr, turning them over occasionally.

Chop the onions and cleaned mushrooms, and strew them in the bottom of a buttered oven-proof dish which will also hold the sausages tightly. Pour in wine just to cover, and season with salt and pepper.

Arrange the sausages side by side on top of the onions and mushrooms and dot with the remaining butter. Cook in a low oven for 30 minutes, turning them over after 20, then increase the heat to medium and leave another 10–15 minutes, depending on the size of the sausages (if, when you turn them over, the vegetables seem too dry, add some more wine, brought to boiling point).

To serve, pour the onion and mushroom mixture over the sausages. Taste for seasoning.

Recommended wine: a Vouvray Cru.

Géline Lochoise
· BRAISED CHICKEN FROM LOCHE ·

Géline is old French for a spring chicken. In this traditional recipe, the chicken is poached prior to braising, and it is a point of honour that the meat should stay quite white. If you can get a corn-fed chicken, so much the better.

——————————— *Ingredients for 4* ———————————

1 young chicken c. 1.5 kg · 3 lb
200 g · 7 oz onions
50 g · 1¾ oz butter
200 ml · 7 fl oz milk
salt, pepper

a bouquet garni: 1 sprig of thyme,
   ¼ bay leaf, 1 sprig of parsley
200 ml · 7 fl oz chicken stock
200 ml · 7 fl oz thick cream

Put the chicken in a casserole with cold water to cover. Bring slowly to the boil and drain.

Meanwhile, on a low heat, in another casserole, toss the sliced onions in the butter so that they are well coated in it, but not browned. Pour in the milk and cook quite hard for 4–5 minutes.

Season inside the chicken with salt and pepper, and put it in the milk and onions, along with the bouquet and stock. Cover the casserole, and cook slowly for 50–60 minutes, turning the bird over halfway through.

Transfer the chicken to a serving dish and keep hot. Remove the bouquet and strain the cooking liquid, pressing the onion through the sieve. Add the cream, return to a low heat, and reduce by a third.

Cut up the chicken and coat with the sauce, having checked the seasoning.

Recommended wine: a mellow Montlouis or Vouvray.

Matelote des Tonneliers
· VEAL CASSEROLE ·

Matelote means cooked in wine. The *tonneliers* were the men who transported the wine on the Loire.

────────────────── *Ingredients for 4* ──────────────────

600 g · 1¼ lb shoulder veal
600 g · 1¼ lb veal flank
2 doz sml onions
200 g · 7 oz carrots
100 g · 4 oz butter
1 tbsp of flour

300 ml · ½ pt Bourgueil or possibly
   a Beaujolais
a bouquet garni: 2 sprigs of thyme,
   1 bay leaf, 2 sprigs of parsley, 1
   or 2 other fresh herbs
salt, pepper

Cut the shoulder veal into 4 cm (1½") cubes and the flank along the line of the cartilage. Bring to the boil, covered in cold water, and drain immediately.

Toss the onions, preferably left whole, and the carrots, diced, in a large frying pan or sauteuse, in half the butter for 10–12 minutes, on a low heat. Sprinkle in the flour and stir for two or three minutes before adding the wine and the bouquet. Bring to the boil and season with salt and pepper.

Add the veal to the pan and simmer for an hour, covered, turning the meat over at halftime.

Discard the bouquet and, off the heat, taste for seasoning and stir in the remaining butter, in small pieces.

Recommended wine: Bourgueil.

Noisettes de Porc aux Pruneaux
· FORELOIN OF PORK WITH PRUNES ·

Tours prunes were popular Paris fare in the sixteenth century, especially during Lent. They came from the plums of the wooded Touraine plateaux. Plums destined to be dried must be picked before sunrise.

────────────────── *Ingredients for 4* ──────────────────

200 g · 7 oz prunes
300 ml · ½ pt Vouvray or other Loire
   white
800 g · 1¾ lb boned foreloin of pork,
   cut into 8 slices

salt, pepper
flour
50 g · 1¾ oz butter
100 ml · 3½ fl oz thick cream
1 tbsp of redcurrant jelly

Simmer the prunes gently in the wine, covered, for 20 minutes.

Rub the pieces of pork with salt and pepper, and flour to dry them.

Sauté in a frying pan, in the butter, on a medium heat, two minutes a side, then reduce the heat and cook a further 4–8 minutes a side. Transfer to a hot dish.

Extract the prunes with a draining spoon, stone them, and arrange on top of the pork. Pour their cooking liquid into the pork juices, together with the cream, and reduce for 3–4 minutes; adjust the seasoning. Away from the heat, stir in the redcurrant jelly and pour over the meat.

Recommended wine: Touraine, Montlouis, Bourgueil, or Chinon.

Fèves à la Tourangelle

Broad beans are very popular in the Touraine and are often just eaten with thin slices of bread dunked in walnut oil.

———————————— *Ingredients for 4* ————————————

2 kg · 4 lb broad beans in the pod
200 g · 7 oz lean uncooked ham or
 gammon
2 dozen sml white new onions
 or lge spring onions

20 g · ³/₄ oz butter
salt, pepper
2 eggs
4–6 sprigs of chervil

Shell the beans, cook them in boiling water for 20 minutes, and drain, saving some of the cooking liquid. Peel off the outer skins.

Dice the ham and soften it with the whole onions in the butter, shaking the pan now and then, for 15 minutes (or less for spring onions). Add bean water just to cover, the beans themselves, and salt, taking account of the saltiness of the ham, and pepper. Cook for 2–3 minutes.

Beat the eggs, and continue beating gradually adding a few spoonfuls of the cooking juices. Off the heat, trickle the egg very slowly into the beans, stirring hard; do not reheat.

Scatter the chervil leaves over it.

Recommended wine: depends on what the beans are accompanying.

Bijane aux Fraises
· STRAWBERRIES WITH CHINON AND BREAD ·

A *bijane* is a cold sweet soup of bread, red wine, and sugar; it comes from Anjou. This is a tricky recipe not readily adaptable to English bread or to other wine.

———————————— *Ingredients for 4* ————————————

pain de campagne to taste
1 bottle Chinon

castor sugar
1 kg · 2 lb strawberries

Slice the bread, dry it out completely in the oven, without letting it brown. Break it up in small pieces into a salad bowl.

Add the wine, and sugar to taste.

Wash and hull the strawberries, drain them on absorbent paper. Leave the small ones whole, cut up the large ones, and mix them into the bread and wine. Cover and refrigerate for several hours before serving.

Recommended wine: Chinon, if wine is essential.

APPENDIX OF BASIC RECIPES

BÉCHAMEL SAUCE

A béchamel sauce is based on a white roux, i.e. one that has not been allowed to brown. Further cooking will make first a blond roux (for a velouté sauce) then a brown roux.

―――――――――――――― *For 500 ml · 17 fl oz* ――――――――――――――

Melt 50 g (1³/₄ oz) of butter slowly in a thick pan, add an equal quantity of flour, and stir until the mixture is well blended.

Pour in 500 ml (17 fl oz) of warmed milk, and stir constantly, ensuring that nothing is sticking, for 10 minutes, to cook the flour.

Season to taste or to need with salt, pepper, and nutmeg.

VARIATIONS: A creamy béchamel: replace a part of the milk with single cream.
Sauce crème: add some double cream, off the heat.
Sauce mornay (Cheese sauce): away from the heat, bind the béchamel with an egg yolk, and add grated cheese (Emmenthal is less cloying than Cheddar).
Sauce soubise (Onion sauce): soften the onions in butter and strain them into the béchamel.

BEURRE D'ÉCREVISSE OU DE CREVETTE·CRAYFISH OR SHRIMP BUTTER

Prepared with crayfish or shrimp shells, the heads sometimes added too. Prawns or lobster may also be used, and the butter is named accordingly. When a mixture of shellfish is used, it is called *beurre rouge*.

Grind the shells finely or put them through a blender, then weigh them.

Soften in a bain-marie with an equal weight of butter, stirring.

With a pestle, press the mixture through a fine sieve into a container of iced water.

Retrieve the hardened butter as it surfaces.

BLANC POUR CUISSONS

A *blanc* is a special *court-bouillon*, its function to keep offal (tongue, etc.) a good colour or to stop vegetables (e.g. cardoons, artichoke hearts, salsifis) discolouring from exposure, once peeled. The mixture of flour and lemon conserves and even accentuates the colour while the fat that is added, being lighter than water, floats to the surface and forms a layer impervious to air. The flour must be cooked first or it will stay at the bottom of the pan and stick.

―――――――――――――― *For 3 lt · 5 pt* ――――――――――――――

Mix 100 g (3¹/₂ oz) of flour with the juice of 2 lemons and 200 ml (7 fl oz) of water, in a saucepan. Heat slowly, stirring almost constantly, scraping the bottom of the pan clean, until the mixture is smooth and thick.

Pour into the cooking pot and mix in 2.5 lt (4 pt) of cold water.

Add 100 ml (3¹/₂ fl oz) of oil or 100 g (3¹/₂ oz) of lard.

BLANCHIR · BLANCHING

The purpose of blanching is: to eliminate either a natural acridity or smell (cabbage) or saltiness owing to conservation (bacon); to make a vegetable more supple so it can be used to wrap round an ingredient or a stuffing; or to prepare a vegetable for conserving or freezing. In the latter cases, blanching helps retain the vegetable's flavour and colour.

To eliminate acridity and saltiness

Put the salted meat or prepared and washed vegetable in a pan and cover it in plenty of water.

Bring the water very slowly to simmering point: the acridity or saltiness is dissolved by long slow heating; if the temperature increases too fast, it will seal in the very elements to be expelled. For a vegetable, draining it as soon as it comes to the boil will usually be enough, while a large piece of salted meat can be left to simmer between 5 and 10 minutes depending on size.

To soften vegetables or prepare them for conserving

Boil the water first (salt may be added if the vegetable is going to be conserved).

Immerse the vegetable as soon as the water boils, and drain the moment it comes back to the boil.

Immediately run it under cold water to revive its colour and to stiffen it up again.

CRÈME ANGLAISE · EGG CUSTARD

The large quantity of eggs will give the custard a good coating consistency. Sometimes the addition of a split vanilla pod is recommended to improve the flavour, but as this gives the custard a bespattered look, it is not advisable if appearance is important. Flavourings may be varied (coffee, caramel, chocolate, tea, etc), but whatever is used it must be either melted or infused in the cooling milk or dissolved in another liquid. If another liquid is being added, the amount of milk should be correspondingly reduced.

For 1 lt · 1 ³/₄ pt of milk

Bring the milk to the boil with the vanilla pod (if that is the chosen flavouring); let it cool.

Cream together 12 egg yolks with 200 g (7 oz) of castor sugar until the mixture forms the ribbon, i.e. is smooth and pale, the sugar completely dissolved.

Discard the vanilla pod, and beat the cooled milk into the mixture, a little at a time.

Transfer the mixture to a saucepan and allow to thicken on a low heat, beating constantly, and scraping the bottom clean, until it starts to simmer. Remove from the heat before it boils.

Strain through a sieve.

CRÈME FRAÎCHE

Proportions are: one part buttermilk or sour cream to two parts double cream. Stir together over a low heat. When the mixture is lukewarm, not more, remove from the heat and leave to stand in a warm place for 5–8 hr or until it has thickened on top but is still liquid underneath. Stir, cover, and refrigerate. *Crème fraîche* will keep for a week or so, and can be used instead of the buttermilk to make a further amount.

CRÈME PÂTISSIÈRE

Crème pâtissière is used mainly in fruit tarts.

———————————— *For 500 ml · 17 fl oz of milk* ————————————

Bring the milk to the boil with the vanilla pod; leave to cool.

Cream 4 egg yolks with 125 g (4 oz) of castor sugar until it forms the ribbon – as for *crème anglaise* – and sprinkle in 60 g (2 oz) of flour, beating constantly.

Remove the vanilla pod and add the milk very slowly, still beating.

In a saucepan, stir the mixture over a low heat, ensuring it is not sticking, for 8–10 minutes to cook the flour (whose presence stops the mixture turning).

Continue beating off the heat, until it is virtually cold and quite smooth.

DESSALER LA MORUE · TO DESALINATE SALT COD

Since even a large quantity of water will become quickly saturated with salt, running water is more effective.

Put the salt cod in a colander: if it's in the piece, have the skinside uppermost so that it doesn't prevent the salty water flowing away.

Stand the colander under cold running water for 12 hr for fillets, 24 for a whole piece (if the sound of running water irritates you, tie a cloth to the tap and drape it into the colander, and the water will flow silently along it).

NAGE · COURT-BOUILLON

A concentrated stock. A fish, *à la nage*, is served in it with all its vegetables.

———————————— *Ingredients for fish for 4* ————————————

Put 2 cleaned, washed, and sliced white leeks, and 2 carrots and a celery stalk, cut into julienne strips, into a large frying pan or sauteuse, along with a bouquet (2 sprigs of thyme, 1/2 bay leaf, and 2 sprigs of parsley), a medium onion, peeled, quartered, and stuck with 1 or 2 cloves, half a bottle of white wine, and 2 lt (3½ pt) of water.

Reduce it, uncovered, on a medium heat, until the carrots begin to soften; season with salt and pepper.

Cook the fish in the stock; when it is ready, transfer to a hot dish.

Discard the onion and bouquet, and reduce to about 1 lt (1¾ pt).

Pour on to the fish, possibly adding other fresh herbs, snipped or chopped, the mixture of herbs being varied, like the *nage* itself, according to the main recipe.

Serve very hot unless required otherwise by main recipe.

NAVETS SALÉS · SALTED TURNIPS

Layer 1.5 kg (3 lb) of finely shredded turnips with 15 g (½ oz) of coarse salt, some 40 juniper berries, and 30 peppercorns interspersed, in a non-metallic container. Cover with a cloth and press down with a plate and a weight. Leave for 24 hr in a cool place

PÂTE À BEIGNETS, PÂTE À FRIRE · FRITTER BATTER, FRYING BATTER

Fritter or frying batter needs to be thin enough to coat but thick enough to adhere to whatever is to be fried, which must itself be very dry, possibly having been rubbed with flour to make it so.

────────── For a batch of fritters for 4 ──────────

Make a well in 125 g (4 oz) of flour and mix in 1 egg yolk, 1 sml tsp of oil, a pinch of salt, ½ sachet dried yeast, followed by, a little at a time, 100–150 ml (⅙–¼ pt) of water, the amount depending on the quality of the flour.

When you are about to use it, fold in a stiffly beaten egg white to make it lighter.

VARIATIONS: Replace the yeast with 2 tablespoons of good lager and allow to stand for 2 hr.
Replace the water with milk. This will make the batter heavier, as will enrichment with egg.
Savoury batters can be flavoured with curry powder, pepper, or saffron, for example; sweet ones with brandy or orange flower water – avoid adding sugar or anything heavily sweetened, like liqueurs, because the sugar will make the batter burn.

PÂTE À BRIOCHE · BRIOCHE DOUGH

Brioche dough may be made with butter, vegetable fat, lard, or other fat, and may be more or less rich in either fat or eggs. But, whatever the proportions, the method is always the same: the yeast is prepared; the basic dough is prepared; the fat and then the yeast are incorporated into the dough; the dough is kneaded.

Pâte à brioche fine · Fine brioche dough

────────── For 500 g · 17 oz of flour ──────────

Dissolve 20 g (¾ oz) of fresh yeast in 75 ml (⅛ pt) of warm water; stir it into 100 g (3½ oz) of flour to make a very sloppy mixture; cover the bowl with a damp cloth and leave to double in volume.

Make a well in the rest of the flour in a bowl; mix in 6 eggs, one by one, 10 g (⅓ oz) of castor sugar (even for a savoury brioche – it helps fermentation of the yeast).

Work in the yeast mixture; let the dough rest for 10–15 minutes before incorporating 300 g (10 oz) of softened butter; shape the dough into a ball, cover the bowl with a damp cloth, and leave to double in volume.

Knead the dough with floured hands on a very lightly floured board, folding it in on itself several times;

make back into a ball and leave another 2–3 hr under a damp cloth or wrap and refrigerate until next day.

If wanting a lard-based brioche dough (*pâte à brioche fine au saindoux*), used mainly for pork dishes, proceed as above, replacing all the butter with lard.

Pâte à brioche allégée ou pâte levée pâtissière ou pâte briochée · Light brioche dough

——————————— *For 500 g · 17 oz of flour* ———————————

Make a well in the flour, and put into it 10 g (¹/₃ oz) salt, 50 g (1³/₄ oz) castor sugar, 2–3 eggs, 20 g (³/₄ oz) fresh baker's yeast, dissolved in 200 ml (7 fl oz) of milk. Mix these together, very gradually incorporating the flour.

When the dough is well blended, knead it by hand; this lightens it by working in air.

Continue kneading, incorporating 150 g (5 oz) of fat (butter, vegetable fat, or lard); make into a ball, cover with a damp cloth, leave to stand for 2–3 hr.

PÂTE BRISÉE · SHORTCRUST PASTRY

The classic pastry for sweet or savoury tarts.

——————————— *For 500 g · 17 oz of flour* ———————————

Make a well in the flour and pour in 50 g (1³/₄ oz) of icing sugar (if sweet pastry required) and 200 g (7 oz) of softened butter; using your finger tips, rub the butter into the flour until you have a powdery mixture.

Make a well in it and add 1 egg and 2 tbsp of water in which 10 g (¹/₃ oz) of salt have been dissolved; mix everything together very gradually.

Knead the dough by taking a spoonful at a time and pressing it flat with the heel of your hand; collect the dough up and make into a ball, and leave for 2 hr in a bowl covered with a damp cloth so that the dough loses its elasticity.

To enrich it (*pâte brisée fine ou enrichie*), add a second egg and 50 g (1³/₄ oz) of butter.

PÂTE FEUILLETÉE · PUFF PASTRY

——————————— *For 500 g · 17 oz of flour* ———————————

Make a well in the flour, add, little by little, 250–300 ml (8–10 fl oz) of water (depending on the flour), in which 10 g (¹/₃ oz) of salt have been dissolved; when the dough is smooth, make a ball, without kneading too much. Leave for 1 hr in a bowl, covered with a damp cloth, for it to lose its elasticity.

Roll out the dough on a lightly floured board (too much flour will change the composition of the dough) to a square about 1 cm (³/₈″) thick; take

350 g (12 oz) of softened butter or vegetable fat and work it by hand to make it more malleable and shape it too into a 1 cm (³/₈″) thick square; place it diagonally on top of the dough; fold the four exposed corners of dough over the fat so that they meet and the fat is completely encased.

Roll it into a rectangle away from you, three times longer than its width; keeping the short side of the rectangle nearest you, fold it in three, like a letter, so it forms a square again; turn the square once, so that one of the folded sides is nearest you, roll it out into a rectangle of the same dimensions again, and fold it again (it has now had two 'turns'); wrap it in clingfilm, handling it as little as possible, and leave for 15–20 minutes, at room temperature if using vegetable fat, in the bottom of the fridge if using butter.

Turn, roll out, and fold twice more and leave as before.

Depending on the needs of the recipe, give another one or two turns: 5 turns makes the pastry puff out more, 6 makes it more stable.

Leave another 10 minutes before rolling out to the desired thickness; and leave the rolled-out pastry another 30 minutes before baking which should be at mark 9 / 240°C, then at mark 7 / 210–220°C.

PÂTE DEMI-FEUILLETÉE · ROUGH PUFF OR FLAKY PASTRY

Made with the trimmings from puff pastry, collected up and rolled out again, sometimes with a little added fat to make it easier to work; or prepare as puff pastry above but with the butter spread on the dough in pieces.

PÂTE À FONCER · VOL-AU-VENT PASTRY

A dough for vol-au-vents, croustades, etc, made like shortcrust pastry but without egg, and, preferably, with lard for a pork dish. This can be enriched (*pâte à foncer fine ou enrichie*) by adding an egg, as for shortcrust pastry; in which case, it may be necessary to increase the fat content slightly.

PÂTE À PAIN ORDINAIRE · BREAD DOUGH

A household dough for pizzas, *pissaladières*, etc.

———————————— *For 500 g · 17 oz of flour* ————————————

Mix 10 g (¹/₃ oz) of fresh baker's yeast with 300 ml (¹/₂ pt) of warm water, adding 10 g (¹/₃ oz) of salt and castor sugar.

Make a well in the flour, work in the yeast mixture gradually, and knead well to give body to the dough; make into a ball, cover the bowl with a damp cloth, and leave for 2–3 hr.

Work the dough with lightly floured hands, deflating it, make into a ball again, cut a cross on it, about 1 cm (³/₈″) deep, and leave another 2 hr to rise.

Shape the dough by hand as required, and leave to rise another 20 minutes before spreading on the filling.

PÂTE À PÂTÉ EN CROUTE · HOT CRUST PASTRY

Hot water gives this dough a kind of pre-cooking which makes it more stable and more impervious to the cooking juices. It can be cut easily.

─────────────── *For 500 g · 17 oz of flour* ───────────────

Make a well in the flour, add 125 g (4 oz) of fat (vegetable fat, butter, or lard, as desired), and rub it into the flour with your finger tips, until it has a powdery consistency.

Make a well again, work in, a little at a time, 150 ml (¼ pt) of hot water (60°C) in which 10 g (⅓ oz) of salt have been dissolved.

Make into a ball, wrap in cling-film and leave in the bottom of the fridge overnight.

SAUMURE · SALTING OR BRINING

Salting or brining inhibits the growth of bacteria, thereby preserving. The process has three side-effects: it alters the flavour of what is preserved; it gives meat a good colour; and it lessens the moisture content.

Saumure sèche · Dry salting

This is the oldest method of curing, the meat being packed in seasoned salt. The juices begin to flow out of the joint into the salt while, simultaneously, the salt starts to penetrate the meat, thus the salt and the juices are reabsorbed into it. The weight of the joint to be cured should be roughly that of the salt.

─────────────── *For 1 kg · 2 lb of salt* ───────────────

Mix the salt with 30 g (1 oz) of saltpetre and brown sugar, 1 teaspoon of pepper, 30 g (1 oz) of juniper berries, 4 bay leaves, 4 cloves, and several sprigs of thyme and rosemary. Rub the meat generously with the mixture and place in a close-fitting, non-metal container. Strew with more of the salt mixture and leave for 4 days per 2.5 cm (1″) thickness of the meat, turning it over once a day. The meat juices will make the salt sticky if not runny.

Grande saumure · Brine

The commoner way of curing, with perhaps a more uniform result, is to immerse the meat in a heavy salt solution.

─────────────── *For 4.5 lt · 1 gallon of water* ───────────────

Bring the water to the boil with 750 g (1½ lb) of salt, 350 g (12 oz) brown sugar, 170 g (6 oz) saltpetre, 8 crushed juniper berries, 6 small pinches of mace or grated nutmeg, 12 whole black peppercorns, 6 cloves, and 2–3 bay leaves and sprigs of thyme. Boil for 10 minutes, skim carefully, and strain through a muslin. Leave to cool completely before submerging the meat in it, holding the joint down with a piece of wood or weights. Meat can be left in brine for up to a month for large pieces, but 3 days is enough for smaller ones. Stir the brine once daily and check it occasionally to see it has not gone sour. The same brine can be used repeatedly but may need strengthening with more salt.

THE MASTER CHEFS OF FRANCE AND THEIR RESTAURANTS

Where a chef has contributed to a chapter, this is indicated by a reference to the chapter after his name, and if he coordinated the research for it, there is a 'c' preceding the reference.

FRANCE

AIN

Antonin, Gérard   *Franche-Comté*
La Terrasse
Place des Mariniers
01980 Loyettes   T. 78·32·70·13

Bechis, Alain
Le Pirate
Avenue de Genève
01210 Ferney Voltaire   T. 50·40·63·52

Blanc, Georges   *Franche-Comté*
Hôtel-Restaurant Georges Blanc
01540 Vonnas   T. 74·50·00·10

Broyer, Gilbert   *Franche-Comté*
Le Chapon Fin
01140 Thoissey   T. 74·04·04·74

Chapel, Alain   *Franche-Comté*
Alain Chapel
01390 Mionnay   T. 78·91·82·02

Douillé, Roger   *Franche-Comté*
Hôtel-Restaurant Douillé
01700 Les Échets   T. 78·91·80·05

Herbelot, Robert   *Franche-Comté*
Hôtel du Rhône
Quai de Gaulle
01420 Seyssel   T. 50·59·20·30

Jantet, Bernard   *Franche-Comté*
Hôtel-Restaurant L'Embarcadère
Avenue du Lac
01130 Nantua   T. 74·75·22·88

Marguin, Jacques   *Franche-Comté*
Hôtel-Restaurant Jacques Marguin
Route de Strasbourg
01700 Les Échets   T. 78·91·80·04

Pauchard, Paul   *Franche-Comté*
Hôtel de France
44 rue du Dr Mercier
01130 Nantua   T. 74·75·00·55

Vullin, Jean-Pierre   *Franche-Comté*
Auberge Bressane
166 bd de Brou
01000 Bourg-en-Bresse   T. 74·22·22·68

AISNE

Courville, Serge   *c. Picardy*
Restaurant La Côte 108
02190 Berry-au-Bac   T. 23·79·95·04

ALLIER

Corlouer, Michel

Le Grenier à Sel
10 rue Vieille Dame
03100 Vieux Montluçon   T. 70·05·53·79

Giraudon, Jean   *Nivernais*
Hôtel-Restaurant Le Chêne Vert
35 boulevard Ledru-Rollin
03500 St-Pourçain-
sur-Sioule   T. 70·45·40·65

Muller, Jacques   *Nivernais*
Le Violon d'Ingres
Rue du Casino
03200 Vichy   T. 70·98·97·70

ALPES-DE-HAUTE-PROVENCE

Gleize, Pierre   *c. Provence*
La Bonne Étape
Chemin du Lac
04160 Château-Arnoux   T. 92·64·00·09

Jourdan, Daniel   *Provence*
Hostellerie La Fuste
Manosque
04210 Valensole   T. 92·72·05·95

Ricaud, Jean-Jacques   *Provence*
Hôtel du Grand Paris
19 boulevard Thiers
04000 Digne   T. 92·31·11·15

ALPES-MARITIMES

Barbate, Roger   *Provence*
Chez les Pêcheurs
18 quai des Docks
06000 Nice   T. 93·89·59·61

Chauveau, Francis
L'Amandier
Place Commandant-Lamy
06250 Mougins-Village   T. 93·90·00·91

Chollet, Serge   *Provence*
Le Moulin de Mougins
Quartier Notre-Dame-de-Vie
06250 Mougins   T. 93·75·78·24

Issautier, Jean-François   *Provence*
Auberge de la Belle Route
06670 St-Martin-du-Var   T. 93·08·10·65

Outier, Louis   *Provence*
L'Oasis
06120 La Napoule   T. 93·49·95·52

Picard, Gilbert   *Provence*
La Réserve de Beaulieu
5 bd Général Leclerc
06310 Beaulieu-sur-Mer   T. 93·01·00·01

Rossolin, Jean   *Provence*
L'Auberge du Logis de la Garde
06440 Escarène-Blausasc   т. 93.79.51.03

Surmain, André   *Provence*
Le Relais à Mougins
Place de la Mairie
06250 Mougins-Village   т. 93·90·03·47

Vergé, Roger   *Provence*
Le Moulin de Mougins
Quartier Notre-Dame-de-Vie
06250 Mougins-Village   т. 93.90.00.91

ARDÈCHE

Gaudry, Jean-Maurice   *Auvergne*
La Vieille Auberge
07800 Charmes-sur-Rhône   т. 75.60.80.10

ARDENNES

Lenoir, Jean   *Champagne*
Hostellerie Lenoir
Auvilliers-les-Forges
08250 Maubert-Fontaine   т. 24·54·30·11

Siegel, Pierre   *Champagne*
Hôtel-Restaurant Le Moderne
Place de la Gare
08300 Rethel   т. 24.38.44.54

AUBE

Paris, Claude   *Champagne*
Hôtel-Restaurant Le Commerce
38 rue Nationale
10200 Bar-sur-Aube   т. 25·27·08·76

AUDE

Rodriguez, J.-C   *Mediterranean Languedoc*
Logis de Trencavel
286 avenue Général Leclerc
11000 Carcassonne   т. 68·71·09·53

BOUCHES-DU-RHÔNE

Bayon, Marc
Hôtel Sofitel Marseilles
36 bd C. Livon
13001 Marseille   т. 91·52·90·19

Clor, Gérard   *Provence*
L'Éscale
Promenade du Port
13620 Carry-le-Rouet   т. 42·45·00·47

Picard, Jacques   *Provence*
Oustau de Baumanière
Les Baux de Provence
13520 Maussane   т. 90·97·33·07

CHARENTE

Ferrière, Jean   *Angoumois*
La Boule d'Or

9 bd Gambetta
16300 Barbezieux   т. 45·78·22·72

Laurent, Bernard   *Angoumois*
L'Auberge de la Chignolle
16430 Champniers   т. 45·95·65·48

CORRÈZE

Husson, Christian   *Limousin*
La Périgourdine
15 avenue Alsace-Lorraine
19100 Brive   т. 55.24.26.55

CÔTE-D'OR

Breuil, Christian
Breuil la Chouette
1 rue de la Chouette
21000 Dijon   т. 80·30·18·10

Crotet, Jean   *Burgundy*
La Côte d'Or
37 rue Thurot
21700 Nuits-St-Georges   т. 80·61·06·10

Minot, François   *Burgundy*
Conseiller Technique
Relais et Châteaux
Velars-sur-Ouche
21370 Plombières-lès-Dijon   т. 80·33·62·43

Parra, André   *Burgundy*
Ermitage Corton
21201 Chorey-lès-Beaune   т. 80·22·05·28

CÔTES-DU-NORD

Guillo, Jacques
Auberge Grand'Maison
1 rue Léon le Cerf
22530 Mur-de-Bretagne   т. 96·28·51·10

Le Saout, Jean-Jacques   *Brittany*
La Cotriade
Port de Piégu
22370 Pléneuf-Val-André   т. 96·72·20·26

Quinton, Georges   *Brittany*
Hôtel-Restaurant Avaugour
1 place du Champ-Clos
22100 Dinan   т. 96·39·07·49

DORDOGNE

Bulot, Régis   *Guyenne*
Le Moulin de l'Abbaye
1 route de Bourdeilles
24310 Brantôme   т. 53·05·80·22

DOUBS

Aubrée, Henri   *Franche-Comté*
Hostellerie du Château d'As
25110 Baume-les-Dames   т. 81·84·00·66

Piguet, Luc   *Franche-Comté*
Auberge de la Charrue d'Or
8 rue Frédéric-Joliot-Curie

25310 Roches-lès-Blamont   T. 81·35·18·40

DRÔME

Chabran, Michel   *Dauphiny*
Restaurant Chabran
Avenue du 45ème parallèle
26600 Pont-de-l'Isère   T. 75·84·60·09

Pic, Jacques   *Dauphiny*
Restaurant Pic
285 avenue Victor Hugo
26001 Valence   T. 75·44·15·32

Reynaud, Jean-Marc
Restaurant Reynaud
82 avenue Président Roosevelt
26600 Tain l'Hermitage   T. 75·07·22·10

EURE

Louet, Yves   *Normandy*
Auberge du Vieux Logis
27210 Contreville
   Beuzeville   T. 32·57·60·16

Pommier, Francis   *Normandy*
Hôtel Le Petit Coq aux Champs
Campigny
27500 Pont-Audemer   T. 32·41·04·19

Simon, Patrick   *Normandy*
Hostellerie Le Clos
27130 Verneuil-sur-Avre   T. 32·32·21·81

EURE-ET-LOIR

Caillault, Robert   *Sologne*
Auberge du Gué des Grues
Montreuil par Dreux
28500 Montreuil   T. 37·43·50·25

Coste, Jacques   *Sologne*
Hôtel de la Forêt
Place du Champ-de-Foire
28250 Senonches   T. 37·37·78·50

FINISTÈRE

Bosser, Adolphe   *Brittany*
Hôtel Le Goyen
Place Jean Simon
29113 Audierne   T. 98.70.08.88

GARD

Alexandre, Pierre   *Med Languedoc*
Hôtel-Restaurant Pierre Alexandre
30128 Garons   T. 66·70·08·99

Itier, Paul   *Med Languedoc*
Maître Itier
30330 Connaux   T. 66·82·00·24

Meissonnier, Michel   *Med Languedoc;*
L'Ermitage Meissonnier   *Provence*
30400 Les Angles   T. 90·25·41·68

Meissonnier, Paul-Louis   *Med Languedoc;*
as previous entry   *Provence*

GARONNE (HAUTE)

Pujol, Marcelin   *Toulousain Languedoc*
Restaurant Pujol
21 avenue Général Compans
31700 Blagnac   T. 61·71·13·58

GIRONDE

Darroze, Claude   *Guyenne*
Hôtel-Restaurant Claude Darroze
95 cours du Général Leclerc
33210 Langon   T. 56·63·00·48

HÉRAULT

Albano, Nicolas   C. *Mediterranean*
Inter-Hôtel La Tamarissière   *Languedoc*
Quai Théophile-Cornu
34300 Agde   T. 67·94·20·87

Alexandre, Paul   C. *Mediterranean*
Terre-Plein de la Capitainerie   *Languedoc*
Alexandre Amirauté
34280 La Grande Motte   T. 67·56·63·63

Furlan, Gilbert
Le Chandelier
3 rue Leenhardt
34000 Montpellier   T. 67·92·61·62

Rousset, Georges   *Mediterranean*
La Crèche   *Languedoc*
Route de Frouzet
34380 St-Martin-de-
   Londres   T. 67·55·00·04

ILLE-ET-VILAINE

Tirel, Roger   *Brittany*
Hôtel-Restaurant Tirel
Gare de la Gouesnière
35350 St-Meloir-des-Ondes   T. 99·89·10·46

INDRE

Bardet, Jean
Restaurant Jean Bardet
1 rue J.-J. Rousseau
36000 Châteauroux   T. 14·34·82·69

Fourré, Maurice   *Berry*
Hôtel d'Espagne
9 rue du Château
36600 Valençay   T. 54·00·00·02

Nonnet, Alain   C. *Berry*
La Cognette
Boulevard Stalingrad
36100 Issoudun   T. 54·21·21·83

INDRE-ET-LOIRE

Lozay, Jean-Pierre

Château du Beaulieu
1 rue de l'Épend
37300 Joué-lès-Tours   T. 47·53·20·26

Sabat, Jean   *Touraine*
Pâtissier-Traiteur
76 rue Nationale
37000 Tours   T. 47·05·34·70

Traversac, René
Château d'Artigny
37250 Montbazon   T. 47·26·24·24

ISÈRE

Achini, Georges   c. *Dauphiny*
Les Mésanges
38330 Montbonnot   T. 76·90·21·57

Chavant, Émile   *Dauphiny*
Chavant à Bresson
38320 Eybens   T. 76·25·15·14

Thivard, Guy   *Dauphiny*
La Pyramide – Madame Point
14 boulevard F. Point
38200 Vienne   T. 74·53·01·96

JURA

Jeunet, André   c. *Franche-Comté*
Hôtel de Paris
9 rue de l'Hôtel de Ville
39600 Arbois   T. 84·66·05·67

LANDES

Coussau, Bernard   c. *Gascony*
Relais de la Poste
40140 Magescq   T. 58·47·70·25

Dando, Max   *Gascony*
Le Hittau
40230 St-Vincent-de-
  Tyrosse   T. 58·77·11·85

Darc, Jacques   *Gascony*
Hôtel-Restaurant Richelieu
13 avenue Victor Hugo
40100 Dax   T. 58·74·81·81

Ducassé, Francis   *Gascony*
Pavillon Landais
26 avenue du Lac
40140 Soustons   T. 58·48·04·49

Guérard, Michel   *Gascony*
Hôtel-Restaurant Les Prés d'Eugénie
Place de l'Impératrice
40320 Eugénie-les-Bains   T. 58·51·19·01

Labadie, Charles   *Gascony*
Hôtel-Restaurant Le Commerce
3 bd des Pyrénées
40800 Aire-sur-Adour   T. 58·76·60·06

LOIR-ET-CHER

Velasco, Robert   *Sologne*

Hôtel du Cheval Rouge
1 place Foch
41800 Montoire   T. 54·85·07·05

LOIRE

Besnier, Jean-Claude
Relais de Roanne
42640 St-Germain-
  Lespinasse   T. 77·71·97·35

Etéocle, Gilles   *Nivernais*
Hostellerie La Poularde
2 rue de St-Étienne
42210 Montrond-les-Bains   T. 77·54·40·06

Farge, Jean   *Nivernais*
Hôtel-Restaurant Le Marcassin
Place de Verdun
42153 Riorges Roanne   T. 77·71·30·18

Randoing, Joannès   *Nivernais*
Hostellierie La Poularde
2 rue de St-Étienne
42210 Montrond-les-Bains   T. 77·54·40·06

Troisgros, Pierre   *Nivernais*
Restaurant Troisgros
22 cours de la République
42300 Roanne   T. 77·71·66·97

LOIRE (HAUTE)

Guichard, Jean
Auberge du Velay
43140 St-Didier-en-Velay   T. 71·61·01·54

LOIRE-ATLANTIQUE

Bernard, Jean-Yves   *Brittany*
Hostellerie Le Domaine d'Orvault
24 chemin des Marais-du-Cens
44700 Orvault   T. 40·76·84·02

Delphin, Joseph   c. *Brittany*
Restaurant Delphin
Bellevue
44470 Ste-Luce   T. 40·49·04·13

LOIRET

Huyart, Paul   *Sologne*
La Crémaillère
34 rue Notre-Dame de Recouvrance
45000 Orléans   T. 38·53·49·17

Jolly, Jean   *Sologne*
Hôtel de la Gloire
74 avenue du Général de Gaulle
45200 Montargis   T. 38·85·04·69

Pipet, Michel
Les Antiquaires
2 & 4 rue au Lin
45000 Orléans   T. 38·53·52·35

LOT

Mommejac, René   *Guyenne*
Le Lion d'Or
8 place de la République
46500 Gramat   T. 65·38·73·18

LOT-ET-GARONNE

Trama, Michel   *Guyenne*
L'Aubergade
52 rue Royale
47270 Puymirol   T. 53·95·31·46

MAINE-ET-LOIRE

Pauvert, Paul
Auberge de la Forge
1 bis place des Piliers
Champtoceaux
49270 St-Laurent-des-
   Autels   T. 40·83·56·23

Piers, Jean-François   *Anjou*
Le Vert d'Eau
9 bd Dumesnil
49000 Angers   T. 41·48·52·86

MANCHE

Bonnefoy, Gérard   *Normandy*
L'Auberge Normande
17 bd de Verdun
50500 Carentan   T. 33·42·02·99

MARNE

Boyer, Gaston   *Champagne*
Boyer – Les Crayères
64 bd Henri Vasnier
51100 Reims   T. 26·82·80·80

Boyer, Gérard   *Champagne*
as previous entry

Lallement, Jean-Pierre
L'Assiette Champenoise
51140 Chalons-sur-Vesle T. 26·49·34·94

Thuet, Joseph   *Champagne*
Réception Le Trianon
Moët & Chandon
9 avenue de Champagne
51200 Épernay   T. 26·54·71·11

MAYENNE

Lemercier, Guy   *Anjou*
Le Bistro de Paris
67 rue du Val-de-Mayenne
53000 Laval   T. 43·56·98·29

Portier, Pierre   *Anjou*
La Gerbe de Blé
83 rue Victor Boissel
53000 Laval   T. 43·53·14·10

MEURTHE-ET-MOSELLE

Roy, Joël   *Lorraine*
Le Prieuré
54630 Flavigny   T. 83·26·70·45

MEUSE

Leloup, Jean
Hostellerie du Coq Hardi
8 avenue de la Victoire
55100 Verdun   T. 29·86·00·68

MORBIHAN

Paineau, Georges   *Brittany*
La Bretagne
13 rue St-Michel
56230 Questembert   T. 97·26·11·12

MOSELLE

Schneider, Jean-Claude   *Lorraine*
Auberge St-Walfrid
58 rue Grosbliederstroff
57200 Sarreguemines   T. 87·98·43·75

Terver, Marcellin   *Lorraine*
La Vénerie
10 rue Porte-de-Trèves
57480 Sierck-les-Bains T. 82·83·72·41

NIÈVRE

Dray, Jean-Claude   *Nivernais*
Hôtel La Renaissance
58470 Magny-Cours   T. 86·58·10·40

Raveau, Jacques   *Nivernais*
L'Espérance
17 rue René Couard
58150 Pouilly-sur-Loire T. 86·39·10·68

Trotier, Henri   *Nivernais*
Auberge Nivernaise
58440 La Celle-sur-Loire T. 86·26·06·23

NORD

Bardot, Robert   c. *Flanders*
Le Flambard
79 rue d'Angleterre
59800 Lille   T. 20·51·00·06

Lelaurain, Francis   *Flanders; Picardy*
La Crémaillère
26 Grand Place
59440 Avesne-sur-Helpe T. 27·61·02·30

Lelaurain, Gilbert
Le Septentrion
Parc du Château du Vert-Bois
59700 Marcq-en-Baroeul
                        T. 20·46·26·98

Lepelley, François   *Flanders*

L'Armorial
Prémesques
59840 Pérenchies ⊤. 20·08·84·24

PAS-DE-CALAIS

Gaudry, Jean-Marc *Picardy*
Auberge du Moulin de Mombreux
Route de Bayenghem
62380 Lumbres ⊤. 21·39·62·44

PUY-DE-DÔME

Bath, Jean-Yves
La Bergerie
Sarpoil
63490 Sauxillanges ⊤. 73·71·02·54

Blanc, Émile *Auvergne*
Le Paradis
Avenue de Paradis
63130 Royat ⊤. 73·35·85·46

Bon, Jean-Claude *Auvergne*
Belle Meunière
25 avenue de la Vallée
63130 Royat ⊤. 73·35·80·17

Legros, Georges *Auvergne*
Hostellerie du Beffroy
63610 Besse-en-Chandesse ⊤. 73·79·50·08

Mioche, Michel *Auvergne*
Hôtel Radio
43 avenue Pierre-Curie
63400 Chamalières ⊤. 73·30·87·83

Sachapt, Antoine *Auvergne*
Les Mouflons
63610 Besse-en-Chandesse ⊤. 73·79·51·31

PYRÉNÉES-ATLANTIQUES

Arrambide, Firmin C. *Béarn*
Hôtel des Pyrénées
19 place du Général de Gaulle
64220 St-Jean-Pied-de-Port ⊤. 59·37·01·01

Bayle, Alain
Chez Mariette
Artiguelouve
64230 Lescar ⊤. 59·83·05·08

Casau, Raymond *Béarn*
Chez Pierre
16 rue Louise-Barthou
64000 Pau ⊤. 59·27·76·86

François, Claude *Béarn*
Hôtel Bakéa
64700 Biriatou ⊤. 59·20·76·36

Jourdan, Patrick *Béarn*
Restaurant Patrick Jourdan
14 rue Latapie
64000 Pau ⊤. 59·27·68·70

Laporte, Pierre *Béarn*

Café de Paril
Place Bellevue
64200 Biarritz ⊤. 59·24·19·53

Relais de Parme
Aérodrome de Biarritz
64600 Anglet ⊤. 59·23·93·84

Moutche, Jean *Béarn*
Le Majestic
9 place Royale
64000 Pau ⊤. 59·27·56·83

PYRÉNÉES (HAUTES)

Rouzard, Louis
La Caravelle
Aéroport de Tarbes-Lourdes
65290 Juillan ⊤. 62·32·99·96

RHIN (BAS)

Husser, Robert *Alsace*
Hostellerie du Cerf
30 rue du Général de Gaulle
67520 Marlenheim ⊤. 88·87·73·73

Jung, Émile *Alsace*
Au Crocodile
10 rue de l'Outre
67000 Strasbourg ⊤. 88·32·13·02

Mischler, Fernand *Alsace*
Auberge du Cheval Blanc
4 rue de Wissembourg
67510 Lembach ⊤. 88·94·41·86

Orth, Jean *Alsace*
À l'Écrevisse
4 avenue de Strasbourg
67170 Brumath ⊤. 88·51·11·08

Westermann, Antoine *Alsace*
Buerehiesel
4 parc de l'Orangerie
67000 Strasbourg ⊤. 88·61·62·24

RHIN (HAUT)

Floranc, René *Alsace*
Auberge du Père Floranc
9 rue Herzog
68920 Wettolsheim ⊤. 89·41·39·14

Gaertner, Pierre *Alsace*
Aux Armes de France
1 Grande Rue
68770 Ammerschwihr ⊤. 89·47·10·12

Haeberlin, Paul *Alsace*
Auberge de l'Ill
Rue de Collonges-au-Mont-d'Or
68150 Illhaeusern-
  Ribeauvillé ⊤. 89·71·83·23

Julien, Francis *Alsace*

Hôtel-Restaurant Central
41 rue Maurice Burrus
68160 Ste-Croix-aux-Mines   T. 89·58·73·27

Schillinger, Jean   *Alsace*
Restaurant Schillinger
16 rue Stanislas
68000 Colmar   T. 89·41·43·17

RHÔNE

Bocuse, Paul   *Lyonnais*
Restaurant Paul Bocuse
Place d'Illhaeusern
69660 Collonges-au-
   Mont-d'Or   T. 78·22·01·40

Constantin, Bernard
Larivoire
Chemin des Îles
69140 Rillieux la Pape   T. 78·88·50·92

Cortembert, Gérard   *Lyonnais*
Le Cep
Place de l'Église
69820 Fleurie   T. 74·04·10·77

Fleury, Jean   *Lyonnais*
Restaurant Paul Bocuse
Place d'Illhaeusern
69660 Collonges-au-
   Mont-d'Or   T. 78·22·01·40

Gervais, Claude   *Lyonnais*
Les Fantasques
47 rue de la Bourse
69002 Lyon   T. 78·37·36·58

Girerd, Guy   *Lyonnais*
Restaurant Les Trois Dômes
Hôtel Sofitel
20 quai Gailleton
69002 Lyon   T. 78·42·72·50

Lacombe, Jean-Paul
Léon de Lyon
1 rue Pleney
69001 Lyon   T. 78·28·11·33

Léron, Daniel   *Lyonnais*
Daniel et Denise
2 rue Tupin
69002 Lyon   T. 78·37·49·98

Lescuyer, Gervais   *Lyonnais*
Restaurant Gervais
42 rue Pierre Corneille
69006 Lyon   T. 78·52·19·13

Nandron, Gérard   *Lyonnais*
Restaurant Nandron
26 quai Jean Moulin
69002 Lyon   T. 78·42·10·26

Orsi, Pierre   *Lyonnais*
Restaurant Pierre Orsi
3 place Kléber
69006 Lyon   T. 78·89·57·68

Robin, Daniel   *Lyonnais*
Les Deschamps
69840 Chénas   T. 85·36·72·67

Roucou, Roger   *Lyonnais*
Roucou La Mère Guy
35 quai J.-J. Rousseau
69350 Lyon-la-Mulatière   T. 78·51·65·37

Vettard, Jean   c. *Lyonnais*
Restaurant Vettard
7 place Bellecour
69002 Lyon   T. 78·42·07·59

SAÔNE-ET-LOIRE

Ducloux, Jean   *Burgundy*
Restaurant Greuze
Rue Thibaudet
71700 Tournus   T. 85·51·13·52

Fauvin, Guy
Les Maritonnes
71570 Romanèche Thorins   T. 85·35·51·70

Lameloise, Jean   c. *Burgundy*
Restaurant Lameloise
36 place d'Armes
71150 Chagny   T. 85·87·08·85

Longueville, Paul   *Burgundy*
Le Commerce
70 quai Jules Chagot
71300 Montceau-les-Mines   T. 85·57·34·18

Raymond, Gérard
Restaurant Raymond
8 rue d'Autun
71140 Bourbon-Lancy   T. 85·89·17·39

SAVOIE

Abry, Jean   *Savoy*
Restaurant Lille
Grand Port
73100 Aix-les-Bains   T. 79·35·04·22

Jacob, Jean   *Savoy*
Le Bâteau Ivre
73370 Le Bourget-du-Lac   T. 79·25·02·66

Rochedy, Michel   *Savoy*
Le Chabichou
Quartier les Chenus
73120 Courchevel 1850   T. 79·08·00·55
(*winter only; for summer see below: Var*)

SAVOIE (HAUTE)

Aubeneau, Jean-Louis
Le Belvédère
7 chemin du Belvédère
74000 Annecy   T. 50·45·04·90

Collon, Bernard   *Savoy*
Auberge de Letraz

Restaurant Bernard Collon
Sévrier
74320 Annecy   T. 50·52·40·36

Crispino, André   *Savoy*
Royal Hôtel
74500 Évian-les-Bains   T. 50·75·14·00

Favre, Robert   *Savoy*
La Diligence et Taverne du Postillon
74160 St-Julien-
en-Genevois   T. 50·49·07·55

Meignan, Pierre   *Savoy*
La Couronne
Grande Rue
74890 Bons-en-Chablais   T. 50·36·11·17

Salino, Fernand   *Savoy*
Restaurant Salino
13 rue Jean Mermoz
74000 Annecy   T. 50·23·07·90

Tuccinardi, Maurice   *Savoy*
Pavillon de l'Ermitage-Chavoires
74290 Veyrier-du-Lac   T. 50·60·11·09

SEINE-MARITIME

Dubuc, Louis-Philippe   *Normandy*
Dubuc
76430 St-Vigor-
d'Ymonville   T. 35·20·06·97

Plaisance, Gilbert
Les Galets
3 rue Victor Hugo
76980 Veules-les-Roses   T. 35·97·61·33

TARN

Galinier, Noël   C. *Toulousain Languedoc*
Hôtel Noël
1 rue de l'Hôtel de Ville
81120 Réalmont   T. 63·55·52·80

VAR

Daviddi, Ephrem   *Provence*
Hôtel-Restaurant Le Roitelet
Canadel-sur-Mer
83820 Le Rayol-Canadel   T. 94·05·61·39

Girard, Claude   *Provence*
Les Santons
83310 Grimaud   T. 94·43·21·02

Hilaire, Jean   *Provence*
Hôtel Bertin
13 & 15 bd Foch
83300 Draguignan   T. 94·68·00·05

Rochedy, Michel
Le Chabichou
Avenue Foch
83990 St Tropez   T. 94·54·80·00
(*summer only; for winter see above: Savoie*)

VAUCLUSE

Gomez, Franck
La Table du Comtat
Séguret
84110 Vaison-la-Romaine   T. 90·46·91·49

Hiély, Pierre   *Provence*
Hiély-Lucullus
5 rue de la République
84000 Avignon   T. 90·86·17·07

Tassan, Primo   *Provence*
Auberge de France
28 place de l'Horloge
84000 Avignon   T. 90·82·58·86

VIENNE

Benoist, Pierre   *Poitou*
Restaurant Pierre Benoist
86240 Croutelle   T. 49·57·11·52

Mercier, Jean   *Poitou*
Restaurant Mercier
Hotel de France
2 bd de Strasbourg
86500 Montmorillon   T. 49·91·00·51

VOSGES

Lagrange, Georges   *Lorraine*
Hôtel de la Paix
88400 Gérardmer   T. 29·63·38·78

Philippe, Michel   *Lorraine*
Hostellerie Bas-Rupts
Bas Rupts
88400 Gérardmer   T. 29·63·09·25

YONNE

Breton, Jean   *Burgundy*
Le Morvan
7 route de Paris
89200 Avallon   T. 86·34·18·20

Godard, Charles   *Burgundy*
Hôtel de Paris et de la Poste
97 rue de la République
89100 Sens   T. 86·65·17·43

Godard, Jean-Claude   *Burgundy*
Modern Hôtel
Rue Robert-Petit
89300 Joigny   T. 86·62·16·28

Lorain, Michel   *Burgundy*
À la Côte St-Jacques
14 faubourg de Paris
89300 Joigny   T. 86·62·09·70

Moret, Michel   *Burgundy*
Relais St-Fiacre
89380 Appoigny   T. 86·53·21·80

BELFORT (TERRITOIRE DE)

Barbier, Gérard
Le Sabot d'Annie
5 rue Aristide Briand
90300 Offemont   T. 84·26·01·71

Clévenot, Roger   *Franche-Comté*
Le Pot d'Étain
90400 Danjoutin   T. 84·28·31·95

Mathy, Dominique   *Franche-Comté*
Hostellerie du Château Servin
9 rue du Général Négrier
90000 Belfort   T. 84·21·41·85

PARIS: THE CENTRE

Barbier, Jean-Jacques   *Ile-de-France*
Hôtel Intercontinental
1 rue Castiglione
75001 Paris   T. (1)42·50·37·80

Barnier, Claude   *Ile-de-France*
Restaurant La Régence
Hôtel Plaza-Athénée
25 avenue Montaigne
75008 Paris   T. (1)47·23·78·39

Bequet, Jean   *Ile-de-France*
La Chaumière des Gourmets
22 place Denfert-Rochereau
75014 Paris   T. (1)43·21·22·59

Besson, Gérard   *Ile-de-France*
Gérard Besson
5 rue du Coq Héron
75001 Paris   T. (1)42·33·14·74

Bonin, Jean-Paul   *Burgundy; Ile-de-France;*
Restaurant Les Ambassadeurs   *Lyonnais*
Hôtel de Crillon
10 place de la Concorde
75008 Paris   T. (1)42·65·24·24

Brazier, Maurice   *Ile-de-France*
Hôtel Méridien
81 bd Gouvion-St-Cyr
75017 Paris   T. (1)47·58·12·30

Burkli, Guy
Au Chateaubriant
23 rue Chabrol
75010 Paris   T. (1)48·24·58·94

Cagna, Jacques   *Ile-de-France*
Restaurant Jacques Cagna
14 rue des Grands-Augustins
75006 Paris   T. (1)43·26·49·39

Chêne, Paul   *Ile-de-France*
Restaurant Paul Chêne
123 rue Lauriston
75016 Paris   T. (1)47·27·63·17

Clessienne, Claude   *Ile-de-France*
Chez Max

19 rue de Castellane
75008 Paris   T. (1)42·65·33·81

Comby, Michel   *Ile-de-France*
Restaurant Michel Comby
116 bd Pereire
75017 Paris   T. (1)43·80·88·68

Deligne, Claude   *Ile-de-France*
Taillevent
15 rue Lamennais
75008 Paris   T. (1)45·61·12·90

Durand, Roland   *Ile-de-France*
Le Relais de Sèvres
Hôtel Sofitel Paris
8–12 rue Louis Armand
75015 Paris   T. (1)45·54·95·00

Fournillier, Aimé   *Ile-de-France*
Potel et Chabot
3 rue de Chaillot
75016 Paris   T. (1)47·20·57·16

Fréon, Jacky
Restaurant Paris
Hôtel Lutetia
45 bd Raspail
75006 Paris   T. (1)45·44·38·10

Gaiga, Raoul
Montparnasse 25
Hôtel Montparnasse Park
19 rue Commandant-Mouchotte
75014 Paris   T. (1)43·20·15·51

Génin, Paul   *Ile-de-France*
Chez Pauline
5 rue Villedo
75001 Paris   T. (1)42·96·20·70

Grondard, Louis   *Ile-de-France*
Jules Verne
Eiffel Tower
75007 Paris   T. (1)45·55·61·44

Jouanin, Gil   *Ile-de-France;*
Restaurant Opéra   c. *Nivernais*
Café de la Paix
5 place de l'Opéra
75009 Paris   T. (1)42·68·12·13

Jouannin, Bernard   *Ile-de-France*
Restaurant Nicolas
12 rue de la Fidélité
75010 Paris   T. (1)42·46·84·74

Lausecker, Clément   *Ile-de-France*
La Coquille
6 rue du Débarcadère
75017 Paris   T. (1)45·74·25·95

Le Divellec, Jacques   *Ile-de-France;*
Restaurant Le Divellec   c. *Angoumois;*
107 rue de l'Université   c. *Poitou*
75007 Paris   T. (1)45·51·91·96

Legay, Guy   *Auvergne; Ile-de-France*
Hôtel Ritz

15 place Vendôme
75001 Paris   т. (1)42·60·38·30

Lenôtre, Gaston   *Ile-de-France*
Le Pré Catalan
Bois de Boulogne
75016 Paris   т. (1)45·24·55·58

Magne, Roland   *Ile-de-France;*
Au Pactole   c. *Touraine*
44 bd St-Germain
75005 Paris   т. (1)46·33·31·31

Marty, Jean-Baptiste   *Ile-de-France*
Le Relais des Pyrénées
1 rue du Jourdain
75020 Paris   т. (1)46·36·65·81

Menant, Michel   *Ile-de-France*
Maxim's
3 rue Royale
75008 Paris   т. (1)42·65·27·94

Normand, Joël
Présidence de la République
75008 Paris   т. (1)42·92·84·13

Pasquet, Michel   *Ile-de-France*
Restaurant Michel Pasquet
59 rue La Fontaine
75016 Paris   т. (1)42·88·50·01

Pibourdin, Jean   *Ile-de-France*
Le Drugstorien
1 avenue Matignon
75008 Paris   т. (1)43·59·38·70

Renty, Joël
Restaurant L'Étoile d'Or
Hôtel Concorde Lafayette
3 place du Général Koenig
75017 Paris   т. (1)47·58·12·84

Roche, Louis-Pierre   *Ile-de-France*
Professeur Principal Cuisine
Centre Technique des Métiers de
  l'Alimentation
11 rue Jean Ferrandi
75006 Paris   т. (1)45·44·38·18

Senderens, Alain   *Ile-de-France*
Lucas Carton
9 place de la Madeleine
75008 Paris   т. (1)42·65·22·90

Tounissoux, Michel   *Ile-de-France*
Chez Michel
10 rue de Belzunce
75010 Paris   т. (1)48·78·44·14

Vandenhende, Francis   *Ile-de-France*
La Ferme St-Simon
6 rue St-Simon
75007 Paris   т. (1)45·48·35·74

Vedel, Pierre   *Ile-de-France;*
Pierre Vedel   *Mediterranean Languedoc*
19 rue Duranton
75015 Paris   т. (1)45·58·43·17

PARIS: SEINE-ET-MARNE

Duvauchelle, Pierre
Restaurant Le Beauharnais
Hôtel de l'Aigle Noir
27 place Napoléon Bonaparte
77300 Fontainebleau   т. (1)64·22·32·65

Esquerre, Gérard   *Ile-de-France*
Aux Vieux Remparts
3 rue Couverte
77160 Provins   т. (1)64·00·02·89

Happart, Alexis   *Ile-de-France*
Hôtel de l'Écu de France
3–7 rue de Paris
77140 Nemours   т. (1)64·28·11·54

Métry, Paul
Le Central
34 place du Marché
77120 Coulommiers   т. (1)64·03·01·69

Tingaud, Alexis-Émile   *Champagne;*
Auberge de Condé   *Ile-de-France*
1 avenue de Montmirail
77260 La-Ferté-sous-
  Jouarre   т. (1)60·22·00·07

Trehet, Édouard   *Ile-de-France*
La Grillade
19 rue Jean-Jaurès
77410 Claye-Souilly   т. (1)60·26·00·68

Vaschalde, Gérard   *Ile-de-France*
Hôtel-Restaurant Le Dauphin
9 bis, rue Aristide-Briand
14 rue du Dauphin
77370 Nangis   т. (1)64·08·00·27

PARIS: YVELINES

Bachelard, Jean-Claude   *Ile-de-France*
Le Cèdre
7 rue d'Alsace
78100 St-Germain-
  en-Laye   т. (1)34·51·84·35

Blanchet, Michel   *Ile-de-France*
Le Tastevin
9 avenue Eglé
78600 Maisons-Lafitte   т. (1)39·62·11·67

Bordier, Jean   *Ile-de-France*
L'Aubergade
78760 Pontchartrain   т. (1)34·89·02·63

Devé, Jean-Pierre   *Ile-de-France*
L'Auberge des Bréviaires
3 route du Matz
Les Bréviaires
78610 Le Perray-
  en-Yvelines   т. (1)34·84·98·47

Marguerite, Claude   *Ile-de-France*
Le Relais du Pavé
20 route de Gambais

Bazainville
78550 Houdan   T. (1)34·87·61·52

Ogier, Lucien   *Dauphiny*
L'Aubergade
78760 Pontchartrain   T. (1)34·89·02·63

Peignaud, Michel   *Berry;*
La Belle Époque   *Ile-de-France*
10 place de la Mairie
78117 Châteaufort   T. (1)39·56·21·66

Philippe, Jean-Pierre   *Ile-de-France*
La Toque Blanche
12 Grande-Rue
Les Mesnuls
78490 Montfort-
    l'Amaury   T. (1)34·86·05·55

Soulat, Jean   *Ile-de-France*
L'Esturgeon
6 cours du 14 Juillet
78300 Poissy   T. (1)39·65·00·04

Toulejbiez, Jean-Pierre   *Ile-de-France*
La Cressonnière
46 route de Port-Royal
78470 St-Rémy-
    lès-Chévreuse   T. (1)30·52·00·41

Vandenameele, Pierre   *Ile-de-France*
La Poularde de Houdan
24 avenue de la République
78550 Houdan   T. (1)30·59·60·50

Vié, Gérard   *Ile-de-France*
Les Trois Marches
3 rue Colbert
78000 Versailles   T. (1)39·50·13·21

PARIS: HAUTS-DE-SEINE

Gasnier, Hubert   *Gascony;*
Restaurant Gasnier   *Ile-de-France*
7 bd Richard Wallace
92800 Puteaux   T. (1)45·06·33·63

PARIS: VAL D'OISE

Cagna, Gérard   *Ile-de-France*
Relais Ste-Jeanne
95830 Cormeilles-
    en-Vexin   T. (1)34·66·61·56

Villamaux, Claude   *Ile-de-France*
Élitair Maxim's Service
Charles-de-Gaulle Airport
Aérogare n°1
95713 Roissy   T. (1)48·62·16·16

CORSICA

Dulucq, Francis
Le Caroubier
Golfe d'Ajaccio
20166 Porticcio   T. 95·25·00·34

GREAT BRITAIN

Bourdin, Michel
Connaught Hotel
Carlos Place
London W1Y 6AL   T. 01-499 7070

Gaume, Bernard
Chelsea Room
Hyatt Carlton Tower
2 Cadogan Place
London SW1X 9PY   T. 01-235 5411

Mouilleron, Guy
Ma Cuisine
113 Walton Street
London SW3   T. 01-584 7585

Roux, Albert
Le Gavroche
43 Upper Brook Street
London W1   T. 01-408 0881

Zarb, Raymond
Les Cèdres
Walford House Hotel
Ross-on-Wye
Herefordshire HR9 5RY   T. 0989 63829

JAPAN

Bruant, Joël
Joël
Kyodo Bldg 2F 5.6.24
Minami Aoyama
Minato-ku
Tokyo   T. 400·7149

Lecomte, André
Pâtisserie Française – Traiteur
New Aoyama Bldg West B.211 1.1.1
Minami Aoyama-Drinado RV
Tokyo   T. 475·1771

Pachon, André
Ile-de-France
Minoto-ku-Roppongi 3 Chome 11.5
Tokyo   T. 404·0384

Pachon
29.18 Sarugaku Cho Shilbuya-ku
Tokyo   T. 476·5025

LUXEMBOURG

Berrino, Michel
Patin d'Or
40 rue de Bettembourg
1899 Kockelscheuer   T. 26·499

SOUTH AFRICA

Guébert, Marc-Edmond
Orient Express
Old Pretoria Road Halfway House
1685 Transvaal   T. 011 805 2906

SWITZERLAND

Bouilloux, Gérard
Vieux Moulin
89 route d'Annecy
1256 Troinex-Geneva   T. 022/422956

Granville, Jacques
Auberge d'Hermance
Rue du Midi 12
1218 Hermance   T. 022/511368

Large, Henri
Auberge du Lion d'Or
5 place Gautier
1223 Cologny-Geneva   T. 022/364432

Pelletier, Louis
Le Marignac
32 avenue Eugène Lance
1212 Grand-Lancy-Geneva   T. 022/940424

Perreard, Jean
Parc des Eaux Vives
82 quai Gustave-Ador
1207 Geneva   T. 022/354140

UNITED STATES

CALIFORNIA

Blanchet, Michel
L'Ermitage
730 N La Cienega Bd
Los Angeles 90069   T. (213)652 5840

Menès, Yves
Hotel Inter-Continental
333 West Harbor Drive
San Diego 92101   T. (619)234 1500

Verdon, René
Le Trianon
242 O'Farrell Street
San Francisco 94102   T. (415)982 9353

CONNECTICUT

Gasparini, Gérard
Wee Burn Country Club
Darien 06820   T. (203)655 1477

DISTRICT OF COLUMBIA

Bell, Maurice
Washington International Club
1800 K Street NW
Washington 20006   T. (202)862 1421

Blanc, Jacques
École de Cuisine
Rear 4822 Yuma Street NW
Washington 20016   T. (202)364 8028

Goyenvalle, Jean-Pierre
Le Lion d'Or
1150 Connecticut Avenue
Washington 20036   T. (202)296 7972

Greault, Robert F.
La Colline
400 North Capitol Street NW
Washington 20001   T. (202)737 0400

Palladin, Jean-Louis
Jean-Louis
Watergate – 2650 Virginia Avenue
Washington 20037   T. (202)298 4488

FLORIDA

Bocuse, Paul
Pavillon de France
Epcot
Orlando

ILLINOIS

Banchet, Jean
Le Français
269 South Milwaukee Avenue
Wheeling
Chicago 60090   T. (313)541 7470

Crétier, Bernard
Le Vichyssois
220 West Road
Mc Henry
Chicago 60050

LOUISIANA

Marcais, Michel
Begue's Restaurant
300 Bourbon Street
New Orleans 70140   T. (504)586 0300

MINNESOTA

Tindillier, Jean-Claude
Le Petit Chef
5932 Excelsior Bd
Minneapolis 53416   T. (612)926 9331

NEW JERSEY

Brecq, Jean-Claude
La Petite Auberge
44 East Madison Avenue
Cresskill 07626   T. (201)569 2270

NEW YORK CITY

Bertrand, Christian   *Champagne*
Lutèce
249 East 50th Street
New York   10022 T. (212)752 2225

Chenus, Roland
Le Chantilly
106 East 57th Street
New York 10022   T. (212)751 2931

Delouvrier, Christian
Maurice

118 West 57th Street
New York 10019   T. (212)245 5000

Drouet, Gérard
The Board Room (private club)
280 Park Avenue
New York 10017   T. (212)687 5858

Dunas, Daniel
Dorset Hotel
30 West 54th Street
New York 10019   T. (212)247 7300

Fessaguet, Roger
La Caravelle
33 West 55th Street
New York. 10019   T. (212)586 4252

Krause, Willy
The Périgord Park
575 Park Avenue
New York 10021   T. (212)752 0050

Passeloup, Claude
Parker Meridien Hotel
118 West 57th Street
New York 10019   T. (212)245 5000

Piquet, Jean-Yves
Le Cygne
55 East 54th Street
New York 10022   T. (212)759 5941

Rachou, Jean-Jacques
La Côte Basque
5 East 55th Street
New York 10022   T. (212)688 6525

Café Lavandou
134 East 61st Street
New York 10021   T. (212)838 7987

Sailhac, Alain
Le Cirque

58 East 65th Street
New York 10021   T. (212)794 9292

Soltner, André
Lutèce
249 East 50th Street
New York 10022   T. (212)752 2225

NEW YORK STATE

Chandelier, Marcel
Germaine Catering Inc
3809 33rd Street
Long Island City 11001   T. (212)392 7284

Morel, Jean
L'Hostellerie Bressane
Hillsdale 12529   T. (518)325 3412

PENNSYLVANIA

Perrier, Georges
Le Bec Fin
1523 Walnut Street
Philadelphia 19102   T. (215)567 1000

TEXAS

Herrmann, Bernard
The Carlyle
5430 Westheimer
Houston 77056   T. (713)840 0153

VIRGINIA

Binon, Bernard
Amelia's in the Underground
1725 Jefferson Davis Highway
Crystal City
Arlington 22202   T. (703)920 6650

OVEN TEMPERATURES

Gas Mark	Fahrenheit	Celsius	
¹/₄	230	110	v. slow
¹/₂	266	130	
1	284	140	slow
2	302	150	
3	338	170	
4	356	180	moderate
5	374	190	medium
6	392	200	
7	428	220	hot
8	446	230	
9	464	240	v. hot
10	482	250	